Lecture Notes in Computer Science　　10128

Commenced Publication in 1973
Founding and Former Series Editors:
Gerhard Goos, Juris Hartmanis, and Jan van Leeuwen

More information about this series at http://www.springer.com/series/7410

Frédéric Cuppens · Lingyu Wang
Nora Cuppens-Boulahia · Nadia Tawbi
Joaquin Garcia-Alfaro (Eds.)

Foundations and Practice of Security

9th International Symposium, FPS 2016
Québec City, QC, Canada, October 24–25, 2016
Revised Selected Papers

 Springer

Editors
Frédéric Cuppens
Télécom Bretagne
Cesson Sévigné
France

Lingyu Wang
Concordia Inst for Info
Concordia University
Montreal, QC
Canada

Nora Cuppens-Boulahia
Cesson-Sevigne
Télécom Bretagne
Cesson Sévigné
France

Nadia Tawbi
Local 3950, pavillon Adrien Pouliot
Université Laval
Quebec, QC
Canada

Joaquin Garcia-Alfaro
Télécom SudParis
Evry
France

ISSN 0302-9743   ISSN 1611-3349   (electronic)
Lecture Notes in Computer Science
ISBN 978-3-319-51965-4   ISBN 978-3-319-51966-1   (eBook)
DOI 10.1007/978-3-319-51966-1

Library of Congress Control Number: 2016961700

LNCS Sublibrary: SL4 – Security and Cryptology

Printed on acid-free paper

This Springer imprint is published by Springer Nature
The registered company is Springer International Publishing AG
The registered company address is: Gewerbestrasse 11, 6330 Cham, Switzerland

Preface

This volume contains the papers presented at the 9th International Symposium on Foundations and Practice of Security (FPS 2016), which was hosted by Université Laval, Québec City, Quebec, Canada, during October 24–26, 2016. Each submission was reviewed by at least three committee members. The review process was followed by intensive discussions over a period of one week. The Program Committee selected 18 regular papers and five short papers for presentation. The accepted papers cover diverse research themes, ranging from classic topics, such as malware, anomaly detection, and privacy, to emerging issues, such as security and privacy in mobile computing and cloud. The program was completed with three excellent invited talks given by François Laviolette (Université Laval), Jean-Yves Marion (Lorraine University, France), and Jeremy Clark (Concordia University).

Many people contributed to the success of FPS 2016. First, we would like to thank all the authors who submitted their research results. The selection was a challenging task and we sincerely thank all the Program Committee members, as well as the external reviewers, who volunteered to read and discuss the papers. We greatly thank the local Organizing Committee, Josée Desharnais and Andrew Bedford, for their great efforts to organize and perfectly control the logistics during the symposium. We also want to express our gratitude to the publication chair, Joaquin Garcia-Alfaro (Télécom SudParis), for his work in editing the proceedings. Last but not least, thanks to all the attendees. As security becomes an essential property in information and communication technologies, there is a growing need to develop efficient methods to analyze and design systems providing a high level of security and privacy. We hope the articles in this proceedings volume will be valuable for your professional activities in this area.

November 2016

Nora Cuppens-Boulahia
Frédéric Cuppens
Nadia Tawbi
Lingyu Wang

Organization

General Chairs

Nadia Tawbi   Université Laval, Canada
Nora Cuppens-Boulahia   Télécom Bretagne, France

Program Co-chairs

Lingyu Wang   Concordia University, Canada
Frédéric Cuppens   Télécom Bretagne, France

Publications Chair

Joaquin Garcia-Alfaro   Télécom SudParis, France

Local Organizing Committee

Nadia Tawbi   Université Laval, Canada
Josée Desharnais   Université Laval, Canada
Andrew Bedford   Université Laval, Canada

Publicity Chair

Raphaël Khoury   Université du Québec à Chicoutimi, Canada

Program Committee

Esma Aimeur   Université de Montréal, Canada
Samiha Ayed   Télécom Bretagne, France
Jordi Castella-Roca   Rovira i Virgili University, Spain
Frédéric Cuppens   Télécom Bretagne, France
Nora Cuppens-Boulahia   Télécom Bretagne, France
Mila Dalla Preda   University of Verona, Italy
Jean-Luc Danger   Télécom ParisTech, France
Mourad Debbabi   Concordia University, Canada
Josée Desharnais   Université Laval, Canada
Nicola Dragoni   Technical University of Denmark, Denmark
Martin Gagné   Wheaton College, USA
Sebastien Gambs   Université du Québec à Montréal, Canada
Joaquin Garcia-Alfaro   Télécom SudParis, France
Jordi Herrera-Joancomarti   Autonomous University of Barcelona, Spain

Chunfu Jia	Nankai University, People's Republic of China
Bruce Kapron	University of Victoria, Canada
Raphaël Khoury	Université du Québec à Chicoutimi, Canada
Hyoungshick Kim	Sungkyunkwan University, South Korea
Evangelos Kranakis	Carleton University, Canada
Pascal Lafourcade	University of Auvergne, France
Giovanni Livraga	University of Milan, Italy
Luigi Logrippo	Université du Québec en Outaouais, Canada
Flaminia Luccio	Ca'Foscari University of Venice, Italy
Ilaria Matteucci	Istituto di Informatica e Telematica, Italy
Mohamed Mejri	Université Laval, Canada
Guillermo Navarro-Arribas	Autonomous University of Barcelona, Spain
Jordi Nin	Universitat Politecnica de Catalunya, Spain
Melek Önen	Eurecom, France
Andreas Pashalidis	Bundesamt für Sicherheit in der Informationstechnik, Germany
Marie-Laure Potet	Ensimag, France
Silvio Ranise	FBK, Security and Trust Unit, Italy
Andrea Saracino	Università di Pisa, Italy
Claudio Soriente	Telefonica Research and Development, Spain
Chamseddine Talhi	Ecole de Technologie Supérieure Montréal, Canada
Nadia Tawbi	Université Laval, Canada
Alexandre Viejo	Rovira i Virgili University, Spain
Lingyu Wang	Concordia University, Canada
Lena Wiese	Göttingen University, Germany
Nicola Zannone	Eindhoven University of Technology, The Netherlands
Nur Zincir Heywood	Dalhousie University, Canada
Mohammad Zulkernine	Queen's University, Canada

Additional Reviewers

Naofumi Homma	Tohoku University, Japan
Omer Yuksel	Eindhoven University of Technology, The Netherlands
Taous Madi	Concordia University, Canada
Maxime Puys	University of Grenoble, France
Stéphane Devismes	University of Grenoble, France
Davide Fauri	Eindhoven University of Technology, The Netherlands
Saed Alrabaee	Concordia University, Canada
Riccardo Focardi	Ca'Foscari University of Venice, Italy
Shahrear Iqbal	Queen's University, Canada
Suryadipta Majumdar	Concordia University, Canada
Feras Aljumah	Concordia University, Canada
Andrew Bedford	Université Laval, Canada
Mahdi Alizadeh	Eindhoven University of Technology, The Netherlands

Steering Committee

Frédéric Cuppens	Télécom Bretagne, France
Nora Cuppens-Boulahia	Télécom Bretagne, France
Mourad Debbabi	University of Concordia, Canada
Joaquin Garcia-Alfaro	Télécom SudParis, France
Evangelos Kranakis	Carleton University, Canada
Pascal Lafourcade	University of Auvergne, France
Jean-Yves Marion	Mines de Nancy, France
Ali Miri	Ryerson University, Canada
Rei Safavi-Naini	Calgary University, Canada
Nadia Tawbi	Université Laval, Canada

Contents

Physical Security

Malware and Anomaly Detection

MalProfiler: Automatic and Effective Classification of Android Malicious Apps in Behavioral Classes

Antonio La Marra, Fabio Martinelli, Andrea Saracino[✉],
and Mina Sheikhalishahi

Istituto di Informatica e Telematica, Consiglio Nazionale delle ricerche, Pisa, Italy
{antonio.lamarra,fabio.martinelli,
andrea.saracino,mina.sheikhalishahi}@iit.cnr.it

Abstract. Android malicious apps are currently the main security threat for mobile devices. Due to their exponential growth in number of samples, it is vital to timely recognize and classify any new threat, to identify and effectively apply specific countermeasures. In this paper we propose MalProfiler, a framework which performs fast and effective analysis of Android malicious apps, based on the analysis of a set of static app features. The proposed approach exploits an algorithm named Categorical Clustering Tree (CCTree), which can be used both as a divisive clustering algorithm, or as a trainable classifier for supervised learning classification. Hence, the CCTree has been exploited to perform both homogeneous clustering, grouping similar malicious apps for simplified analysis, and to classify them in predefined behavioral classes. The approach has been tested on a set of 3500 real malicious apps belonging to more than 200 families, showing both an high clustering capability, measured through internal and external evaluation, together with an accuracy of 97% in classifying malicious apps according to their behavior.

1 Introduction

In the last years we have witnessed an exponential increase in the number of malicious applications (apps) for mobile devices [1,14]. Their continuously increase and the considerable relevance that the phenomenon of malicious apps has on users, draw the attention of developers, researchers and security software vendors. Currently more than 98% of existing malicious apps are targeting Android devices [7], which is the most popular operating system, with more than 80% of the mobile device market share. Malicious apps exploit different techniques to damage Android device users, generally aiming at private data, or money, stealing them directly or through social engineering. Academic researchers and antivirus software companies are daily striving to tackle the actions of malicious developers by (i) collecting malicious apps found in the wild, performing

This work has been partially funded by the EU Funded Projects H2020 C3IISP, GA #700294, H2020 NeCS, GA #675320, EIT Digital MCloudDaaS.

© Springer International Publishing AG 2017
F. Cuppens et al. (Eds.): FPS 2016, LNCS 10128, pp. 3–19, 2017.
DOI: 10.1007/978-3-319-51966-1_1

analysis which is generally manual inspection, (ii) extracting signatures to be used to detect malicious apps in marketplaces and on device, and (iii) defining active countermeasures to dynamically recognize and block malicious behaviors, on device at runtime.

To simplify this complex tasks, malicious apps have been divided in malware families, i.e. sets of malicious apps including the same malicious code. Among 1 M android malicious apps which can be find in the wild, about 200 families of malware have been defined starting from 2011 [21] and this classification has been adopted by the main antivirus software houses. Still this classification is not sufficient for an easy analysis of malicious apps, nor to design countermeasures. In fact, several families, even if showing different source code, they produce the same or very similar effects. This moved researchers to perform a better grouping by defining malware classes [17]. Malware classes group together several families showing similar behaviors, causing a similar negative effect for the device or user. However, this analysis task is tedious and time consuming, based on manual analysis of malicious apps to infer their behavior and classifying them accordingly. Indeed, malicious apps are generally collected in large databases where malicious apps are either divided per family, or simply by the year of discovery. Considering that family names are not standardized, the same malware can be easily found under different names, further complicating this analysis task.

In order to simplify this analysis and to automate the classification of brand new threats, commonly known as zero-day, in this paper we propose *MalProfiler*, a novel framework based on the Categorical Clustering Tree (CCTree) algorithm to perform both automated grouping and classification of malicious apps in behavioral classes. The proposed framework brings a two-fold contribution to simplify the malware analysis task: (i) it divides (clusters) large amount of unlabeled (unclassified) malicious applications into smaller homogeneous sets where the contained apps are structurally similar and show the same behavior, (ii) builds a classifier out of a labeled dataset which can be used to classify new unknown malicious apps. The analysis is based on a set of static features, extracted directly from the app's `apk` file, which are representative of both the app structure and of the performed behaviors. This easy-to-extract features are very effective when exploited by the CCTree algorithm, which returns very homogeneous and meaningful clusters, as demonstrated through both external and internal evaluation. The contributions of this paper can be summarized as follows:

- We introduce MalProfiler, a fast, lightweight and accurate analysis framework which allows both clustering and classification of Android malicious apps.
- We present a set of static features extracted from apk files, effective in representing both the app structure and capabilities.
- We discuss the usage of the CCTree clustering algorithm to build an accurate supervised learning-based classifier.
- An evaluation of the clustering algorithm with the presented set of features is reported, through both internal and external evaluation.

– The capability of the algorithm in classifying malicious apps according to their behavior is evaluated on a set of 3500 malicious apps. An analysis for feature selection is also discussed.

The rest of the paper is organized as follows: in Sect. 2 we report some background information on the CCTree algorithm and on Android native security mechanisms. Section 3 describes the MalProfiler framework components and the envisioned workflows. Section 4 reports the results on clustering, classification experiments and performance overhead. Other related work in Android malicious apps detection is presented in Sect. 5. Finally Sect. 6 concludes proposing some future directions.

2 Background

In this section we first briefly introduce the mechanisms for security natively included in Android, with the emphasis on the permission system needed to understand some specific malicious behavioral patterns. Afterwards, we recall notions on the Categorical Clustering Tree (CCTree) algorithm, presented in [2,19], recalling the terminology and construction methodology.

2.1 Android Security Mechanisms

Given the level of threat, the Android framework includes several elements to enforce security on the physical device, applications and user data. The Android native security mechanisms are the Permission System and Application Sandboxing, which enforce, respectively, access control and isolation. Through the permission system, every security critical resource (e.g., camera, GPS, Bluetooth, network, etc.), data or operation is protected by mean of a permission. If an application needs to perform a security critical operation or access a security critical resource, the developer must declare this intention in the app AndroidManifest.xml (manifest for short) file asking the permission for each needed resource or operation. Permissions declared by the application are shown to users when installing the app, to decide if he wants to consider the application secure or not. If the application tries to perform a critical operation without asking the permission for it, the operation is denied by Android. The manifest file is bound to the application by means of digital signature. The integrity check is performed at deploy time, thus the Android system ensures that if an application has not declared a specific permission, the protected resource or operation cannot be accessed.

On the other hand, isolation is enforced through the synergy of two elements: the isolated runtime environment implemented through Virtual Machines (VM) and the underlying Linux kernel. In Android every application runs in a VM named Dalvik Virtual Machine (DVM) up to release 4.4 and Android Runtime Environment (ART) in the following releases. DVM and ART are an optimized version of the Java Virtual Machine, in particular ART also includes the support for Ahead of Time compilation for improved performance. In DVM and

ART each application has its own memory space, can act like it is the only application running on the system and is isolated from other apps. Moreover each VM instance is registered as a separate user of the Linux kernel. This means that each installed app is considered a user at the kernel level, able to run its own processes and with its own home folder. The home folder of each application stores application files on the device internal memory, thus it is protected from unauthorized access by the Linux kernel itself. In fact, files stored in the home folder can be accessed only by the application itself. However, since the device internal memory is limited, the amount of data that can be stored in the home folder is limited and generally using the internal memory is a deprecated practice.

2.2 CCTree Construction

CCTree [2] is constructed iteratively through a decision tree-like structure, where the leaves of the tree are the desired clusters. The root of the CCTree contains all the elements to be clustered. Each element is described through a set of *categorical* attributes, such as the *Language* of a message. Being categorical each attribute may assume a finite set of discrete values, constituting its domain. For example the attribute *Language* may have its domain as {*English, French, Spanish*}. At each step, a new level of the tree is generated by splitting the nodes of the previous levels, when they are not homogeneous enough. *Shannon Entropy* is used both to define a homogeneity measure called *node purity*, and to select the attribute used to split a node. In particular non-leaf nodes are divided on the base of the attribute yielding the maximum value for Shannon entropy. The separation is represented through a branch for each possible outcome of the specific attribute. Each branch or edge extracted from parent node is labeled with the selected feature which directs data to the child node. For additional information on the CCTree algorithm we refer the reader to [19]. An example of CCTree is reported in Fig. 1.

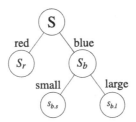

Fig. 1. A small CCTree

3   MalProfiler Framework

MalProfiler is a versatile framework which can be used either to cluster large amount of unlabeled malicious apps, dividing them in smaller, easy to handle, homogeneous sets of malicious apps, or to classify them in one of the aforementioned behavioral classes.

Figure 2 represents the logical components of MalProfiler and the possible operative workflows. The three components of the framework are the Feature Extractor, which takes as input the apk file of apps to be analyzed and extract the features generating the feature vector (element) to be clustered or classified. The CCTree Clustering is the component which generates a CCTree, according to the model described in Sect. 2.2, from a dataset of elements representing the apks. Finally the classifier performs supervised learning classification on elements, assigning them a label which represents the behavioral class. Being modular, MalProfiler can also use an alternative classifier in the place of the CCTree, which however is very accurate. As shown in Fig. 2, there are three main workflows represented by the three different arrow patterns. The training workflow is performed when is available a set of malicious apk whose behavioral label is already known, to be used as a training set. After feature extraction, the elements are used to generate a CCTree classifier. The CCTree classifier is like a normal CCTree where the leaves with their labels represent the classifier's knowledge. The classification workflow assumes that a trained classifier already exists in the framework. This workflow takes any number of unlabeled malicious apk, extracts the feature vectors through the extractor, and assigns a label to them through the classifier. This workflow can be used for example to classify zero day threats, or sets of malicious apps for which a label is not provided, or is classified differently from different antivirus software. The clustering workflow is instead exclusively applied to large datasets of unclassified malicious apps. After feature extraction, the CCTree will divide malware in homogeneous clusters, maximizing the cluster homogeneity related to the defined behavioral classes. In particular, the target of this instance of CCTree is the one of minimizing the probability that two or more elements, belonging to different behavioral classes do not fall in the same leaf cluster. After clustering, if a trained classifier is

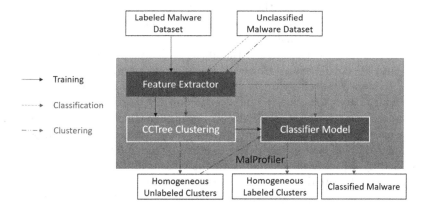

Fig. 2. MalProfiler logical model.

available, it is possible to classify the element of each cluster. This brings a double advantage to malware analyzer, since at the end of the clustering and classification process, the result are homogeneous sets of malicious grouped by similarity, whose behavior is known [18]. In the following we will detail the various components both on conceptual and implementation aspects.

3.1 Feature Extraction

The Feature Extractor is a software which takes in input an apk file, exploiting different tools to extract information on its internal files. The apk can be considered, in fact, a compressed archive, containing all the files which describe and define the behavior of the application. In particular, the feature extractor analyzes the `AndroidManifest.xml` file to extract information related to permissions and number of app components. Furthermore, it analyzes the `resources.arsc` file to extract information on the static resources included in the app (multimedia, documents, etc.) and decompiles the executable files (dex), looking for invocation of critical libraries[1].

We introduce now the set of 18 attributes (features) extracted by the Feature Extractor component, which are representative of structural properties of malware and of their behaviors. The selected attributes extend the set of features discussed in [9]. The attributes and a brief description are presented in Table 1.

Since the clustering algorithm is *categorical*, selected features are either binary or categorical as well. Numerical features are turned into categorical by defining intervals and assigning a feature value to each interval defined in such a way. The intervals have been according to the *ChiMerge* discretization method [13], which returns outstanding results for discretization in decision tree-like problems [11].

As shown in Table 1, the extracted features represent the capability of the malicious apps to maliciously exploit security critical resources and operations, together with information on the whole app structure. The rational of malprofiler is that specific combinations of these features identify specific behavioral classes. For this analysis, especially for those aspects concerning Android permissions, we leverage the results of [8,10]. The Internet permission is generally exploited by applications to send out (sensitive) information, or to receive commands from an external server under the control of the attacker. These are typical behaviors of spyware and botnet malware. However, the Internet permission by itself is not sufficient to identify specific threats, since it is a permission normally required by any app which needs to access the Internet to download or send information. The SMS permission is referred to the `SEND_SMS` permission which is mandatory to send text messages. This permission is not very common between standard apps, since normally in Android text messages are handled by a default messenger app, still it is needed by all malware belonging to the class of SMS Trojan. The permissions to read and write data on the external memories are respectively typical of two classes of malware: spyware, to access data stored on external memory, and to installers, which push malicious payload on external memory before installing it.

---

[1] We made the software available at: www.android-security.it/RetrieveFeatures.jar.

Table 1. List of static features extracted from malicious apps.

Attribute	Description
`Internet Permission`	Allows to access network interfaces. (BIN)
`SMS Permission`	Permission for sending text message. (BIN)
`Read SD card`	Read-only access to external memory. (BIN)
`Write SD card`	Write access to external memory. (BIN)
`Permission to install package`	Used to install additional apks. (BIN)
`Administrator permission`	Get administrator privileges. (BIN)
`Accessibility service permission`	Allows keylogging. (BIN)
`Permission to start at boot`	Self-Start of app at boot. (BIN)
`Permission to read contacts`	Accesses contact list. (BIN)
`Phone Status Permission`	Accesses sensitive info such as IMEI/IMSI. (BIN)
`Number of Permissions`	Amount of specified permissions. (CAT)
`Camera permission`	Permission to start camera and record video. (BIN)
`Microphone permission`	Permission to register voice from microphone. (BIN)
`Reputation score`	App reputation calculated according to [8]. (CAT)
`App components`	Number of components specified in the manifest. (CAT)
`Resource Size`	Size of static resource files. (CAT)
`Hidden Application`	App not visible in launcher. (BIN)
`Use cryptographic function`	Includes crypto API. (BIN)
`Custom permissions`	Requires custom permissions. (CAT)

Accessibility services, camera and microphone related permissions are all related to different attempts to spy user actions. Camera and microphone can be exploited to record picture, video and voices to infer information about the user. Moreover, the accessibility service permission, if maliciously exploited, allows an attacker to read the movement pattern on the device screen, including key-logging. The analysis on the size of the static resources included in the app can be meaningful to identify installer malware, since often they include in the asset folder of the apk, the payload of the other malicious app they will attempt to install. Some applications that only perform tasks in background may be configured by developers to not be shown in the main launcher interface, though it is still possible to see it in the apps list in Settings. This feature can be maliciously exploited especially by botnet and spyware apps attempting to pass unnoticed to users. The access to library for cryptographies is instead a behavior observed in the last generations of ransomware, which attempt to encrypt all the files on the SDCard. For this misbehavior, the permission to write on external memory is also needed. Finally the last feature specify if the application requires custom permissions, i.e. permissions defined by developers to protect interfaces of their applications. Some malicious apps, in particular botnet and spyware requires these permissions to access interfaces of apps with privacy sensitive data, or to perform confused deputy attacks, combining permissions of different malicious apps.

3.2   CCTree Clustering

The CCTree Clustering is a component which takes as input the feature vectors related to malicious apps and divides them in homogeneous clusters exploiting the fast and effective CCTree algorithm [19]. Being a divisive clustering algorithm, it requires that all the elements to be clustered are presented to the algorithm all together. Hence this component will be mainly used to group large sets of unlabeled malicious apps.

As discussed in Sect. 2.2, CCTree algorithm requires two stop conditions as input, i.e. the minimum number of elements (μ) and the minimum purity in a cluster (ϵ). Henceforth, the notation $\texttt{CCTree}(\epsilon, \mu)$ will be used to refer to the specific implementation of the CCTree algorithm.

In order to find the optimum stop conditions parameters and to evaluate our proposed methodology, in the following we introduce two well known approaches in clustering evaluations, named *internal* and *external* evaluation. Due to the fact that each evaluation approach contains a wide range of metrics, in this work we apply *silhouette* and *cluster homogeneity* as *internal* and *external* metrics, respectively.

Internal Evaluation: Internal evaluation measures the ability of a clustering algorithm in obtaining homogeneous clusters. A high score on internal evaluation is given to clustering algorithms which maximize the *intra-cluster similarity*, i.e. elements within the same cluster are similar, and minimize the *inter-cluster similarity*, i.e. elements from different clusters are dissimilar. The cluster dissimilarity is measured by computing the distances between elements (data points) in various clusters. The used distance function changes for the specific problem. In particular, for elements described by categorical attributes, the common geometric distances, e.g. Euclidean distance, cannot be used. Hence, in this work the *Hamming* distance measures [12] are applied. Internal evaluation can be performed directly on the dataset on which the clustering algorithm operates, i.e. the knowledge of the classes (desired clusters) is not a prerequisite.

Silhouette: Let $d(x_i)$ be the average *dissimilarity* of data point x_i with other data points within the same cluster. Also, let $d'(x_i)$ be the lowest average dissimilarity of x_i to any other cluster, except the cluster that x_i belongs to. Then, the *silhouette* $s(i)$ for x_i is defined as:

$$s(i) = \frac{d'(i) - d(i)}{\max\{d(i), d'(i)\}} = \begin{cases} 1 - \frac{d(i)}{d'(i)} & d(i) < d'(i) \\ 0 & d(i) = d'(i) \\ \frac{d'(i)}{d(i)} - 1 & d(i) > d'(i) \end{cases}$$

where the definition result in $s(i) \in [-1, 1]$. As much as $s(i)$ is closer to 1, the more the data point x_i is appropriately clustered. The average value of $s(i)$ over all data of a cluster, shows how tightly related are data within a cluster. Hence, the more the average value of $s(i)$ is close to 1, the better is the clustering result [12].

External Evaluation: The external evaluation is a standard technique to measure the capability of a clustering algorithm to correctly classify data. To this end, external evaluation is performed on a dataset, whose classes, i.e. the desired clusters, are known beforehand. This small dataset must be representative of the operative reality, and it is generally separated from the dataset used for clustering. A common index used for external evaluation is *cluster homogeneity*.

Cluster Homogeneity: *Cluster homogeneity* [3] is an essential quality property of a clustering algorithm. Cluster homogeneity states that the resulted clusters must be homogeneous, i.e. they should not mix elements belonging to different classes. In this study, we measure the cluster homogeneity as follows. Let D be the dataset desired to be clustered, the elements of D belong to categories (class labels) $\mathcal{L}' = \{L_1, L_2, \ldots, L_m\}$. For example, the labels belonging to $\mathcal{L}$ in our problem are represented by the behavioral classes defined in the following subsection. Moreover, suppose that $\mathcal{C} = \{C_1, C_2, \ldots, C_k\}$ are the resulted k clusters by our clustering algorithm. Considering:

$$p(C_i, L_j) = \frac{|\{d_{it} \in C_i | l(d_{it}) = L_j\}|}{|C_i|}$$

where $|.|$ returns the number of elements in a dataset and $l(x)$ returns the label of element x; we compute the homogeneity of clustering algorithm as the following:

$$\sum_{i=1}^{k} \sum_{j=1}^{m} p(C_i, L_j)$$

where k and m ranges over the number attributes and class labels, respectively.

3.3   Classifier

This component is embodied by a supervised learning-based classifier, which classifies feature vectors in five behavioral classes. Being configurable, virtually any classifier can be used as specific instance of this component. However, in this specific implementation, we are using a novel classifier, which is based on the CCTree algorithm. We present here the methodology exploited to construct a classifier inspired by the structure of CCTree clustering algorithm, hence named *CCTree classifier*. To this end, suppose a set of labeled dataset D is given.

Figure 3 depicts the structure of CCTree classifier and how it is utilized to label new unlabeled Android malicious app. As shown, the classifier is generated as a normal CCTree, starting from a large set of malicious apps. The only difference in the generation process lays in the stop conditions for splitting nodes:

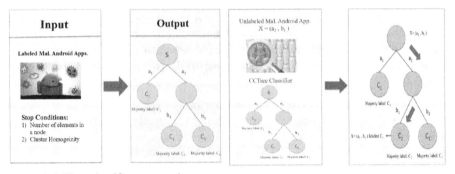

(a) CCTree classifier construction.   (b) Classification process.

Fig. 3. CCTree classifier construction and classification process.

(i) the number of elements in the node if fewer than a threshold, say μ, or (ii) the node cluster homogeneity (as defined for external evaluation) is better than a specific threshold δ. When the tree is generated, every leaf is labeled with the majority class present in that leaf, completing thus the classifier training. In the case that two or more class labels have the same frequency, or a leaf contain no element, then it is labeled as the majority label of the parent node. It is worth noting that, thanks to the high homogeneity of CCTree-generated clusters and to the novel stop condition based on cluster homogeneity, the situation in which a leaf contains elements of different classes is quite unlikely. This statement is supported by the experimental results presented in Sect. 4. Once the classifier is trained, the classification of single elements happens by walking the tree from root to leaves, according to the associated feature values. A formal description of the algorithm is given in Algorithm 1. It is worth noticing that CCTree classifier is different from boht CCTree clustering and standard decision tree classifiers [15]. We remark the differences in the following:

- *CCTree classifier vs CCTree clustering:* for constructing a CCTree classifier, differently from CCTree clustering, the set of data are labeled. Consequently, a node is considered as a leaf of a CCTree clustering, when the node purity (measured through similarity of features) is better than a specified threshold. However, in CCTree classifier, a node is considered as a leaf if the cluster homogeneity, computed from the labels of elements, is better than a threshold.
- *CCTree classifier vs Decision tree:* CCTree classifier is different from decision trees in splitting criteria. Basically, in decision trees the attribute causing the maximum information gain depending to attribute distribution and the labels of elements in a node, is selected to split the data belonging to a node. In CCTree classifier, the splitting attribute is selected as CCTree clustering, i.e. the one which has the highest entropy in terms of attribute values.

Input: Labeled data points D , Attributes $A = \{A_1, A_2, \ldots, A_k\}$,
   $cluster\_homogeneity\_threshold$, max_num_elem
Output: A set of labeled leaves $L = \{l_1, l_2, \ldots, l_m\}$
Root node N_0 takes all labeled data points D
for *each node N_i!=leaf node* **do**
$\quad$ **if** *cluster_homogeneity$_i$ < cluster_homogeneity_threshold*||
$\quad num\_elem_i < max\_num\_elem$ **then**
$\quad\quad N_i \to L$ & $l_i =$ majority labels in N_i
$\quad\quad$;
$\quad$ **else**
$\quad\quad$ **for** *each attribute A_j* **do**
$\quad\quad\quad$ **if** *A_j yields max Shannon entropy* **then**
$\quad\quad\quad\quad$ split N_i on A_j;
$\quad\quad\quad\quad$ generate new nodes $N_{i_1}, \ldots, N_{i_t}$;
$\quad\quad\quad$ **end**
$\quad\quad$ **end**
$\quad$ **end**
end

Algorithm 1. CCTree Classifier algorithm

3.4 Definition of Classes

As discussed, the amount of malicious Android apps is continuously increasing and currently counts to millions [14], whilst malware families count to hundreds. However, Android malicious apps show for the majority a quite limited set of common behavior which can be grouped into a more limited and manageable number of classes. To this end, referring to the model presented in [17], we discuss the behavioral classes which are used in the MalProfiler classification problem.

1. **SMS Trojan**: malware that send SMS messages stealthily and without the user consent, generally to subscribe the user to a premium services, send spam messages to user contacts, or exploit SMS-based authentication mechanism of some bank institutes to authorize unwanted transactions.
2. **Spyware**: malware that steals pieces of private data from the mobile device, such as IMEI and IMSI, contacts, messages or social network account credentials. The stolen information are sent to the attacker either through text messages, or, more commonly, through Internet.
3. **Installer**: this malware do not carry malicious code by itself, reducing the possibilities it is detected. However, once installed, they stealthily push on the device additional apps without the user consent, which generally contain the effective malicious code, belonging to any other of the behavioral classes defined. The most typical methodology exploited to stealthily install malicious apps consists of maliciously taking Linux super user privileges (rooting) to have full read/write access to all folders, then pushing the new malicious apps.
4. **Botnet**: malware opening a backdoor on the device, waiting for commands which can arrive from an external server or an SMS message.

5. **Ransomware**: malware that prevent the user from interacting with the device, by continuously showing a web page asking the user to pay a ransom to remove the malware. Other possible behavior consists of encrypting personal user files asking a ransom to retrieve the decryption key.

4   Clustering and Classification Results

In this section we will present experimental results to evaluate clustering capabilities, classification accuracy and performance overhead. All experiments have been performed on a set of 3525 real malicious apps, which have been extracted from three datasets, namely the Genome dataset [21], the Drebin [4] dataset and a set of malware extracted from the Contagio Mobile website[2]. The malware are divided as follows in the 5 behavioral classes: (i) 1927 SMS Trojan, (ii) 562 Installer, (iii) 1001 Spyware, (iv) 7 Botnet and (v) 28 Ransomware.

4.1   Clustering Evaluation

In order to evaluate the clustering capability of the CCTree Clustering component, it is necessary to compute the indexes for internal and external evaluation discussed in Sect. 3. Since CCTree is a parametric algorithm, we will study the variation of silhouette, number of clusters (internal evaluation) and cluster homogeneity (external evaluation), at the variation of these parameters. Table 2 shows the values for silhouette and cluster homogeneity at the variation of the purity parameter (ϵ). The results are also matched with the amount of clusters and the number of outliers, i.e. the number of clusters containing a single element, which we attempt to minimize.

Table 2. Internal/External evaluation results of CCTree, $\mu = 1$ and ϵ varies.

Metric	CCTree $- \mu = 1$			
	$\epsilon = 0.0001$	$\epsilon = 0.001$	$\epsilon = 0.01$	$\epsilon = 0.1$
Silhouette	1	1	0.9899	0.7295
Total number of clusters	483	483	469	231
Outliers	215	215	204	43
Cluster homogeneity	0.9991	0.9991	0.9899	0.9495

As the number of clusters is affected by the ϵ parameter, it is possible to choose the optimal value of ϵ knowing the optimal number of clusters. The problem of estimating the optimal number of clusters for hierarchical clustering algorithms is discussed in [16], by determining the point of maximum curvature (*knee*) on a graph showing the inter-cluster distance in function of the number

---

[2] http://contagiominidump.blogspot.com.

of clusters. Recalling that silhouette index is inversely related to inter-cluster distance, it is sound to exploit the same methodology, finding the knee on the graph of Fig. 4 computed with the silhouette on the dataset used for internal evaluation, with four different values of $\epsilon(\in \{0.0001, 0.001, 0.01, 0.1\})$. To simplify our analysis we fix the value of $\mu = 1$, thus the only stop condition affecting the result is the node purity ϵ.

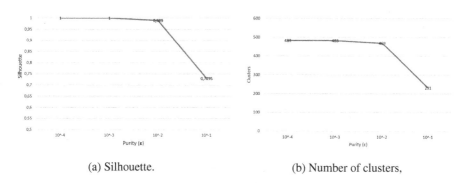

(a) Silhouette.   (b) Number of clusters,

Fig. 4. Knee analysis for silhouette and number of generated clusters in function of the ϵ parameter with $\mu = 1$.

As shown in Fig. 4, the purity value and generated clusters reach the maximum and almost stabilize when $\epsilon = 0.01$, which is effectively the knee in the graph, with a very high silhouette value of 0.989 and an acceptable number of clusters.

Fixed ϵ it is possible to study the variation of silhouette changing the value of μ. Table 3 shows silhouette, number of clusters, outliers, and the cluster homogeneity which we have previously defined for five different values of μ.

Table 3. Internal/External evaluation results of CCTree, $\epsilon = 0.01$ and μ varies.

Metric	CCTree $- \epsilon = 0.01$				
	$\mu = 1$	$\mu = 2$	$\mu = 3$	$\mu = 4$	$\mu = 5$
Silhouette	0.9899	0.9636	0.9413	0.9172	0.9004
Total number of clusters	469	426	391	354	329
Outliers	204	118	83	69	57
Cluster homogeneity	0.9985	0.9943	0.9909	0.9843	0.9807

As expected, $\mu = 1$ returns the highest number of clusters and outliers (i.e., clusters with one element), whilst the internal purity (silhouette) and cluster homogeneity are very high. On the other hand, by increasing the value of μ, the number of generated clusters decreases, as the internal purity overall cluster homogeneity. However, it is worth noting how even for higher value of μ which causes a consistent reduction of outliers, the overall cluster homogeneity and silhouette are still consistently high, which proves the validity of our approach. In fact, the CCTree algorithm, with the proposed set of features is able to divide malware in homogeneous clusters (silhouette), which are also very well divided for the behavioral classes, having only few clusters where malware from different classes are mixed. Also, when $\mu = 5$ the number of outliers drops to 57, out of a dataset of 3525 analyzed malware. The value of μ can be considered as a parameter to be changed according to the preference of the malware analyzer, and to specific structures of the dataset under analysis.

4.2   Classification Results

To verify the capability of correctly classifying Android malicious application in behavioral classes, the whole dataset of 3525 malicious apps is used for supervised learning and K-fold validation of the CCTree classifier. Also the results are compared with a set of well known classifiers, which are the best representatives of the various classifier sets, namely the K-star, C4.5, Bayes Network, and Support Vector Machine. The performance evaluation has been done through the K-fold ($K = 5$) validation method, i.e. classifying the data for K times using each time $K - 1/K$ of the dataset as training set and the remaining elements as testing set. Table 4 reports True Positive Rate (TPR) and False Positive Rate (FPR) for the five classifiers, reporting the detailed result for each class.

As shown, all classifiers have fair values of both TPR and FPR globally, which remarks the effectiveness of the selected features for this specific classification problem. However, the CCTree classifier shows better results both globally and for each behavioral class, both on the side of TPR and FPR. The tested instance of CCTree has the purity set to 0.01 and the minimum number of elements set to 1. This configuration reported the best results for our analysis, which is similar, still not equivalent to the clustering process. As can be observed, all classifiers perform quite well in classifying SMS Trojan and Spyware, while they find more difficult to classify elements from ransomware and botnet classes. This is due to the strongly unbalanced dataset used, which tricks the classifiers

Table 4. Classification results evaluated on 5-fold cross validation.

Algorithm	K-star		C4.5		BayesNet		SVM		CCTree (0.01,1)	
Measure	TPR	FPR	TPR	FPR	TPR	FPR	TPR	FPR	TPR	FPR
SMS.Trojan	0.995	0.048	0.989	0.019	0.991	0.142	0.991	0.126	0.989	0.012
Spyware	0.932	0.008	0.95	0.014	0.709	0.017	0.785	0.023	0.971	0.012
Installer	0.945	0.008	0.952	0.012	0.916	0.032	0.891	0.023	0.948	0.007
Ransomware	0.821	0	0.643	0.003	0.536	0.002	0	0	0.821	0.002
Botnet	0	0	0.143	0	0	0.001	0	0	0.857	0
Global	0.966	0.029	0.968	0.016	0.893	0.088	0.907	0.079	0.974	0.011

in labeling elements with the majority class, reducing thus the error probability, while increasing the FPR for that class. The CCTree classifier does not considers in its training process the error probability, which yields better results also for the minority classes. Even if overall results might benefit from a dataset balancing, it is worth noting that the present dataset is representative of the reality, where malware belonging to the first three classes of Table 4 are the larger majority of existing malware for Android. This aspect has to be considered both for the training process, which imposes to train any classifier to recognize the reality in which it will operate, and for the specific analysis task of malware analyzers that might have to operate on datasets that is not possible to balance.

Performance Analysis. One of the advantage of the CCTree algorithm, both if used for clustering or classification is the low (linear) complexity and high efficiency [2]. MalProfiler, is intended to work on large scale data, hence designed for being effective and scalable. In the performed experiments, the average time for clustering the set of 3525 malicious vector is below 1 s (878 ms), on a medium performance PC, for different configuration of the ϵ and μ parameters, and, as discussed it scales linearly if the amount of data to be considered increases. The bottleneck of the analysis process is the feature extraction process, which takes 3, 5 s in average for analyzed apps, which might increase for apps of large dimension. However, it is worth noting that this process is totally independent for each app and can thus be easily parallelized.

5   Related Work

As discussed, several efforts have been done in the direction of classifying malicious application. In [21], the authors collect and classify a set of malicious apps extracted from Chinese unofficial marketplaces. The study provided the first publicly available dataset of Android malicious apps and a set of typical behaviors of malicious apps. However, the authors do not propose techniques for automatic app classification, nor sets of features to be analyzed. In [5] the authors propose a methodology for behavior-based clustering of malicious applications for PCs. The analysis is based on dynamic features, hence it requires the application to be run. On the other hand, MalProfiler is able to cluster and then classifying Android malware by analyzing easy-to-extract static features. The authors of [20] present a methodology for Android malware classification using API dependency graphs. The designed approach is effective and able to detect zero-day attacks. Still, the classification requires an analysis of invoked API and graph generation not suitable for fast analysis. Another work which extracts and analyzes static features of Android apps for fast malware detection is presented in [8]. The approach is effective in determining if an application is malicious, still does not provide any information about the misbehavior which could be performed by the app. A framework which could benefit from a synergy with MalProfiler is the one presented in [9,17]. This work defines different dynamic per-app malware control strategies, defined on the base of the behavioral class of malicious applications, similar to the one proposed in the present work. In fact, the analysis of specific behavioral classes may bring the definition of new strategies (policies) specifically designed to counter specific behavior of novel threats. Another framework for static analysis of Android malware is presented in [6]. This framework exploits n-grams analysis, extracted after decompiling apps, to train classifiers in recognizing malicious patterns. The framework has a fair detection, accuracy, still it is more directed to detect malicious apps from benign ones, without giving detail on the possible malicious behavior performed by the app.

6   Conclusion

Since malicious apps for Android devices are growing exponentially, tools to simplify the analysis by security experts, for timely discovery and classification of new threats are a needed asset. In this paper we have presented MalProfiler a framework which exploits a categorical clustering algorithm to group and classify malicious Android apps according to behavioral classes. This paper shows another successful application of the CCTree algorithm, already used as a security tool for clustering spam emails. By grouping malicious apps in very homogeneous clusters, MalProfiler is a valuable tool in helping finding groups of apps showing the same behavior. Furthermore, operating as a classifier, MalProfiler can easily profile zero-day attacks, assigning to them their behavioral classes and finding apps previously classified which show similar features. As future work, MalProfiler will be extended to consider additional sets of features, including dynamically extracted ones, also proposing an implementation as web service publicly available, which allows the submission of large sets of apps for both clustering and classification.

References

1. Sophos mobile security threat reports (2014). http://www.sophos.com/en-us/threat-center/mobile-security-threat-report.aspx. Accessed 21 July 2017
2. Alishahi, M.S., Mejri, M., Tawbi, N.: Clustering spam emails into campaigns. In: ICISSP 2015 - Proceedings of the 1st International Conference on Information Systems Security and Privacy, ESEO, Angers, Loire Valley, France, 9–11 February 2015, pp. 90–97 (2015)
3. Amigó, E., Gonzalo, J., Artiles, J., Verdejo, F.: A comparison of extrinsic clustering evaluation metrics based on formal constraints. Inf. Retr. **12**(4), 461–486 (2009)
4. Arp, D., Spreitzenbarth, M., Hübner, M., Gascon, H., Rieck, K.: Drebin: effective and explainable detection of android malware in your pocket. In: Proceedings of NDSS (2014)
5. Bayer, U., Comparetti, P.M., Hlauschek, C., Kruegel, C., Kirda, E.: Scalable, behavior-based malware clustering. In: NDSS, vol. 9, pp. 8–11. Citeseer (2009)
6. Canfora, G., Lorenzo, A.D., Medvet, E., Mercaldo, F., Visaggio, C.A.: Effectiveness of opcode ngrams for detection of multi family android malware. In: 10th International Conference on Availability, Reliability and Security, ARES 2015, Toulouse, France, 24–27 August 2015, pp. 333–340 (2015)

7. Christian Funk, M.G.: Kaspersky security bullettin 2013, December 2013. http://media.kaspersky.com/pdf/KSB_2013_EN.pdf
8. Dini, G., Martinelli, F., Matteucci, I., Petrocchi, M., Saracino, A., Sgandurra, D.: Evaluating the trust of android applications through an adaptive and distributed multi-criteria approach. In: 2013 12th IEEE International Conference on Trust, Security and Privacy in Computing and Communications, pp. 1541–1546, July 2013
9. Dini, G., Martinelli, F., Saracino, A., Sgandurra, D.: MADAM: a multi-level anomaly detector for android malware. In: Proceedings of Computer Network Security - 6th International Conference on Mathematical Methods, Models and Architectures for Computer Network Security, MMM-ACNS 2012, St. Petersburg, Russia, 17–19 October 2012, pp. 240–253 (2012)
10. Felt, A.P., Chin, E., Hanna, S., Song, D., Wagner, D.: Android permissions demystified. In: Proceedings of the 18th ACM Conference on Computer and Communications Security, CCS 2011, Chicago, Illinois, USA, 17–21 October 2011, pp. 627–638 (2011)
11. Garcia, S., Luengo, J., Saez, J.A., Lopez, V., Herrera, F.: A survey of discretization techniques: taxonomy and empirical analysis in supervised learning. IEEE Trans. Knowl. Data Eng. **25**(4), 734–750 (2013)
12. Han, J., Kamber, M., Pei, J.: Data Mining: Concepts and Techniques, 3rd edn. Morgan Kaufmann Publishers Inc., San Francisco (2011)
13. Kerber, R.: Chimerge: discretization of numeric attributes. In: Proceedings of the Tenth National Conference on Artificial Intelligence, AAAI 1992, pp. 123–128. AAAI Press (1992)
14. Kindsight Security Labs: Kindsight security labs malware report h1 2014 (2014). http://resources.alcatel-lucent.com/?cid=180437
15. Quinlan, J.R.: Induction of decision trees. Mach. Learn. **1**(1), 81–106 (1986). http://dx.doi.org/10.1023/A:1022643204877
16. Salvador, S., Chan, P.: Determining the number of clusters/segments in hierarchical clustering/segmentation algorithms. In: Proceedings of the 16th IEEE International Conference on Tools with Artificial Intelligence, ICTAI 2004, pp. 576–584. IEEE Computer Society, Washington, DC (2004)
17. Saracino, A., Sgandurra, D., Dini, G., Martinelli, F.: Madam: effective and efficient behavior-based android malware detection and prevention. IEEE Tran. Dependable Secure Comput. (2016)
18. Sheikhalishahi, M., Saracino, A., Mejri, M., Tawbi, N., Martinelli, F.: Digital waste sorting: a goal-based, self-learning approach to label spam email campaigns. In: Foresti, S. (ed.) STM 2015. LNCS, vol. 9331, pp. 3–19. Springer, Heidelberg (2015). doi:10.1007/978-3-319-24858-5_1
19. Sheikhalishahi, M., Saracino, A., Mejri, M., Tawbi, N., Martinelli, F.: Fast and effective clustering of spam emails based on structural similarity. In: Garcia-Alfaro, J., Kranakis, E., Bonfante, G. (eds.) FPS 2015. LNCS, vol. 9482, pp. 195–211. Springer, Heidelberg (2016). doi:10.1007/978-3-319-30303-1_12
20. Zhang, M., Duan, Y., Yin, H., Zhao, Z.: Semantics-aware android malware classification using weighted contextual API dependency graphs. In: Proceedings of the 2014 ACM SIGSAC Conference on Computer and Communications Security, CCS 2014, New York, NY, USA, pp. 1105–1116. ACM (2014)
21. Zhou, Y., Jiang, X.: Dissecting android malware: characterization and evolution. In: Proceedings of the 2012 IEEE Symposium on Security and Privacy, SP 2012, pp. 95–109. IEEE Computer Society, Washington, DC (2012)

ANDRANA: Quick and Accurate Malware Detection for Android

Andrew Bedford[1]([✉]), Sébastien Garvin[1], Josée Desharnais[1], Nadia Tawbi[1],
Hana Ajakan[1], Frédéric Audet[2], and Bernard Lebel[2]

[1] Laval University, Quebec, Canada
andrew.bedford.1@ulaval.ca
[2] Thales Research and Technology Canada, Quebec, Canada

Abstract. In order to protect Android users and their information, we
have developed a lightweight malware detection tool for Android called
ANDRANA. It leverages machine learning techniques and static analysis
to determine, with an accuracy of 94.90%, if an application is malicious.
Its analysis can be performed directly on a mobile device in less than a
second and using only 12 MB of memory.

Keywords: Malware detection · Android · Static analysis · Machine
learning

1 Introduction

Android's domination of the mobile operating system market [30] has attracted
the attention of malware authors and researchers alike. In addition to its large
user base, what makes Android attractive to malware authors is that, contrarily
to iOS users, Android users can install applications from a wide variety of sources
such as first and third-party application markets (e.g., Google Play Store, Sam-
sung Apps), torrents and direct downloads. Malware on mobile devices can be
damaging due to the large amounts of sensitive information that they contain
(e.g., emails, photos, banking information, location).

In order to protect users and their information, researchers have begun to
develop malware detection tools specifically for Android. Traditional approaches,
such as the signature-based and heuristics-based detection of antiviruses can
only detect previously known attacks and hence suffer from a low detection rate.
One possible solution is to use Machine Learning algorithms to determine which
combinations of features (i.e. characteristics and properties of an application)
are typically present in malware. These algorithms learn to detect malware by
analyzing datasets of applications known to be malicious or benign.

The features used in Machine Learning are typically dynamically detected by
executing the application in a sandbox (an isolated environment where applications can be safely monitored) where events are simulated [7,20,21]. This approach has two major problems, the first being the time needed. Analyzing each
malware takes between 10 and 15 min (depending on the number of events sent
to the simulator). The infrastructure required to keep such a tool up-to-date

F. Cuppens et al. (Eds.): FPS 2016, LNCS 10128, pp. 20–35, 2017.
DOI: 10.1007/978-3-319-51966-1_2

needs to be of considerable size, as more than 60 000 applications are added to Google's Play Store each month [4]. The second problem is that this approach cannot take into account all possible executions of the application, only those that happen in the time allocated. Furthermore, sophisticated malwares can exploit this fact by stopping their malicious behavior when they detect that the current execution is in a sandbox.

To address these issues, we built a new malware detection tool for Android called ANDRANA. It uses static analysis to detect features, and Machine Learning algorithms to determine if these features are sufficient to classify an application as a malware. Static analysis can be performed quickly and directly on a mobile device. This means that no sandbox and no external infrastructure is required. Also, because static analysis considers all possible executions, it can detect attempts to evade analysis by the application. ANDRANA analyzes applications in three steps. First, the application is disassembled to obtain its code. Then, using static analysis, the application's features are extracted. Finally, a classification algorithm decides from the set of present features if the application is malicious.

One of the most important obstacle to static analysis is *obfuscation*. A code is obfuscated to make it hard to understand and analyze while retaining its original semantics. Although obfuscation has its legitimate uses (e.g., protection of intellectual property), it is often used by malware authors in an attempt to hide the malicious behaviors of their applications. ANDRANA can identify a number of obfuscation techniques and takes advantage of this information to improve the precision of its analysis.

In summary, our contributions in this paper are:

- We introduce ANDRANA, a malware detection tool able to quickly and accurately determine if an application is malicious (Sect. 3).
- We present the set of features that ANDRANA uses to classify applications. It includes the obfuscation techniques used by the application (Sect. 4).
- We have trained and tested classifiers using different machine learning algorithms on a dataset of approximately 5 000 applications. Our best classifier has an accuracy of 94.90 % and a false negative rate of 1.59 %. (Sect. 5).
- We report on two of our experiments to improve the overall accuracy and usability of ANDRANA: (1) using string analysis tools to improve the detection rate of API calls, (2) executing ANDRANA on a mobile device (Sect. 6).

2 Android

Before presenting ANDRANA, we must first introduce a few Android-related concepts and terminology, namely, the components of Android applications, Android's permission system and the structure of application packages.

2.1 Components

Android applications are composed of four types of components:

- **Activities**: An activity is a single, focused task that the user can do (e.g., send an email, take a photo). Applications always have one main activity (i.e., the one that is presented to the user when the application starts). An application can only do one activity at a time.

– **Services**: A service is an application component that can perform operations in the background (e.g., play music). Services that are started will continue to run in the background, even if the user switches to another application.
– **Intents**: An intent is a message that can be transmitted to another component or application. They are usually used to start an activity or a service.
– **Content Providers**: Content providers manage access to data. They provide a standard interface that allows data to be shared between processes. Android comes with built-in content providers that manage data such as images, videos and contacts.

2.2   Permissions

Android uses a permission system to restrict the operations that applications can perform. Android permissions are divided into two categories:

– **Normal**: Normal permissions are ones that cannot really harm the user, system or other applications (e.g., change the wallpaper) and are automatically granted by the system [2].
– **Dangerous**: Dangerous permissions are ones that involve the user's private information or that can affect the operation of other applications [24]. For example, the ability to access the user's contacts, internet or SMS are all considered to be dangerous permissions. These permissions have to be explicitly granted by the user.

2.3   Application Packages

Android applications are packaged into a single *.apk* file which contains:

– **Executable**: Android applications are written in Java and compiled to Java bytecode (*.class* files). The *.class* files are then translated to Dalvik bytecode and combined into a single Dalvik executable file named *classes.dex*.
– **Manifest**: Every Android application is accompanied by a manifest file, named *AndroidManifest.xml*, whose role is to specify the metadata of the application (e.g., title, package name, icon, minimal API version required) as well as its components and requested permissions.
– **Certificate**: Android applications must be signed with a certificate whose private key is known only to its developers. The purpose of this certificate is to identify (and distinguish) application authors.
– **Assets**: The assets used by the application (e.g., images, videos, libraries).
– **Resources**: They are additional content that the code uses such as user interface strings, layouts and animation instructions.

3   Overview of ANDRANA

ANDRANA analyzes applications in three steps: disassembly, feature extraction and classification (see Fig. 1).

Fig. 1. General flow of ANDRANA

Step 1: Disassembly. To analyze the code of the application and extract its features, we must first disassemble it. Fortunately, Android applications are based on Java, which is easy to disassemble and decompile. Moreover, Java forces multiple constraints on the structure of the code, which prevents manipulations that could make static analysis less effective (e.g., explicit pointer manipulations).

To disassemble the application, we use a tool called Apktool [3]. It converts Dalvik bytecode into Smali [29], a more readable form of the bytecode.

Step 2: Feature Extraction. Once the application has been disassembled, its features are extracted using static analysis. These features, presented in Sect. 4, are characteristics and properties that the classifier will use in Step 3 to distinguish malicious from benign applications. It is the most computationally intensive step of the analysis.

Step 3: Classification. Finally, the detected features are fed to a binary classifier that classifies the application as either "benign" or "malware". To generate the most accurate classifier possible, we have tried a variety of Machine Learning algorithms (see Sect. 5). They were trained and tested on a dataset of approximately 5 000 applications.

The whole process takes on average 30 s and 280 MB of memory (see Fig. 2) on a desktop computer (Intel Core i5-4200U with 4 GB of RAM). We were able to produce an optimized Android version which utilizes a reduced set of significant features and whose analysis takes on average less than a second and 12 MB of memory (see Sect. 6).

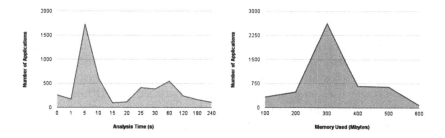

Fig. 2. Analysis time and memory usage distributions.

4   Feature Extraction

In this section, we present the features extracted by ANDRANA. These features characterize the behavior of an application and are used by the classifier to determine if an application is malicious or benign. In addition to the features that are typically extracted in similar tools (see Sect. 7), such as requested permissions and API calls, ANDRANA also detects a number of obfuscation techniques and tools used by the application.

4.1   Features Extracted from the Manifest and Certificate

Requested Permissions. We extract the permissions requested by the application from the manifest file. Certain combinations of requested permissions can be indicative of a malicious intent. For example, an application that requests permissions to access the microphone and start a service could be covertly listening in on conversations.

Components. From the manifest file, we extract the application's components and determine if the application executes code in the background, which intents it listens to and which content providers it accesses.

Invalid Certificate. We verify the validity of certificates using a utility called *jarsigner*. An invalid certificate indicates that the application has been tampered with.

4.2   Features Extracted from the Code

API Calls. We extract API calls from the code and, when possible, we also extract the value of their parameters. The latter are useful, for example, when trying to detect the attempt to send an email. This is done by looking for the function call `Activity.startActivity("act=android.intent.action.sendto dat=mailto:")`. ANDRANA considers that this feature is present if there is a call to this function and a string containing the value `"act=android.intent.action.sendto dat=mailto:"` somewhere in the code.

Necessary Permissions. By analyzing the API functions used in the code, we extract the permissions that are actually necessary to run the application. This allows to detect incongruities between the permissions requested by the application and those needed. Missing permissions could indicate that the application uses a root exploit to elevate its privileges during execution. To extract this information, ANDRANA uses an exhaustive mapping between the API calls and their required permissions. This mapping, which Google does not offer, is generated using PScout [25]. Note that since PScout's mapping is only an approximation, it may lead to false positives (i.e., reporting that there are missing permissions when, in fact, it is not true).

Obfuscation Techniques Used. We identify the obfuscation techniques possibly used by the application. The common techniques are: renaming, reflection, encryption and dynamic loading [23]. Note that their presence does not necessarily mean that the application uses obfuscation, only that it *may* have. It is the role of the learning algorithm to consider this feature as important or not.

Renaming. A simple way to obfuscate a code is to rename its packages, classes, methods and variables. For example, a class "Car" could be renamed "diZx9cA" or " ছতীপরীক্ষা " (Java supports unicode characters). This technique is particularly effective against human analysts as the purpose of a class or method has to be guessed from its content. It also makes it harder to recognize the method elsewhere in the code.

To detect the use of renaming, we exploit the fact that class names usually contain common names (e.g., File, Car, User) and methods contain verbs (e.g., getInstance, setColor). Knowing this, the first strategy of ANDRANA is to look for classes that have single-letter names (e.g., b.class). If there are many of them, then we assume that renaming has been used. If none are found, then we use an n-gram-based language detection library [18] to detect the language used to name the classes and functions of the application. If the result varies widely across the application, then we assume that renaming has been used.

Reflection. Reflection refers to the ability of the code to inspect itself at runtime. It can be used to get information on available classes, methods, fields, etc. More importantly, it can also be used to instantiate objects, invoke methods and access fields at runtime, without knowing their names at compile time. For example, using reflection, an instance of `ConnectivityManager` is created and method `getActiveNetworkInfo` is invoked in Listing 1.1.

```
Class c = Class.forName("android.net.ConnectivityManager");
Object o = c.newInstance()

Method m = c.getDeclaredMethod("getActiveNetworkInfo", ...);
method.invoke(o, null);
```
Listing 1.1. Instantiating an object and calling a function using reflection

The use of reflection itself can be detected easily, by looking for standard reflection API calls.

Encryption. Encryption can be used to obfuscate the strings of the code. For instance, it could be used to statically hide the names of classes instanced using reflection, as in the following listing.

```
String className = decrypt(encryptedClassName);
Class c = Class.forName(className);
```
Listing 1.2. Instanciating an object of a statically unknown class using reflection

To detect the possible use of encryption, ANDRANA looks for standard cryptography API calls.

Dynamic Loading. Java's reflection API also allows developers to dynamically load code (.apk, .dex, .jar or .class files). This code can be hidden in encrypted/-compressed assets or data arrays. However, to load this code, applications must use Android's API `getClassLoader` function. Once loaded, the reflection API must be used to access the classes, methods and fields of the dynamically loaded code. Android applications can also dynamically load native libraries through the *Java Native Interface* (JNI). This not only allows Java code to invoke native functions, but also native code to invoke Java functions. According to Zhou et al. [34], approximately 5% of Android applications invoke native code.

To detect the use of dynamic loading, ANDRANA looks for instances of classes `DexClassLoader` and `ClassLoader`. To detect the use of native libraries, we look for calls to the API `System.loadLibrary`. Note that, for the moment, ANDRANA only detects the use of dynamic loading and native libraries: the libraries are not analyzed.

Commercial Obfuscation Tools. While developers can manually obfuscate the code themselves, most of them use commercially available obfuscation tools. ANDRANA is able to detect the use of these tools using the techniques described by Apvrille and Nigam [5]. The obfuscation tools that are currently detected are ProGuard, DexGuard and APKProtect.

– ProGuard renames packages, classes, methods and variables using either the alphabet (default behavior) or a dictionary of words. ProGuard comes with the Android SDK and runs automatically when building an application in release mode. As such, it is the most popular obfuscation tool. ANDRANA can detect the use of ProGuard by looking for strings such as "a/a/a->a" in smali code.
– DexGuard is the commercial version of ProGuard. It also renames the packages, classes, methods and variables, but uses by default non-ASCII characters which reduces even more the readability of the code. It also encrypts the strings present in the code. ANDRANA detects the use of DexGuard by looking for names that contain non-ASCII characters.
– APKProtect can be detected by searching for the string `"apkrotect"` in the *.dex* file.

Sandbox Detection. Certain malwares have the ability to deactivate their malicious behaviors when they detect that they are in a sandbox. This may indicate a malicious intent, as it could invalidate the results of a dynamic analysis. It does not affect static analyses, of course.

To detect the use of sandbox detection, we look for strings whose values are typically present in Android sandboxes. Vidas and Christin [31] enumerate some of the most common ones.

Disassembly Failure. While disassembly works in most cases, it can sometimes fail. Disassembly failure clearly indicates an attempt to thwart analysis. For this reason, it is part of our feature set.

5   Classification and Evaluation

In this section, we evaluate the performance of multiple Machine Learning algorithms.

5.1   Dataset

To train and test our algorithms, we have collected and analyzed a dataset of approximately 5 000 applications, 80% of which were malwares. To avoid overfitting, the malware samples were randomly selected from two repositories: Contagio [12] and Virus Share [32]. The benign samples came from Google's Play Store various "Top 25". We noted that 47% of the samples used some kind of obfuscation.

Our dataset contains more malware samples than benign samples for two reasons. The main reason is that it is hard to obtain benign applications. Indeed, while there are many repositories of malicious Android applications, we found none that contained certified benign applications. Had we taken a larger number of applications from the Play Store, we would have risked introducing malicious samples into our dataset of benign samples. Another reason for using more malware samples is that it has a desirable side effect on the learning algorithm: it will lead the algorithm to try to make fewer bad classifications on this class. Hence, the number of false negatives (i.e., applications classified as "benign" when they are in fact malicious) will be naturally lower than the number of false positive.

5.2   Learning Algorithms

In order to obtain the best classifier possible, we have experimented with different learning algorithms: Support Vector Machines (SVM), k-Nearest Neighbors (KNN), Decision Trees (DT), Adaboost and Random Forest (RF).

Support Vector Machines (SVM) [13] is a learning algorithm that finds a maximal margin hyperplane in the vector space induced by the examples. The SVM can also take into account a *kernel function*, which encodes a notion of similarity between examples. Instead of producing a linear classifier in the *input space*, the SVM can produce a linear classifier in the space induced by the chosen kernel function. In our experiments, we use the *Radial Basis Function* (*RBF*) kernel $k(x, x') = e^{-\gamma ||x - x'||_2^2}$, where γ is a parameter of the kernel function. The SVM also considers a hyperparameter C that controls the trade-off between maximizing the margin and permitting misclassification of training examples.

k-Nearest Neighbors (KNN) [14] is a learning algorithm that classifies a new data point by considering the k most similar training examples and by choosing the most frequent label among these examples. Here, k is a hyperparameter of the algorithm: different values of k might give different results. The most similar examples are computed using any similarity function, such as the Euclidean distance.

Decision Tree (DT) [9] is a learning algorithm that classifies examples by applying a decision rule at each internal node. The label of the example is decided at a leaf of the tree. Decision trees are learned by considering a measure of quality for a split such as the Gini impurity or the entropy for the information gain. In our experiment, we use the Gini impurity.

Adaboost [27]. is an *ensemble classifier*, that considers many *base classifiers* and learns a weighted combination of these classifiers. At each iteration, a new base classifier is chosen (or generated) to focus on examples that are incorrectly classified by the current weighted combination. The algorithm usually stops after a fixed number of iterations, or when the maximum number of base classifiers is attained. This maximum number of base classifiers is a hyperparameter of the algorithm.

Random Forest (RF) [8] is, similarly to adaboost, an ensemble classifier. It builds a majority vote of decision tree classifiers, by considering sub-samples of the data and by controlling the correlation between the trees. The number of trees or tree construction parameters such as the maximal depth are hyperparameters of the algorithm.

5.3   Performance Metrics

To evaluate the performance of the resulting classifiers, we measured their True Positive Ratio (TPR). It represents the proportion of malware applications that are correctly classified:

$$\text{TPR} = \frac{\text{TP}}{\text{TP} + \text{FN}}$$

where TP is the number of malware applications that are correctly classified and FN is the number of malware applications that are classified as "benign". Similarly, we measured their True Negative Ratio (TNR), which represents the proportion of benign application that are correctly classified:

$$\text{TNR} = \frac{\text{TN}}{\text{TN} + \text{FP}}$$

where TN is the number of benign applications that are correctly classified and FP is the number of benign applications that are classified as "malware". Finally, we measured their overall accuracy, which represents the proportion of applications that are correctly classified:

$$\text{Accuracy} = \frac{\text{TP} + \text{TN}}{\text{TP} + \text{TN} + \text{FP} + \text{FN}}.$$

5.4   Evaluation

According to Hoeffding's bound [16], with at least 600 test samples, the real risk is almost equal to the risk on test with 95% confidence. Hence, we chose to use

Table 1. Considered values for each hyperparameter, for each algorithm.

Learning algorithm	Hyperparameter	Values
SVM	C	$\{0.001, 0.01, 0.1, 1, 10, 100, 1000\}$
	γ	$\{100, 10, 1.0, 0.1, 0.01, 0.001, 0.0001\}$
KNN	k	$\{1, 2, 3, 4, 5, 10, 15, 20, 25, 50, 100\}$
Decision Trees (DT)	max_leaf_nodes	$\{5, 10, 15, 20, 25, 30, 40, 50\}$
	min_samples_leaf	$\{1, 2, 3, 5, 10, 20\}$
AdaBoost	n_estimators	$\{5, 10, 25, 50, 100, 250, 500, 1000\}$
RandomForest (RF)	n_estimators	$\{2, 5, 10, 25, 50, 100, 500, 1000, 2000, 3000\}$

Table 2. A comparison of the classifiers' metrics, Accuracy, True Positive Ratio and True Negative Ratio, using different machine learning algorithms.

Learning algorithm	Accuracy%	TPR%	TNR%
SVM	94.72	**98.64**	78.43
KNN	94.11	97.74	79.06
Decision Trees (DT)	93.20	97.43	75.62
AdaBoost	94.11	98.26	76.87
RandomForest (RF)	**94.90**	98.41	**80.31**

the following splitting scheme in our experiments: 2/3 (∼3300 samples) for the training set and 1/3 (∼1700 samples) for the testing set. For each algorithm, we chose the hyperparameters using a 5-folds cross-validation on the training set and chose the hyperparameter values that optimized the accuracy. Table 1 shows the hyperparameter values on which the cross-validation was performed for each algorithm. Finally, we trained the algorithm using the whole training set, and predicted the examples of the testing set. Note that all reported values are metrics calculated on the testing set, containing examples that have not been seen during training time. Table 2 shows the resulting accuracies for each algorithm.

We now discuss on whether an increase in the size of the training dataset can possibly improve the learning algorithms' performance. For this experiment, we first split the dataset into a training set (2/3) and a test set (1/3). Then, we followed the same procedure as above, but applied exclusively to a ratio of the training set and without altering the test set. Figure 3 shows that an increase of the training ratio leads to a fluctuating improvement of the accuracy. The non-monotonous behavior of the accuracy is a common occurrence in statistical learning and is mainly caused by noise in the dataset. Still, one can see that the accuracy tends to increase when the training ratio increases. So, we can expect a higher performance by using a larger dataset.

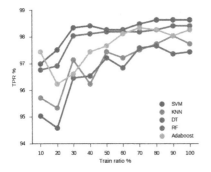 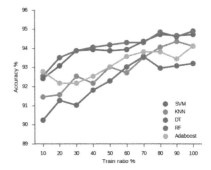

Fig. 3. The progression of true positives ratio and accuracy on the test set for different ratios of training set and for each learning algorithm. It is calculated using the best configuration of hyperparameters outputted by a 5-fold cross-validation.

6 Additional Experiments

This section presents the various experiments that we did in order to improve the overall accuracy and usability of ANDRANA.

6.1 E1: Using String Analysis Tools

As previously mentioned, API calls can be invoked through reflection. To detect those calls, we look for their class and method names in the strings of the code. Of course, strings are not necessarily hard coded, they can also be dynamically built. For instance, in Listing 1.3, the class instantiated could be either "java.lang.String" or "java.lang.Integer".

```
String a = "java.lang.";
String b;
if (random) { b = "String"; } else { b = "Integer"; }
String className = a + b;
Class c = Class.forName(className);
Object o = c.newInstance();
```
Listing 1.3. Dynamically built class name

To take into account cases where the class and/or function names are dynamically created, we have experimented with a tool called *Java String Analyzer* (JSA) [11,17]. JSA performs a static analysis of Java programs to predict the possible values of string variables. This allows us to determine that the possible values for the string variable `className` in Listing 1.3 are {"java.lang.String", "java.lang.Integer"}.

However, JSA is not able to analyze entire Android applications in a reasonable time or without running out of memory. Li et al. [19] encountered similar problems with JSA and hypothesize that this problem is due to the fact that it uses a variable-pair-based method to do the global inter-procedural aliasing analysis. This method has an $O(n^2)$ memory complexity, where n is the number of variables in the application.

We have also experimented with another string analysis tool called *Violist* [19]. While it is considerably faster than JSA and can actually be used to analyze Android applications, it still requires too much time (around 4 min) and resources (up to 2.4 GB of memory) for our purpose: the analysis has to be executable on a mobile device. Furthermore, in our test on 10 applications that used reflection, it did not lead to the detection of additional features. For these reasons, we chose to not use them in ANDRANA. Besides, as seen in the previous section, it turns out that a precise string analysis is not required to accurately classify applications. This is because ANDRANA uses a wide variety of features to classify applications, some of which are not affected by obfuscation techniques (e.g., permissions, certificate, disassembly failure).

6.2   E2: Executing ANDRANA on a Mobile Device

Mobile devices generally have low computing power and memory compared to desktop computers. Consequently, if ANDRANA is to run directly on such devices, it must be very efficient. To evaluate ANDRANA's runtime performance on mobile devices, we have implemented a version of it for Android (see Fig. 4). In order to minimize ANDRANA's analysis time on Android, we chose to use the decision tree as the classifier. As previously shown, it is accurate (93.20%) and requires only a small subset of our features to classify applications (between 3 and 9 features). We also optimized ANDRANA's Android version so that it uses as little memory as possible. We analyzed 150 randomly selected applications from our dataset on a Nexus 5X and, on average, the analysis took only 814 milliseconds and 12 MB of memory, much quicker than our desktop version which extracts *all* features. Besides its performance, another advantage of using the decision tree classifier is that it is simple to understand and interpret.

Fig. 4. ANDRANA's interface on Android.

7 Related Work

Research on malware detection tools for Android has been very active in recent years. We present in this section the approaches that are most similar to ours.

Static Malware Detection Tools for Android. Sato et al. [26] present a method to calculate the malignancy score of an application based entirely on the information found in its manifest file. Namely, the permissions requested, intent filters (their action, category and priority), number of permissions defined and application name. They trained their classifier on a dataset of 365 samples and report an accuracy of 90%.

Aafer et al. [1] present a classifier, named DroidAPIMiner, that uses the API calls present in the code of the application to determine whether an application is benign or malicious. To determine the most relevant API calls for malware detection, they statically analyzed a large corpus of malware and looked at the most frequent API calls. They report a maximum accuracy of 99% using a KNN classifier.

Arp et al. [6] present another classifier, named Drebin, which uses statically detected features. Namely, they extract the hardware components (e.g., GPS, camera, microphone) used by the application by looking at the permissions requested in the manifest file, the requested permissions, the API calls present in the code, IP addresses and URLs found in the code. They use the SVM machine learning algorithm to produce a classifier. It has an accuracy of approximately 94%. Their Android implementation requires, on average, 10 seconds to return a result.

Since the datasets used in these approaches are not actually available for analysis, we cannot directly compare their performance with ANDRANA's. We also do not know if their samples were as heavily obfuscated as ours. All we can say is that ANDRANA seems to equal them in terms of accuracy and surpass them in terms of speed. We expect that by using a larger dataset of applications, like the 20 000 used by DroidAPIMiner, we could improve even more our accuracy. So that others may compare their results with ours, our dataset is available online [22].

There are also various antiviruses available on Google's Play Store (e.g., AVG, Norton, Avira). Antiviruses mostly use pattern matching algorithms to identify known malware (i.e., they look for specific sequences of instructions). This means that different patterns must be used to detect variations of the same malware. ANDRANA's main advantage over antiviruses is that it can not only detect known malware and their variations, but also unknown malware.

Dynamic and Hybrid Malware Detection Tools for Android. Crowdroid [10], Andromaly [28] and MADAM [15] detect malware infections by looking for anomalous behavior. To detect anomalies, they monitor system metrics such as CPU consumption, number of running processes, number of packets sent through WiFi and/or the API calls performed at runtime by an application.

Machine learning techniques are then used to distinguish standard behaviors from those of an infected device.

DroidRanger [34] use both static and dynamic analysis to perform a large-scale study of several application markets. Instead of using machine learning techniques to automatically learn to classify applications, they use a variety of heuristics. Using their tool, they were able to identify 211 malicious applications present on the markets, 32 of which were on Google's Play Store.

DroidDolphin [33] inserts a monitor into applications to log their API calls and then executes them. The authors generate a classifier using this information and a dataset of 34 000 applications. They report an accuracy of 86.1%.

Andrubis [21] and its successor Marvin [20] uses approximately 500 000 features, detected using a combination of static and dynamic analyses, to train and test their classifier on a dataset of over 135 000 applications. They report an accuracy of 98.24%.

ANDRANA's main advantages over these approaches are that it introduces no runtime overhead and that its analysis can be performed on the user's mobile device, very quickly.

8   Conclusion

In this paper, we have presented ANDRANA, a lightweight malware detection tool for Android. It uses static analysis to extract an application's features and then uses a classifier to determine if it is benign or malicious. We have trained and tested multiple classifiers using a variety of Machine Learning algorithms and a dataset of approximately 5 000 applications, 4 000 of which were malwares. The dataset is available online [22]. Its samples came from multiple sources to avoid overfitting. Our best classifier has an accuracy of 94.90% and a false negative rate of 1.59%, which is comparable to other similar tools. As indicated by the upward trends of Fig. 3, the use of larger datasets should lead to even higher accuracies.

As almost half of our dataset used reflection, we considered using two string analysis tools, JSA and Violist, to improve the detection rate of our features, but their use turned out to be too computationally expensive for our purpose.

We have implemented a version of ANDRANA for Android and our tests reveal that, on average, it can analyze applications in less than a second using only 12 MB of memory, faster and more efficiently than any similar tools. Since our implementation uses a decision tree as its classifier, users can easily understand what lead the application to be classified as malware/benign.

Future Work. Benign applications may also compromise the security of a user's information, generally by accident. For this reason, we are working on a way to enforce information-flow policies by inlining a monitor in Android applications. In theory, this type of mechanism could allow users to execute applications safely, that is, without compromising the confidentiality of their information or the integrity of their system.

We are also working on our own string analysis tool. Our goal is to make it as lightweight as possible so that it can be executed on a mobile device.

Acknowledgments. We would like to thank François Laviolette for his suggestions and Souad El Hatib for her help with the string analysis tools. This project was funded by Thales and the NSERC.

References

1. Aafer, Y., Du, W., Yin, H.: DroidAPIMiner: mining API-level features for robust malware detection in Android. In: Zia, T., Zomaya, A., Varadharajan, V., Mao, M. (eds.) SecureComm 2013. LNICST, vol. 127, pp. 86–103. Springer, Heidelberg (2013). doi:10.1007/978-3-319-04283-1_6
2. Android operating system security. http://developer.android.com/guide/topics/security/permissions.html. Accessed 5 July 2016
3. Apktool. https://ibotpeaches.github.io/Apktool/. Accessed 5 July 2016
4. Appbrain. http://www.appbrain.com/stats/number-of-android-apps. Accessed 18 July 2016
5. Apvrille, A., Nigam, R.: Obfuscation in android malware, and how to fight back. Virus Bull. 1–10 (2014)
6. Arp, D., Spreitzenbarth, M., Hübner, M., Gascon, H., Rieck, K., Siemens, C.: DREBIN: effective and explainable detection of Android malware in your pocket. In: Proceedings of the Annual Symposium on Network and Distributed System Security (NDSS) (2014)
7. Atzeni, A., Su, T., Baltatu, M., D'Alessandro, R., Pessiva, G.: How dangerous is your Android app? An evaluation methodology. In: Proceedings of the 11th International Conference on Mobile and Ubiquitous Systems: Computing, Networking and Services, pp. 130–139. ICST (Institute for Computer Sciences, Social-Informatics and Telecommunications Engineering) (2014)
8. Breiman, L.: Random forests. Mach. Learn. **45**(1), 5–32 (2001)
9. Breiman, L., Friedman, J., Stone, C.J., Olshen, R.A.: Classification and Regression Trees. CRC Press, Boca Raton (1984)
10. Burguera, I., Zurutuza, U., Nadjm-Tehrani, S.: Crowdroid: behavior-based malware detection system for Android. In: Proceedings of the 1st ACM Workshop on Security and Privacy in Smartphones and Mobile Devices, pp. 15–26. ACM (2011)
11. Christensen, A.S., Møller, A., Schwartzbach, M.I.: Precise Analysis of String Expressions. Springer, New York (2003)
12. Contagio. http://contagiominidump.blogspot.ca/. Accessed 16 July 2016
13. Cortes, C., Vapnik, V.: Support-vector networks. Mach. Learn. **20**(3), 273–297 (1995). http://dx.doi.org/10.1007/BF00994018
14. Cunningham, P., Delany, S.J.: k-nearest neighbour classifiers. In: Multiple Classifier Systems, pp. 1–17 (2007)
15. Dini, G., Martinelli, F., Saracino, A., Sgandurra, D.: MADAM: a multi-level anomaly detector for Android malware. In: Kotenko, I., Skormin, V. (eds.) MMM-ACNS 2012. LNCS, vol. 7531, pp. 240–253. Springer, Heidelberg (2012). doi:10.1007/978-3-642-33704-8_21
16. Hoeffding, W.: Probability inequalities for sums of bounded random variables. J. Am. Stat. Assoc. **58**(301), 13–30 (1963)
17. Java string analyzer (JSA). http://www.brics.dk/JSA/. Accessed 5 July 2016

18. Language detection library. https://github.com/shuyo/language-detection. Acessed 5 July 2016
19. Li, D., Lyu, Y., Wan, M., Halfond, W.G.: String analysis for Java and Android applications. In: Proceedings of the 2015 10th Joint Meeting on Foundations of Software Engineering, pp. 661–672. ACM (2015)
20. Lindorfer, M., Neugschwandtner, M., Platzer, C.: MARVIN: efficient and comprehensive mobile app. classification through static and dynamic analysis. In: 39th Annual Computer Software and Applications Conference (COMPSAC), vol. 2, pp. 422–433. IEEE (2015)
21. Lindorfer, M., Neugschwandtner, M., Weichselbaum, L., Fratantonio, Y., Van Der Veen, V., Platzer, C.: Andrubis-1,000,000 apps later: a view on current Android malware behaviors. In: 2014 Third International Workshop on Building Analysis Datasets and Gathering Experience Returns for Security (BADGERS), pp. 3–17. IEEE (2014)
22. LSFM. http://lsfm.ift.ulaval.ca/recherche/andrana/. Accessed 30 Sep 2016
23. Maiorca, D., Ariu, D., Corona, I., Aresu, M., Giacinto, G.: Stealth attacks: an extended insight into the obfuscation effects on Android malware. Comput. Secur. **51**, 16–31 (2015)
24. Permissions classified as dangerous. http://developer.android.com/guide/topics/security/permissions.html#normal-dangerous. Accessed 5 July 2016
25. Pscout. https://github.com/dweinstein/pscout. Accessed 5 July 2016
26. Sato, R., Chiba, D., Goto, S.: Detecting Android malware by analyzing manifest files. In: Proceedings of the Asia-Pacific Advanced Network, vol. 36, pp. 23–31 (2013)
27. Schapire, R.E., Singer, Y.: Improved boosting using confidence-rated predictions. Mach. Learn. **37**(3), 297–336 (1999)
28. Shabtai, A., Kanonov, U., Elovici, Y., Glezer, C., Weiss, Y.: "Andromaly": a behavioral malware detection framework for Android devices. J. Intell. Inf. Syst. **38**(1), 161–190 (2012)
29. Smali/baksmali. https://github.com/JesusFreke/smali. Accessed 20 July 2016
30. Smartphone OS market share, q1 2015 (2015). http://www.idc.com/prodserv/smartphone-os-market-share.jsp. Accessed 7 July 2016
31. Vidas, T., Christin, N.: Evading android runtime analysis via sandbox detection. In: Proceedings of the 9th ACM Symposium on Information, Computer and Communications Security, pp. 447–458. ACM (2014)
32. Virus share. https://virusshare.com/. Accessed 14 July 2016
33. Wu, W.C., Hung, S.H.: DroidDolphin: a dynamic Android malware detection framework using big data and machine learning. In: Proceedings of the 2014 Conference on Research in Adaptive and Convergent Systems, pp. 247–252. ACM (2014)
34. Zhou, Y., Wang, Z., Zhou, W., Jiang, X.: Hey, you, get off of my market: detecting malicious apps in official and alternative android markets. In: NDSS, vol. 25, pp. 50–52 (2012)

Micro-signatures: The Effectiveness of Known Bad N-Grams for Network Anomaly Detection

Richard Harang[1(✉)] and Peter Mell[2]

[1] United States Army Research Laboratory, Adelphi, MD, USA
richard.e.harang.civ@mail.mill
[2] National Institute of Standards and Technology, Gaithersburg, MD, USA
peter.mell@nist.gov

Abstract. Network intrusion detection is broadly divided into signature and anomaly detection. The former identifies patterns associated with known attacks and the latter attempts to learn a 'normal' pattern of activity and alerts when behaviors outside of those norms is detected. The n-gram methodology has arguably been the most successful technique for network anomaly detection. In this work we discover that when training data is sanitized, n-gram anomaly detection is not primarily anomaly detection, as it receives the majority of its performance from an implicit non-anomaly subsystem, that neither uses typical signatures nor is anomaly based (though it is closely related to both). We find that for our data, these "micro-signatures" provide the vast majority of the detection capability. This finding changes how we understand and approach n-gram based 'anomaly' detection. By understanding the foundational principles upon which it operates, we can then better explore how to optimally improve it.

Keywords: Network intrusion detection · Anomaly detection · Microsignatures

1 Introduction

Anomaly based intrusion detection systems attempt to learn a 'normal' pattern of activity and then produce security alerts when behavior outside of those norms is detected. This has been an active area of research since at least the late 1980's [1–3]. In the late 1990's, the use of n-grams was discovered to be useful for host based anomaly detection [4]. N-grams are simply a collection of arrays of length n obtained by applying a sliding window of length n to whatever activity is being monitored (e.g., system calls) [5], and were first applied to analyze network payloads in the PAYL model [6] in 2004 but were limited to 1-grams, as the number of different n-grams that can be acquired can approach a^n where a is the number of characters available (UTF-8 encoding has 1,114,112 code points [7]). In 2006, the seminal Anagram approach introduced using an n of greater than 1 by storing the acquired n-grams in Bloom filters [8]. As a minor enhancement, Anagram introduced the idea of using known bad n-grams to augment its ability to identify malicious traffic.

The rights of this work are transferred to the extent transferable according to title 17 U.S.C. 105.

© Springer International Publishing AG 2017
F. Cuppens et al. (Eds.): FPS 2016, LNCS 10128, pp. 36–47, 2017.
DOI: 10.1007/978-3-319-51966-1_3

While not discussed in [8], use of the bad n-grams represented a significant shift away from pure anomaly detection. In this approach, a corpus of malicious packet payloads or intrusion signatures can be used to generate n-grams and these n-grams are filtered to exclude any that have been observed to occur in normal benign traffic. The remaining n-grams are then added to a known bad content filter comprised of what we refer to as automatically generated micro-signatures. In operation, any time an n-gram is analyzed that matches one in the bad content filter, the score for the overall packet increases pushing it towards being labelled anomalous/malicious. The good n-gram filter works in an opposite fashion in that the score for the overall packet increases if an n-gram is evaluated that is not in the good filter (thus truly looking for anomalies).

In our work, we re-implement the Anagram approach and attempt to reproduce the results of [8]. We experiment with the Hypertext Transfer Protocol (HTTP) to provide a direct comparison with one of the protocols examined in [8]. We also analyze Anagram performance relative to Domain Name System (DNS) requests, which was not previously done. This traffic is of interest because – while previous work [9] found that n-gram analysis of purely binary protocols was not feasible – DNS requests contain both binary components (e.g., record types and number of requests are encoded as byte fields) and textual components (e.g., the domain name itself is encoded in human-readable ASCII text with length fields acting as separators).

We focus our evaluation on the extent to which the automatically generated micro-signatures in the known bad n-gram filter contribute to the overall performance of Anagram. To do this, we constructed a standalone intrusion detection system (IDS) consisting only of the known bad filter. Unlike the original Anagram, which used bad n-grams derived from IDS signatures and virus samples, we derived our n-grams from known malicious packets to align it with our data sets. We refer to our known bad n-gram IDS as the micro-signature approach.

We find that the Anagram and micro-signature approaches have very similar performance characteristics with the Receiver Operating Curves (ROC) of the full Anagram approach providing only small improvements over the micro-signature ROC curves. In the best case, we found that the Anagram approach provided an increase in area under the ROC of only .0028 compared to the micro-signature approach. This means that the vast majority of the detection capability of Anagram (at least when applied to our data sets) is derived from the known bad component.

The known bad component was portrayed in [8] as a minor enhancement and has received little attention in any other paper in our literature survey. Thus, our results suggests that future research and development of network anomaly detection systems should focus on n-grams of malicious behavior as a primary detection method to be supplemented by the more traditional n-grams of normal behavior. This is the reverse of what is currently discussed in the literature. The utility of automatically generated micro-signatures is an open area for future IDS research.

We should emphasize that this result does not imply that the known good content filters are useless or that the Anagram approach is flawed. On the contrary, the full Anagram approach slightly outperforms the micro-signature approach across a wide range of false positive rates (e.g., false positive rates of .0001 to .001). However, the vast majority of true positives are still attributed to the micro-signature approach, supporting the primary conclusion of our paper. In the worst case with one data set, at a false positive rate of 0 the micro-signature true positive rate exceeds Anagram's by .03. In the best case with the same data set, the Anagram true positive rate exceeds the micro-signature's by .12 at a false positive rate of .0001. For the vast majority of non-zero false positive rates, the Anagram true positive rate had some small advantage over the micro-signature true positive rate.

In summary, the primary findings of this paper are the following:

1. The Anagram approach of using high order n-grams remains effective for analysis of two ubiquitous network protocols (HTTP and DNS).
2. For our data sets, the known bad n-gram filter accounts for the vast majority of the detection capability, and the identification of anomalous n-grams provides only an incremental improvement.
3. Automatically generated micro-signatures provide an effective detection abstraction and can be used to create standalone n-gram based IDSs that can be viewed as an interesting hybrid of an anomaly detection technique (n-grams), standard signature detection, and automated analyses of malicious packets.

The rest of this paper is organized as follows. Section 2 discusses our data. Section 3 summarizes our experiments and Sect. 4 discusses the results. Section 5 provides related work and Sect. 6 concludes.

2 Data

We used three sets of data to compare the effectiveness of Anagram and the micro-signature approach. The first two are sets of HTTP requests and the last is a set of DNS requests.

For the first set, we collected HTTP requests to an operational web server over the course of 24 h. We obtained 769,838 distinct requests, of which 605 were known to be malicious due to signature-based analysis. The first 10,000 requests in this file were closely examined by hand by network security personnel to verify that they were benign.

For the second set, we generated a data set of 393,814 malicious requests from a combination of scanning, vulnerability assessment, fuzzing, and exploit tools from the Kali Linux distribution that were targeted at a virtual machine running an identical web stack to the operational web server. We restricted the data to consider only incoming TCP packets delivered via port 80; all packet headers were discarded, and no stream reassembly was performed.

For the third set, we obtained DNS requests gathered via monitoring traffic crossing the network boundary of an active network. Due to the high volume of requests, we examined only the first 3,000,000 requests that were obtained, and restricted the data to UDP packets with a destination port of 53 and containing a valid DNS header. As with the HTTP data, all transport layer headers were discarded. Based on a pre-existing analysis, 28 packets were known to be malformed and deliberately altered to contain non-DNS data from the 32nd byte onwards. An additional 72,914 packets were known to contain properly formatted requests, but requested domain names that encoded non-DNS information in some fashion (such as base16 or base32 encoding). Many of these appeared to be commercial security products using DNS as a communication channel, presumably to avoid being blocked by firewalls.

3   Experiment Design

For each of the two types of data sets (HTTP and DNS), we define training sets used to generate the n-gram based content filters (both 'good' and 'bad'). We then construct both Anagram and micro-signature IDSs from the content filters and, from each of the three data sets, we define a validation set used to test the IDSs' effectiveness.

3.1   Training Sets

For HTTP, we constructed a 'normal traffic' training set consisting of the 10,000 hand verified requests along with 100,000 randomly selected requests from the remaining 759,838 requests (excluding the 605 known bad requests). We constructed a malicious training set consisting of 10,000 randomly chosen requests from the set of 393,814 generated malicious requests.

For DNS, we constructed a 'normal traffic' training set consisting of 10,000 randomly selected requests from the 2,927,058 not known to be malicious. We constructed a malicious training set consisting of 10,000 randomly chosen requests from the set of 28 malformed and deliberately altered requests and the 72,914 requests encoded with non-DNS information.

3.2   Intrusion Detection System Construction

We followed the procedure as described in [8] to build and train the known good and known bad content filters and to construct the Anagram IDS. We used just the known bad filter to construct the micro-signature IDS. Note that different good and bad content filters were generated specific to each protocol (HTTP and DNS). The Bloom filters used for the content filters were constructed using a 2^{24} bit index with 3 hash functions per item and using SHA-1 as the hash function, as in [8]. We used an n-gram size of 5 as [8] cited this as being good for 'general' purpose experiments.

For HTTP, we first generated n-grams from the 10,000 hand-verified known good requests to populate what we call a 'gold' content filter (there was no name for this in [8]). We then constructed the bad content filter by generating n-grams from our malicious request training set and including them in the filter if they didn't also occur in the gold filter. Note that this is the only use of the gold filter and it is not used again. Finally, we generated n-grams from the normal traffic training set. For each HTTP request, if the proportion of n-grams that appear in the bad content filter is less than 5%, then we add those n-grams to the good content filter that did not occur in the bad content filter. If this ratio exceeded 5% then the entire HTTP request was ignored.

For DNS, we followed the same methodology. For this though, we had no gold content filter and we populated the known bad filter directly from the malicious request training set. The good content filter was constructed using the 'normal traffic' training set using the same methodology as with the HTTP traffic (using the 5% rule and the bad content filter to eliminate candidate n-grams).

To score a particular request (HTTP or DNS) using our content filters, we recorded the number of n-grams in that request that were not found in either content filter (i.e., new n-grams), the number found in the known bad filter, and the total number of n-grams in the request. Three scoring rules were applied: the Anagram rule of $\frac{5 \times \#\{\text{bad ngrams}\} + \#\{\text{new ngrams}\}}{\#\{\text{ngrams in packet}\}}$, our micro-signature rule of $\frac{\#\{\text{bad ngrams}\}}{\#\{\text{ngrams in packet}\}}$, and a "non-normalized" micro-signature rule which involves simply counting the number of bad n-grams without normalization against the size of the packet. However, this final non-normalized version produced worse results, which we do not display.

3.3   Validation Data Sets

To test the effectiveness of the Anagram and micro-signature approaches, we generated three validation data sets. For each set, receiver operator characteristic (ROC) curves were generated for the Anagram and micro-signature approaches.

The first HTTP validation set was focused on testing IDS effectiveness in detecting 'real' attacks. It consisted of 659,838 requests. This was the total set of 769,838 distinct requests minus the 110,000 used in the training set for the good content filter. This set includes the 605 known malicious requests. There was thus no overlap between the training and testing data.

The second HTTP validation set was focused on testing IDS effectiveness in detecting our generated attacks (from the use of security and exploit tools). It consisted of 1,043,652 requests. We started with the total set of 769,838 distinct HTTP requests and removed the 605 known malicious requests. Then we removed the 110,000 requests used in the training set for the good content filter. Lastly, we added the 383,814 generated malicious requests that were not used in the training set for the bad content filter.

The DNS validation set consisted of 2,980,000 requests. We started with the 3,000,000 total requests and subtracted the 10,000 used to train the good content filter and then subtracted the 10,000 used to train the bad content filter. This then included 62,942 known malicious requests that were not used in any of the training sets.

4   Results

The results of our experiments indicate that, for our data sets, the Anagram and micro-signature approaches provide very similar performance. This is surprising as the micro-signature approach is portrayed in the literature as simply a minor augmentation to the overall Anagram approach. We first provide a look at the overall area under the ROC curves for all data sets and then look specifically at the HTTP and DNS results in more detail.

The area under the ROC curves for all three validation sets are shown in Tables 1 and 2. In the very best case for Anagram, it has an area under the curve of just 0.0028 more than the micro-signature approach. In the worst case (DNS), it slightly under-performs micro-signatures, although by such a thin margin that the difference is likely

Table 1. HTTP results

	Area under ROC curve per data set	
	Real attacks	Generated attacks
Anagram	0.9648	0.9998
Micro-signatures	0.9620	0.9997

Table 2. DNS results

	Area under ROC curve
Anagram	0.999963
Micro-signatures	0.999996

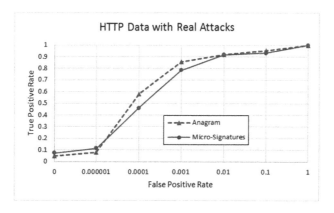

Fig. 1. Full ROC curve for the HTTP validation set with real attacks

not significant. It is especially interesting that the micro-signature approach was able to achieve this performance having been trained on only 10,000 malicious packets and tested against data sets with up to 3 million requests.

In Fig. 1 we show the full ROC curve where Anagram has the greatest advantage over micro-signatures with respect to the area under the curve (the HTTP validation set with the real attacks). Notice the similarities between both algorithms. While some differences do exist, the visual impact of this is highly exaggerated by the logarithmic scaling of the x-axis. While such scaling is not common for ROC curves, we will do this to highlight the importance of the true positive rate (TPR) values at very small false positive rates (FPRs). This is because for network anomaly detection, the number of packets is typically very high and an IDS will thus only be useful if it can operate at extremely low false positive rates [10].

We now review each of the validation sets in detail and analyze the portions of the ROC curves that best show the distinctions between the two approaches under analysis.

4.1   HTTP Results

As shown in Fig. 1 for the real HTTP attacks, Anagram has a better TPR than the micro-signature approach at FPRs at .0001 and above. At extremely low FPRs (.000001 and below), the micro-signature approach has a slight advantage. The largest Anagram advantage is at a FPR of .0001 where the Anagram TPR exceeds that of the micro-signatures by .12. The largest micro-signature advantage is at a FPR of 0 where the micro-signature TPR exceeds that of Anagram by .03. Both methods converge in performance at an FPR of .01.

In Fig. 2 we see how, for generated attacks, the Anagram TPR at most exceeds that of the micro-signature TPR by .0015 at a FPR of .0001. At the lowest observed FPRs, micro-signatures once again have an extremely small advantage over Anagram. Both methods converge in performance at FPRs of .001 and higher.

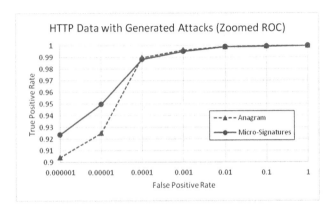

Fig. 2. Zoomed ROC curve for HTTP validation set with generated attacks

4.2   DNS Results

Analogous to our previous results, Fig. 3 shows how Anagram exceeds the micro-signature approach with our DNS dataset, but only by a very small margin. Note how at best Anagram has a TPR .013 higher than the micro-signature approach at the same FPR. The DNS data is of particular interest as it contains a mixture of binary encoded header information with (mostly) textual domain information at the end of the packet. Previous work [9] has suggested that binary protocols are difficult to analyze with n-gram methods; however, it appears that in this particular case the distributions over malicious and benign traffic in both the textual and binary encoded portions of the payloads are sufficiently dissimilar to permit accurate classification. In contrast to the HTTP data, Anagram outperforms the micro-signatures (albeit by extremely fine margins) at all FPR values. Note the extremely small range of y-axis values in Fig. 3, indicating the close similarity of the two approaches at all FPRs.

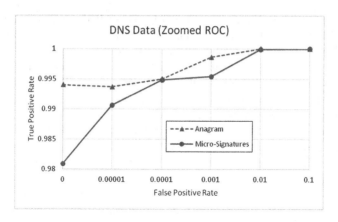

Fig. 3. Zoomed ROC curve for DNS validation set

5   Discussion

The results clearly show the effectiveness of the overall Anagram approach for the HTTP and DNS request datasets. Quite surprisingly, the micro-signatures performed almost as well as the full Anagram approach when considering the area under the ROC curves. At the very best with the HTTP generated attack validation set, Anagram had an ROC curve with an area .0028 greater than the corresponding micro-signature ROC curve. This overall similarity hides the fact that Anagram does outperform micro-signatures at most (but not all) operating points (although our data sets are substantially smaller than those described in [8], which may also account for the slightly poorer performance of the anomaly detection portion). In the best case at a .0001 FPR with the HTTP real attack validation set, Anagram achieves a TPR .12 higher than the micro-signatures. However, the micro-signatures still account for the vast majority of detections at all operating points and validation sets tested. This means that, relative to our datasets, the seminal Anagram anomaly detection system that proved the usefulness of n-grams for network packet inspection achieves the majority of its effectiveness from a subsystem that is effectively signature based.

However, this signature based subsystem is very different from typical signature based systems. The signatures are automatically generated from known malicious packets and are very small in size. It is the presence of groups of signatures that are indicative of an attack, not just single signatures as is the case with standard signature based IDSs. This means that, while clearly signature based, micro-signatures can also potentially generalize to new attacks. This micro-signature paradigm is then a hybrid anomaly-signature system that, in our literature survey, has not been explicitly investigated before. Micro-signatures are not a new discovery (having been included within Anagram in 2006), but they were not highlighted as a major contributor and were not separately evaluated. In this work, we have empirically shown the importance of this component and suggest that micro-signatures can provide a new avenue of IDS research.

An interesting aspect of micro-signatures (that is newly discovered in this research) is that their accuracy can be extremely high even with a small training set. We used 385,751 bad n-grams for the HTTP data set and achieved similar HTTP detection results to the original Anagram paper [8], which used 30 million bad n-grams. For the DNS work, while we can't compare the results directly to [8], we achieve a high detection capability with only 78,532 bad n-grams. This suggests that the micro-signatures generalize to attacks not present in training data, although further research is necessary to quantify this. With a training set of just 10,000 malicious DNS requests, the micro-signatures were able to detect a set of 62,942 malicious requests with a TPR of .995 at a FPR of .0001. This may be potentially explained by considering micro-signatures as a form of supervised learning, while the anomaly detection component of Anagram is more closely related to a one-class unsupervised learning problem. Supervised learning approaches for intrusion detection using n-grams have been shown to be successful elsewhere [11], although they are typically significantly more complex than the simple set membership tests we consider here.

One consideration in the use of micro-signatures, is their resilience to evasion attacks. In particular, the normalization to packet length in our micro-signature approach could lead to an evasion attack where a malicious packet is stuffed with a lot of normal data; this "content mimicry" attack is considered within the original Anagram paper, where it is addressed via subsampling of the packet payload [8]. While the mimicry resistant approach suggested in the original Anagram paper will likely not be as effective for micro-signatures, another potential avenue for handling content mimicry might be through not normalizing the micro-signature counts to packet length. Not shown in this paper are results which find that this idea is effective, but has worse performance than normalized micro-signatures.

6   Related Work

The difficulty of applying machine learning in general to intrusion detection is discussed by Sommer and Paxson [12], which points out several features of intrusion detection problems that make it difficult to successfully apply machine learning; this includes the rareness of attacks, the high cost of diagnosing detected attacks, and the complexity of the input data. A more probabilistic argument is made in [10] in terms of the base rate fallacy. Nevertheless, multiple examples of anomaly-based and unsupervised network intrusion detection methods can be found in the literature.

One of the earliest n-gram approaches is that of the PAY-L system [6], which clusters network traffic based on the distribution of 1-grams. The Anagram system [8], which forms the basis of our analysis, extends the length of the n-grams to between 5 and 9, while also addressing the issue of "content mimicry". In perhaps the most general case, the issue of anomaly detection via n-grams in non-textual, binary protocols is considered by Hadžiosmanović et al. [9], building on the work of [6, 8]; this work examines classifiers that make no use of any protocol-specific domain knowledge and concludes that n-gram based methods generally perform poorly for binary protocols, with an unavoidable tradeoff between high detection rate and low false positive rate. This is formalized in the work of [14], which in addition to evaluating the settings in which n-gram based tools may be expected to perform well, also empirically examines a number n-gram based intrusion detection systems, including the Anagram system. While they do examine the "benign" filter alone and in conjunction with the malicious content filter, they do not examine the contribution of the malicious content filter alone. Finally, similarly to the clustering described in [6], the work of [13] examines the use of a self-organizing map for on-line clustering of packets.

Domain-specific knowledge, in the form of partial parses of protocols, can be used to extract more specific sets of features that help in the identification of anomalous content. In Robertson et al. [15], for instance, web requests are processed by specializing to particular web components, and then learning simple specialized models conditional on each field and component – in effect learning a mixture of site-specific 'sub-protocols' within HTTP. Guangmin [16] performs similar tokenization for use in an artificial immune system model. Ingham et al. [17] attempt to learn deterministic finite automata (DFAs) for normal HTTP traffic while detecting, parsing, and transforming known features (such as email addresses) in order to control complexity. The high degree of structure in the underlying grammar (HTTP) combined with the generally limited character set all contribute to the ability of such systems to be effective. However, these systems are also highly specialized to their particular domain of application and so cannot extend to more general intrusion detection scenarios.

Finally, as machine learning techniques have developed, anomaly-based IDS work has kept pace. More advanced approaches to the problem include that of Gornitz et al. [18]. Here, active learning is used to request that specific packets be labeled by an outside mechanism (e.g. a human analyst) thus maximizing the discriminative power of the learning algorithm within a limited budget of time and effort. While such systems do require more resources to train initially, they typically result in significantly improved performance over purely unsupervised systems. The use of the bad content model in the Anagram system [8] may be viewed as a non-active, simplified version of this semi-supervised approach.

7   Conclusion

The n-grams methodology has arguably been the most successful technique for anomaly detection within packet payloads, with Anagram [8] being the seminal work. We tested the Anagram anomaly detection system on two ubiquitous network protocols, confirming its effectiveness on HTTP requests and newly demonstrating its effectiveness on DNS requests. We analyzed the two primary components of Anagram and showed that, for our data, the known bad n-gram filter accounted for the vast majority of the detection capability and that the identification of anomalous n-grams provided only a marginal improvement. Furthermore, we showed that the automatically generated micro-signatures (comprising the known bad n-gram filter) provide an effective detection abstraction and can be used to create standalone n-gram based IDSs, which have performance comparable to Anagram under a wide range of operating conditions.

This study strongly suggests that the effectiveness of Anagram is not primarily due to its core anomaly detection filter but instead to a novel signature detection methodology (i.e., micro-signatures) that was never highlighted in the literature. Thus, this result may indicate a new avenue for IDS research that is not pure anomaly detection but that also deviates greatly from standard signature detection. Unlike anomaly detection, it uses signatures and requires some reference set of malicious traffic. Unlike standard signature detection, it neither looks for arbitrary and variable length substrings or patterns within packet data nor does it require humans to write complete descriptions of indicators of malicious traffic. Instead, it can automatically construct n-gram based signatures automatically from malicious traffic, once that traffic is identified.

In future work, we plan to evaluate how to most effectively use micro-signatures. We plan to create micro-signatures from existing IDS signatures and compare the micro-signature IDS performance against the standard signature based IDS performance. We also need to evaluate the extent to which a group of micro-signatures can hinder an attacker from creating variations of attacks that evade current signature sets. Building on this, we need to evaluate how much micro-signatures generalize within classes of attacks or even between different classes. The various parameters that can be set for the micro-signatures, including the length of the n-gram used, the parameterization of the Bloom filter (or other data structure), and methods for selecting the threshold parameter in the absence of extensive validation data, all require further study. Methods for providing additional situational awareness around positive results from micro-signatures should also be considered; we need to either identify the portions of the packet in which micro-signatures were found or (if the micro-signatures were created from existing signatures) find a way to link the micro-signature to source data for easier interpretation. Finally, the effectiveness of micro-signatures across multiple protocols must be examined, including the potential of combining micro-signatures for multiple protocols into a single, larger Bloom filter.

References

1. Smaha, S.E.: Haystack: an intrusion detection system. In: Aerospace Computer Security Applications Conference (1988)
2. Denning, D.E.: An intrusion-detection model. IEEE Trans. Softw. Eng. **2**, 222–232 (1987)
3. Vaccaro, H.S., Liepins, G.E.: Detection of anomalous computer session activity. In: IEEE Symposium on Security and Privacy (1989)
4. Forrest, S., Hofmeyr, S., Somayaji, A.: Computer immunology. Commun. ACM **40**(10), 88–96 (1997)
5. Damashek, D.: Gauging similarity with n-grams: language independent categorization of text. Science **267**(5199), 843–848 (1995)
6. Wang, K., Stolfo, S.J.: Anomalous payload-based network intrusion detection. In: Jonsson, E., Valdes, A., Almgren, M. (eds.) RAID 2004. LNCS, vol. 3224, pp. 203–222. Springer, Heidelberg (2004). doi:10.1007/978-3-540-30143-1_11
7. The Unicode Standard Version 6.0- Core Specification, February 2011. http://www.unicode.org/versions/Unicode6.0.0/ch01.pdf

8. Wang, K., Parekh, Janak, J., Stolfo, Salvatore, J.: Anagram: a content anomaly detector resistant to mimicry attack. In: Zamboni, D., Kruegel, C. (eds.) RAID 2006. LNCS, vol. 4219, pp. 226–248. Springer, Heidelberg (2006). doi:10.1007/11856214_12

9. Hadžiosmanović, D., Simionato, L., Bolzoni, D., Zambon, E., Etalle, S.: N-Gram against the machine: on the feasibility of the N-Gram network analysis for binary protocols. In: Balzarotti, D., Stolfo, Salvatore, J., Cova, M. (eds.) RAID 2012. LNCS, vol. 7462, pp. 354–373. Springer, Heidelberg (2012). doi:10.1007/978-3-642-33338-5_18

10. Axelsson, S.: The base-rate fallacy and the difficulty of intrusion detection. ACM Trans. Inf. Syst. Secur. 3(3), 186–205 (2000)

11. Chang, R., Harang, R.E., Payer, G.S.: Extremely lightweight intrusion detection (ELIDe), Army Research Laboratory (2013)

12. Sommer, R., Paxson, V.: Outside the closed world: on using machine learning for network intrusion detection. In: Security and Privacy (2010)

13. Bolzoni, D., Zambon, E., Etalle, S., Hartel, P.: Poseidon: a 2-tier anomaly-based intrusion detection system, arXiv.preprint.cs/0511043 (2005)

14. Wressnegger, C., Schwenk, G., Arp, D., Rieck, K.: A close look on n-grams in intrusion detection: anomaly detection vs. classification. In: 2013 ACM workshop on Artificial intelligence and security (2013)

15. Robertson, W., Vigna, G., Kruegel, C., Kemmerer, R.A.: Using generalization and characterization techniques in the anomaly-based detection of web attacks. In: NDSS (2006)

16. Guangmin, L.: Modeling unknown web attacks in network anomaly detection. In: Third International Conference on Convergence and Hybrid Information Technology (2008)

17. Ingham, K.L., Somayaji, A., Burge, J., Forrest, S.: Learning DFA representations of HTTP for protecting web applications. Comput. Netw. 51(5), 1239–1255 (2007)

18. Görnitz, N., Kloft, M., Rieck, K., Brefeld, U.: Active learning for network intrusion detection. In: Proceedings of the 2nd ACM Workshop on Security and Artificial Intelligence (2009)

19. Axelsson, S.: Intrusion detection systems: a survey and taxonomy (2000)

20. Paxson, V.: Bro: a system for detecting network intruders in real-time. Comput. Netw. 31, 2435–2463 (1999)

21. Roesch, M.: Snort: lightweight intrusion detection for networks. In: LISA (1999)

22. Rieck, K., Laskov, P.: Detecting unknown network attacks using language models. In: Büschkes, R., Laskov, P. (eds.) Detection of Intrusions and Malware & Vulnerability Assessment. LNCS, pp. 74–90. Springer, Heidelberg (2006)

23. Rieck, K., Laskov, P., Müller, K.-R.: Efficient algorithms for similarity measures over sequential data: a look beyond kernels. In: Franke, K., Müller, K.-R., Nickolay, B., Schäfer, R. (eds.) DAGM 2006. LNCS, vol. 4174, pp. 374–383. Springer, Heidelberg (2006). doi:10.1007/11861898_38

24. Cretu-Ciocarlie, G.F., Stavrou, A., Locasto, M.E., Stolfo, S.J.: Adaptive anomaly detection via self-calibration and dynamic updating. In: Kirda, E., Jha, S., Balzarotti, D. (eds.) RAID 2009. LNCS, vol. 5758, pp. 41–60. Springer, Heidelberg (2009). doi:10.1007/978-3-642-04342-0_3

25. Perdisci, R., Ariu, D., Fogla, P., Giacinto, G., Lee, W.: McPAD: a multiple classifier system for accurate payload-based anomaly detection. Comput. Netw. 53(6), 864–881 (2009)

Intrusion Response

Multi-Criteria Recommender Approach for Supporting Intrusion Response System

Tarek Bouyahia[✉], Nora Cuppens-Boulahia, Frédéric Cuppens, and Fabien Autrel

Télécom-Bretagne, 35576 Cesson Sévigné, France
{tarek.bouyahia,nora.cuppens,frederic.cuppens,
fabien.autrel}@telecom-bretagne.eu

Abstract. Recommender systems are tools for processing and organizing information in order to give assistance to the system users. This assistance is provided by analyzing their own preferences or the preferences of their community. This paper introduces an approach based on content-based recommendation for efficient security administrators assistance in the context of reaction against intrusion detection. The proposed methodology considers the set of active contexts while analyzing the security administrator decisions historic. It provides better recommendation depending on the contexts in which the system is operating. For instance, in an automotive system, given an attack scenario, the fact that a vehicle is operating on downtown or on a highway influences countermeasures selection.

1 Introduction

Decisions making against an attack detection is a complex task, because applying an inappropriate countermeasure given a specific attack could be more harmful than the attack itself and could have deleterious effects on the system. In other words, a countermeasure that remedies to a specific attack while causing the minimum loss on the nominal system functional behavior (e.g., performance, availability) should always be preferred over other proposed countermeasures. Moreover, an appropriate countermeasure should depend on the context in which the system is operating. For instance, when considering a database server in a private network of a company, the availability criterion should be favored during work time when employees are using the system's database, but the performance criterion should be preferred outside the working hours when database backups are created.

We believe that the goal of modern security systems is not only to maintain the system in safe conditions but also to satisfy the system requirements. Thus, we propose in this paper an approach based on a recommender system using Multi-Criteria Decision Making (MCDM) method for assisting system security administrators while selecting the appropriate countermeasures against a specific attack scenario. This approach considers the different effects a countermeasure

© Springer International Publishing AG 2017
F. Cuppens et al. (Eds.): FPS 2016, LNCS 10128, pp. 51–67, 2017.
DOI: 10.1007/978-3-319-51966-1_4

could have on the system as criteria to be considered when selecting the appropriate countermeasures. The objective of this paper is not to replace the security administrator during the countermeasures selection process, but rather to recommend system responses based on the security administrator decisions historic. This approach permits also to automatically select appropriate countermeasures in critical cases where the system security administrator is unable to select them. We apply the proposed methodology to automotive systems use case to show how countermeasures could be recommended, given a detected attack scenario and according to the contexts in which the system is operating.

The paper is organized as follows: Sect. 2 presents related works. In Sect. 3, we show how the system responses set is generated given an intrusion scenario. Section 4 introduces the MCDM approach for security administrator assistance. Section 5 shows how to integrate the MCDM module into an existing system response against intrusion detection. We present deployment scenarios highlighting how our approach is applied in the use case of automotive system in Sect. 6. Section 7 concludes the paper and outlines future work.

2   Related Work

2.1   Automated System Response

There have been various models and architectures proposed for dynamic decision making based Intrusion Response Systems (IRS). The aim of such systems is to respond in real time to the attack in progress. Dynamic decision making based IRS involves a reasoning process about an ongoing attack based on detecting alerts and selecting the most appropriate response. The authors in [1] propose a dynamic intrusion response approach that evaluates the response effects on the system using a dependency tree structure. This approach allows to select the response which has the minimal negative effect on the system. However, the work presented in [1] is not providing countermeasures that depend on the context in which the system is operating. In [2] the authors propose a gain matrix, which formulates the effects of selecting a specific response on the system. This formulation is based on two metrics; the probability of the system to be on a specific step from the attack scenario and the benefit from applying a system response on a specific system state. The main limitation of this approach is the large number of countermeasures to be selected especially when the corresponding attack scenario is constituted of a large number of attack steps. The challenge in such IRS systems is to select the optimal set of candidate responses in real time. Existing works propose approaches that rely on heuristics to reduce the size of candidate responses given a detected attack scenario. In [3] the authors present an approach called ADEPTS that considers only the countermeasures that are applicable in the sites where the detected alert was generated. This approach limits the size of the system responses set. ADEPTS is not evaluating the candidate system responses according to the response effect on the overall system. The proposed approach considers only the system response effect on the specific service where it is deployed. In our work, we propose a dynamic decision making based IRS that generates an optimal system responses set called the preferred extension using argumentative logic. The proposed approach considers the multi criteria aspect of systems to provide responses satisfying the different objectives the system administrator could have. Moreover, this approach analyzes the security administrator decisions historic to provide a better assistance when detecting a new intrusion alert.

2.2   Multi-Criteria Decision Making (MCDM)

The aim of this section is to address the recommendation problem from the MCDM perspective and to demonstrate the interest of applying MCDM methods to design multi-criteria recommender systems. There are three basic approaches for recommender systems: the content-based recommendation [4], collaborative filtering [5] and a hybrid approach [6] that combines collaborative and content-based methods. The collaborative filtering approach consists in collecting evaluations about the different contents and generating predictions for the user about a specific content by comparing them with the evaluations done by users with similar tastes and preferences.

The Content-based approach focuses only on the user evaluations to generate recommendations. This approach consists in analyzing the user evaluations historic to identify the user common features of interest. The work done in [4] presents an approach that collects user evaluations of the interest of visited pages on the World Wide Web. The authors show that a user profile can learn from this information and use it to recommend other pages that may interest the user.

There exists several contributions showing recommender systems that engage some MCDM methods as presented in [7,8]. The authors in [9] propose a framework to support strategic decision making in an organization. The proposed framework employs Multi-Criteria Decision Analysis to support decision making in strategy workshops. This framework takes into account the organization modern nature which is less hierarchic and more participative with a more distributed knowledge and decision taking. The approach proposed in [9] considers the multiple objectives aspect that must satisfy the organization strategic decision. However, this framework presents a high level of uncertainty. In [10], Zeleny proposes to increase the decider confidence and to limit to the post-decision regrets. Zeleny proves how pre-decision and post-decision steps are interdependent. In [11], the authors propose to model the MCDM process using Model Driven Engineering approaches. The proposed approach offers a guidance for the analyst and improves the communication between deciders and analysts. More related to the security field, the authors in [12] propose a novel approach that combines an MCDM approach called KAPUER with classic access control tools to assist users while writing high level permission rules. This approach includes algorithms that converge after the first phase of initializing user preferences.

In this paper, we propose a recommender system based on the content-based approach to assist the system security administrator in choosing the most appropriate countermeasures according to his/her requirements, given a specific attack scenario. Using a simple recommender system is not appropriate in the context of system response against intrusion detection. It cannot take into account the multiple dimensions of the impact that a countermeasure could have on the system state. The recommended tool proposed in this work applies MCDM methods to consider the multiple criteria nature of countermeasures.

3   Responses Set Generation Process

In our previous work, we proposed an approach for system response against intrusion detection. This approach allows to anticipate the attacker's intentions by generating potential future actions that the attacker may perform and by generating a response set that remedy to the potential attack scenario. The authors used the argumentative logic [13] for this purpose by designing the Contextual Value-based Argumentation Framework (CVAF) which is an extension of the Value-based Argumentation Framework (VAF) [14]. This approach is used to generate an optimal response set according to a detected intrusion based on an argumentation reasoning. However, it does not provide a tool to recommend better countermeasures corresponding to the security administrator preferences and requirements. This tool is necessary especially when the generated response set is large and the decisions of security administrator must be provided in a real-time. Besides, security administrators may not have the required knowledge about an ongoing attack or about the proposed countermeasures. In such cases, a recommending module is useful to overcome these issues. In our work, we opted for this approach and we extend it by integrating an MCDM module. In this section, we present briefly the proposed approach for generating system responses against intrusion.

3.1   Argumentative Logic

Due to the dynamic nature of modern systems, we argue in [15] that using a static argumentation framework in intrusion response context is not adapted. Thus, we extend the definition of *VAF* [14] to that of a contextual *VAF* (*CVAF*).

Definition 1. *A contextual value-based argumentation framework, denoted CVAF, is a 6-tuple $\langle AR, attacks, V, val, \mathcal{C}, ContPref \rangle$ where:*

- *AR is a set of arguments and attacks is a relationship over $AR \times AR$*
- *V is a non-empty set of values*
- *val is a function which maps elements from AR to elements of V*
- *$\mathcal{C}$ is a set of contexts. A context is either active or inactive. At a given time multiple contexts can be active*
- *ContPref is a transitive, irreflexive and asymmetric preference relation on $V \times V$ which depends on the set of active contexts in $\mathcal{C}$*

3.2   Generating Potential Attack Scenario

Purpose: In modern attacks, the attacker can execute several actions in order to make the execution of other actions possible until reaching a certain intrusion objective. The aim of generating potential attack scenario is to anticipate the attacker's intentions by generating correlated sequences of virtual actions instances starting from a malicious action detection. An action A is said to be correlated to an action B if the effects of action A are a subset of action B preconditions. In other words, two actions are said to be correlated, if the execution of one action has a positive influence on the execution of the other one.

Correlation Module: Once an alert is generated, the models instantiation module instantiates the action corresponding to the detected alert as well as other potential actions and intrusion objectives. As shown in Fig. 1, the correlation module generates a sequence of detected actions, correlated virtual actions instances and potential intrusion objectives. This constitutes the potential intrusion scenario for the detected action. Actions, intrusions objectives and countermeasures are modeled in the proposed approach in Lambda [16].

3.3   Constructing the Set of Arguments

Given a detected alert, the proposed approach considers the arguments set AR as the conjunction of the detected action, the potential actions hypothesis, the potential intrusion objectives and the countermeasures that mitigate the effects of the attack scenario different steps. The *attacks* relation role in this approach is to select all countermeasures that are anti correlated to the attack scenario steps (i.e., a countermeasure is said to be anti correlated to an action, if the countermeasure effects on the system block the action execution).

3.4   Generating the Preferred Extension

Purpose: *Attacks* relation between arguments is also used in this approach to formalize conflicts between countermeasures. Two countermeasures are said to

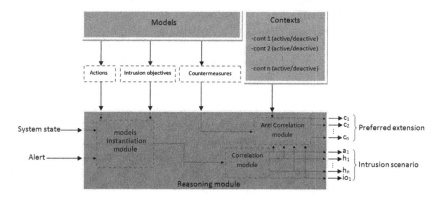

Fig. 1. Generating preferred extension architecture

be in conflict, when the effects of a countermeasure block the execution of the other one (e.g., *filter_host* countermeasure requires, in its preconditions, that wifi must be on, whereas *disable_wifi* turns the wifi off). To avoid such problem, the authors propose the Anti Correlation Module (ACM) that allows to generate a set of coherent countermeasures.

Anti Correlation Module: The authors use the *CVAF* to generate a set of preferred extension starting from the set of arguments, given an intrusion scenario. The preferred extension constitutes the maximal set (with respect to set inclusion) of coherent countermeasures according to the security administrator preferences. The preferences are statically predefined according to the different combination of active contexts and using the notion of *defeat* between countermeasures. This notion is used in the proposed approach, by a mono-criterion comparison. Each countermeasure being assigned to a simple nominal system functional behavior (e.g., precaution for *disable_wifi*), which constitutes the value of the corresponding countermeasure. According to the *CVAF*, when two countermeasures are attacking each other, the defeated one is the one which has the lower value. In this work, we consider the multi-criteria nature of countermeasures; the *defeats* notion is implemented to compare the concerned countermeasures scores. The generating responses system architecture proposed in [15] is presented in Fig. 1.

4   Multi-Criteria Decision Making Module

We designed an MCDM module to support security administrator during system response against intrusion detections. The recommender system we designed follows a cyclical process as shown in Fig. 2. This cycle is triggered when the system detects an intrusion and generates its preferred extension. The security administrator selects countermeasures among recommended ones generated from the preferred extension. The system consults selected countermeasures evaluations according to a predefined criteria list. The criteria list presents a list of nominal system functional behavior (e.g., availability, integrity, performance). The evaluation consists in assigning to each criterion, a mention that describes the impact level the countermeasure could have on the system state. The possible evaluations are (Very Low(0), Low(1), Medium(2), High(3), Very High(4)). "Very High" implies that the countermeasure has the highest impact level on the system according to the considered criterion (e.g., countermeasures that disable wifi connection ensure a very high level of precaution). This evaluation is done by functional experts that study the different effects a countermeasure could have on the system state (e.g., level of availability loss). Then, the system checks the list of active contexts during countermeasures selection time by the security administrator. To learn more about the security administrator way of reacting, we propose a learning module which learns about the security administrator preferences and requirements according to his/her decisions historic. Preferences in intrusion response context are considered in our approach as the

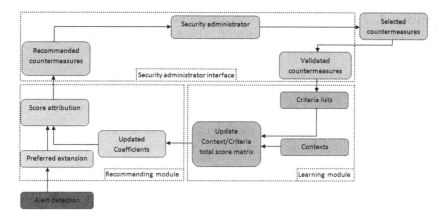

Fig. 2. Recommender system architecture

criteria having the highest score according to a specific combination of active contexts. We define the Context/Criteria matrix, which constitutes the core of the learning phase and which allows to analyze choices made by the security administrator. It is often called an options matrix or a decision table. This matrix is updated when countermeasures are selected by the security administrator and depending on the context on which the system is operating. For instance, when a security administrator always selects countermeasures having a high score on "precaution" criterion in a critical context, Criteria/Context matrix generates "precaution" as the most preferred criterion by the security administrator in this critical context. Thus, the recommendation of some countermeasures among all the preferred extension refers to each criterion score provided by the Context/Criteria matrix. Different parts are involved in the Multi-Criteria Decision Making process such as the learning module, the recommending module, and the security administrator interface.

4.1   Learning Module

We define the learning part as the different process allowing to give a visibility about the security administrator way of reacting and the different parameters influencing his/her decisions. This part is supplied by the security administrator decisions historic by analyzing the score of different criteria. Each time the security administrator validates a decision, the Context/Criteria matrix is updated with the selected countermeasure values according to each criterion. The update process of the Context/Criteria matrix according to n selected countermeasures is established as follows:

Definition 2. *Let Mat be a Context/Criteria matrix, Mat is a matrix of integers, $j \in card(criteria)$ and $criteria(CM_i, j)$ a function returning the jth criterion evaluation corresponding to the CM_i countermeasure.*

$$Mat_{updated}[contconfig][j] = Mat_{current}[contconfig][j] + \sum_{i=1}^{n} criteria(CM_i, j)$$

Where $contconfig$ presents the current combination of active contexts, and $criteria(CM_i, j) \in [0, 4]$ as described in the previous section.

4.2   Recommending Module

The recommendation phase is based on the Context/Criteria matrix to determine the decider favored criteria per context. The recommending module calculates the jth coefficient criterion as follows:

Definition 3. *Let Mat be a Context/Criteria matrix, $n = card(criteria)$ and $j \in \{1..n\}$*

$$coeff(j, contconfig) = \frac{Mat[contconfig][j]}{\sum\limits_{i=1}^{n} Mat[contconfig][i]}$$

Where $coeff(j, contconfig) \in [0, 1]$

Coefficients are then used in the score assignment phase where candidate countermeasures are evaluated based on their value per criterion and the criterion coefficient. The score of each candidate countermeasure must be calculated upon dynamic criteria coefficients to reflect a score compatible with the importance the security administrator assigned to each criterion according to each set of active contexts. The score assignment presents the last phase of recommendation, which consists in a dynamic assignment of score to each proposed countermeasure so that the system can compare them and recommend the most relevant ones. There exists several MCDM methods for calculating alternatives scores (e.g., SAW [17], TOPSIS [18], ELECTRE [19], AHP [20]). In this approach, we opted for SAW (Simple Additive Weighting) method which evaluates alternatives based on two metrics: the performance value of the alternative in term of a specific criterion, and the relative weight of importance of this criterion. Alternatives scores are calculated using SAW method as follows:

Definition 4. *Simple Additive Weighting (SAW) method*

$$\forall i \in \{1, N\}, S_i = \sum_{j=1}^{M} w_j \times r_{ij}$$

Where: S_i is the overall score of the ith alternative, r_{ij} is the rating of the ith alternative for the jth criterion, w_j is the weight (importance) of the jth criterion, N the number of alternatives and M the number of criteria.

SAW method is applicable only when all alternatives are evaluated in the same unit. Otherwise, other methods, such AHP for example, that allow to standardize alternatives evaluations, should be applied. As presented in this section, possible evaluations of all countermeasures are standardized (i.e., possible countermeasures evaluations according to each criterion are: 1, 2, 3 and 4). Thus, SAW method is applicable in our case of study. In addition, SAW is known as the simplest and the faster MCDM method. This will be helpful when designing systems response against intrusion detection since such systems must respond to real-time constraints especially in critical contexts. The score of each proposed countermeasure is calculated using SAW method as follows:

Definition 5. *Let* CM *be a countermeasure,* $n = card(criteria)$, $j \in \{1..n\}$ *and* $criteria(CM, j) \in [0, 4]$

$$Score(CM, contconfig) = \sum_{j=1}^{n} (criteria(CM, j) \times coeff(j, contconfig))$$

4.3 Security Administrator Interface

The aim of the recommending system is not only to replace security administrators and to make decisions in their places, but also to assist and show them the points that alone they are not able to see. As explained in Sect. 4.1, the security administrator provides information that supply the learning module. Each time the security administrator selects some countermeasures, he/she is asked to validate his/her decision. The validation phase allows the learning module to consider only the decisions that satisfy the security administrator, the learning module does not consider the administrator regrettable countermeasures. Once the administrator validates his/her decisions, the learning module updates the Context/Criteria matrix, to take into account the new decisions.

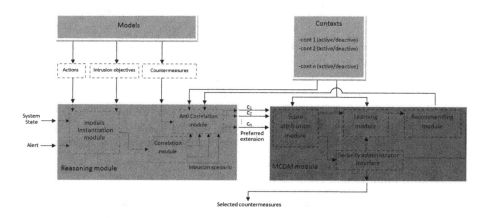

Fig. 3. Overall system architecture

5   MCDM Module Integration with Intrusion Response System

The overall system architecture is described in Fig. 3, where the MCDM module is integrated with the intrusion response architecture presented in [15]. In our previous work, the reasoning module refers to a criteria order called "rationale order" which is manually predefined by the system expert. In this work, we integrate the MCDM module to the existing architecture. In this approach, the criteria order will be automatically established by referring to the security administrator decisions historic. The overall system process can be summarized in four steps.

5.1   Prediction Phase

Reacting in a critical context against an attack after its execution can not always mitigate the adverse effects of the attack. In these cases it is essential to anticipate the attacker's intentions and to take precautionary measures to prevent the attacker from reaching his/her intrusion objective. For this purpose, the approach proposed in [15] consists on instantiating actions hypothesis correlated to the detected malicious action. The authors consider, as an example, that the system detects an action consisting on cracking the wifi passkey. This action is modeled in Lambda as follows:

$name : wifi\_passkey\_crack(A, T)$
$pre : \quad role(T, wifi\_gateway) \land is\_on(T)$
$post : \quad network\_access(A, T, wifi)$

The system instantiates correlated attack hypothesis that the attacker may execute. The system considers $message\_saturation$, which consists in overflowing the ITS server with messages, as a correlated action. This action is modeled as following:

$name : message\_saturation(A, T, M)$
$pre : \quad network\_access(A, T, M) \land role(T, its\_server) \land is\_on(T)$
$post : \quad dos(T)$

$Message\_saturation$ is considered as a correlated action, since $wifi\_passkey\_crack$ postconditions are a subset of $message\_saturation$ preconditions. The system generates as well $manipulation\_relayed\_messages$ as a potential intrusion objective correlated to $message\_saturation$.

$Manipulation\_relayed\_messages$ is then considered as the intrusion objective that the attacker can achieve starting from $wifi\_passkey\_crack$ and through the $message\_saturation$ attack. This intrusion objective is modeled as follows:

$name : \quad manipulation\_relayed\_messages$
$condition : manipulate(A, T) \land dos(T)$

According to the example, an attack scenario $\{wifi\_passkey\_crack, message\_saturation, \ manipulation\_relayed\_messages\}$ is to be considered in the responses generation phase and not only the $wifi\_passkey\_crack$.

5.2   System Response Generation Phase

In this phase, the Anti Correlation Module selects countermeasures that are anti correlated to the generated attack scenario. To avoid generating a response set containing conflictual countermeasures, we proposed in [15] an approach that refers to a mono criterion evaluation to determine which countermeasure should be selected. In this work, we propose a more enhanced approach than the one proposed in [15] by integrating the MCDM module. This module allows a more adaptive evaluation between countermeasures by comparing their scores. This allows an evaluation that covers all the countermeasures impacts on the system, rather than considering the main effect of a countermeasure on the system as the only criterion to be considered. MCDM module intervenes in the proposed framework at two levels: (1) It automatically updates the criteria order according to the set of active contexts in the preferred extension generation phase; (2) It generates the recommended countermeasures among the preferred extension.

5.3   Recommendation Phase

Once a preferred extension is generated according to a specific attack scenario, all generated countermeasures are subdivided into criteria evaluations. The recommender system refers to the current Context/Criteria matrix to generate the criteria order and coefficients as described in Sect. 4. Then, the system calculates countermeasures scores starting from countermeasures criteria evaluations and the criteria order and coefficients as defined in Definition 5. Countermeasures having highest scores will be recommended over the other system responses from the preferred extension. Security administrators are asked to select countermeasures that satisfy their preferences and requirements according to the current set of active contexts. This module is summarized in Algorithm 1.

Theorem 1. *Given a set of N generated countermeasures and M criteria, the complexity of the Algorithm 1 is $\mathcal{O}(N \times M + Nlog(N) + 2M)$ in time.*

Proof. According to Algorithm 1, the loop from line 2 to line 4 costs $\mathcal{O}(M)$. The second loop (from line 5 to line 7) costs also $\mathcal{O}(M)$. The nested loops (from line 8 to line 13) costs $\mathcal{O}(N \times M)$. Finally, the execution of the function "order" (line 14)costs in the worst case $\mathcal{O}(Nlog(N))$, since it uses merge sort. Therefore, the overall time complexity of Algorithm 1 is $\mathcal{O}(N \times M + Nlog(N) + 2M)$.

5.4   Matrix Update Phase

The Context/Criteria matrix is updated when countermeasures are selected by the security administrator and depending on the context in which the system is operating. When the security administrator selects countermeasures from the preferred extension, the Context/Criteria matrix is updated by adding selected countermeasures evaluations according to each criterion to the matrix current scores. This phase provides information concerning the security administrator

---

Algorithm 1. ConstructRecommendedList(PreferredExt,contconfig)

1: $Sum\_per\_context = 0$
2: **for all** $criterion \in Criteria$ **do**
3:     $Sum\_per\_context \leftarrow Sum\_per\_context + Mat[contconfig][criterion]$
4: **end for**
5: **for all** $criterion \in Criteria$ **do**
6:     $coeff(criterion, contconfig) \leftarrow Mat[contconfig][criterion] / Sum\_per\_context$
7: **end for**
8: **for all** $argument \in PreferredExt$ **do**
9:     $Score(argument, contconfig) = 0$
10:     **for all** $criterion \in Criteria$ **do**
11:         $Score(argument, contconfig) \leftarrow Score(argument, contconfig) +$
        $criteria(argument, criterion) \times coeff(criterion, contconfig)$
12:     **end for**
13: **end for**
14: $Recommended\_Countermeasure\_List \leftarrow order(PreferredExt, contconfig)$
15: **return** $Recommended\_Countermeasure\_List$

---

preferences and requirements using his/her personal decisions historic organized according to the different criteria. It provides criteria order according to each set of active contexts as well as the coefficient of importance to give to each criterion. In this work, the Context/Criteria matrix supports the generation of preferred extension by updating the criteria order and coefficients, which allows to apply the *defeat* notion between countermeasures by comparing their scores.

6   Application to the Automotive Case of Study

We show in this section, the deployment of our approach in the automotive system as an example of a case study.

6.1   Automotive Systems

Modern automotive system consists of one hundred micro-controllers, called Electronic Control Units (ECU) installed in the architecture specific components and connected by bridges. Vulnerabilities in automotive system are mainly due to the large number of enforcement points in the system architecture. Security vulnerabilities can be exploited to affect automotive system different components (e.g., lock/unlock car wheel at speed, disable brakes, kill engine, disable cylinders) [21,22]. Such attacks are always originating form compromise Internet or Bluetooth connection increasingly available in modern vehicles. Three main contexts are considered in this approach: *in_car* context which is defined to activate or deactivate specific activity in the vehicle, *V2V* context which is defined to manage communication within vehicles and *V2I* context which is defined to manage communication between vehicle and infrastructure. Extra contexts are considered as well, describing the environment on which the vehicle may operate (e.g., high way, parking, rainy day, night).

6.2 Deployment Scenario

We consider in this section, the attack scenario S presented in Fig. 4. As an output of the reasoning module presented in [15], the system generates a preferred extension that consists in a coherent set of candidate countermeasures. The generation process of the preferred extension depends on the current active contexts. The Figs. 4 and 5 show that the preferred extension corresponding to S scenario are $Ex\_pref_{\{in\_car\}}$ and $Ex\_pref_{\{in\_car,high\_way\}}$ respectively, for $\{in\_car\}$ and $\{in\_car, high\_way\}$ context. The shadowed nodes represent the defeated countermeasures. Where:

$Ex\_pref_{\{in\_car\}}$ ={Filter_host, Reduce_frequency, Add_source_auth, Limit_traffic, Digitally_sign_message, Remove_requirement, No_Cryp_ch-ecksum}.

$Ex\_pref_{\{in\_car,high\_way\}}$ = {Disable_wifi, Reduce_frequency, Add_source_auth, Limit_traffic, Digitally_sign_message, Remove_requirement}.

We consider the Context/Criteria matrix presented in Table 1. Once the security administrator selects and validates countermeasures, the Context/Criteria matrix is updated by evaluations corresponding to each criterion. Values in bold present the security administrator most preferred criterion according to the different combination of active contexts. The recommending module generates the criteria order and coefficients using Definition 3 in Sect. 4.2. Table 2

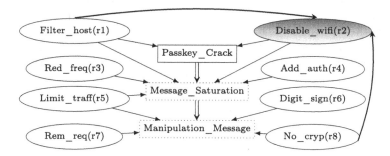

Fig. 4. System response against crack passkey attack in {in_car} context

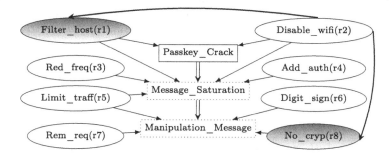

Fig. 5. System response against crack passkey attack in {in_car,high_way} context

Table 1. Context/Criteria matrix

Contexts	Integrity	Availability	Confidentiality	Performance	Precaution
{in_car}	64	88	**110**	104	22
{in_car, high_way}	81	72	**127**	112	103
{V2V}	77	**102**	97	67	54

Table 2. Criteria order and coefficients provided by the Context/Criteria matrix depending on the active contexts

(a) {in_car} context		Coeff	(b) {in_car, high_way} context		Coeff	(c) {V2V} context		Coeff
	Criteria	Coeff		Criteria	Coeff		Criteria	Coeff
1	Confidentiality	0.284	1	Confidentiality	0.257	1	Availability	0.257
2	Performance	0.268	2	Performance	0.226	2	Confidentiality	0.244
3	Availability	0.227	3	Precaution	0.208	3	Integrity	0.194
4	Integrity	0.165	4	Integrity	0.164	4	Performance	0.169
5	Precaution	0.057	5	Availability	0.145	5	Precaution	0.136

presents the criteria order and coefficients according to three contexts configurations ({in_car},{in_car,high_way},{V2V}). This table is provided by the Context/Criteria matrix. The criteria coefficients reflect the importance to be attached to each criterion at the recommendation phase. Once the system generates a preferred extension corresponding to a specific attack scenario, the system refers to the criteria order and coefficients tables to calculate the score of each proposed countermeasure. For instance, the preferred extension generated in *in_car* context and corresponding to S, contains two countermeasures: *Reduce_frequency* and *Add_source_auth*. In the following, we present the recommendation process for both countermeasures. We denote by Rf and Asa respectively, *Reduce_frequency* and *Add_source_auth* countermeasure. Evaluations done by functional experts corresponding to both countermeasures are presented in Table 3. To determine which countermeasures should be recommended, the system calculates the score of each countermeasure using the Definition 5 in Sect. 4.2. For instance, the score attribution of *Reduce_frequency* and *Add_source_auth* is calculated as follows:

$$Score(Rf, in\_car) = \sum_{i=1}^{5}(criteria(Rf, i) \times Coeff(i, in\_car))$$

$$Score(Rf, in\_car) = 0.165 \times 3 + 0.284 \times 2 + 0.057 \times 4 = 1.291$$

The *Add_source_auth* score in *in_car* context is calculated with the same formula as *Reduce_frequency*, we obtain $Score(Asa, in\_car) = 2.337$.

Thus, *Add_source_auth* countermeasure will be recommended over *Reduce_frequency* countermeasure. Figure 6 summarizes the score assignment

Table 3. Examples of countermeasures values per criteria

(a) *Reduce_frequency*		(b) *Add_source_auth*	
Criteria	Value	Criteria	Value
Integrity	High (3)	Integrity	High (3)
Availability	Very Low (0)	Availability	High (3)
Confidentiality	Medium (2)	Confidentiality	Medium (2)
Performance	Very Low (0)	Performance	Medium (2)
Precaution	Very High (4)	Precaution	Low (1)

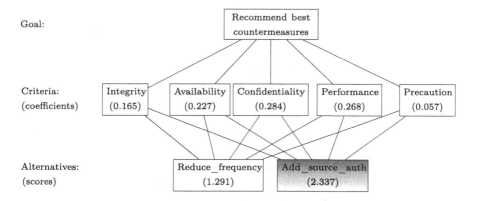

Fig. 6. Score assignment using SAW method for reduce_frequency and add_source_authentification countermeasures in {*in_car*} context

Table 4. Updated Context/Criteria matrix

Contexts	Integrity	Availability	Confidentiality	Performance	Precaution
{*in_car*}	67	91	**112**	106	23
{*in_car, high_way*}	81	72	**127**	112	103
{*V2V*}	77	**102**	97	67	54

process for both countermeasures. The shadowed node represents the recommended countermeasure.

The main goal of our approach being to assist the decider rather than replacing him, the user can select the recommended countermeasures as well as other proposed countermeasures from the preferred extension. Once the decider selects a countermeasure, the system updates the Context/Criteria matrix as presented in Table 4 (when the decider selects *Add_source_auth* countermeasure) and calculates the new criteria coefficients per contexts. This constitutes the learning phase of the recommendation process.

6.3   Evaluation

As explained in Sect. 4.2, we opted for SAW method for its low computational costs. Indeed, we showed in Sect. 5.3 that the complexity in time of the proposed algorithm is polynomial. Thus, our approach provides recommendations of system responses in real-time for a reasonable number of criteria and countermeasures included in the generated preferred extension. We can notice that the proposed approach does not provide the same results after a finite number of executions. Once a countermeasure is applied and validated by the security administrator, the Context/Criteria matrix is updated by the selected countermeasure evaluations. This update induces a change in criteria coefficients and may as well change the criteria order, which may provide different results in next executions.

7   Conclusion and Future Works

In order to assist security administrators when selecting countermeasures, it is necessary to have a recommender system that analyzes the security administrator decisions historic to determine his/her different preferences and requirements. We consider the content-based approach the most appropriate to achieve this objective. The content-based approach considers the user decisions historic and analyses them to provide appropriate recommendations. In this work, we proposed an approach based on content-based recommendation for efficient security administrator assistance when selecting the appropriate countermeasures, given a specific attack scenario. This approach considers the set of active contexts in different steps of generation system response as well as in the recommendation phase. Future research and development will focus on the evaluation of the approach efficiency by testing different scenarios and checking if this approach is applicable in the context of real-time system constraints.

References

1. Toth, T., Krügel, C.: Evaluating the impact of automated intrusion response mechanisms. In: 18th Annual Computer Security Applications Conference, 9–13 December 2002, Las Vegas, NV, USA, pp. 301–310. IEEE Computer Society (2002)
2. Balepin, I., Maltsev, S., Rowe, J., Levitt, K.: Using specification-based intrusion detection for automated response. In: Vigna, G., Kruegel, C., Jonsson, E. (eds.) RAID 2003. LNCS, vol. 2820, pp. 136–154. Springer, Heidelberg (2003). doi:10.1007/978-3-540-45248-5_8
3. Foo, B., Wu, Y., Mao, Y., Bagchi, S., Spafford, E.H.: ADEPTS: adaptive intrusion response using attack graphs in an e-commerce environment. In: 2005 Proceedings of the International Conference on Dependable Systems and Networks (DSN 2005), 28 June - 1 July 2005, Yokohama, Japan, pp. 508–517, IEEE Computer Society (2005)
4. Pazzani, M.J., Billsus, D.: Learning and revising user profiles: the identification of interesting web sites. Mach. Learn. **27**(3), 313–331 (1997)

5. Resnick, P., Iacovou, N., Suchak, M., Bergstrom, P., Riedl, J.: GroupLens: an open architecture for collaborative filtering of netNews. In: Proceedings of the Conference on Computer Supported Cooperative Work, CSCW 1994, pp. 175–186. ACM (1994)
6. Balabanovic, M., Shoham, Y.: Content-based, collaborative recommendation. Commun. ACM **40**(3), 66–72 (1997)
7. Manouselis, N., Costopoulou, C.: Analysis and classification of multi-criteria recommender systems. World Wide Web **10**(4), 415–441 (2007)
8. Adomavicius, G., Manouselis, N., Kwon, Y.: Multi-criteria recommender systems. In: Ricci, F., Rokach, L., Shapira, B., Kantor, P.B. (eds.) Recommender Systems Handbook, pp. 769–803. Springer, New York (2011)
9. Montibeller, G., Franco, A.: Multi-criteria decision analysis for strategic decision making. In: Zopounidis, C., Pardalos, P.M. (eds.) Handbook of Multicriteria Analysis, vol. 103, pp. 25–48. Springer, Heidelberg (2010)
10. Zeleny, M.: Multiple Criteria Decision Making. McGraw-Hill, New York (1982)
11. Chiprianov, V., Meyer, P., Simonin, J.: Towards a model-based multiple criteria decision aid process (2013)
12. Oglaza, A., Laborde, R., Zaraté, P.: Kapuer: un assistant à l'écriture de politiques d'autorisation pour la protection de la vie privée. Ingénierie des Systèmes d'Information **19**(6), 91–115 (2014)
13. Dung, P.M.: On the acceptability of arguments and its fundamental role in nonmonotonic reasoning, logic programming and n-person games. Artif. Intell. **77**(2), 321–357 (1995)
14. Bench-Capon, T.J.M.: Persuasion in practical argument using value-based argumentation frameworks. J. Log. Comput. **13**(3), 429–448 (2003)
15. Bouyahia, T., Autrel, F., Cuppens-Boulahia, N., Cuppens, F.: Context aware intrusion response based on argumentation logic. In: Lambrinoudakis, C., Gabillon, A. (eds.) CRiSIS 2015. LNCS, vol. 9572, pp. 91–106. Springer, Heidelberg (2016). doi:10.1007/978-3-319-31811-0_6
16. Cuppens, F., Ortalo, R.: LAMBDA: a language to model a database for detection of attacks. In: Debar, H., Mé, L., Wu, S.F. (eds.) RAID 2000. LNCS, vol. 1907, pp. 197–216. Springer, Heidelberg (2000). doi:10.1007/3-540-39945-3_13
17. Afshari, A., Mojahed, M., Yusuff, R.M.: Simple additive weighting approach to personnel selection problem. Int. J. Innov. Manag. Technol. **1**(5), 511 (2010)
18. Hwang, C., Lai, Y., Liu, T.: A new approach for multiple objective decision making. Comput. OR **20**(8), 889–899 (1993)
19. Bouyssou, D., Roy, B.: Aide multicritere a la decision: Methodes et cas. Economica, Paris (1993)
20. Saaty, T.: The Analytic Hierarchy Process. McGraw-Hill, New York (1980)
21. Koscher, K., Czeskis, A., Roesner, F., Patel, S., Kohno, T., Checkoway, S., McCoy, D., Kantor, B., Anderson, D., Shacham, H., Savage, S.: Experimental security analysis of a modern automobile. In: 31st IEEE Symposium on Security and Privacy, S&P 2010, pp. 447–462. IEEE Computer Society (2010)
22. Checkoway, S., McCoy, D., Kantor, B., Anderson, D., Shacham, H., Savage, S., Koscher, K., Czeskis, A., Roesner, F., Kohno, T.: Comprehensive experimental analyses of automotive attack surfaces. In: USENIX Association (2011)

An Optimal Metric-Aware Response Selection Strategy for Intrusion Response Systems

Nadine Herold[(✉)], Matthias Wachs, Stephan-A. Posselt, and Georg Carle

Technical University of Munich (TUM),
Boltzmannstr. 3, 85748 Garching bei München, Germany
{herold,wachs,posselt,carle}@net.in.tum.de
https://www.net.in.tum.de

Abstract. Due to the ever increasing number and variety of security incidents, incident management is an important and challenging aspect of operating indispensable services. Self-protection capabilities ensure service continuity by detecting and counteracting security incidents. Within this process, determining the set of countermeasures to be applied is essential. But detecting and analyzing security incidents in a complex network environment—especially under the pressure of an ongoing incident—is a challenge usually too complex for human comprehension and capabilities. As a consequence, often catastrophic and exaggerated actions are chosen when manually antagonizing security incidents.

In this paper, we propose a novel approach towards automatic response selection to counteract security incidents in complex network environments and, by relieving network operators, increase network security. Our approach is based on defining response selection as a mathematical optimization problem and providing a proven optimal combination of countermeasures. Our approach pays respect to user-defined cost metrics for countermeasures and supports restrictions like conflicting countermeasures and resource restrictions in the network. To ensure the usability and scalability of our approach, we evaluate the performance and show the applicability in different network settings.

Keywords: Self-protection · Intrusion response · Optimization

1 Introduction

Computer networks are the backbone infrastructure of many companies and organizations. The availability of services provided by such networks are companies' key economic assets. A security incident can easily generate huge losses and even human casualties. Therefore, security is a key requirement especially nowadays, with digital crimes, industrial espionage and cyber-attacks being omnipresent threats. Self-protection capabilities for network environments get more and more important, particularly when critical infrastructures need to guarantee service continuity. One approach towards self-protection is to monitor the network for security incidents, detect and counteract them by taking appropriate countermeasures (often called *responses*).

© Springer International Publishing AG 2017
F. Cuppens et al. (Eds.): FPS 2016, LNCS 10128, pp. 68–84, 2017.
DOI: 10.1007/978-3-319-51966-1_5

Contemporary computer networks consist of a large number of components and connected subnetworks creating inherently hard to manage complexity. More or less sophisticated *Intrusion Detection Systems (IDS)* (often multiple products at the same time) monitor network traffic, components, and systems for security incidents. In case of a security incident, IDSes may report a large, uncorrelated number of alerts to network operators. Without systems assisting human operators, it is impossible for them to identify the incident, analyze its source, distinguish between parallel but uncorrelated incidents and determine suitable countermeasures for the whole security incident in a timely manner.

Responses have varying efficacy, affect different targets, can be mutually exclusive, and create negative impact, e.g. downtime of services. Determining a *response strategy* and a set of non-contradictory *responses*, which mitigate the incident for all affected systems with few negative impact, easily overwhelms human operators under the pressure of ongoing attacks. Such situations can lead to sub-optimal or catastrophic decisions not increasing but instead decreasing network security. *Intrusion Response Systems (IRS)* extend traditional IDS-functionality beyond detection by evaluating and applying suitable responses.

In this paper, we evaluate how automated response selection can help to increase network security by providing a proven optimal response strategy to mitigate security incidents. This strategy can be applied autonomously or with the confirmation of a network operator. We present a model for incident response strategies, along with a transformation to an optimization problem, which allows us to solve this problem with mixed integer linear programming. This formalization includes costs for responses on multiple metrics, resource restrictions, and conflicts among responses. It provides a mathematically proven optimal response strategy. To evaluate the viability of this approach with respect to cost and execution time, we compare this approach to two greedy heuristics while varying different network settings. With this evaluation, we determine the network characteristics the performance of this approach depends on, and determine the benefit of using optimization in comparison to simplistic, greedy heuristics.

2 Related Work

Response selection is an essential part in the field of IRS. Different surveys on IRS [1,6,23] show the evolution IRS went through with respect to response selection strategies. Earlier IRS started with static mappings that connect an alert to a predefined response. In [4], the authors focus on intrusion detection methods and block suspicious transactions. No selection process is applied and anomalies are directly mapped to responses. As static mappings based on simple tables, are not a sufficient solution for complex networks, and cannot cope with environmental changes [29], IRS became more flexible using more dynamic response selection strategies. Several systems emerged, e.g. Cooperating Security Managers (CSM) [31], EMERALD [20] or AAIRS (Adaptive, Agent-based Intrusion Response) [21] that can cope with environmental changes using different metrics.

Later on, cost-sensitive mappings [16] were introduced using estimated damage and intrusion costs. They are balanced against each other to find a good solution. The cost-sensitive approach was improved over time to become more precise in terms of estimating response costs and damages [26,27]. Additionally, calculations for distributed systems were proposed [32]. [29] presents an approach using dependency trees to model network configurations and a cost model to estimate the effects of responses. To cope with uncertainty what an intruder really did, a specification-based response on the host level was proposed [2]. To improve the scope of decision making to more than one goal, timing aspects between selected responses were considered [18]. In [19], the effectiveness of a response is evaluated after its execution and fed back to response selection. In [8,9], the costs of a response plan are evaluated and the best plan is chosen. This approach needs to generate all possible response plans and calculate the resulting costs of each of them.

Approaches for particular domains, or to antagonize specific attacks, were presented: relational database systems [12], wireless sensor networks [28], mobile ad-hoc networks [10,30], and denial of service attacks [25].

However, existing approaches lack in finding an optimal solution employing a holistic approach to counteract the whole security incident. Neither the possibility that a single response can cover more than one network entity nor conflicting responses are respected by the work described before.

3   System Model

In this section, we define a model of the relationships between network entities, incidents, and responses. The idea is that a real-world IRS will generate an instance of this model from the parameters of a current incident. In the next section, we will show an automatic transformation of this model into a *mixed integer linear programming (MILP)* problem which can be solved programmatically. As a result, the IRS obtains an optimal sub-set of responses to execute.

3.1   Definition of Elements and Relations

The sets and symbols we use to define our system model are summarized in Table 1. A network consists of various entities, such as hosts, routers, and firewalls. In this model, all of these entities are contained in the set $S = \{s_1, s_2, \ldots\}$. A subset of these entities is affected by the current incident: $A = \{a_1, a_2, \ldots\} \subseteq S$. The set $R = \{r_1, r_2, \ldots\}$ contains all responses available to the IRS. A response, if successfully executed, will mitigate the effects of the incident to one or several entities of A. This is captured by the function $f\colon A \times R \to \mathbb{B}$ with $\mathbb{B} = \{0, 1\}$. $f(a, r)$ evaluates to 1 for *true* if r "frees" entity a, otherwise to 0 for *false*.

The function $x\colon S \times R \to \mathbb{B}$ describes which entity can *execute* a response. If another entity can execute a semantically equivalent response, those responses are treated as distinct responses. A response is executable by exactly one entity. Thus, the following property holds: $\forall r \in R\colon \sum_{i=1}^{|S|} x(s_i, r) = 1$.

If a response is executed, costs incur. Costs are measured by a set of metrics: $M = \{m_1, m_2, \ldots\}$. These metrics can be defined freely by the system designer.

Table 1. Sets and symbols used in the system model

Symbol	Set	Meaning
s	S	Set system entities
a	$A \subseteq S$	Set of entities affected by incident
r	R	Set of responses
m	M	Set of metrics
c	$R \times M \to \mathbb{R}_{\geq 0}$	Cost of a response in metric
d	$M \to \mathbb{R}_{\geq 0}$	Cost of inaction ('damage')
x	$S \times R \to \mathbb{B}$	Is response executed by entity?
f	$A \times R \to \mathbb{B}$	Does response 'free' entity?
o	$R \times R \to \mathbb{B}$	Do responses conflict?

An example for such a metric is the execution time of a response. The rationale behind this approach is that a service may be down while the response is still running. The *cost* of a response is given by the function $c : R \times M \to \mathbb{R}_{\geq 0}$. There is also a cost associated with not mitigating the incident at all. This is the *damage* $d: M \to \mathbb{R}_{\geq 0}$, measured in the same metrics. This damage limits the effort put into the incident mitigation: if the total cost of the selected responses exceeds the damage, it is cheaper to do nothing.

Metrics of different domains are, in general, not comparable. To be able to choose the "best" responses, we will later convert and weight all metrics to get a single cost domain with the range $[0, \infty)$.

Two responses may conflict with each other. A conflict implies that only one of those responses can be executed, but not both. A conflict can occur because of resource restrictions of the executing entity or counteracting effects. The function $o: R \times R \to \mathbb{B}$ describes conflicting responses. In our model, o is symmetric and non-reflexive, so $\forall r_1, r_2 \in R: o(r_1, r_2) = o(r_2, r_1)$ and $\forall r \in R: o(r, r) = 0$ hold.

3.2 Scope

The detection and identification of incidents, and the selection of possible responses are out of the scope of this work. These tasks are well studied among IDSes, both for hosts and networks. We assume that for a certain incident, the sets R, S, and A are given. We assume that responses and attacks can be assessed appropriately, as related work provides suitable techniques [7,13,15,33].

4 Designing the Selection Strategy

In this section, we show a transformation from the presented model into the linear equations of an optimization problem. The goal is to find the optimal combination of responses which mitigates the incident on all affected hosts. This problem can be solved with MILP.

4.1 Linear Programming

Linear programming is a well-known and well-researched technique originating from the field of operations research. While a linear programming problem can be solved in polynomial time, the restriction of (some) variables to integral values makes the problem one of Karp's 21 NP-complete problems [14]. Well-known methods to solve linear programming problems are *Basic-Exchange* algorithms, for example the *Simplex*-algorithm proposed by Dantzig [5], or *Interior Point* methods [14]. A beneficial property of these algorithms is the possibility of a *warm start-over*, where an optimal solution from a previous solution run can be re-used. This property has a positive impact on solution performance when a problem has to be solved repeatedly with modified matrix coefficients. To solve an *integer linear problem* (ILP), first the corresponding linear problem, called the relaxation of the ILP, is solved. Based on the optimal solution of the relaxation, exact methods like *Branch and Bound* algorithms or *Cutting-Plane* methods can be applied to find the integer optimal solution.

4.2 Formulating the Optimization Problem

The model from Sect. 3 describes the network environment, the security incident, and responses available. The corresponding optimization problem formalizes the following question: *In a given model instance, which subset from the set of responses available*

- *frees all affected entities from an incident,*
- *has minimal cost within the given set of metrics, and*
- *has lower cost than the incident being unmitigated?*

When transforming a problem to the form required to solve it as a linear programming problem, it is common to distinguish between two kinds of constraints: *feasibility constraints* and *optimality constraints*. Feasibility constraints force the solution to be within the constraints of a valid solution whereas the optimality constraints drive the solution into the desired direction of minimization or maximization. The constraints defined in Sects. 4.5 and 4.6 are explicitly formulated to be linear and directly applicable to a mixed integer linear optimization problem.

4.3 Inputs and Output

From the system model in Sect. 3, we get the inputs to the optimization problem as depicted in Table 1. The solution of the optimization problem states as output in a vector $\vec{n}$ for each response $r_i \in R$ whether it should be executed ($n_i = 1$) or not ($n_i = 0$). Since these are integral values, the problem is a MILP problem. In addition, the solution also offers the total cost c_{total} of all selected responses. If no valid solution exists, the solver reports the problem as infeasible.

4.4 Objective Function

The goal of the optimization problem is to minimize the cost of the responses selected to counter the incident. Therefore the objective function is defined as:

$$\min(\sum_{i=1}^{|R|}\sum_{j=1}^{|M|} n_i c_{i,j}) = \min(n_1 c_{1,1} + \cdots + n_{|R|} c_{|R|,|M|})$$

4.5 Feasibility Constraints

Without any feasibility constraints, the optimal solution would be to select no responses at all. Then, the total cost of the selected responses would be 0. The following feasibility constraints force the optimization towards a practically useful solution.

All Affected Entities Are Freed. Every entity affected by the incident has to be freed. Such an entity has to be affected by at least one selected $(n_j = 1)$ response:

$$\forall a \in A: \sum_{j=1}^{|R|} n_j f_{a,j} \geq 1$$

Each Response Can only Be Executed once. We define that a response $r \in R$, if executed once, is fully effective and does not need to be executed multiple times:

$$\forall r_i \in R: 0 \leq n_i \leq 1$$

Total Cost of Responses Has to Be Below Cost of Damage. Based on the damage an incident inflicts in the network, we do not want responses to generate more cost than the incident itself. Therefore, we add a constraint limiting the cost of the responses to be below the expected cost of damage:

$$\forall m \in M: \sum_{i=1}^{|R|} n_i c_{i,m} \leq d_m$$

If no damage is given for a metric m_i, it is set to $d_i = \infty$.

No Conflicting Responses Are Executed. We prevent conflicting responses to be selected at the same time:

$$\sum_{i=1}^{|R|}\sum_{j=1}^{|R|} o_{i,j} n_i n_j = 0$$

4.6 Optimality Constraints

The objective of this optimization problem is to determine the set of responses with minimal costs fulfilling the feasibility constraints defined in Sect. 4.5.

$$\forall m \in M : c_{m_{total}} = \sum_{i=1}^{|R|} n_i c_{i,m} \Rightarrow$$

$$\forall m \in M : c_{m_{total}} - \sum_{i=1}^{|R|} n_i c_{i,m} = 0$$

Based on this formalization, the size of the resulting optimization problem depends on the size of input sets:

– Number of variables: $|M| + |R|$
– Number of constraints: $2|M| + 2|R| + |A|$
– Number of non-zero elements in the problem matrix:
  $\sum_{i=1,j=1}^{|A|,|R|} f_{i,j} + 2|R||M| + |M| + 2\sum_{i=1,j=1}^{|R|,|R|} h_{i,j}$

Since the number of metrics is expected to be more or less constant and small, the size of the problem and its complexity is dominated by the number of available responses and the number of affected entities.

5 Alternative Cost Function

The objective function returns the combined cost of all responses as a single metric, which is minimized by the solver. The given model supports more than one metric per response, so the individual metrics need to be combined to a single cost metric for the objective function. The objective function in Sect. 4.4 simply adds up all metrics. This requires the metrics to already be normalized in a single domain. In this section, we look at suitable metrics and propose a different cost function which is more practically useful.

One of the most common metrics used is the downtime t_{g_i} of components g_i as a side-effect of executed responses [11,22,24]. In [24], this metric is split up into the downtime of critical components and at critical points in time. Another prominent metric is the success probability p_r of response r, or its counterpart, the error-proneness $(1 - p_r)$, expressing how reliable a response is to cope with the incident [3,11,17]. The effectiveness e_r of a response expresses how completely the incident is resolved, or how high the improvement of availability is after applying the response [11,22]. Other metrics to measure a response were proposed including the complexity or severity of a response during execution [17].

The cost functions depends on the system and may be fine-tuned towards special use cases. However, the following cost function is a good starting point:

$$c(r, m) = \frac{1}{p_r} \cdot \frac{1}{e_r} \cdot \sum_{g_i} (t_{g_i} \cdot w_{g_i} \cdot c_{g_i}).$$

The first term $\frac{1}{p_r}$ is the inverse success probability of the response. We assume that executions of responses are independent events and factor in the number of executions to get an expectancy value of 1. The second term $\frac{1}{e_r}$ represents the effectiveness of a response. We assume that coping with the remainder of the incident will be proportional to the calculated costs. The last term includes additional costs: w_{g_i} is a *weighting* factor translating the unit and scale of the *cost* c_{g_i} to embed it into the single cost function. t_{g_i} is the duration over which the cost occurs. This is well suited to resources like bandwidth and memory.

Those calculations are independent from the response selection process and other metrics can be used as well. This proposed alternative cost function is not part of the implementation where the straight-forward way of summing up metrics is used.

6   Implementation

To be able to evaluate the applicability and performance of the presented approach, we implement the proposed design and use this implementation for the evaluation in Sect. 7.

The main tasks of this implementation are the generation of network environment and incident scenario datasets, to transform these datasets into a linear optimization problem and to instrument established MILP solvers to solve this problem and obtain the computed solution.

This functionality is realized by a controller written in Python. First, a network environment is generated where the controller accepts the number of entities, responses, and conflicts between responses, as well as the coverage rate of responses as input. It assigns randomized costs to response and defines relations between responses, and responses and entities. In a second step, a specific incident scenario is obtained by specifying the number of affected hosts. The controller selects them from the network environment and filters information to only contain applicable responses. Additionally, the user can restrict the number of responses and conflicts to be used.

Based on this input, the controller generates the corresponding optimization problem (see Sect. 4.1), and instruments existing MILP solvers to solve the optimization problem and return the computed solution to the controller. Optionally, a problem description file can be generated that can be used as input for both solvers.

The controller interfaces with well-established and optimized linear programming solutions: The *GNU Linear Programming Kit* (GLPK)[1] and the *IBM ILOG CPLEX Optimization Studio* (CPLEX)[2]. To interface with GLPK the controller uses *Python-GLPK*[3] and *pycpx*[4] to interface with CPLEX. Solving a MILP problem is often stated as computationally expensive and time consuming.

---

[1] https://www.gnu.org/software/glpk/.
[2] http://www.ibm.com/software/commerce/optimization/cplex-optimizer/.
[3] http://www.dcc.fc.up.pt/~jpp/code/python-glpk.
[4] http://www.stat.washington.edu/~hoytak/code/pycpx/index.html.

To be able to compare the MILP-based approach, the controller additionally implements two simplistic heuristics to find a solution for the incident as a point of reference for the performance of the optimization:

The **Cheapest-First-Algorithm** orders all available responses with respect to their cost. For each affected entity, the cheapest response is selected. In case the selected response covers more than one entity, no response will be selected for the other entities since they are already covered.

The **Coverage-First-Algorithm** sorts the available responses with respect to their coverage. The responses that help the most affected entities are considered first. On a tie, the cheapest is selected. Responses are drawn as long as there are hosts left which were not covered. Responses which help only hosts which are already covered are ignored.

7   Evaluation

The goal of this evaluation is to analyze whether the presented approach relying on MILP is suitable for response selection, how MILP compares to simplistic approaches like heuristics and to determine how different problem properties influence the performance of both the MILP and heuristic approaches towards response selection.

7.1   Evaluation Methodology

Based on the implementation presented in Sect. 6, we analyze and compare both the performance of the MILP approach and both heuristics and the quality of the solution (i.e. the cost to counteract the security incident) by all approaches. We analyze the behavior of the presented MILP approach and both heuristics in different incident scenarios by increasing problem complexity. We raise the problem complexity by increasing (one at a time) the

1. number of responses
2. number of entities
3. number of conflicts
4. number of entities a response is applicable to (coverage factor)

in the problem while keeping the number of remaining problem parameters fixed.

We employ seven datasets for network environments with differing average and maximum *response coverage factors*. The response coverage factor g is the number of hosts a response frees. The first 6 datasets have an average coverage factor rising from 1 to 25 using a step size of 5 and a maximum coverage factor rising from 1 to 50 using a step size of 10. The last dataset has an average coverage factor of 50 and a maximum coverage factor of 100. If not stated differently, the dataset with an average coverage factor of 10 is used in the evaluation since it represents expected average values for responses.

In order to avoid overhead from Python bindings and the Python interpreter itself, we use the command line clients provided by the GLPK and CPLEX solver and give them generated problem description files in CPLEX format as input.

We execute the evaluation using a system equipped with an Intel Xeon E3-1275 CPU running at 3.4 GHz with 4 physical cores and Hyper-Threading enabled, and 16 GB of RAM. The operating system is Ubuntu 15.10 64-Bit with Python 2.7.10, GLPK 4.55, and CPLEX 12.6.1. GLPK does not support multiple CPU cores and therefore uses only one of the CPU cores. CPLEX supports multiple cores and can therefore benefit from the multicore system used in this evaluation. All test runs are executed five times using the same random instance of the incident scenario. All solutions are based on the same incident scenario as well. In the remainder of this evaluation, all figures depict the average execution time and response costs for each measurement. Additional information including standard deviation is described in the corresponding text for each measurement.

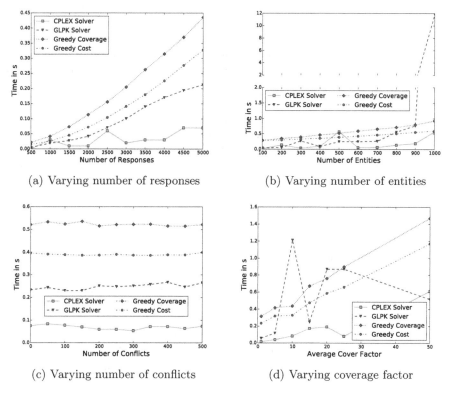

(a) Varying number of responses

(b) Varying number of entities

(c) Varying number of conflicts

(d) Varying coverage factor

Fig. 1. Performance evaluation with increasing problem complexity in one of the following dimensions: number of responses, entities, conflicts, or coverage factor

7.2   Evaluation of Solver Performance

To evaluate the applicability of the presented approach and its performance and to be able to analyze the impact of different problem properties, we evaluate the execution time based on different input settings with increasing complexity. The execution time of both solvers includes reading the problem from the file, setting up the optimization problem and calculating the optimal solution. This evaluation has shown that problem creation and reading from a file has only negligible impact on the execution time and is therefore not separately depicted in the figures. The execution time of both heuristics includes the ordering of the data as described in Sect. 6.

Increasing Number of Responses. With the first evaluation, we analyze the impact of responses in the incident scenario. The evaluation starts with a number of 500 responses which is raised up to 5000 responses using a step size of 500. The number of entities in the scenario is fixed to 500 and the number of conflicts between responses is 100. The resulting average execution time is depicted in Fig. 1a. The maximum standard deviation for all iterations, all approaches and all complexity settings is 0.007 s. Therefore, the results are very stable.

The number of responses increases the problem size in multiple dimensions: with each additional response, the number of terms in the objective function grows, additional constraints are added (cf. Sect. 4.5), and the number of terms in the constraints increases (cf. Sect. 4.5). But still, both the GLPK and the CPLEX solver are faster than both heuristics. We assume that the reason for this is that both heuristics are implemented in Python. As both heuristics have to order the list of responses with respect to costs and in case of the coverage-first algorithm additionally with respect to the coverage factor, the execution time increases with the number of responses. As both algorithms are dominated by the search, the growth is expected to be $n\,log(n)$.

Increasing Number of Entities Next, we analyze the impact of entities in the incident scenario. The evaluation starts with a number of 100 entities which is raised up to 1000 using a step size of 100. The number of responses in the scenario is fixed to 5000 and the number of conflicts between responses is 100. The resulting execution time is depicted in Fig. 1b. The maximum standard deviation for all iterations, all approaches and all complexity settings is 0.045 s. Therefore, the results are very stable.

The number of constraints increases with the number of hosts (cf. Sect. 4.5). Those constraints have several terms as they reflect which response can help which entity. However, this seems to have a moderate impact on the performance of CPLEX for small values apart from the measurement with a number of 500 entities. But only after a number of 800 entities, the execution time increases significantly. With CPLEX we have a solver capable of solving the problem faster than both heuristics. In comparison, GLPK's execution time increases significantly with increased problem complexity. In the final measurement for GLPK with 1000 entities, the execution time is many times higher than with 900 entities.

Increasing Number of Conflicts. In this setting, we analyze the impact of conflicts between responses in the incident scenario. The evaluation starts with a number of 0 conflicts which is raised up to 500 using a step size of 50. The number of responses in the scenario is fixed to 5000 and the number of entities is 500. The resulting execution time is depicted in Fig. 1c. The maximum standard deviation for all iterations, all approaches, and all complexity settings is 0.03 s. Therefore, the results are very stable.

Comparing the results from this and the previous section, the measurement results look very different. Adding more conflicts leads to an increased number of constraints (cf. Sect. 4.5), but the structure of those constraints is different compared to constraints that are added with a rising number of entities. Constraints describing conflicts have a limited number of terms and have, therefore, a much simpler structure.

This observation is reflected in the measurements, as an increasing number of conflicts has no significant impact on the execution time of all tested approaches. As a conclusion, conflicts do not harm performance, as long as only few responses conflict with each other.

Increasing Coverage Factor. For this analysis, we use datasets with varying coverage for responses, as described in Subsect. 7.1. The maximum value for the average factor is increased from 1 to 25 using a step size of 5. Additionally, a average coverage factor of 50 is used for the final measurement. For all tests the number of entities is fixed to 500, the number of responses is fixed to 5000, and a number of 100 conflicts is used. The results are shown in Fig. 1d. The maximum standard deviation for all iterations, all approaches and all complexity settings is 0.038 s. Therefore, the results are very stable.

A higher coverage factor for responses leads to a higher number of terms in the constraints as described in Sect. 4.5, because a response will appear more often within those constraints as the response is capable of freeing a higher number of entities. An increasing coverage factor has the highest impact on performance within the evaluation. The time consumption of both heuristics is growing rapidly, but linear with an increasing coverage factor. From the measurements, the behavior of GLPK is unclear as the time consumption goes up and down without clear trend. CPLEX has one outlier with a coverage factor of 25. The rest of the measurements show a rising tendency. Nevertheless, CPLEX performance beats both heuristics and shows that the presented approach is usable even with complex network environments.

7.3 Solution Quality

Besides performance with respect to execution time, another important aspect to consider is the quality of solutions provided by MILP in comparison to solutions of heuristic solvers. While the solution provided by MILP solvers is optimal within the given objective function, the quality of a heuristic need not be optimal in any way. We therefore compare the proven optimal solutions provided by the

MILP approach and the solutions provided by the Greedy Coverage-First and the Greedy Cheapest-First heuristic for all scenarios used for the performance analysis. In Fig. 2a the number of responses is increased, in Fig. 2b the number of entities, in Fig. 2c the number of conflicts between responses, and in Fig. 2d the coverage factor of a response.

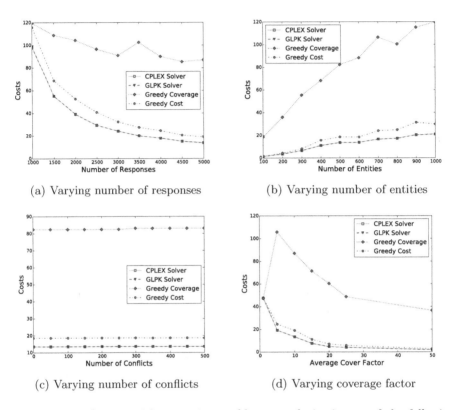

(a) Varying number of responses   (b) Varying number of entities

(c) Varying number of conflicts   (d) Varying coverage factor

Fig. 2. Cost evaluation with increasing problem complexity in one of the following dimensions: number of responses, entities, conflicts, or coverage factor

In the following, we point out the potential cost benefits in case an optimizer instead of the Cheapest-First heuristic is used. The Coverage-First metric offers in all scenarios results worse than the Cheapest-First metric. In case the number of responses increases, the average cost saving potential is nearly 33%. At minimum 17.6% costs can be saved, at maximum around 39% are possible. The percentaged cost saving possibilities slightly decrease during the scenario. In case the number of entities increases, the average cost saving potential is around 36% and lies between 15% at minimum and 54% at maximum. The percentaged cost saving potential increases slightly with an increasing number of entities. In case additional conflicts are added, the cost saving potential stays nearly constant around 38%. Within the datasets the optimal solution was rarely impacted with additional conflicts. In case the coverage factor increases, the percentaged cost saving potential increases slightly. The first measurement shows, that all approaches find the optimal solution in case one response can free only one entity. With an increasing coverage factor the cost calculated drift apart. At minimum a 27%, at maximum 53%, and in average 37% cost can be saved by using an optimizer. In summary, an average cost saving of 36% is possible for all tested scenarios. The smallest potential saving is a still notable amount around 15%.

8   Future Work

We only consider a selection of responses a valid solution if the incident is completely mitigated, i.e. each entity in A is covered by at least one response: $\forall a \in A \colon \sum_{r \in R} f(a, r) \geq 1$. Partial solutions covering only a subset of affected entities are part of future work. Additionally, we plan to integrate response dependencies, i.e. responses have to be executed in conjunction. This allows to specify a more fine-grained response plan. The calculated costs of selected responses can be further decreased, as multiple responses may depend on the same prerequisite responses.

9   Conclusion

In this paper, we present an novel approach towards automated response selection to counteract security incidents in complex network environments. The focus of this work is to relieve network operators from having to select countermeasures in case of an ongoing security incident and hereby increasing network security. With this work, we showed that automated response selection based on linear optimization is a beneficial approach and can provide response strategies much faster and with higher quality than simplistic heuristics.

This work is based on a problem model to represent security incidents. This model is transformed to a linear formulation to solve the problem of response selection as an optimization problem using mixed integer linear programming (MILP). This transformation respects use case-specific metrics and constraints and provides a mathematically proven optimal response strategy. With our evaluation, we have shown that our approach and using established MILP solvers can provide solutions with much higher quality (i.e. lower cost) than heuristics. Compared to heuristics, MILP optimization— often said to be computationally expensive— provides a scalable and competitive approach towards response selection in very complex network environments.

Acknowledgments. This work has been supported by the German Federal Ministry of Education and Research (BMBF) under support code 16KIS0145, project SURF.

References

1. Anuar, N., Papadaki, M., Furnell, S., Clarke, N.: An investigation and survey of response options for intrusion response systems (irss). In: Information Security for South Africa (ISSA) (2010)
2. Balepin, I., Maltsev, S., Rowe, J., Levitt, K.: Using specification-based intrusion detection for automated response. In: Vigna, G., Kruegel, C., Jonsson, E. (eds.) RAID 2003. LNCS, vol. 2820, pp. 136–154. Springer, Heidelberg (2003). doi:10. 1007/978-3-540-45248-5_8
3. Carver, C.A., Hill, J.M., Pooch, U.W.: Limiting uncertainty in intrusion response. In: Proceedings of the IEEE Workshop on Information Assurance and Security (2001)
4. Costante, E., Fauri, D., Etalle, S., den Hartog, J., Zannone, N.: A hybrid framework for data loss prevention and detection. In: Proceedings of the Workshop on Research for Insider Threats (WRIT) (2016)
5. Dantzig, G.: Linear Programming and Extensions. Princeton University Press, Princeton (1963)
6. Foo, B., Glause, M.W., Howard, G.M., Wu, Y.S., Bagchi, S., Spafford, E.H.: Intrusion response systems: a survey. In: Qian, Y., Joshi, J., Tipper, D., Krishnamurthy, P. (eds.) Information Assurance: Dependability and Security in Networked Systems. Morgan Kaufmann, Burlington (2008)
7. Gonzalez Granadillo, G., Débar, H., Jacob, G., Gaber, C., Achemlal, M.: Individual countermeasure selection based on the return on response investment index. In: Kotenko, I., Skormin, V. (eds.) MMM-ACNS 2012. LNCS, vol. 7531, pp. 156–170. Springer, Heidelberg (2012). doi:10.1007/978-3-642-33704-8_14
8. Gonzalez-Granadillo, G., Alvarez, E., Motzek, A., Merialdo, M., Garcia-Alfaro, J., Debar, H.: Towards an automated and dynamic risk management response system. In: Brumley, B.B., Röning, J. (eds.) NordSec 2016. LNCS, vol. 10014, pp. 37–53. Springer, Heidelberg (2016). doi:10.1007/978-3-319-47560-8_3
9. Granadillo, G.G., Motzek, A., Garcia-Alfaro, J., Debar, H.: Selection of mitigation actions based on financial and operational impact assessments. In: 11th International Conference on Availability, Reliability and Security (ARES) (2016)
10. Hasswa, A., Zulkernine, M., Hassanein, H.: Routeguard: an intrusion detection and response system for mobile ad hoc networks. In: IEEE International Conference on Wireless and Mobile Computing, Networking and Communications (WiMob) (2005)
11. Jahnke, M., Thul, C., Martini, P.: Graph based metrics for intrusion response measures in computer networks. In: 32nd IEEE Conference on Local Computer Networks (LCN) (2007)
12. Kamra, A., Bertino, E.: Design and implementation of an intrusion response system for relational databases. IEEE Trans. Knowl. Data Eng. **23**, 875–888 (2011)
13. Kanoun, W., Cuppens-Boulahia, N., Cuppens, F., Dubus, S., Martin, A.: Intelligent response system to mitigate the success likelihood of ongoing attacks. In: 6th International Conference on Information Assurance and Security (IAS) (2010)
14. Karp, R.: Reducibility among combinatorial problems. In: Miller, R.E., Thatcher, J.W., Bohlinger, J.D. (eds.) Complexity of Computer Computations. Plenum Press, New York (1972)
15. Kheir, N., Cuppens-Boulahia, N., Cuppens, F., Debar, H.: A service dependency model for cost-sensitive intrusion response. In: Gritzalis, D., Preneel, B., Theoharidou, M. (eds.) ESORICS 2010. LNCS, vol. 6345, pp. 626–642. Springer, Heidelberg (2010). doi:10.1007/978-3-642-15497-3_38

16. Lee, W., Miller, M., Stolfo, S.J., Fan, W., Zadok, E.: Toward Cost-sensitive Modeling for Intrusion Detection and Response. IOS Press, Amsterdam (2002)
17. Mateos, V., Villagrá, V.A., Romero, F., Berrocal, J.: Definition of response metrics for an ontology-based automated intrusion response systems. Comput. Electr. Eng. **38**, 1102–1114 (2012)
18. Mu, C.M., Li, Y.: An intrusion response decision-making model based on hierarchical task network planning. Expert Syst. Appl. **37**, 2465–2472 (2010)
19. Ossenbühl, S., Steinberger, J., Baier, H.: Towards automated incident handling: how to select an appropriate response against a network-based attack? In: 9th International Conference on IT Security Incident Management IT Forensics (IMF) (2015)
20. Porras, P.A., Neumann, P.G.: EMERALD: event monitoring enabling responses to anomalous live disturbances. In: National Information Systems Security Conference (1997)
21. Ragsdale, D., Carver, C., Humphries, J., Pooch, U.: Adaptation techniques for intrusion detection and intrusion response systems. In: IEEE International Conference on Systems, Man, and Cybernetics (2000)
22. Scarfone, K.A., Grance, T., Masone, K.: Computer security incident handling guide (spp. 800–61 rev. 1.). Technical report, National Institute of Standards & Technology (2008)
23. Shameli-Sendi, A., Ezzati-jivan, N., Jabbarifar, M., Dagenais, M.: Intrusion response systems: survey and taxonomy. Int. J. Comput. Sci. Netw. Secur. (IJCSNS) **12**, 1–14 (2012)
24. Sowa, A., Fedtke, S.: Metriken - Der Schlüssel Zum Erfolgreichen Security und Compliance Monitoring: Design, Implementierung und Validierung in Der Praxis. Vieweg+Teubner Verlag, Heidelberg (2011)
25. Sterne, D., Djahandari, K., Wilson, B., Babson, B., Schnackenberg, D., Holliday, H., Reid, T.: Autonomic response to distributed denial of service attacks. In: Lee, W., Mé, L., Wespi, A. (eds.) RAID 2001. LNCS, vol. 2212, pp. 134–149. Springer, Heidelberg (2001). doi:10.1007/3-540-45474-8_9
26. Strasburg, C., Stakhanova, N., Basu, S., Wong, J.: A framework for cost sensitive assessment of intrusion response selection. In: 33rd Annual IEEE International Computer Software and Applications Conference (COMPSAC) (2009)
27. Strasburg, C., Stakhanova, N., Basu, S., Wong, J.S.: Intrusion response cost assessment methodology. In: Proceedings of the 4th International Symposium on Information, Computer, and Communications Security (ASIACCS) (2009)
28. Sultana, S., Midi, D., Bertino, E.: Kinesis: a security incident response and prevention system for wireless sensor networks. In: Proceedings of the 12th ACM Conference on Embedded Network Sensor Systems (SenSys) (2014)
29. Toth, T., Kruegel, C.: Evaluating the impact of automated intrusion response mechanisms. In: Proceedings of 18th Annual Computer Security Applications Conference (2002)
30. Wang, S.-H., Tseng, C.H., Levitt, K., Bishop, M.: Cost-sensitive intrusion responses for mobile ad hoc networks. In: Kruegel, C., Lippmann, R., Clark, A. (eds.) RAID 2007. LNCS, vol. 4637, pp. 127–145. Springer, Heidelberg (2007). doi:10.1007/978-3-540-74320-0_7
31. White, G., Fisch, E., Pooch, U.: Cooperating security managers: a peer-based intrusion detection system. IEEE Netw. **10**, 20–23 (1996)

32. Wu, Y., Liu, S.: A cost-sensitive method for distributed intrusion response. In: 12th International Conference on Computer Supported Cooperative Work in Design (CSCWD) (2008)
33. Zhang, Z., Ho, P.H., He, L.: Measuring ids-estimated attack impacts for rational incident response: a decision theoretic approach. Comput. Secur. **28**, 605–614 (2009). Elsevier Advanced Technology Publications

Attack Mitigation by Data Structure Randomization

Zhongtian Chen[1](✉) and Hao Han[2]

[1] University High School of Indiana, Carmel, USA
zeroday00@163.com
[2] EMC, Wenzhou, China
haoh@163.com

Abstract. Address Space Layout Randomization (ASLR) and Control Flow Integrity (CFI) have been regarded as the most effective defenses against control flow hijacking attacks. However, researchers have recently shown that data-oriented attacks can circumvent both ASLR and CFI, and are even Turing-complete. These attacks often leverage encapsulated data structures to achieve malicious behaviors. To defeat data structure oriented attacks (DSOA), we propose data structure layout randomization techniques. Our method not only randomizes the data structure layout at compile time, but also inserts the padding bytes to increase entropy. Experimental results show that our method can defeat DSOA with low performance overhead (2.1% on average).

1 Introduction

Control flow integrity [3,10,17,18] has been regarded as an effective defense against control flow hijacking attacks. However, recently, data oriented attacks [11,12] are proposed to be able to circumvent control flow integrity checks, thus demonstrating their Turing-completeness. Encapsulated data structures, such as structs and classes in C/C++, are vulnerable to data oriented attacks as they usually contain security sensitive data (e.g., uid, `password`). In this paper, we denote data oriented attacks that focus on data structures as data structure oriented attacks (DSOA). Address Space Layout Randomization (ASLR) [2,6,8,16], enforcement of Data Flow Integrity (DFI) [9] and Data Space Randomization (DSR) [7] are all state-of-the-art defenses against data oriented attacks. ASLR randomizes the base address of the code/data segments to prevent the attacker from knowing the base address of the targets. However, ASLR does not randomize the layout of data structures. Once an attacker knows the offsets of data fields in a data structure, he/she is then empowered to manipulate these fields to serve their purposes. For example, by exploiting the buffer overflow vulnerability related to the KEY_ARG array in OpenSSL (CVE-2002-0656) [1], the attacker can read a leaked pointer value. Knowing the offset of the target data structure from the address pointed by the pointer, the attacker can acquire the base address of the data structure, effectively rendering ASLR meaningless. Enforcement mechanisms of DFI generates data flow graphs (DFG) and checks

© Springer International Publishing AG 2017
F. Cuppens et al. (Eds.): FPS 2016, LNCS 10128, pp. 85–93, 2017.
DOI: 10.1007/978-3-319-51966-1_6

whether the data flow follows the DFGs at runtime. However, complete enforcement of DFI suffers from high performance overhead, thus making it difficult to apply DFI checks into everyday practices. DSR encrypts data objects and decrypts them at time of usage. However, DSR does field insensitive pointer analyses. Therefore, if any attack utilizes a bug found overwriting inner fields of a data structure, it could not be prevented by DSR. In addition, DSR also suffers from high performance overhead. In this paper, we propose a novel defense against DSOAs - a customized compiler that defenders may use to generate programs with randomized data structure layouts. To further increase their entropy, the compiler inserts paddings of flexible lengths into the data structures generated. Experimental results show that this method can defeat DSOAs with low performance overhead.

Our contributions in this work are summarized as follows:

- We propose a novel defense against DSOAs with a new randomization algorithm and flexible length padding insertion.
- We propose a method that determines which data structure can be randomized.
- We evaluate the effectiveness and overhead of the system. Experimental results show that the runtime overhead is only 2.1% on average.

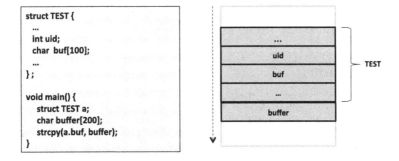

Fig. 1. An example of DSOA

2   Overview

2.1   Threat Model

Our threat model focuses on data structure oriented attacks. We assume the target programs contains memory corruption bugs and the attacker can leverage the bug to overwrite/overread any fields in the data structure. We assume that there are no memory disclosure bugs, however, as existing defenses [4,5] can mitigate such attacks. Take the program in Fig. 1 as an illustrating example. The goal of the attack is to modify field uid in struct instance a to escalate privilege. An attacker, knowing the base address of a, may get the layout of a based on the definition of TEST. Then, he may write a maliciously-crafted value to a->uid by exploiting the buffer overflow bug as shown.

2.2   Key Idea

We propose a novel method for mitigating DSOAs by randomizing the data structure layouts of the programs. We compile programs with a customized compiler (i.e., a modified GNU GCC) so that the relative offsets of fields in data structures can be shuffled every time the program is compiled. By doing so, each copy of the program will be different and when an attacker launches a DSOA attack, the layout of data structure he/she uses will be obsolete.

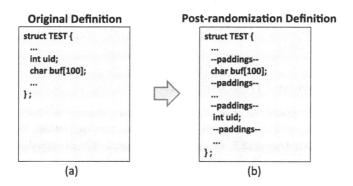

Fig. 2. Comparison of original definition with after-randomized definition.

For instance, consider a program that contains structure TEST as shown in Fig. 2(a). An attacker, upon discovering a buffer-overflow vulnerability that can overflow the string buffer buf in the data structure, may change security sensitive field uid, and perform a privilege escalation attack. However, if the program is compiled by a compiler that shuffles data structure layouts, the attack could be defeated. Consider a randomized data structure layout inside struct TEST as shown in Fig. 2(b). The attacker, referencing the original layout of the program, will end up accessing completely irrelevant fields in most situations and fail to change uid, resulting in an unsuccessful attack.

3   Challenges

In this section, we discuss the challenges in modifying the GNU GCC compiler to include the data structure randomization process.

3.1   Flexible Array Members

Flexible array members are objects of incomplete array types that must be placed at the end of a structure as defined by the C standard. This poses a challenge to the implementation of the special compilers previously mentioned because the flexible array members have to be identified and their positions preserved in the data structure randomization process.

3.2 Data Structure Initialization

As the definitions of structures are altered, initialization statements have to be changed to match the new definitions. Refer to the structure TEST as shown in Fig. 2 for example. To initialize struct instance s with the original definition of TEST, we may use:

$$\text{struct TEST s} = \{\ldots, \ 0, \ \texttt{"Hello World!"}, \ldots\};$$

However, if this initialization is used for the new definition in Fig. 2(b), the fields' values would mismatch. Then, the problem either could not finish compilation with type-mismatching errors or, even worse, would raise unexpected errors during execution.

3.3 Pointer Involved Data Structures

Another challenge posed by randomizing data structures is that it disrupts direct pointer arithmetic based on the original structure definition. Still consider the example of structure TEST. Originally, it is perfectly acceptable to do the following:

```
char *p;
struct TEST x;
x.uid = 1;
p = &x.uid;
*(p+4) = "Hello_World!";
```

However, the last statement will fail in the new definition of TEST as *(p+4) now refers to some padding element rather than buf[100].

3.4 Dynamic Library Parameter Involved Data Structures

When a randomized data structure instance is passed to a dynamic library function, the function will handle this instance based on its original definition, which will lead to unexpected results. For example, when a program calls bind in GNU LIBC with an instance of data structure sockaddr, the sockaddr instance might be randomized. However, bind would still attempt to use the sockaddr instance based on its original definition. This will obviously lead to an execution error.

4 Design and Implementation

In this section, we introduce our randomization algorithm, illustrate how challenges mentioned in Sect. 3 may be solved, and calculate the post-randomization entropy of the data structures.

4.1 Randomization Algorithm

We implement the following randomization algorithm in GCC to randomize field declarations in objects.

Algorithm 1. Randomization Algorithm

Input: Random value R, Original sequence of field declarations seq[1...m]
Output: The reordered declaration sequence seq[1...m]
   Initialization: n ← m
   while n > 1 **do**
      i ← R %n + 1; /*Assign a random number between 1 and n to i */
      t ← seq[i]; /* Swap the ith and n^{th} elements of the sequence */
      seq[i] ← seq[n];
      seq[n] ← t;
      n=n-1; /* Decrease n by 1 */
   end while

4.2 Special Cases

Flexible Array Members. In the implementation, we are able to identify flexible arrays with these two sets of criteria:

(1) The declaration in question is for an object of type array; and
(2) The declaration is incomplete.

After the flexible array members are identified, they are easily removed from the randomization process.

Finding Randomizable Data Structure. As shown in Sect. 3, the randomization of data structure can cause serious issues. Some of them can be worked around easily, some cannot. Therefore, we propose a blacklisting mechanism for finding randomizable data structures. The compiler, with the randomization feature enabled, first tries to compile the source code with the potential problems. The output is parsed, and whenever an error caused by data structure randomization is raised, the name of the related structure object is logged in a blacklist. Then the compiler would try to compile the source code again, smartly omitting the randomization process for the structures on the blacklist. If more randomization related problem occurs, the names of the related structure will be appended to the blacklist. The process repeats itself until all randomization related errors are cleared.

4.3 Padding Insertion Algorithm

We implement the following padding insertion algorithm in GCC after the data structure randomization process has completed to increase randomization entropy. Algorithm 2 shows the details. For each field, we insert 1–4 padding variables in the data structure with the same size of the field. This method will increase entropy. For example, suppose a data structure has m fields with total l bytes. If we only randomize the data structure layout, the attacker has to guess l times to overwrite a specific field's value. If we add the paddings to the data structure, the length of the randomized data structure is l' (l' ∈ [2l,5l]). As such, the attacker has to guess at least 2l times, but at most 5l times.

Algorithm 2. Padding Insertion Algorithm

Input: Random value R, Randomized sequence of field declarations seq[1...m]
Output: The padded declaration sequence seq'[1...(m+k)] (k ∈ [m,4m])
   Initialization: n ← 1, i ← 1
   while n <= m **do**
     seq'[i] ← seq[n];
     a ← 0 /* Initialize local variable a to 0 */
     while a < R%4+1 **do**
       i=i+1;
       seq'[i] ← a copy of seq[n]
       a=a+1;
     end while
     i=i+1;
     n=n+1;
   end while

---

5   Evaluation

We chose to implement our data structure randomization feature in the open source compiler, GNU GCC 4.5.0. In addition to randomization, the modified compiler also adds paddings with arbitrary sizes in between each field declaration to increase randomization entropy. In this section, we present our evaluation of the effectiveness and performance overhead of the Data Structure Randomization technique. The testing environment is a Redhat Linux 7.3 with 2 GB RAM and Intel i7 CPU.

5.1   Effectiveness

Using the modified GCC, we test the effectiveness of the Data Structure Randomization technique by recompiling Apache Server v. 1.3.23 and OpenSSL v. 0.9.6d with known heap overflow vulnerability when used within our testing environment. The attack tool used is openssl-too-open [1], which exploits the KEY_ARG buffer overflow vulnerability to open a shell for the attacker. Experimental results show that the recompiled Apache Server and the Openssl package are able to defeat the buffer overflow attack, thus proving the randomization technique is indeed effective against Data Structure Manipulation Attacks.

5.2   Performance Overhead

The performance of the recompiled Apache Server is tested against that of the original one with Apache Benchmark. The configurations of the two servers are identical except for the directory paths their related files are in. The Apache Benchmark is set to send a total of 100,000 requests in groups of 500 per round per server with the keep-alive option enabled. The exact command used is `ab -n 100000 -c 500 -k http://localhost/index.html`. Five rounds of testing are administered to both servers and all requests completed with success. The data collected is shown in Table 1. This result indicates that the recompiled server introduces low performance overhead. Interestingly, randomized servers may sometimes be even faster than the original servers due to program locality.

Table 1. Server performance data

Round #	New server (reqs/sec)	Original server (reqs/sec)	Overhead (%)
Round 1	4384.04	4325.63	1.3
Round 2	4339.15	4274.78	1.5
Round 3	4375.22	4264.03	2.6
Round 4	4346.88	4247.19	2.3
Round 5	4344.05	4234.24	2.6
Average	4357.87	4269.17	2.1

6   Related Work

6.1   Memory Safe Protection

Memory corruption bugs, which are leveraged by the attacker to achieve data oriented attacks [11,12], exist in languages like C/C++ because these languages are type-unsafe. Cyclone [13] and CCured [15] propose a type-safe alternative to C. SoftBound with CETS [14] provides bound checking and identifier matching to achieve complete memory safety. However, both of these defenses suffer from high performance overhead.

6.2   Data Space Randomization

Data Space Randomization (DSR) [7] encrypts all data objects at their definition and decrypts them at usage. However, DSR performs field insensitive analyses and thus does not prevent DSOAs that overflow the inside of a data structure. In addition, DSR suffers from high performance overhead. Our method prevents the DSOA with low performance overhead.

7   Conclusion

To defeat data structure oriented attacks (DSOA), we propose Data Structure Layout Randomization techniques. During compilation, our method not only randomizes data structure layouts, but also inserts padding bytes to increase entropy. Experimental results show that our method can defeat DSOA with low performance overhead.

References

1. Openssl speed. http://www.openssl.org/docs/apps/speed.html
2. Pax aslr documentation. http://pax.grsecurity.net/docs/aslr.txt
3. Abadi, M., Budiu, M., Erlingsson, U., Ligatti, J.: Control-flow integrity. In: ACM Conference on Computer and Communications Security (CCS 2005) (2005)
4. Backes, M., Holz, T., Kollenda, B., Koppe, P., Nürnberger, S., Pewny, J.: You can run but you can't read: preventing disclosure exploits in executable code. In: ACM SIGSAC Conference on Computer and Communications Security (CCS 2014) (2014)
5. Backes, M., Nürnberger, S.: Oxymoron: making fine-grained memory randomization practical by allowing code sharing. In: USENIX Security Symposium (Security 2014) (2014)
6. Bhatkar, E., Duvarney, D.C., Sekar, R.: Address obfuscation: an efficient approach to combat a broad range of memory error exploits. In: Proceedings of the 12th USENIX Security Symposium, pp. 105–120 (2003)
7. Bhatkar, S., Sekar, R.: Data space randomization. In: International Conference on Detection of Intrusions and Malware, and Vulnerability Assessment (DIMVA 2008) (2008)
8. Bhatkar, S., Sekar, R., DuVarney, D.C.: Efficient techniques for comprehensive protection from memory error exploits. In: Proceedings of the 14th Conference on USENIX Security Symposium, Berkeley, CA, USA, vol. 14, p. 17 (2005)
9. Castro, M., Costa, M., Harris, T.: Securing software by enforcing data-flow integrity. In: Proceedings of the 7th Symposium on Operating Systems Design and Implementation (OSDI 2006) (2006)
10. Davi, L., Dmitrienko, A., Egele, M., Fischer, T., Holz, T., Hund, R., Nrnberger, S., Sadeghi, A.-R.: Mocfi: a framework to mitigate control-flow attacks on smartphones. In: Annual Network and Distributed System Security Symposium (NDSS 2012) (2012)
11. Hu, H., Chua, Z. L., Adrian, S., Saxena, P., Liang, Z.: Automatic generation of data-oriented exploits. In: Proceedings of the 24th USENIX Security Symposium (Security 2015) (2015)
12. Hu, H., Shinde, S., Adrian, S., Chua, Z.L., Saxena, P., Liang, Z.: Data-oriented programming: on the expressiveness of non-control data attacks. In: IEEE Symposium on Security and Privacy (Oakland 2016) (2016)
13. Jim, T., Morrisett, J.G., Grossman, D., Hicks, M.W., Cheney, J., Wang, Y.: Cyclone: a safe dialect of C. In: General Track of the Annual Conference on USENIX Annual Technical Conference, ATEC 2002 (2002)
14. Nagarakatte, S., Zhao, J., Martin, M.M., Zdancewic, S.: Softbound: highly compatible and complete spatial memory safety for C. In: Proceedings of the 30th ACM SIGPLAN Conference on Programming Language Design and Implementation (PLDI 2009) (2009)

15. Necula, G.C., McPeak, S., Weimer, W.: CCured: type-safe retrofitting of legacy code. In: 29th ACM SIGPLAN-SIGACT Symposium on Principles of Programming Languages (POPL 2002) (2002)
16. Pax Team: Pax address space layout randomization (aslr). http://pax.grsecurity. net/docs/aslr.txt
17. Wang, Z., Jiang, X.: Hypersafe: a lightweight approach to provide lifetime hypervisor control-flow integrity. In: IEEE Symposium on Security and Privacy (Oakland 2010) (2010)
18. Zhang, C., Wei, T., Chen, Z., Duan, L., McCamant, S., Szekeres, L., Song, D., Zou, W.: Practical control flow integrity and randomization for binary executables. In: IEEE Symposium on Security and Privacy (Oakland 2013) (2013)

Vulnerability Analysis and Security Metrics

Vulnerability Analysis of Software Defined Networking

Salaheddine Zerkane[1]([⊠]), David Espes[2], Philippe Le Parc[2],
and Fréderic Cuppens[3]

[1] IRT B<>COM, UBO, Télécom Bretagne, 35510 Cesson-Sévigné, France
Salaheddine.ZERKANE@b-com.com
[2] IRT B<>COM, UBO, 29200 Brest, France
{David.espes,Philippe.Le-Parc}@univ-brest.fr
[3] IRT B<>COM, Télécom Bretagne, 35510 Cesson-Sévigné, France
Frederic.Cuppens@telecom-bretagne.eu

Abstract. Security of Software Defined Networking (SDN) is an open issue because of many reasons. Security requirements were not considered in the primary definition of SDN. Consequently, SDN enlarges the network vulnerability surface by introducing new vulnerabilities that do not exist in the conventional networking architecture. In addition, there are neither security risk management processes nor mathematical models that specifically address SDN security and the influence of its specific features. We provide a vulnerability analysis for SDN to study these weaknesses and to measure their impacts. Our analysis specifies a model of SDN assets that needs to be protected. Then, it derives 114 SDN generic vulnerabilities using standardized security objectives. It relies on an open standardized semi qualitative semi quantitative scoring system to calculate the severities of theses vulnerabilities. Then, it adapts them to SDN specific features using Analytical Hierarchical Process (AHP).

Keywords: Software defined networking · Information security · Vulnerability analysis · CVSS · Analytical hierarchical process · Security metrics

1 Introduction

Computer security risk management [1] faces many issues such as uncertainty, lack of adequate data and technological changes. The later challenge becomes the most impressive driving force for the overhaul of security risk management in computer systems. Especially with the advent of emerging technologies, such as Internet of things (IOT), Big Data, Machine Learning and Software Defined Networking (SDN), security risk management needs to cover the specific characteristics of these technologies in order to enable stakeholders to take effective security decisions.

SDN [2–4] is an evolution of programmable networks. It is based on decoupling the control plane from the data plane. The former is logically centralized while the latter is distributed in the network. The major benefits of this separation are the network global view empowering the control plane, the rapid innovation through the development of automatized network functions, and the abstraction from hardware concerns.

© Springer International Publishing AG 2017
F. Cuppens et al. (Eds.): FPS 2016, LNCS 10128, pp. 97–116, 2017.
DOI: 10.1007/978-3-319-51966-1_7

However, SDN is facing substantial challenges in security because it inherits security flaws from classical network architecture. In addition, it reinforces these flaws and introduces new vulnerabilities. Security risks are magnified within the control plane, because it becomes a single point of failure in an SDN environment and because it relies heavily on automation [5].

Vulnerability analysis is an important process in security risk management because it enables discovering the weaknesses of a system and their impacts on its security. In turn, analyzing a system to detect its unidentified weaknesses is still a complex and a subjective process [6] because there is neither a universal classification nor a standardized methodology in vulnerability analysis. This fact is particularly amplified in a dynamic and emerging environment such as SDN where there are no historical and well known SDN vulnerabilities.

While the goal of SDN is the convergence of all network actors around a mutual standardized set of technologies, in practice, it is still not the case. SDN is deployed and implemented in different ways using different technologies that are not yet converging. For example, the lack of standardized northbound API or East/West API (or the non-standardization of controllers) pause many issues related to interoperability and deployment. Moreover, each organization deploys and configures SDN in different ways according to its specific needs and goals. Thus, a generic vulnerability analysis for SDN is necessary to improve SDN security and understand its weaknesses. Such analysis provides a generic classification of SDN vulnerabilities and evaluates their impacts on SDN security. These outcomes enable organizations to know the impacts of their conceptual and implementation choices. They aid them to adopt suitable countermeasures against security attacks by making the best security decisions.

In order to perform robust vulnerability analysis, we rely on the Common Vulnerability Scoring System (CVSS) [7, 8] to estimate the impacts of security vulnerabilities. CVSS is based on qualitative and quantitative metrics that define the impacts of the security vulnerabilities. Its computation procedures integrate three dimensions related to the different characteristics of classical networks (or generally computer systems): the intrinsic generic features of computer systems, their temporal features, and their environment related factors.

However, there are significant factors, specific to SDN, which are not covered by CVSS. These factors affect the security of SDN and enlarge its vulnerability surface. For example, the centralization of the Controller transforms its components to precarious shared resources among other SDN assets. In this case, all the SDN assets are exposed by the vulnerabilities of the Controller.

Thus, a proper vulnerability analysis also needs to integrate specific SDN features into the evaluation of vulnerability impacts. We rely on decision making procedures to measure the intensities of SDN features on its security because these characteristics are intangible.

Decision making is the process to choose among alternatives based on multiple factors [9]. Although decisions are subjective judgments and they depend on the knowledge and experience of domain experts, there are methods that can be used to rationalize decisions and quantify them mathematically. The Analytical Hierarchy Process (AHP) [10, 11] is one of these approaches. It is a multi-criteria decision making procedure. It is used to define and evaluate the importance of decision alternatives in the decision making process. It decomposes complex problems into many levels of connected sub problems. Then, it evaluates the intensity of each sub problem in the overall set of problems. Within this framework, AHP enables us measuring the overall intensities of SDN characteristics on the severities of its vulnerabilities.

Our work provides a new input into the arena of SDN. We are the first to propose generic vulnerability analysis for SDN. Our contributions in this paper are as follows:

- We propose an SDN meta-model, its instantiation and a set of standardized security objectives.
- We construct a matrix of generic SDN vulnerabilities.
- We evaluate the impacts of vulnerabilities on SDN security using the CVSS.
- We adapt the severity scores by integrating SDN specific features into the CVSS using the AHP.

The outline of this article is organized as the following. In Sect. 2, we discuss the research works related to SDN security analysis. We provide in Sect. 3 a meta-model of SDN assets. In Sect. 4, we derive new SDN vulnerabilities using standardized security objectives. In Sect. 5, we use CVSS to compute the severities of the SDN vulnerabilities, and in Sect. 6, we enhance the results using AHP. Finally, in Sect. 7, we conclude our work by highlighting the future directions.

2 Related Work

Lu et al. [12] propose a security assessment methodology for Software Defined Networking Based Mobile Networks (SDN-MN). The mechanism uses attack graphs to define and to generate attack paths while taking into account SDN-MN's specific features. In addition, it uses AHP to quantify the influence of SDN-MN dynamic factors on its security in terms of attacks costs.

Many works [13–17] focus on the security assessments of OpenFlow [18] (SDN's southbound Interface). Kloti et al. [19] provides an Openflow risk analysis based on attack trees and the STRIDE[1] approach [20]. A brief overview of Openflow vulnerabilities is discussed in [21]. The article highlights the OpenFlow vulnerabilities that are currently deployed by hardware and software vendors.

The article in [22] proposes seven new threat vectors of SDN that can exploit its vulnerabilities. The work considers the programmability and centralization features of SDN as honeypots. According to its authors, these features attract attackers and expose the SDN vulnerabilities. The proposed vectors are as follows: (1) Forged or faked traffic flows. (2) Attacks on vulnerabilities in switches. (3) Attacks on control plane communications. (4) Attacks on/and vulnerabilities in controllers. (5) Lack of mechanisms to ensure trust between the controller and management applications. (6) Attacks on/and vulnerabilities in administrative stations. (7) Lack of trusted resources for forensics and remediation.

---

[1] STRIDE is a threat model proposed by Microsoft. Its name comes from the initials of the following security categories: Spoofing identity, Tampering with data, Repudiation, Information disclosure, Denial of service, and Elevation of privilege.

There are some researches that survey security in SDN [23, 24]. The authors in [25] introduce a set of SDN specific vulnerabilities and provide a list of SDN attacks. It categorizes SDN security issues by type with respect to the SDN layer/interface affected by each issue. The issues are split into seven main categories (Unauthorized Access, Data Leakage, Data Modification, Malicious/Compromised Application, Denial of Service, configuration issues and System Level SDN Security). For each problem, the survey provides examples how attacks might occur.

The aforementioned literature provides a general view of SDN vulnerabilities without measuring their severities and the impacts of SDN characteristics. Furthermore, many of these works are only focused on the aspects of Openflow security and do not tackle the rest of the SDN architecture. Our work fills these gaps. It is the first work that quantifies vulnerability assessment and customizes it to SDN's characteristics. First, it provides more complete and detailed SDN vulnerabilities based on a generic SDN architecture covering all SDN components. Second, it measures the severities of these vulnerabilities. It captures the impact of SDN's inherent characteristics on them. Finally, it adapts the previous measures by including these impacts.

3 SDN Assets Classification

SDN is organized into four layers [26–28]. On the top, an *Application layer* defines different network services such as load balancing, firewalls, and VoIP. The *Control layer* manages the infrastructure's resources and provides the *Application layer* with network state and network data. Both layers interact through northbound Application programming interfaces (APIs), which allow the *Application layer* to program the network. Besides, the *Control layer* supervises the behavior of the *Data Plane layer*, which processes and executes network forwarding functions, through southbound APIs. The three aforementioned layers are governed by a *management layer* that manages all the administrative tasks of the network, spreads network policies, and allocates SDN resources.

We propose a meta-model for SDN and its instantiation in Fig. 1. The meta-model corresponds to a generic abstraction of SDN architecture. The SDN architecture model is an example of a specialization of the SDN meta-model. It is based on the following technologies. The *Management layer* corresponds to the Openstack solution [29]. Openstack is a set of open source software that controls large pools of compute, storage, and networking resources. The later are managed through a dashboard that gives administrators control while empowering their users to provision resources through a web interface. The *Application layer* corresponds to a set of Security and Networking Applications such as Firewalls, etc. The *Control layer* example is the RYU *Controller*. RYU [30] is a component based Software Defined Networking Framework. The *Data Plane layer* corresponds to Open Virtual Switch (OVS) [31]. OVS is a multilayer virtual switching solution designed to enable massive network automation and distribution across multiple physical servers.

Table 1 describes the assets of our system under study. It explains all the entities of the aforementioned models. The assets are the logical objects of our system under study that need to be protected.

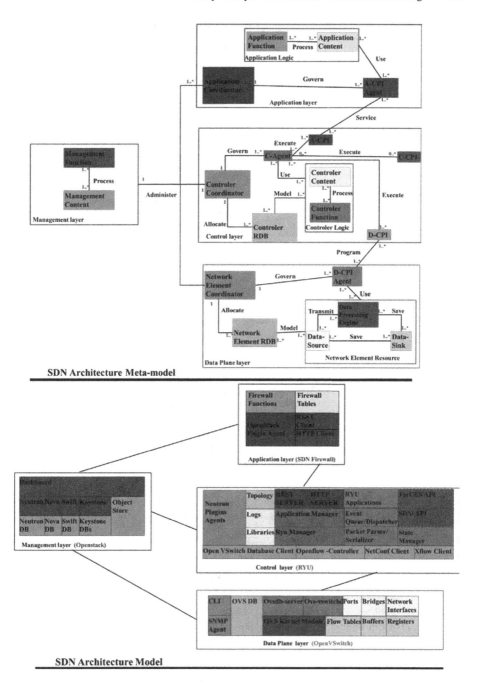

Fig. 1. SDN Architecture Metamodeling.

Table 1. Assets of the system under study.

Asset Class	Asset Component	Location	Describtion	Instanciation
Application	Application Function	Application layer	It defines the operations and processes of network Service	SDN Firewall
	Application Content		It defines the information used and generated by the network Service	
Controller	Controller Content	Control layer	It encompasses the control behaviour expressed by different operations	Packets parser/Serialiser, RYU Applications, Event Queue/Dispatcher, State Manager
	Controller Function		All the data produced or consumed by Controller Function	
	C-Agent	Controller Agent exposes the	Ryu manager, App-Manager	
	Controller RDB	Controller's functions and its abstractions to other entities (Application and Controller)	Controller Resource Data Base conceptualizes all the information on the Controller's resources in a data base model	Topology, Libraries
Network element	Data Processing Engine	Data plane layer	It is a set of functionalities that process data traffic and store it	OVS Kernel Module
	Data Source	It delivers and transmits data traffic	Ports, Bridges, Network Interfaces	
	Data Sink	It is a memory space that stores the data received from the two previous entities	Buffers, Registers, Flow Tables	
	Network Element RDB	It stores the data plane resources information	OVS DB	
SDN Interface	A-CPI Agent	Application layer	Application-Control Plane Agent provides Application Logic entity with network information. Also, it exposes the capabilities of the Application Function (Application) to the later	REST Client, HTTP Client

(*continued*)

Table 1. (*continued*)

Asset Class	Asset Component	Location	Describtion	Instanciation
	A-CPI	Control layer	Application Control Plane Interface allows Application to express its requirements and to react programmatically to network states	REST Server, HTTP server
	C-CPI	Control layer	Controller-Controller Programming Interface offers a view of Controller resources to another Controller	SDNi API, ForCES API
	D-CPI	Control layer	Data-Controller Programming Interface allows the Control layer programming the behavior of the data plane and sharing its resources	Openflow-Controller, Open vSwitch Database Client, NETCONF Client, XFlow Client
	D-CPI Agent	Data plane layer	It executes the Controller's instructions using the resources of Network Element and exposes the capabilities of the later to Controller	Ovsdb-server, Ovs-vswitchd
Manager	Management Function	Management layer	It performs administration operations and allows thir parties entities to allocate SDN resources	Neutron, Nova, Swift, Keystone, Dashboard
	Management Content	Management layer	It contains all the information data such as Resource information, storage data, Metrics	Nova DB, Swift DB, Neutron DB, Object Store, Keystone DBs
Coordinator	Application Coordinator	Application layer	It installs customer specific requirements and network policies received from the Management layer on the Application Layer	Openstack plugins agents

(*continued*)

Table 1. (*continued*)

Asset Class	Asset Component	Location	Describtion	Instanciation
	Controller Coordinator	Control layer	It installs customer specific configurations and network policies received from the Management layer on the control Layer	Neutron plugins agents
	Network Element Coordinator	Data plane layer	It installs customer specific configurations received from the Management layer on the data plane Layer	CLI, SNMP Agent

4 SDN Vulnerability Construction

Security vulnerability [32] is a weakness in a system; when it is exploited, it triggers the transition of the system to a flawed state. It can also expose parts of the system and lead to the violation of its security characteristics. It is crucial to identify the vulnerabilities of our system in order to correct them, because most of the attacks exploit them in order to achieve their goals; therefore, by eliminating and correcting vulnerabilities, we can prevent attacks from happening.

In contrast to our study, we propose a set of SDN generic vulnerabilities. These vulnerabilities are not related to the implementation of the SDN components nor to any specific technology; but rather to the SDN architecture design and its distinctive characteristics. Our objective is to identify the new vulnerabilities introduced by the SDN design apart from the known vulnerabilities in any network.

We have built these vulnerabilities by applying a set of inverted security principals to the assets of our system under study. The security objects [33] that we took into consideration are access control, authentication, confidentiality, non-repudiation, integrity and availability. We obtain 114 generic vulnerabilities (see Table 4 in the Annex) after applying the following vulnerability construction procedure:

1. Reverse the security object (see Table 2).
2. Combine each reversed security object to all the identified assets.
3. Delete from the new combinations all the unfeasible mappings.
4. If all the asset components have the same vulnerability and the same impact, generalize the combination to their asset class.

The generated vulnerabilities are a generalization of all the intrinsic vulnerabilities that may occur in an SDN architecture. They are used to measure the impacts on SDN security. They can be also adapted to the environment and temporal variables if these later change in the subject architecture. For example, vulnerability *V1* with an impact *I1* in the class *C-Agent* is passed to its instances *Ryu Manager* and *Application Manager*.

Table 2. Reversion of security object.

Security object	Reversion	Description
Access Control	Open Access	Susceptibility to be accessed by any element without restriction
Authentication	Nonidentification	Lack of identification in a distinctive way
Confidentiality	No-secrecy	Reveling its features and disclosing its communications
Non-Repudiation	Non-traceability	Not tracking its actions, its events and their actors
Integrity	Alterability	Susceptibility to be tampered in whole or in part
Availability	Disruption	Resources are partially or totally inaccessible

A threat that affects *C-Agent* availability uses a *Disruption* weakness in this class. Therefore, *C-Agent Disruption* is the inferred vulnerability. An instance of this vulnerability can be a *Lack of Exception Handling Mechanism* in *Ryu Manager*. An attacker can interrupt *Ryu Manager* by generating an unhandled exception event. In this case, the lack of a proper exception handler in *Ryu Manager* leads to an uncaught exception (with the termination of *Ryu Manager*) or blocks *Ryu Manager*.

5   SDN Vulnerabilities Scoring

We use the CVSS in order to evaluate the severities of the vulnerabilities on SDN security. It offers an open framework to assess the impacts of computer security vulnerabilities. It uses a set of standardized metrics to score vulnerabilities and compute their severity scores. The metrics in the base group evaluate the unchangeable characteristics of vulnerabilities not influenced by time or by user environments. On the other hand, the metrics of the temporal group process the characteristics that are subject to change over time and those in the environment group focus on the proprieties that are influenced by user environments.

Table 3 describes all the CVSS metrics according to SDN requirements. It covers all the SDN attributes inherited from the conventional network architecture. The vulnerabilities scores are scaled in an interval of [0, 10]. They are mapped to the following ratings: None (0.0), Low (0.1–3.9), Medium (4–6.9), High (7–8.9), Critical (9–10). We use CVSS 3.0 Calculator offered by [34] to calculate the impacts of the assessed SDN vulnerability in the three metric groups.

We compute the severities using the following assumptions. In the base group, the attacks on the assets of the *Application* and *Data Plane layer*s can come from the Network and may require user or external processes to succeed; however, the threats on the *Control layer* come from a limited vector (adjacent neighbors) and do not require user interactions. Besides, the attacks on the SDN interfaces and agents amplify the scope of the attack. In the temporal group, *Exploit Code Maturity* is between *Unproven* and *Proof-Of-Concept* because there is not a threat code that works in any SDN situation. The *Remediation Level* value is set to *Official Fix* only when the deployment of TLS (Transport Layer Security protocol) [35] mitigates or prevents the exploit.

Table 3. CVSS vulnerabilities metrics applied on SDN.

Group	Metric	Definition
Base	Attack Vector	The path by which an attacker exploits the vulnerability. Remote: from an external network (internet), Adjacent: from a neighboring network that shares the same infrastructure, Local: within the SDN network, Physical: physically accessing the assets
	Complexity	The conditions and the efforts that need the attacker in order to exploit the vulnerability. Low: conditions and efforts are identified through SDN specifications and standards, High: efforts need the attacker to invest in reconnaissance, preparation, pen testing, and more steps in order to exploit the vulnerability
	Privilege required	The rights that the attacker needs to exploit the SDN vulnerability. None, Low: user privileges, High: management privileges
	User Interaction	Determines if an SDN user is needed to participate or not in the process of vulnerability exploitation
	Scope	Determines if the vulnerability exploitation impacts other assets
	Confidentiality	The impact of the vulnerability exploitation on SDN contents, communications and data bases confidentiality. None, Low: Assets information leaks to authorized entities, High: Asset information leaks to unauthorized entities
	Integrity	The impact of the vulnerability exploitation on the veracity and trustworthiness of SDN informational resources (contents, communications and data bases). None, Low: the attacker does not control the process neither measures the consequences, High: the attacker control the process of modification and the consequences
	Availability	The impact of the vulnerability exploitation on SDN resource accessibility. None, Low: asset availability is partially impacted whether it is unavailable for a certain time only or available all the time with some interruptions, High: asset is completely inaccessible
Temporal	Exploit Code Maturity	The likelihood of the SDN vulnerability being exploited based on current state of exploit techniques and exploit code availability. Unproven: No exploit is available, Prove of Concept: the exploit code is not functional and not Practical in SDN, Functional: the code works only on the vulnerable asset, High: exploit code works in SDN and is widely-available, reliable, and easy to use

(continued)

Table 3. (*continued*)

Group	Metric	Definition
	Remediation Level	The level of fixes and patches to correct the SDN vulnerability. Official Fix: A complete SDN vendor solution is available, Temporal: a temporal tool or hotfix is available, Workaround: unofficial fix and a non-vendor patch is available, Unavailable: there is no solution to correct the vulnerability
	Report Confidence	The degree of confidence on the SDN vulnerability and the level of its technical knowledge. Unknown: there are documents reporting the vulnerability but its causes are not identified, Reasonable: significant details are available but the vulnerability is not proven in practice, Confirmed: detailed vulnerability reports are available and functional reproduction is possible
Environmental	Confidentiality Requirement	Enable to customize the importance of confidentiality for the SDN asset relatively to other metrics in order to adapt the score
	Integrity Requirement	Enable to customize the importance of integrity for the SDN asset relatively to other metrics in order to adapt the score
	Availability Requirement	Enable to customize the importance of availability for the SDN asset relatively to other metrics in order to adapt the score
	Modified Base Metrics	The eight metrics customize the base metrics according to available modifications in the SDN environment. An example is the existence of protection mechanisms such as TLS in Openflow and https in Rest API

We have also observed in the literature that the majority of security reports are focused on the interface between the control plane and the data plane (Openflow). Therefore, we assign a *Reasonable Report Confidence* for the threats on *D-CPI* and *D-CPI Agent*. In the environment group, we assume that TLS is deployed in the interfaces between the *Control layer*, the *Data Plane layer* and the *Application layer*. This security measure modifies the required privileges to High. Finally, we assign different values to the metrics *Confidentiality*, *Integrity* and *Availability* according to the security objective of the vulnerability. For example, the vulnerability *Controller Function Alterability* impacts *Integrity* but does not affect *Availability* and *Confidentiality*.

Kandoi et al. [36] discusses a Denial-of-Service (DoS) attack on the *Control layer*. The attacker sends a large traffic to the *Data Plane layer*. The latter encapsulates the unknown traffic and forwards it to the *Control layer*. *Controller Function* processes the traffic, installs the corresponding rules on the *Data Plane layer* and sends the traffic back. One target of the attacker is to overload the *Control layer* by misusing *Network Element Resource*. In this case, *Data Processing Engine* floods *Controller Function* with large encapsulated packets, especially, if the size of the traffic and the sending rate exceed the absorption capacity of *Controller Function*. The latter becomes impotent to respond because its resources (memory, buffer, bandwidth and CPU) are busy, resulting in a DoS attack on *Controller Function*. The attack exploits at least the vulnerability *Controller Function Disruption*.

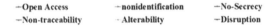

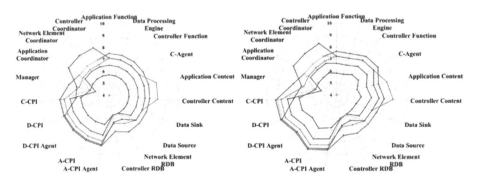

Fig. 2. SDN base scores spider.   **Fig. 3.** Enhanced SDN Base scores spider.

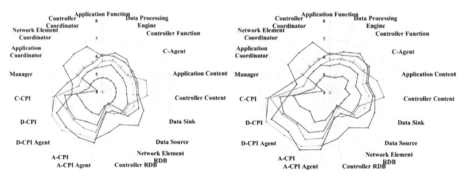

Fig. 4. SDN Temporal scores spider.   **Fig. 5.** Enhanced SDN Temporal scores spider.

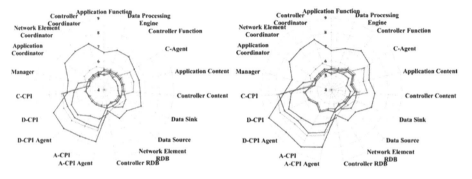

Fig. 6. SDN environment scores spider.   **Fig. 7.** Enhanced SDN environment scores spider.

Thus, we proceed according to the following logic to estimate the severity of *Controller Function Disruption*. In the base group, the Attack Vector of the vulnerability is *adjacent* because the flooding source is *Data Processing Engine*. The complexity of the attack is low because the attacker misuses the default behavior of *Network Element Resource* and he can repeat the attack. He does not need special privileges and user Interactions. Furthermore, this vulnerability impacts highly the availability of *Controller Function* and in some cases it can lead the target to alter the contents it receives and to interrupt the communications with other entities. As a result, the base group score of *Controller Function Disruption* is 7.1. There are a proof-of-Concept related to the exploit technic with a non-official solution and reasonable reports discussing this DoS Attack. Therefore, the vulnerability score in the temporal group is 6.3. In the environment group, the TLS deployment modifies the privileges to Low. Thus, *Network Element Resource* needs to open a secure channel before talking with the *Control layer*. The attacker cannot misuse a non TLS *Network Element Resource*. As a consequence the score in the environment group reduces to 6.9.

We compute the scores of the assessed SDN vulnerabilities in the base, temporal and environment groups. We display them respectively in Figs. 2, 4 and 6. We observe that the vulnerability surface is between 8.3 (High) and 5.2 (Medium) in the base group spider diagram (Fig. 2). The different interfaces and their agents (*A-CPI, A-CPI Agent, D-CPI, D-CPI Agent* and *C-CPI*) have the highest scores because they expose other assets in different layers and enlarge the attack scope. Furthermore, the vulnerabilities related to Open Access and Disruption are the most severe.

In the Temporal group (Fig. 4) the vulnerability surface becomes between 7.2 and 4.3. This decrease is due to the unavailability of mature malicious code and attacker techniques. As a result the exploitation of the vulnerabilities is more difficult and expensive, especially for the *Control layer*. Besides, the majority of the vulnerability exploits (excluding Disruption and Alterability in *Application Logic* and *Network Element Resource*) are not reported.

The vulnerability surface becomes between 8.0 and 5.0 in the environment score spider (Fig. 6). However, it is not Open Access vulnerabilities (such as in the base group) that have the most severe impact. The Disruption vulnerabilities of the interfaces become the most severe. The SDN specification recommends the deployment of TLS in the southbound and in the northbound interfaces. This deployment reduces the severities of Open Access vulnerabilities (and those of Non-Secrecy, Alterability. and Nonidentification).

We note also that the vulnerabilities of *C-CPI* diverges from the other interfaces vulnerabilities scores in the temporal and environment groups. The main reason is because *C-CPI's* security is unexplored and an untapped subject.

The results indicate a significant relation between SDN assets. In the Base group, the vulnerabilities scores of *Controller Function, C-Agent,* and *Controller Content* are equal to the vulnerabilities scores of *Application Function, Application Content, Data Processing Engine, Data Sink* and *Data Source* (there are minor disparities in the temporal and environment groups). The same equality relation is observed between the different interfaces in the *Control layer* and their respective agents in the *Application layer* and the *Data Plane layer*. For example another target of the aforementioned DoS attack is the Openflow tables (*Data Sink*). *Controller Function* answers with Flow rules and packet-out *Data Processing Engine*. However, because flow table size is limited, the tables can overflow. As a result, *Data Processing Engine*'s performance reduces and it rejects the new Openflow rules (including those for legitimate traffic). In this scenario, the DoS attack abuses the limited size of Openflow tables which corresponds to the vulnerability *Data Sink Disruption*. The scores of this vulnerability in the 3 groups (respectively 7.1, 6.3 and 6.9) equal the scores of *Controller Function Disruption*; however there is an issue with this equality. The DoS attack on *Controller Function* disturbs the entire network and enlarges the impacts to other layers. Other network elements (and Applications in the upper SDN layer) will experience large answer delays (and even communication interruptions) from the *Control layer*. At the same time the other attack on the *Data Plane layer* remains in its scope. Therefore, the severities of the *Control layer* vulnerabilities should be higher than the others.

The reasons of these observations are related to the functions and space of CVSS method. They focus only on the characteristics of conventional network systems. They do not take into account the specific features of SDN neither the importance of each SDN asset towards the others. Therefore we need to enhance the CVSS in order to take into account the characteristics of SDN and obtain more accurate scores reflecting SDN features.

6   Vulnerabilities Scores Enhancement

In addition to the conventional features that define the severity of vulnerabilities, SDN has its own specific characteristics that affect its vulnerabilities. These specific SDN characteristics increase the severities of its vulnerabilities because they expose the characteristics of its assets. Thus, the CVSS approach without taking into consideration this aspect is incomplete.

In order to enhance the CVSS values and adjust them according to SDN specific features, we integrate the latter in the quantification of the vulnerabilities scores. We use AHP to define the impact of each SDN feature on SDN assets. We measure the weight of each asset. Then, we integrate the weight of each asset into its vulnerability scores to quantify the new CVSS. We undertake the following steps:

1. We describe SDN specific criteria and construct the hierarchy tree according to AHP.
2. We calculate the weights of each SDN asset using the AHP tree and the weights of each criterion.
3. We enhance the CVSS scores by integrating the assets weights scores into the calculations of CVSS.

A. SDN hierarchy tree

The construction of the factors tree is the first step in the AHP process. The root of the tree corresponds to the objective of our analysis which is the evaluation of the impacts of SDN assets on security. The first level of the hierarchy represents the SDN features that affect SDN security. The last level of the tree refers to the SDN assets.

We define three SDN specific characteristics [37] that impact the severities of SDN vulnerabilities. Programmability is an SDN feature that allows configuring, managing, deploying automatically network operations, and adapting them dynamically to network changes. This criterion increases the vulnerabilities of the SDN assets because it gives attackers a way to automatize their threats, adapt them to the evolution of the network and spread them dynamically and widely to other assets. Another feature is Centralization. It defines the density of assets links and their reliance. A centralized asset is critical and its vulnerabilities affect other assets. The third feature is neutrality. SDN is neutral from any specific technology proprietary or from any constructor hardware. This feature enables an attacker to extend their exploits to all SDN organizations since they share a common technology.

B. SDN Assets weights

AHP uses pairwise comparisons to evaluate individual alternatives, to derive weights for the criteria and to construct their overall ratings [38]. We follow the following AHP steps:

a. We calculate the pairwise matrix A (3X3) for the first level criteria. The values of the matrix (see Table 4) represent the overall intensities of the impacts of the SDN features on security. These values fulfil a standardized AHP scaling [39] form 1 (same intensity) to 9 (extremely intense). The entries a_k^j and a_j^k satisfy the following constraint:

$$a_k^j * a_j^k = 1. \tag{1}$$

b. We normalize the matrix A (n, m) into the Matrix A' according to the equation:

$$a_k^{'j} = \frac{a_k^j}{\sum_{l=1}^m a_l^k}. \tag{2}$$

c. We compute the criteria weight vector W based on the Eigen vector method. The weights are derived according to the equation:

$$w_j = \frac{\sum_{l=1}^m a_j^{'l}}{m}. \tag{3}$$

d. We define the pairwise matrixes of the second level. Each matrix expresses the impacts intensities of each SDN criterion on the asset. In the Annex is an example of a pairwise Matrix for the Programmability Criteria.
e. We repeat steps 2 and 3 for each pairwise matrix and calculate the criteria weight vectors.
f. We construct the Matrix S where each column corresponds to a criteria weight vector (see in the Annex).
g. We compute the impact overall intensities in Vector V (see below) based on the equation:

$$v_k = \sum_{j=1}^{m} S_k^j * W_j \tag{4}$$

A =	Pairwise comparisons among SDN Features	Programmability	Centralization	Neutrality
	Programmability	1,00	0,75	1,25
	Centralization	1,33	1,00	2,25
	Neutrality	0,80	0,44	1,00

W =	Weights
	0,3129
	0,4604
	0,2267

Application Function	0,0198
Application Content	0,0197
Controller Function	0,0826
Controller Content	0,0765
C-Agent	0,1000
Controller RDB	0,0538
Data Processing Engine	0,0195
Data Source	0,0161
Data Sink	0,0240
Network Element RDB	0,0227
A-CPI Agent	0,0492
A-CPI	0,1174
C-CPI	0,1174
D-CPI	0,1174
D-CPI Agent	0,0492
Manager	0,0256
Application Coordinator	0,0220
Controller Coordinator	0,0453
Network Element Coordinator	0,0220

V = (the table above)

We see in vector V that *Control layer* components have the highest weights (0.1174 for the APIs and 0.0826 for *Controller Function*) because SDN architecture is based on the separation, the programmability, and the centralization of the *Control layer*. In contrast, *Application* and *Network Element Resource* have lower intensities (0.0198 for *Application Function* and 0.0161 for *Data Source*) because SDN does not affect their designs. It enables organizations to develop their own *Application* and *Network Element Resource* separately from the architecture. SDN requires the ability of these entities to interact with the interfaces agents; whereas, it offers to Applications a way to configure and program the network.

C. CVSS adaptation

We integrate the final weights to CVSS computation according to the following equation:

$$CVSS_i' = CVSS_i + (CVSS_i * v_i) \tag{5}$$

Because the scale of the new CVSS moves from the interval [0, 10] to [0, 10 + (10 * Max (v_i))], we adjust the new values according to the original interval by the following equation:

$$CVSS_i'' = CVSS' * 10/(10 + (10 * Max(v_i))) \tag{6}$$

The new results are displayed in Figs. 3, 5, and 7. In contrast to the previous results, we observe that the vulnerability surface increases in the 3 groups. It becomes in the base group between 9.2 and 5.3. We see also an important shift. All the *Control layer* vulnerabilities scores become the highest. The leading scores belong to *D-CPI*

(9.2, 7.6, and 8.8), *D-DPI* (9.2, 7.6, and 8.5), and *C-CPI* (9.2, 7.5, and 7.4), and in some extent to *Controller Function, C-Agent* and *Controller Content.* The CVSS scoring enhancement breaks the equality relation between the *Control layer* assets and the other assets in the *Data Plane layer* and *Application layer.* In the example of the DoS Attack we found that it abuses two vulnerabilities which are *Controller Function Disruption* and *Data Sink Disruption.* Both have equal scores in the 3 groups (7.1, 6.3 and 6.9) according to CVSS despite they belong to two different layers. The CVSS enhancement resolves this incoherence. It gives more weight to *Controller Function Disruption.* Hence, the new scores are 7.6, 6.8 and 7.4 for *Controller Function Disruption* and 7.3, 6.4 and 7.0 for *Data Sink Disruption.*

7 Conclusion

In this paper, we analyze the vulnerabilities of SDN. We propose a meta-model of SDN architecture and its instantiation. Then, we construct a list of generic SDN vulnerabilities by inversing security objectives for each SDN entity. We use CVSS to compute the severities of theses generic vulnerabilities. Besides, we integrate to these results the intensities of specific SDN features in order to adapt CVSS to SDN.

Our findings indicate that SDN has a lot of vulnerabilities with high and medium severities because of the weaknesses inherited from classical network architecture and due to its specific characteristics. Overall, vulnerabilities related to Open Access are the most severe in the base group, while the severities of disruption increase in the environment group. We show that CVSS is agnostic to SDN specific features. It assigns to different entities in different layers equal scores. We resolve this issue by integrating AHP to CVSS and adapting the latter to SDN specific features.

We will continue to address security issues of SDN by using these results in a risk assessment of SDN. The future study will highlight the threats that exploit these SDN vulnerabilities. Also, we envision the development of a tool that probes SDN weaknesses by using our vulnerabilities as a reference data base.

Annex

See Table 4.

Table 4. Second level weights Matrix (S Matrix).

Second level weights	Programmability	Centralization	Neutrality
Application function	0,027142086	0,016239548	0,0167123
Application content	0,026359221	0,016239548	0,0174059
Controller function	0,050904506	0,126487023	0,0373873
Controller content	0,04401356	0,120464331	0,0322212
C-Agent	0,083174392	0,120590266	0,0813329
Controller RDB	0,036267175	0,073223348	0,0383662
Data processing engine	0,026934327	0,014980384	0,0184423
Data source	0,018064438	0,014015702	0,0174084
Data sink	0,036091425	0,015690439	0,0241956
Network element RDB	0,026078155	0,018940867	0,0255563
A-CPI agent	0,080774805	0,019206794	0,0663608
A-CPI	0,12481917	0,09748963	0,1475272
C-CPI	0,12481917	0,09748963	0,1475272
D-CPI	0,12481917	0,09748963	0,1475272
D-CPI agent	0,080774805	0,019206794	0,0663608
Manager	0,016525796	0,03703465	0,0148234
Application coordinator	0,024145933	0,014828434	0,033615
Controller coordinator	0,024145933	0,065524546	0,033615
Network element coordinator	0,024145933	0,014828434	0,033615

References

1. Soo Hoo, K.J.: How Much Is Enough? A Risk Management Approach to Computer Security, Center for International Security and Cooperation, Palo Alto, CA (2000)
2. Ranjan, P., Pande, P., Oswal, R., Qurani, Z., Bedi, R.: A survey of past, present and future of software defined networking. Int. J. Adv. Res. Comput. Sci. Manage. Stud. **2**(4), 238–248 (2014)
3. Hu, F., Hao, Q., Bao, K.: A survey on software-defined network and OpenFlow: from concept to implementation. IEEE Commun. Surv. Tutorials **16**(4), 2181–2206 (2014)
4. Nunes, B.A.A., Mendonca, M., Nguyen, X.N., Obraczka, K., Turletti, T.: A survey of software-defined networking: past, present, and future of programmable networks. IEEE Commun. Surv. Tutorials **16**(3), 1617–1634 (2014)
5. Fanning, E.: Software-defined networks. COMPUTERWORLD, Framingham (2015)
6. Igure, V.M., Williams, R.D.: Taxonomies of attacks and vulnerabilities in computer systems. IEEE Commun. Surv. Tutorials **10**(1), 6–19 (2008)
7. Scarfone, K.: Common Vulnerability Scoring System (CVSS) Version 2. National Institute of Standards and Technology (NIST), USA (2007)
8. FIRST and C. SIG teams, Common Vulnerability Scoring System v3.0: Specification Document, Morrisville (2015)
9. Teknomo, K.: Analytic Hierarchy Process (AHP) Tutorial, Revoledu.com (2012)
10. Saaty, T.L.: Decision making with the analytic hierarchy process. Int. J. Serv. Sci. **1**(1), 83–98 (2008)

11. Wang, Z., Zeng, H.: Study on the risk assessment quantitative method of information security. In: 3rd International Conference on Advanced Computer Theory and Engineering (ICACTE), pp. 529–533 (2010)
12. Luo, S., Dong, M., Ota, K., Wu, J., Li, J.: A Security Assessment Mechanism for Software-Defined Networking-Based Mobile Networks, Sensors 2015, pp. 31843–31848, 9 November 2015
13. Open Networking Foundation, Principles and Practices for Securing Software-Defined Networks, ONF, Palo Alto (2015)
14. Wasserman, M., Hartman, S.: Security Analysis of the Open Networking Foundation (ONF) OpenFlow, Network Working Group (2013)
15. Kulkarni, V., Kawli, J.: Analysis of OpenFlow Networks (2013)
16. You, W., Qian, K., He, X., Qian, Y.: OpenFlow security threat detection and defense services. Int. J. Adv. Networking Appl. 6(3), 2347–2351 (2014)
17. Romão, D., Van Dijkhuizen, N., Konstantaras, S., Thessalonikefs, G.: Practical Security Analysis of Openflow. University of Amsterdam, Amsterdam (2013)
18. Open Networking Foundation, OpenFlow Switch Specification, ONF, Palo Alto (2014)
19. Kloti, R.: OpenFlow: A Security Analysis, Master dissertation, Zurich (2013)
20. Palanive, M., Selvadurai, K.: Risk-driven security testing using risk analysis with threat modeling approach. Springerplus 3(754), 1–14 (2014)
21. Benton, K., Camp, L.J., Small, C.: OpenFlow Vulnerability Assessment, SIGCOMM HOTSDN, pp. 151–152 (2013)
22. Kreutz, D., Ramos, F.M.V., Verissimo, P.: Towards secure and dependable software-defined networks, SIGCOMM HotSDN, pp. 55–60, (2013)
23. Coughlin, M.: A Survey of SDN Security Research. University of Colorado Boulder (2014)
24. Taha Ali, S., Sivaraman, V., Radford, A., Jha, S.: A survey of securing networks using software defined networking. IEEE Trans. Reliab. 64(3), 1086–1097 (2015)
25. Scott-Hayward, S., Natarajan, S., Sezer, S.: A survey of security in software defined networks. IEEE Commun. Surv. Tutorials 18(1), 623–654 (2016)
26. Open Networking Foundation, SDN architecture, ONF, Palo Alto (2014)
27. Jarraya, Y., Madi, T., Debbabi, M.: A survey and a layered taxonomy of software-defined networking. IEEE Commun. Surv. Tutorials 16(4), 1955–1980 (2014)
28. Rowshanrad, S., Namvarasl, S., Abdi, V., Hajizadeh, M., Keshtgary, M.: A survey on SDN, the future of networking. J. Adv. Comput. Sci. Technol. 3(2), 232–248 (2014)
29. openstack, Rackspace Cloud Computing. http://www.openstack.org/. Accessed 25 Sept 2016
30. RYU Community, Component-Based Software Defined Networking Framework (2014). http://osrg.github.io/ryu/. Accessed 25 Sept 2016
31. Production Quality, Multilayer Open Virtual Switch, Linux Foundation (2016). http://openvswitch.org/. Accessed 25 Sept 2016
32. Bazaz, B., Arthur, J.D.: Towards a taxonomy of vulnerabilities. In: Proceedings of the 40th Hawaii International Conference on System Sciences, pp. 163–174 (2007)
33. Standardization and Telecommunication Sector, Security architecture for systems providing end-to-end communications, International Communication Union, Geneva, Switzerland (2003)
34. FIRST Team, Common Vulnerability Scoring System Version 3.0 Calculator, FIRST.org (2016). https://www.first.org/cvss/calculator/3.0. Accessed 24 June 2016
35. Rescorla, E.: The Transport Layer Security (TLS) Protocol Version 1.3, Network Working Group (2015)

36. Kandoi, R., Antikainen, M.: Denial-of-service attacks in OpenFlow SDN networks. In: IFIP/IEEE International Symposium on Integrated Network Management (IM), pp. 1322–1326, 11–15 May 2015
37. Jain, R., Paul, S.: Network virtualization and software defined networking for cloud computing: a survey. IEEE Commun. Mag. Cloud Networking Commun. **51**(11), 24–31 (2013)
38. Antonio, J.: Alonso. Consistency in the analytic hierarchy process: a new approach, international journal of uncertainty, fuzziness and knowledge-based systems **14**(4), 445–459 (2006)
39. Alexander, M.: Decision-making using the analytic hierarchy process (AHP) and SAS/IML. In: 20th Annual South East SAS Users Group (SESUG) Conference, pp. 1–12 (2012)

Towards Metric-Driven, Application-Specific Visualization of Attack Graphs

Mickael Emirkanian-Bouchard and Lingyu Wang[✉]

Concordia Institute for Information Systems Engineering,
Concordia University, Montreal, Canada
wang@ciise.concordia.ca

Abstract. As a model of vulnerability information, attack graph has seen successes in many automated analyses for defending computer networks against potential intrusions. On the other hand, attack graph has long been criticized for the lack of scalability when serving as a visualization model for conveying vulnerability information to human analysts. In this paper, we propose two novel approaches to improving attack graph visualization. First, we employ recent advances in network security metrics to design metric-driven visualization techniques, which render the most critical information the most visible. Second, existing techniques usually aim at an one-size-fits-all solution, which actually renders them less effective for specific applications, and hence we propose to design application-specific visualization solutions for network overview and situational awareness. We discuss the models, algorithms, implementation, and simulation results.

1 Introduction

Computer networks have long become the nerve system of enterprise information systems and critical infrastructures. On the other hand, the scale and severity of security threats to computer networks have continued to grow at an ever-increasing pace. To defend computer networks against potential attacks, an important starting point is to understand the networks' weaknesses and flaws. To that end, a network security administrator or analyst should be capable of assessing the security posture of a network quickly and efficiently. However, the amount of vulnerability information in a network increases quickly in the network's size, mostly because vulnerabilities are seldom independent and attackers may combine them in sophisticated ways for attack propagation or privilege escalation. Therefore, conveying a large amount of vulnerability information to human analysts is a challenging issue for most networks.

Attack graph is an established model of vulnerability information in networks [1,22]. By encoding potential exploits of vulnerabilities and linking them through their common pre- and post-conditions, an attack graph provides a clear picture about how attackers may potentially break into a network and subsequently compromise network assets. Attack graphs have seen successes in many automated analyses for assessing, monitoring, and hardening computer networks.

© Springer International Publishing AG 2017
F. Cuppens et al. (Eds.): FPS 2016, LNCS 10128, pp. 117–134, 2017.
DOI: 10.1007/978-3-319-51966-1_8

On the other hand, attack graph has long been criticized for its poor scalability when serving as a visualization model for human analysts to comprehend, since even a small network may yield an attack graph that is too complex to understand [17].

The visualization of attack graphs has received limited attention (a more detailed review of related work will be given in Sect. 5). The scalability may be partially improved by abstracting and hiding low-level details [17], although the improvement is often limited since the method still relies on the same node-link representation of attack graphs. The clustered adjacency matrices [18] address the scalability issues but lead to a highly abstract model unsuitable for human interpretation. GARNET [24] and NAVIGATOR [6] employ tree-based structures to represent host configuration, but they both lack sufficient details about connectivity and exploit relationships.

In this paper, we propose two novel approaches to improving attack graph visualization. First, we employ recent advances in network security metrics to design *metric-driven visualization* techniques. Such techniques prioritize the visualization based on relative metric scores. This will allow the most critical information to be best highlighted or magnified in order to guide human analysts to explore the most pertinent threats. Second, we observe that most existing attack graph visualization techniques aim at an one-size-fits-all solution, which actually renders them less effective for specific applications; we then propose to design *application-specific visualization* solutions. In this paper, we focus on two such solutions, namely, the *radial attack treemaps* for network overview and the *topographic attack trees* for situational awareness. We discuss models, algorithms, implementation, and simulation results.

The rest of this paper is organized as follows. Section 2 reviews background information on attack graph, security metrics, and relevant visualization techniques. We will then introduce two novel attack graph visualization models for network overview and situational awareness in Sects. 3 and 4, respectively. Finally, Sect. 5 reviews related work and Sect. 6 concludes the paper.

2   Preliminaries

To be self-contained, this section reviews background information on attack graph, security metrics and visualization techniques.

2.1   Attack Graph and the Scalability Issue

Attack graph models vulnerabilities and their inter-dependency inside a network [1,22]. An attack graph can be represented as a directed graph, with exploits and conditions as vertices, and the causal relationships between exploits and conditions as edges.

The left-hand side of Fig. 1 shows our running example which will be used throughout the paper to illustrate different visualization methods. On the right-hand side of the figure is a toy network and on the left side the corresponding attack graph, in which each predicate *vulnerability(source host, destination host)* inside an oval indicates a self-explanatory exploit, and each plaintext *condition(host₁,host₂)* or *condition(host)* indicates a security-related condition. Edges point either from an exploit's pre-conditions to the exploit (e.g., a user privilege on host 1 is a pre-condition for exploits originated from host 1), or from the exploit to its post-conditions. Note the numbers inside the attack graph can be ignored for now, and they will be needed in later discussions. More formally,

Definition 1. *An attack graph G is a directed graph $G(E \cup C, R_r \cup R_i)$ where E is a set of exploits, C a set of conditions, $R_r \subseteq C \times E$ the require relation, and $R_i \subseteq E \times C$ the imply relation.*

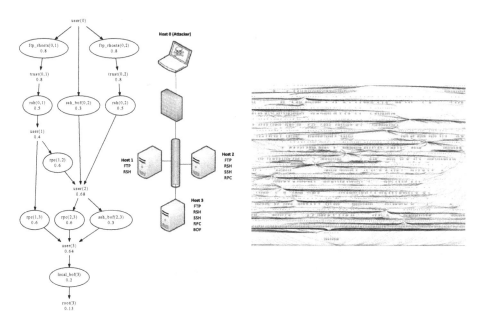

Fig. 1. The running example (Left) and attack graph of a 14-host network (Right)

The above basic representation of attack graphs is more suitable for automated analysis than for visualization-based human analysis. Enumerating all the exploits, their pre- and post-conditions, and edges between them in a single directed graph will inevitably lead to very high node and edge density, a significant amount of crossings between edges, highly complex edge paths, and a high average edge length. These characteristics render the attack graph messy and difficult to comprehend, and prevent human analysts from interpreting the attack graph and cross validating with results of automated analysis. As an example, the right-hand side of Fig. 1 shows a messy and illegible attack graph. It may be surprising to note that this attack graph actually represents a small network composed of only 14 machines, each of which has less than 10 vulnerabilities. Clearly, the basic representation of attack graphs is not a viable visualization solution.

2.2 Security Metrics

Scoring and ranking vulnerabilities and networks based on their relative severity and security has drawn significant attentions. Among existing efforts, the
Common Vulnerability Scoring System (CVSS) is a widely recognized standard
for security vendors and analysts to assign numerical scores to vulnerabilities to
reflect their relative severity [21]. The approach in [8] first assigns a normalized
CVSS score as the conditional probability of successfully executing each exploit
of the vulnerability given satisfied pre-conditions. The assigned probabilities are
then used to build a Bayesian network based on causal relationships between
exploits and used to find the probability that critical assets are compromised,
which provides a security metric for the whole network. For example, in Fig. 1,
a number inside an oval is the aforementioned conditional probability and under
each condition is the probability of satisfying that condition.

In this paper, we extend the above Bayesian network-based security metric
by introducing the notion of *asset value* to attack graphs, which is a numerical
value between 0 and 10 (corresponding to the domain of CVSS scores) assigned
by administrators to each condition in the attack graph based on the condition's
relative significance with regards to confidentiality, integrity, and availability.
From this assigned asset value, we calculate the *risk* at multiple hierarchical
levels for conditions, hosts, groups of hosts (subnets), and networks. Here we
adopt the common approach of defining risk as the product of the asset value
and attack likelihood (that is, the probability obtained using the aforementioned
Bayesian network approach). More specifically,

Definition 2. *Given the probability of executing each exploit $P(e)$ and that of
satisfying a condition $P(c)$ inside an attack graph $G(E \cup C, R_r \cup R_i)$, and an
asset value assignment function $AV(.) : C \to [0, 10]$, we define*

- *the risk of a condition c as $R_c(c) = \frac{P(c)*AV(h)}{10}$.*
- *the risk of a host h as $R_h(h) = R_c(< root, h >)$.*
- *the risk of a group of hosts (or the whole network) G as $R_g(G) = \sum_{h \in G} R_h(h)$.*

2.3 Applying Existing Visualization Models

We apply several existing visualization models to attack graph to demonstrate
their limitations and motivate further discussions.

Balloon Attack Graph. Due to the hierarchical nature of most networks, an
obvious approach for improving the scalability of attack graphs is to grouping
or clustering certain nodes which share similar characteristics (e.g., residing on
the same or adjacent hosts [17]). However, such an approach will meet difficulty
to maintain readability without losing valuable information due to the relatively
high edge density and crossings in a usually highly-connected attack graph.

In Fig. 2, we apply to our running example a clustering method with multiple cluster centers in order to form clusters of nodes without a pre-defined top-down path or a particular directional layout, based on the clustering method proposed by Melancon et al. [16] which aims to achieve a balanced layout, namely, a *balloon attack graph*.

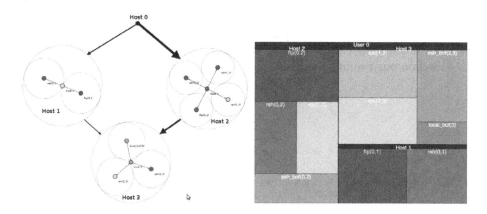

Fig. 2. Balloon attack graph and attack treemap

From the example, it is clear that this visualization model can improve the density of nodes as well as the readability to some extent, through clustering exploits associated to the same host. However, it is equally clear that the edges cannot be fully displayed (without breaking the balloons), leading to a significant loss of information; the improvement of scalability is also quite limited.

Attack Treemap. An issue with conventional node-edge attack graph is the difficulty of expressing the hierarchical relationships between exploits, hosts, and networks. The above balloon attack graph addresses this through clustering nodes into balloons, but it also wastes much visualization space to explicitly depict the hierarchical relationships.

To that end, treemaps allow for implicit representation of hierarchical information inside a rectangular display, where the entirety of the visualization space is put to use [11]. Figure 2 shows an *attack Treemap* using our running example, built with the JavaScript InfoVis Toolkit [3] using the binary tiling algorithm [23]. In the attack treemap, each rectangle with a black bar at the top represents a host, inside which each colored rectangle represents an exploit. The color denotes the CVSS score, and the relative size of rectangles denotes the risk value as calculated before.

Clearly, treemap is a dense and relatively scalable visualization model. In addition, GARNET [24] has shown how to add reachability results to treemaps by interactively displaying them through semantic substrates. However, most of the connectivity information and edges in attack graphs are still missing here, and adding them as overlying edges will clearly lead to a messy result. We will address this issue in Sect. 3.

Hyperbolic Attack Tree. As attack graphs get larger, screen size becomes a concern, and forcing an analyst to zoom or pan on sections of an attack graph will likely lead to a loss of context or awareness of the overall network. To this end, the hyperbolic geometry offers opportunities for creating a fisheye-lens effect, with the center of the graph (the focus) occupying the most space and the remainder of the graph condensed and pushed outwards, which helps to maintain the context and awareness of the whole graph [2]. Figure 3 shows a *hyperbolic attack tree* based on our running example.

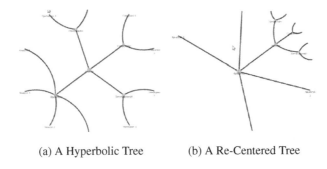

(a) A Hyperbolic Tree   (b) A Re-Centered Tree

Fig. 3. Hyperbolic attack tree

The constant contextual awareness makes hyperbolic attack trees an appealing choice for applications like situational awareness. We will revisit this approach in Sect. 4.

3   Radial Attack Treemaps

This section introduces a scalable, metric-driven visualization model, the *radial attack treemap*, for the purpose of obtaining a quick overview of a network's vulnerability information. We first give an overview, followed by the description of models and algorithms, and finally we present simulation results.

3.1   Overview

Enabling a security analyst to acquire a quick overview of the entire network's vulnerability information is a key tactical advantage in assessing networks' security. The goal here is to encode as much legible details as possible inside a given size canvas. Section 2.3 mentioned treemaps as a visualization model that provides relatively high information density and scalability by occupying the entirety of the canvas. On the other hand, the main shortcoming of treemaps lies in the difficulty of displaying edges between exploits.

Intuitively speaking, our main idea here is to *bend the treemap into a ring, and display edges inside that ring.* As to the actual display of edges, we turn to radial graphs, which allows a fixed-size layout with high information density, element proximity, and edge management [14]. Unlike conventional graphs in which an edge may be obstructed by a node, in a radial graph, a line between two points on a circle is an unobstructed line. Moreover, the edges in a radial graph can be hierarchically bundled with crossings between edges minimized.

By combining key concepts of treemaps and radial graphs, we propose a metric-driven and treemap-based radial visualization, namely, the *radial attack treemap.* We summarize the key features and advantages of this novel visualization model in the following, while leaving details of the model and implementation to later sub-sections:

- The model provides a quick overview of exploits, chains of exploits (that is, paths in an attack graph), hosts, and causal relationships between exploits in a network.
- The color and size of each slice of the outside ring represents the CVSS score and risk of the corresponding exploit, respectively.
- The stacking of slices and sub-slices in the outside ring implicitly represent hierarchical relationships between exploits, exploit chains, and hosts, reducing the number of edges that need to be explicitly displayed (in contrast to the original attack graph).
- The center of the ring displays edges in a bundled way to minimize the number of crossings between edges, leading to a cleaner visualization result.
- Layout of the bent treemaps is optimized such that the lower level details are displayed more towards the outer side of the ring in order to occupy more space.

Figure 4 illustrates an example of radial attack treemap, which is based on our running example shown in Fig. 1.

3.2   Models and Algorithms

Definition 3 more precisely describes the radial attack treemap.

Definition 3 (Radial Attack Treemap). *Given an attack graph $G(E \cup C, R_r \cup R_i)$ with hosts H and the risk function R_c, R_h, and R_g, a radial attack treemap is composed of a ring R and a collection of links L, where*

- *R is divided into a collection of slices S, with each slice $s \in S$ corresponding to a host $h \in H$.*
- *each slice s is divided into a collection of subslices SS, with each subslice $ss \in SS$ corresponding to an exploit chain (a sequence of exploits involving the destination host h, the same source host, and leading to $< root, h >$.*
- *each subslice ss is further divided into a collection of subsubslices SSS, in which each subsubslice $sss \in SSS$ corresponds to an exploit e in the exploit chain.*

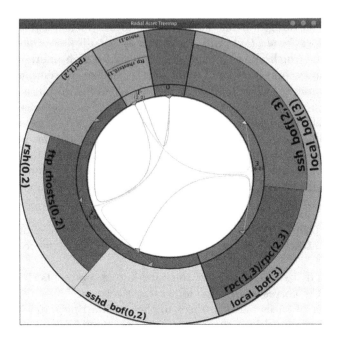

Fig. 4. Radial attack treemap

- *the relative size of each slice, subslice, and subsubslice is proportional to the risk score (Definition 2) of corresponding host, exploit chain, and exploit, respectively (details will be provided later).*
- *the color of each subsubslice represents the CVSS score of the corresponding exploit (details will be provided later).*
- *each link in L points from a slice corresponding to host h, to a subslice corresponding to an exploit chain involving the source host h.*
- *all the links in L are bundled and routed through the center of the ring R.*

Data Structures. We now describe the data structures required for implementing the proposed visualization model. Specifically, to implement the model, we need to compute the aforementioned risk metrics and convert a given attack graph into a suitable data structure. We then derive geometric information necessary to the final rendering of the model. Therefore, for each element in the model, there will be a corresponding view element containing additional information necessary to the visualization, as detailed below.

- *Exploit & Subsubslice:* Each exploit is a list of five attributes, an identifier, a set of pre-conditions and post-conditions, a CVSS score, and a risk value. Correspondingly, a subsubslice, as the view representation of the exploit, is a list of attributes including a label, a color derived from a normalized CVSS score, as well as a size proportional to the risk value of exploit chain.

- *Exploit Chain & Subslice:* Each exploit chain is a list of attributes including an identifier, a risk value, as well as the source host involved. Correspondingly, a subslice is a list of attributes including references to the composing subsubslices, a label, a size derived from the risk value, an anchor point which is a set of coordinates used as destination points for incoming links, and a color derived from the CVSS scores of the corresponding exploits.
- *Host & Slice:* A host is a list of attributes including the references to the composing exploit chains, an identifier, and a risk value. Correspondingly, a slice is a list of attributes including the host name, references to the composing subslices, a label, a color derived from the CVSS scores, a size derived from the risk value of the host, and two anchor points, with the first being a set of coordinates used as intermediate destination points for incoming links and the second being a set of coordinates used as the source points for outgoing links from this host.
- *Link:* A link is a pair $< h, ec >$ indicating the source host h involved by exploits in the exploit chain ec. Correspondingly, the link is visualized using the Bézier spline composed of two curves, a cubic Bézier curve and a quadratic Bézier curve [20]. The former contains three sets of coordinates, namely, a start point, an end point and a control point, while the latter has four, namely, a start point, an end point and two control points.

Algorithms. This subsection discusses two series of algorithms. The first converts a given attack graph to the data structures mentioned in the previous sub-section. The second is for computing geometric information used in creating the view structures.

First, in the following, Algorithm 1 uses a recursive depth-first search in the input attack graph to obtain all paths from user-access conditions to the root condition of the target host (Algorithm 2). For each path obtained, we verify that all exploit sequences leading to this condition have all their pre-conditions satisfied and that the path generated is valid (detailed algorithm is omitted due to space limitations).

Second, we discuss how the view data structures may be generated (detailed algorithms are omitted due to space limitations). The ring is generated by converting exploits, exploit chains and hosts into subsubslices, subslices and slices, respectively. Host and exploit chain risk scores are expressed by the angle of ring

---

Algorithm 1. GETALLEXPLOITCHAINS

Input: An attack graph, a set of host-access conditions *Host*
Output: A set of Hosts possessing exploit chains and exploits
1 **foreach** *Host to* $\in$ *Hosts* **do**
2   **foreach** *Host from* $\in$ *Hosts* **do**
3          $paths_{from->to}[\ ][\ ] \leftarrow getAllPaths(from, to)$;
4   **foreach** *path* $p \in paths_{from->to}$ **do**
5   **if** $isValid(true, path, from, initialconditions)$ **then**
6                  $to.addExploitChain(path)$;

Algorithm 2. GETALLPATHS

Input: A Linked List of visited nodes *visited*, the end condition *end*
1 $Node\ n = visited.last();$
2 $Node[]\ nodes = n.getNexts();$
3 **foreach** $Node\ n \in Nodes$ **do**
4   **if** $visited.contains(node)$ **then**
5    $\lfloor\ continue;$
6   $visited.add(n);$
7   $Node[]\ path \leftarrow visited;$
8   $allPaths.add(path);$
9   $visited.removeLast();$
10 **foreach** $Node\ n \in Nodes$ **do**
11   **if** $visited.contains(n)\ ||\ n = end$ **then**
12    $\lfloor\ continue;$
13   $visited.addLast(n);$
14   $getPath(visited, end);$
15   $visited.removeLast();$

---

segments they occupy. $Host_0$, representing the initial attacker-controlled host, possesses a fixed angle, α_0. The slices representing a given host x will have an angle α_x of value:

$$\alpha_x = (360 - \alpha_0) * \frac{score_x}{\sum_{i=1}^{n} score_i} \tag{1}$$

Similarly, the angle α_y of an exploit chain $ec \in h_x$, relative to risk of the other exploit chains of the host – will have a value of:

$$\alpha_y = \alpha_x * \frac{score_{ec}}{\sum_{ec \in h} score_{ec}} \tag{2}$$

For an exploit $e \in ec$, the angle of ring segment it occupies is the same as that by its exploit chain parent, and occupied area thus depends on the length of the radius segment between the current exploit and the next exploit (or the ring's two edges), depending on the risk scores of these exploits' post-conditions. The color of subsubslice is derived from the normalized CVSS scores of the vulnerabilities using a *color ramping algorithm* similar to the one described by Bourke in [4].

The links displayed at the center are Bézier splines [20] computed using the method by Holten in [9]. The spline is composed of two Bézier curves, the *origin curve*, a cubic Bézier curve with two control points starting at the origin host's anchor point denoted by point 0 and ending on the destination host's projection on the host circle, and the *destination curve*, a quadratic Bézier curve starting at the end of the origin curve and ending at the exploit chain anchor point. Finally, the link color is derived from the score of the first exploit in the exploit chain of the destination, using a color ramping algorithm.

3.3 Implementation and Simulation

A prototype was built using Java and the Graphics2D and Curve2D libraries, included in the JavaSE package. It is built using the Model-View Controller [12] (MVC) pattern. A GraphViz [7] .dot file parser reads an input attack graph and loads it into memory. The graph is then traversed to generate exploits, exploit chains, and hosts, using Algorithms 1 and 2. This model is then converted into slices, subslices, subsubslices, and links, in order to generate the ring and links.

We now study the density and scalability of the visualization model through simulation using randomly generated attack graphs (we note that although an experiment using real world data is certainly more desirable, to the best of our knowledge, a publicly available dataset containing a significant number of attack graphs is not currently available). We generate 1200 attack graphs using Python programs from small seed graphs based on real world attack graphs. The simulation environment is a dual-core Intel Core i5 processor with 8 GB of RAM running Debian 7. The entire application was written in Java and runs on OpenJDK 6.

We compare the scalability of radial attack treemaps with that of the input attack graphs. As a radial asset treemap is designed as a fixed-size visualization, we set a threshold value for the smallest allowable subsubslice, at $1000px^2$ (leaving approximately 10 characters at 8pt. font size), and we ensure all subsubslices in a radial attack treemap to be legible by scaling them according to this threshold. Figure 5 shows the average canvas size of both models in relation to the number of hosts.

The simulation clearly confirms that radial attack treemaps offer a higher information density than conventional attack graphs. Figure 5 shows that, on average, 10 hosts can be represented on a canvas of merely 900×900 pixels, while the corresponding attack graphs would require a canvas of over 2800×2800 pixels.

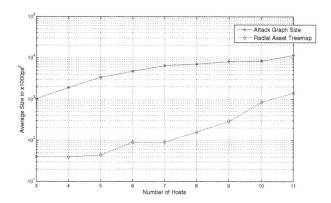

Fig. 5. The Comparison of average sizes

Next, we study the degree of reduction in the number of edges/links by implicitly representing edges in the radial attack treemaps (through stacking subsubslices). We note that, in addition to this reduction in the number of edges/links, the radial attack tree maps have other advantages in terms of displaying links, as mentioned already in the previous subsection. Figure 6 compares the number of edges/links in relation to the number of hosts in the graph.

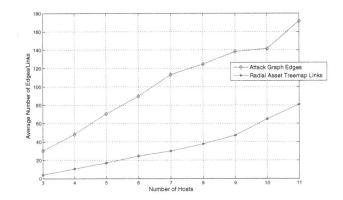

Fig. 6. Average number of Edges/Links

This simulation indicates that the amount of edges/links has been reduced to approximately a third those of conventional attack graphs. The implicit relationships between host, exploit chains and exploits allow for such a significant edge reduction.

We note that, Fig. 5 seems to indicate that the rate of growth of radial asset treemap is greater than that of conventional attack graphs. This is a consequence of the ring's tiling algorithm: regardless of the size of the canvas, an exploit chain's partition angle will remain the same. When compared to a two-dimensional graph canvas, both size increases are quadratic but with the partition size depending on the angle of its parent exploit chain, leading to a lower rate of growth of partition surface compared to the available surface of a rectangular canvas.

3.4   Discussions

The proposed metric-driven radial attack treemap provides a viable visualization solution for human analysts to quickly grasp an overview of the vulnerability information in a network. Nonetheless, the model in its current form still has a few limitations. First, due to the limited level of hierarchy in the treemaps, it will be difficult to visualize a large network in a single view. Developing a new tiling algorithm to support more levels of hierarchy or using interactivity to vary the hierarchy levels of slices or filtering out certain nodes are both viable solutions. How well those solutions would scale to larger networks with hundreds of hosts will need to be confirmed through experiments. Second, the trade-off between the areas occupied by the ring and by links requires developing algorithms to optimize such a trade-off for clarify on both sides.

4   Topographic Hyperbolic Trees

This section introduces the novel *topographic hyperbolic tree* model for monitoring and predicting real time progress of attacks.

4.1   Overview

One important aspect of visualization in the application of cyber-situational awareness is to allow administrators to see both the current focus of an ongoing attack and most likely next steps. Another important aspect is to provide a sense of *distance* between potential attack steps based on the number of intermediate steps or relative difficulty of such steps [24,25]. In Sect. 2.3, we have shown that the hyperbolic tree model is a suitable model for the first purpose. As to express the attack distance, we are inspired by geographical topographic maps, in which contour lines are used to indicate fixed increases in altitude. Therefore, the main idea here is to *enhance the hyperbolic attack tree model with contour lines representing attack steps at similar distance*. Again, we summarize the key features and advantages of this novel visualization model in the following, while leaving details of the model and implementation to later sub-sections:

- It provides an interactive visualization of ongoing attacks and plausible next steps.
- The hyperbolic tree creates a fisheye-lens effect that allows administrators to focus on the current attack and its closest future steps, while not losing context or awareness of other steps that may be further away but are still possible, such as the ultimate goal of the attack.
- The contour lines provide a rough idea about future attack steps that are at similar distance from the current step.
- In addition, the relative length of different edges represent (after taking into account the fisheye-lens effect) the relative difficulty of the corresponding exploit.

Figure 7 shows the topographic hyperbolic tree for our running example.

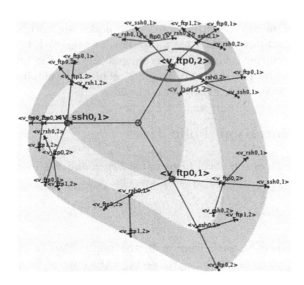

Fig. 7. Topographic hyperbolic tree

4.2   Model and Algorithms

Definition 4 formally describes the topographic hyperbolic tree.

Definition 4. *Given an attack graph $G(E \cup C, R_r \cup R_i)$ with hosts H and the risk function R_c, R_h, and R_g, a topographic hyperbolic tree is composed of a hyperbolic attack tree $T(E, C)$, which has the exploits E as nodes and conditions C as edges, and a collection of contour lines L linking all the exploits sharing the same depth in the tree. The relative length of an edge is based on the risk metric score of the corresponding condition as well as the depth of the node (more details will be provided later).*

The construction of a topographic hyperbolic tree from an input attack graph involves a few steps. We first load the attack graph into memory. Then, for each time the graph is recentered, we apply the tree generation algorithms. We then layout the tree on the canvas and generate the contour lines. More specifically (detailed algorithms are omitted due to space limitations),

1. We start by establishing the context required to initiate the graph traversal using (Algorithm 3), and then recursively perform the graph traversal and tree construction using Algorithm 4, while limiting the maximal depth of any tree branch to be a pre-defined parameter MAX_DEPTH in order to avoid the explosion of possible paths.
2. We then layout nodes on the canvas. We compute the coordinates of every node by calculating the length of a link as well as the angle at the origin. The length of an edge is a function of the risk of the pre-conditions of the exploit represented, as well as the number of steps from the center: $distance_{child} = \frac{score_{child}}{c} * (MAX\_DEPTH - step_{child} + 1)$. The angle of a node's children

will depend on the angle of the parent as well as the number of children this parent possesses: $\alpha_c = \frac{180 - c*step}{nbChildren}$.

3. Finally, we generate and draw the contour lines. Three main steps are required for the drawing. First, after obtaining all points at a given level i, we ensure that the polygon formed by these points completely includes the polygon formed by the points at a previous level $i - 1$. Otherwise, we add the points of polygon $i - 1$ lying outside of polygon i to the polygon i. Second, we ensure that each polygon is convex. If the polygon is concave, we apply a convex-hull algorithm commonly called the Gift-Wrapping Algorithm [10]. Finally, we smooth the lines by interpolating the points using the Catmull-Rom Algorithm [5].

Algorithm 3. THE TRAVERSAL INITIATION FUNCTION

Input: A tree $tree$, an attack graph $graph$, a list of conditions $attackerKnowledge$
Output: A tree $tree$ representing all possible attacker paths from given initial conditions

1 $Node[\ ]\ firstNextSteps \leftarrow getNextSteps(initialConditions)$;
2 **for** $Node\ n \in firstNextSteps$ **do**
3 $\quad$ $knowledge.add(n)$;
4 $\quad$ $knowledge.add(n.getNexts())$;
5 $\quad$ $traverse(tree, n, knowledge, 1)$;
6 **return** $tree$;

Algorithm 4. THE TREE GENERATING ALGORITHM

Input: A tree node $previous$, an attack graph node $graphnode$, a list of conditions
$\quad$ $attackerKnowledge$ a depth $depth$
Output: The fully expanded tree representing all possible attacker paths

1 $Node\ current = graphNode$;
2 **if** $previous = FINAL\_CONDITION\ \&\&\ depth \leq MAX\_DEPTH$ **then**
3 $\quad$ $previous.addNext(current)$;
4 $\quad$ $current.addPrevious(previous)$;
5 $\quad$ $Node[]\ nextSteps = getNextSteps(attackerKnowledge)$;
6 $\quad$ **for** $Node\ n \in nextSteps$ **do**
7 $\quad\quad$ **if** $(!\ attackerKnowledge.contains(n.getNexts()))$ **then**
8 $\quad\quad\quad$ $attackerKnowledge.add(n.getNext())$;
9 $\quad\quad\quad$ $attackerKnowledge.add(n)$;
10 $\quad\quad\quad$ **return** $traverse(current, n, attackerKnowledge, depth + 1)$

We have implemented a prototype using Java and the Graphics2D library. Our simulation (detailed results omitted due to space limitations) shows that both the visualization result and the running time are easily manageable with the maximal depth set to about six, whereas unsurprisingly there is a sharp increase in both thereafter. Given the interactive nature of this visualization model, we believe the model is still useful for many practical applications. On the other hand, further study is needed to improve the tree expansion algorithms in order to avoid the exponential explosion, and to find more efficient ways for incrementally updating the model after each centering operation.

5   Related Work

Sheyner *et al.* firstly employ a model checker to generate all possible attack paths for a network, namely, an attack graph [22]. Since such a model-checking technique suffers from scalability issues, the *monotonicity assumption* stating that an attacker never relinquishes a gained privilege, is employed to achieve a polynomial complexity [1], which is further improved by Ou *et al.* in developing the MulVAL tool [19]. Related efforts on security metrics include the Common Vulnerability Scoring System (CVSS) which is a widely recognized standard for scoring and ranking vulnerabilities [21]. Frigault *et al.* [8] convert attack graphs into Bayesian networks to analyze vulnerability metrics using a probabilistic model. As to related efforts on visualization, Treemaps are introduced as a graphical representation of a weighted tree by recursively partitioning rectangles depending on the weight assigned to the node [11]. The shape of the partitions is dictated by *tiling algorithms*, as reviewed in [23]. Hyperbolic trees (or hypertrees) are introduced by Lamping *et al.* [13] as a *focus+context* technique to create a fisheye effect for viewing and manipulating large hierarchies. There has recently been much focus on radial visualization models across different scientific fields, such as VisAware [15], a radial visualization system representing situational awareness in a generalized way, which is further adapted for intrusion detection in VisAlert [14]. Attack graph visualization presents additional challenges due to their specific requirements. Noel *et al.* [17] present a framework for hierarchically aggregating nodes in an attack graph. Noel et al. [18] also make use of clustered adjacency matrices to compute the reachability and distance similar to a heatmap. GARNET [24] is an Attack Graph visualization tool which outputs treemaps with semantic substrates to visualize a network and its reachability. GARNET later evolves into the NAVIGATOR (Network Asset VIsualization: Graphs, ATtacks, Operational Recommendations) [6], with improvements like the possibility of zooming-in to the host level and displaying port numbers and possible exploits on these ports.

6   Conclusion and Future Work

We have proposed two novel approaches to attack graph visualization, namely, metric-driven visualization and application-specific visualization. Specifically, we proposed a new visualization model by combining treemaps with radial graph for the use case of network overview. Second, we enhanced hyperbolic attack trees with contour lines borrowed from topological maps for the purpose of situational awareness. In addition to future work already mentioned in Sects. 3 and 4, we will also pursue metric-driven visualization models for other applications of attack graphs.

Acknowledgements. The authors thank the anonymous reviewers for their valuable comments. This work is partially supported by Natural Science and Engineering Research Council of Canada under Grant N01035.

References

1. Ammann, P., Wijesekera, D., Kaushik, S.: Scalable, graph-based network vulnerability analysis. In: Proceedings of the 9th ACM Conference on Computer and Communications Security, pp. 217–224. ACM (2002)
2. Anderson, J.W.: Hyperbolic Geometry. Springer, New York (2007)
3. Belmonte, N.G.: The JavaScript InfoVis toolkit. http://www.thejit.org. Accessed 2 Mar 2013
4. Bourke, P.: Colour ramping for data visualization. http://local.wasp.uwa.edu.au/pbourke/texture_colour/colourramp/. Accessed 18 Nov 2012
5. Catmull, E., Rom, R.: A class of local interpolating splines. Comput. Aided Geom. Des. **74**, 317–326 (1974)
6. Chu, M., Ingols, K., Lippmann, R., Webster, S., Boyer, S.: Visualizing attack graphs, reachability, and trust relationships with navigator. In: Proceedings of the Seventh International Symposium on Visualization for Cyber Security, pp. 22–33. ACM (2010)
7. Ellson, J., Gansner, E., Koutsofios, L., North, S.C., Woodhull, G.: Graphviz— open source graph drawing tools. In: Mutzel, P., Jünger, M., Leipert, S. (eds.) GD 2001. LNCS, vol. 2265, pp. 483–484. Springer, Heidelberg (2002). doi:10.1007/3-540-45848-4_57
8. Frigault, M., Wang, L., Singhal, A., Jajodia, S.: Measuring network security using dynamic Bayesian network. In: Proceedings of the 4th ACM workshop on Quality of protection, QoP 2008, pp. 23–30. ACM, New York (2008)
9. Holten, D.: Hierarchical edge bundles: visualization of adjacency relations in hierarchical data. IEEE Trans. Visual. Comput. Graph. **12**, 741–748 (2006)
10. Jarvis, R.A.: On the identification of the convex hull of a finite set of points in the plane. Inf. Process. Lett. **2**(1), 18–21 (1973)
11. Johnson, B., Shneiderman, B.: Tree-maps: a space-filling approach to the visualization of hierarchical information structures. In: Proceedings of the IEEE Conference on Visualization 1991, pp. 284–291, October 1991
12. Krasner, G.E., Pope, S.T., et al.: A description of the model-view-controller user interface paradigm in the smalltalk-80 system. J. Object Oriented Program. **1**(3), 26–49 (1988)
13. Lamping, J., Rao, R., Pirolli, P.: A focus+context technique based on hyperbolic geometry for visualizing large hierarchies. In: Proceedings of the SIGCHI conference on Human Factors in Computing Systems, CHI 1995, pp. 401–408. ACM Press/Addison-Wesley Publishing Co., New York (1995)
14. Livnat, Y., Agutter, J., Moon, S., Erbacher, R.F., Foresti, S.: A visualization paradigm for network intrusion detection, pp. 92–99 (2005)
15. Livnat, Y., Agutter, J., Moon, S., Foresti, S.: Visual correlation for situational awareness. In: IEEE Symposium on Information Visualization, INFOVIS 2005, pp. 95–102. IEEE (2005)
16. Melancon, G., Herman, I.: Circular drawings of rooted trees. In: Reports of the Centre for Mathematics and Computer Sciences (1998)
17. Noel, S., Jajodia, S.: Managing attack graph complexity through visual hierarchical aggregation. In: Proceedings of the 2004 ACM Workshop on Visualization and Data Mining for Computer Security, pp. 109–118. ACM (2004)
18. Noel, S., Jajodia, S.: Understanding complex network attack graphs through clustered adjacency matrices. In: ACSAC, pp. 160–169 (2005)

19. Xinming, O., Govindavajhala, S., Appel, A.W.: MulVal: a logic-based network security analyzer. In: 14th USENIX Security Symposium, pp. 1–16 (2005)
20. Prautzsch, H., Boehm, W., Paluszny, M.: Bézier and B-Spline Techniques. Springer, New York (2002)
21. Schiffman, M.: The common vulnerability scoring system (CVSS), November 2005
22. Sheyner, O., Haines, J., Jha, S., Lippmann, R., Wing, J.M.: Automated generation and analysis of attack graphs. In: 2002 Proceedings of the IEEE Symposium on Security and Privacy, pp. 273–284. IEEE (2002)
23. Shneiderman, B., Wattenberg, M.: Ordered treemap layouts. In: 2001 IEEE Symposium on Information Visualization, INFOVIS 2001, pp. 73–78 (2001)
24. Williams, L., Lippmann, R., Ingols, K.: GARNET: a graphical attack graph and reachability network evaluation tool. In: Visualization for Computer Security, pp. 44–59 (2008)
25. Williams, L., Lippmann, R., Ingols, K.: An interactive attack graph cascade and reachability display. In: VizSEC 2007, pp. 221–236 (2008)

Insider Threat Likelihood Assessment for Access Control Systems: Quantitative Approach

Sofiene Boulares[✉], Kamel Adi, and Luigi Logrippo

Département d'informatique et d'ingénierie,
Université du Québec en Outaouais, Gatineau, QC, Canada
{bous42,kamel.adi,luigi.logrippo}@uqo.ca

Abstract. Organizations need to use flexible access control mechanisms where the access decisions to critical information assets are taken dynamically. In this paper, we present a framework for insider threat likelihood assessment within the context of access control systems. Our approach takes into account information flows, the trustworthiness of subjects, the sensitivity of objects and the security countermeasures. We identify and formally describe a set of properties to be satisfied within this approach. These properties are, then used for quantitatively assessing the insider threat likelihood.

Keywords: Information Security · Access control · Information flow · Insider threat · Threat likelihood assessment · Risk assessment

1 Introduction

Risk-based access control provides support for flexible access control decisions and facilitates information sharing. Consider a situation where a workflow architect asks an IT security specialist to determine which combinations of operations are less risky for the tasks composing a workflow, given the subjects, objects and actions involved in each operation. The decisions could be based on the evaluation of access risks, by selecting the combinations giving the lowest risk values.

An access control system that can give employees risky accesses can cause insider security incidents. According to the US firm Forrester Research, insider incidents within organizations represent 46% of security breaches [11]. In addition, the survey Global Corporate IT Security Risks 2013 [6], conducted by Kaspersky Lab, shows that 85% of companies worldwide have experienced an insider computer security incident.

Bishop et al. [3] distinguish two categories of insider threats:

1. violation of access control policy by using authorized access,
2. violation of security policy by obtaining unauthorized access.

Our approach for threat likelihood estimation of access requests deals with the first category of insider threats which includes cases where an employee uses his legitimate access to perform an action that violates the access control policy:

© Springer International Publishing AG 2017
F. Cuppens et al. (Eds.): FPS 2016, LNCS 10128, pp. 135–142, 2017.
DOI: 10.1007/978-3-319-51966-1_9

discloses sensitive data to a third party, releases information to untrusted environments, etc. Our method can be seen as an approach to estimate the threat likelihood of the violation of an access control policy, caused by the authorization of other access requests.

The rest of the paper is organized as follows. Section 2 presents an overview of our work and the contribution of this paper. In Sect. 3, we present our threat assessment approach. In Sect. 4, we compare our work with notable work of the literature and we present the limitations of our approach. Finally, we draw conclusions for this paper and outline opportunities for future work in Sect. 5.

2   Overview and Contribution

Assessing the threat likelihood for different types of events with their predicted impacts is a common way to assess IT risks. OWASP [9] defines the risk R as "the product of the likelihood L of a security incident occurring times the impact I that will be incurred by the organization due to the incident, that is: $R = L \times I$".

Our approach differentiates between the *intrinsic threat likelihood* which is the probability that the risk in question will occur in the absence of security countermeasures and *threat likelihood* which considers the reduction of risk by the application of countermeasures [5]. The security countermeasures could be devices, procedures, or techniques that reduce the likelihood of threat on the security of information that is processed, stored or transmitted. Examples of such countermeasures are enabled access logs, data encryption, etc.

Let us assume the existence of the following entities: S a set of subjects, O a set of objects, A a set of actions, L_c a set of secrecy levels, and SC a set of security criteria. We limit the set A to two actions, read and write, which will be collectively called *accesses*. We also limit the set SC to two criteria: Secrecy and Integrity. We define a function $Threat\_likelihood : S \times A \times O \times SC \rightarrow [0, 1]$ that represents the threat likelihood value when a subject $s \in S$ requesting an action $a \in A$ on an object $o \in O$ when a security criterion $sc \in SC$ is intended. Secrecy will be abbreviated c.

3   Assessment of Threat Likelihood When Secrecy
Is Intended

In this section, we propose our approach to estimate threat likelihood on secrecy in access control systems. This approach considers the following factors: the intended security criteria (secrecy in this section), the requested action (read or write), the secrecy level of subjects requesting access, the secrecy level of objects to be accessed and the security countermeasures. We assume that threat likelihood depends on the importance of information flow between objects and subjects, determined by the difference between their security levels.

In our approach, the likelihood of threat on secrecy increases when information flows down. Consider, for example, the information flow when a *Top Secret* subject writes in a *Public* object, such information flow is more important than the one when the same subject writes in a *Secret* object. In the first case, *Top Secret* information could be leaked to the public, in the second case this information would remain secret. It is reasonable to assume that the threat likelihood would be higher in the first case. The reasoning for integrity is dual.

We define a total order on L_c and for each secrecy level in L_c, we assign a numerical value in accordance with the defined order, where higher numbers denote higher security levels. Throughout this paper, the following functions will be needed to develop our approach:

- $csl : S \rightarrow L_c$ formally represents the assignment of secrecy levels to subjects that reflects the trust bestowed upon each of them.
- $col : O \rightarrow L_c$ formally represents the assignment of secrecy levels to objects that reflects the protection needs of the data.

3.1 Defining "Threat Likelihood"

Instead of adopting the binary vision of the *Bell La Padula* model [2] to assess the threat likelihood of read and write requests, we propose the following principles: we consider that permitting a subject s to read an object o, such that $csl(s) < col(o)$ or permitting a subject s to write in an object o, such that $csl(s) > col(o)$, presents by itself a measurable threat likelihood.

In this section, we define the "threat likelihood" on secrecy as follows: we say that the likelihood of threat on secrecy is non null if a subject $s \in S$ is able to read an object $o \in O$, such that $csl(s) < col(o)$. But for any attempt by a subject s to read an object o, such that $csl(s) \geq col(o)$ the threat likelihood is null. Any measure of read threat likelihood on secrecy in the first case is affected by the following two general principles:

- **Principle 1:** the likelihood of threat on secrecy increases (or decreases) as the object's secrecy level increases (respectively decreases).
- **Principle 2:** the likelihood of threat on secrecy increases (or decreases) as the subject's secrecy level decreases (respectively increases).

The reasoning for write accesses is dual.

We define the relation $<_T$ in the following way: $(s, a, o, sc) <_T (s', a', o', sc)$ iff $Threat\_likelihood(s, a, o, sc) < Threat\_likelihood(s', a', o', sc)$.

3.2 Read Threat Likelihood Assessment for Secrecy

We assume the existence of the subjects: s_1, s_2, s_3, s_4, s_5 and s_6, and the objects o_1 and o_2. Table 1(a) and (b) illustrate the secrecy levels of these entities.

Table 1. Secrecy levels for running examples

Subjects	s_1	s_2	s_3	s_4	s_5	s_6
Secrecy levels	4	3	2	1	1	1

(a)

Objects	o_1	o_2
Secrecy levels	5	4

(b)

3.2.1 Read Threat Likelihood Assessment for Secrecy: Qualitative Approach

Assume that access for data objects has been requested by subjects who are employees of the business that owns the objects (trusted and reliable to some degree by the system). In this case, data owners might be more concerned about the secrecy levels of objects than the secrecy levels of subjects. Hence, our approach for threat likelihood assessment in this paper is primarily based on the *secrecy levels of objects*.

Let us assume that a workflow architect asked an IT security specialist to define a set of tasks composing a workflow by selecting the least threatening combinations of subjects, objects and actions for the secrecy of data. Task T_1 can be executed by s_2 reading from objects o_1 or o_2, task T_2 can be executed by either s_3 or s_4 reading from o_2 and task T_3 can be executed by either s_5 or s_6 reading from o_1. The last two subjects request access from two distant sites where s_5 is connected via an unencrypted public network and s_6 via VPN.

To determine the least threatening combinations of subjects, objects and actions on secrecy we follow this method:

Method 1: A read threat likelihood assessment technique that is primarily based on object secrecy levels should support the following:

1. always apply **Principle 1**: read threat likelihood always increases as object secrecy level increases,
2. whenever object secrecy levels are the same, apply **Principle 2**: read threat likelihood increases as subject secrecy level decreases,
3. apply **Principle 3**: threat likelihood of accesses increases (or decreases) as the effect of security countermeasures reducing the threat likelihood decreases (respectively increases).

The least threatening combinations of our example according to **Method 1** are as follows: T_1 should be executed by s_2 reading from o_2 since $col(o_2) < col(o_1)$ $((s_2, r, o_2, c) <_T (s_2, r, o_1, c))$, T_2 should be executed by s_3 reading from o_2 since $csl(s_3) > csl(s_4)$ $((s_3, r, o_2, c) <_T (s_4, r, o_2, c))$ and T_3 should be executed by s_6 reading from o_1 since $csl(s_5) = csl(s_6)$ and only s_6 is connected via VPN which is a countermeasure that reduces threat likelihood by preventing disclosure of information $((s_6, r, o_1, c) <_T (s_5, r, o_1, c))$. Indeed, VPNs typically allow remote access using tunnelling protocols and encryption techniques.

3.2.2 Read Threat Likelihood Assessment for Secrecy: Quantitative Approach

Let us consider task T_4 that can be executed by either s_1 or s_2 reading from o_1 where s_1 is connected via an unencrypted public network and s_2 via VPN. According to **Principles 1** and **2**, allowing s_2 to read object o_1 has a greater likelihood of threat on secrecy than allowing s_1 to read object o_1. However, **Principle 3** tells us that this may not be true in the presence of countermeasures such as the VPN, that can reduce the threat likelihood of s_2 reading o_1. Hence, we can see that priority orders such as the one outlined in Sect. 3.2.1, can not permit threat likelihood comparison in all cases. However, quantitative measures which correspond to this threat likelihood ordering may be useful, such as in the case of task T_4. There can be many different formulas which respect the properties of our approach and can measure the threat likelihood of granting access. In this section, we propose a formula and describe its construction.

ISO/IEC 27001 [10] requires regular verification of computer security. In order to determine to which extent the countermeasures are producing the desired outcome to meet the security requirements, the security administrator measures the contribution of the implemented countermeasures in the reduction of risks. In this work, we consider the effect of countermeasures in the calculation of threat likelihood. In Table 2, each rule determines a countermeasure and its effect corresponding to an access request identified by the subject's security level, the object's security level, the action requested and the security criteria intended.

Table 2 shows a representation of all possible read accesses by subjects to objects when secrecy is intended. Note that when $csl(s) > col(o)$, the threat likelihood is null. Hence, entries of Table 2 are empty along or below the diagonal. Otherwise, each table entry $[i, j]$ includes a set of couples (measure, value) that represents the countermeasures and their contribution in the reduction of threat likelihood of a subject s reading an object o, where $csl(s) = i$ and $col(o) = j$. The sum of all countermeasures values in each entry is bound between 0 and 1.

The rule of entry $[2, 4]$ shows that if a subject having a secrecy level 2 reads an object having a secrecy level 4, then the countermeasures m_3 and m_4 can respectively reduce the likelihood of threat on secrecy by 0.5 and 0.2.

$Counter(s, a, o, sc)$ denotes the sum of the effects of the different implemented countermeasures to reduce threat likelihood if s executes an action a on an object o when the security criteria sc is intended. For example, we can see from Table 2 that if a subject s having a secrecy level of 1 requests to read an object o having a secrecy level of 5 when secrecy is intended and all three countermeasures are applied, we have $Counter(s, r, o, c) = 0.5 + 0.2 + 0.2 = 0.9$.

We define the following additional principles for the calculation of the threat likelihood of access requests, which we assume to be bound between 0 and 1.

- **Principle 4:** The threat likelihood of an access request is equal to zero, if the cumulative effect of the corresponding security countermeasures is equal to or greater than the value of the intrinsic threat likelihood.

- **Principle 5:** The threat likelihood of an access request increases (or decreases) when the intrinsic threat likelihood increases (respectively decreases).

Table 2. The effect of countermeasures in the reduction of the read threat likelihood

Subjects secrecy levels	Objects secrecy level 1	Objects secrecy level 2	Objects secrecy level 3	Objects secrecy level 4	Objects secrecy level 5
1		$(m_5, 0.5)$	$(m_5, 0.5)$	$(m_3, 0.5)$	$(m_1, 0.5)$
					$(m_2, 0.2)$
					$(m_4, 0.2)$
2			$(m_2, 0.2)$	$(m_3, 0.5)$	$(m_2, 0.2)$
			$(m_4, 0.2)$	$(m_4, 0.2)$	$(m_4, 0.2)$
3				$(m_3, 0.5)$	$(m_4, 0.2)$
4					$(m_4, 0.2)$
5					

We now introduce the concept of threat likelihood indexing. We associate a numerical value representing the threat likelihood index from the set $\{0, \cdots, |L_c| - 1\}$ to each subject and object having a secrecy level in L_c. In the case of read accesses when secrecy is intended, from the point of view of subjects, we expect the threat likelihood to increase as subject secrecy levels decrease. Hence, subject threat likelihood index values decrease with subject secrecy levels. For $level$ in L_c, we write $\overset{\frown}{level}$ to denote a subject threat likelihood index. Formally, $(\overset{\frown}{level}) = |L_c| - level$. For example, when $L_c = \{$Top secret, Secret, Confidential, Restricted, Public$\}$, $(\overset{\frown}{Secret}) = 5 - 4 = 1$. However, object threat likelihood indexes increase with object secrecy levels. We write $\overset{\smile}{level}$ to denote an object threat likelihood index. Formally, $\overset{\smile}{level} = level$ -1. For example, $\overset{\smile}{Secret} = 4 - 1 = 3$.

If we assume that $|L_c| = 5$ there can be at most $5 \times 5 = 25$ combinations of subject-object accesses. We define a function $Intrinsic : S \times A \times O \times SC \rightarrow [0, 1]$ that represents the intrinsic threat likelihood value of a subject $s \in S$ requesting an action $a \in A$ on an object $o \in O$ when a security criterion $sc \in SC$ is intended.

$$Intrinsic(s, r, o, c) = \begin{cases} \frac{(|L_c| \times \overset{\smile}{col(o)} + \overset{\frown}{csl(s)})}{(|L_c|^2) - 1}, \textbf{if} csl(s) < col(o) \\ 0, \textbf{ Otherwise.} \end{cases} \quad (1)$$

A formula that respects the principles of **Method 1** and **Principles 4** and **5** for measuring the threat on secrecy likelihood of granting read access to a subject s for an object o, is given below:

$$Threat\_likelihood(s, r, o, c) = \begin{cases} Intrinsic(s, r, o, c) - Counter(s, r, o, c), \\ \textbf{if } csl(s) < col(o) \textbf{ and} \\ Counter(s, r, o, c) < Intrinsic(s, r, o, c) \\ 0, \textbf{ Otherwise.} \end{cases} \quad (2)$$

The numerator of formula (1) is intuitive. Since we require that more importance be given to the threat likelihood index of objects, we multiply the object threat likelihood index by $|L_c|$ that equals the cardinality of the set of secrecy levels L_c. Then, we add the threat likelihood index of the subject. The numerator of the formula maps all possible read accesses by subjects to objects into an interval $[0 \cdots (|L_c|^2) - 1]$, where a higher value represents a greater threat likelihood. In order to have intrinsic likelihood threat values into an interval $[0, 1]$, we divide the value obtained from the numerator by $(|L_c|^2) - 1$. In formula (2), we subtract the value representing the effect of the different implemented countermeasures corresponding to the request in question. The resultant value represents the object-based read threat likelihood that respects the principles of **Method 1** and **Principles 4** and **5**.

Let us consider that the coutermeasure m_2 in Table 2 represents the encryption of data and we apply formula (2) to our example stated in Sect. 3.2.2. We have $Counter(s_1, r, o_1, c) = 0$ and $Counter(s_2, r, o_1, c) = 0.2$. We get the following: $Threat\_likelihood(s_1, r, o_1, c) = Intrinsic(s_1, r, o_1, c) - Counter(s_1, r, o_1, c) = 0.87$ (1) and $Threat\_likelihood(s_2, r, o_1, c) = Intrinsic(s_2, r, o_1, c) - Counter(s_2, r, o_1, c) = 0.91 - 0.2 = 0.71$ (2). From (1) and (2), we have $Threat\_likelihood(s_2, r, o_1, c) < Threat\_likelihood(s_1, r, o_1, c)$.

Future papers will show how to derive formulas giving values representing the object-based likelihood of threat on secrecy when write access is requested and the likelihood of threat on integrity when write and read accesses are requested. Note that threat likelihood on integrity increases when information flows up.

4 Related Work and Limitations

Cheng et al. propose Fuzzy Multi-Level Security (Fuzzy MLS), which quantifies the risk of an access request in multi-level security systems as a product of the value of information and probability of unauthorized disclosure [4]. Unlike Fuzzy MLS which is limited to the estimation of the threat likelihood of read accesses forbidden by Bell La Padula, our approach estimates the threat likelihood of read and write accesses, is applicable when the objective of integrity is of interest (is not limited to secrecy) and considers security countermeasures mitigating the threat likelihood.

Bartsch proposes a policy override calculus for qualitative risk assessment in the context of role-based access control systems [1]. This work presents a qualitative estimation of threat likelihood. In comparison with the work of Bartsch, our approach is both qualitative and quantitative, developed in the context of generic access control systems and is not limited to RBAC.

Threat likelihood assessment in our framework cannot cover unexpected threats such as those in which several other socio-technical parameters must be taken into consideration for reflecting the reality of insider threats such as users' access history, behavior, collusion with other users, etc.

5 Conclusion

The main contribution of this paper is a quantitative approach for threat likelihood assessment in the context of access control systems. Our approach considers primarily the security levels of objects, and thus gives more priority to the sensitivity of data. This is only one possibility and our approach can be easily modified to accommodate other views, such as those presented in [7,8]. In order to be compliant with IT Risk standards and guidelines, and to obtain realistic values of threat likelihood, our approach takes account of the effect of the security countermeasures mitigating the threat likelihood of access requests.

In this paper, we have focused on quantitative threat likelihood assessment, which is a pre-requisite for estimating access risks. However, our ultimate goal is to develop a framework for estimating the risk of access requests.

Acknowledgements. This research was partially supported by the Natural Sciences and Engineering Research Council of Canada.

References

1. Bartsch, S.: A calculus for the qualitative risk assessment of policy override authorization. In: Proceedings of the 3rd International Conference on Security of Information and Networks, pp. 62–70. ACM (2010)
2. Bell, D.E., La Padula, L.J.: Secure computer system: unified exposition and multics interpretation. Technical report, DTIC Document (1976)
3. Bishop, M., Gates, C.: Defining the insider threat. In: Proceedings of the 4th Annual Workshop on Cyber Security and Information Intelligence Research, p. 15. ACM (2008)
4. Cheng, P.-C., Rohatgi, P., Keser, C., Karger, P.A., Wagner, G.M., Reninger, A.S.: Fuzzy multi-level security: an experiment on quantified risk-adaptive access control. In: 2007 IEEE Symposium on Security and Privacy (SP 2007), pp. 222–230. IEEE (2007)
5. Clusif. MEHARI 2010 principes fondamentaux et spécifications fonctionnelles. Club de la sécurité de l'information français (2009)
6. IT Global Corporate. Security risks (2013)
7. Khambhammettu, H., Boulares, S., Adi, K., Logrippo, L.: A framework for threat assessment in access control systems. In: IFIP International Information Security Conference, pp. 187–198. Springer (2012)
8. Khambhammettu, H., Boulares, S., Adi, K., Logrippo, L.: A framework for risk assessment in access control systems. Comput. Secur. **39**, 86–103 (2013)
9. Meucci, M., Muller, A.: The owasp testing guide 4.0 (2014)
10. International organization for Standardization: ISO/IEC 27001: Information Technology, Security Techniques, Information Security Management Systems, Requirements. ISO/IEC (2005)
11. Shey, H., Mak, K., Balaouras, S., Luu, B.: Understand the state of data security, privacy: 2013 to 2014. Forrester Research Inc., 1 October 2013

Privacy and Verification

An Enhancement of Privacy-Preserving Wildcards Pattern Matching

Tushar Kanti Saha$^{(\boxtimes)}$ and Takeshi Koshiba

Division of Mathematics, Electronics, and Informatics,
Graduate School of Science and Engineering, Saitama University,
255 Shimo-Okubo, Sakura, Saitama 338-8570, Japan
{s15dm054,koshiba}@mail.saitama-u.ac.jp

Abstract. We consider secure pattern matching for some alphabet set, where gaps are represented by the character '*'. Generally, we know that a wildcard character '*' in the pattern is used to replace zero or more letters in the text. Yasuda et al. (ACISP 2014) proposed a new packing method for somewhat homomorphic encryption for handling wildcards pattern where the wildcards replace one letter in the text. We extend the secure pattern matching so that the wildcards are replaced with any sequences. We propose a method for privacy-preserving wildcards pattern matching using somewhat homomorphic encryption in the semi-honest model. At the same time, we also propose another packing method for executing homomorphic operations between plaintext and encrypted wildcards pattern in three homomorphic multiplications rather than $3k$ multiplications required by Yasuda et al. method to handle k sub-patterns. Moreover, we have been able to improve the communication complexity of Yasuda et al. method by a factor k denoting the total number of sub-patterns appearing in the pattern. In addition, our practical implementation shows that our method is about k-times faster than that of Yasuda et al. Here, we show some applications of our packing method to computing secure Hamming and Euclidean distances.

Keywords: Privacy-preserving · Repetitive-wildcards · Pattern matching computation · Somewhat homomorphic encryption · Bioinformatics · Biometrics · Hamming and Euclidean distances

1 Introduction

Pattern matching computation (PMC) has vast applications in various fields like biometrics authentication, speech and image recognition, bioinformatics, search engine, forensics, etc. Now computer professionals and scientists are thinking how these computations can be done securely without revealing any information to the public. So encryption is one of the techniques to secure data. But we need to do computation on encrypted data for security. So the solution is homomorphic computation which was introduced by Rivest et al. [1]. Moreover, data is increasing day by day. So users are interested in storing it online not only

© Springer International Publishing AG 2017
F. Cuppens et al. (Eds.): FPS 2016, LNCS 10128, pp. 145–160, 2017.
DOI: 10.1007/978-3-319-51966-1_10

for saving space of local computers but also access it anytime and anywhere from the world. Cloud service providers like Amazon, Google, Microsoft, etc. are facilitating massive storage service along with computation. But securing data and search over secured data are needed at the same time. Homomorphic encryption (HE) has allowed service providers to facilitate these services to their users. But at the early stages, cryptosystem of Goldwasser and Micali [20], El Gamal [21], Cohen and Fischer [22], Paillier [23] allowed only single homomorphic computation either addition or multiplication but not both. In 2005, Boneh et al. enabled us to perform both operations at the same time [3]. But they have the limitation of doing multiple additions but single multiplication. After that Gentry [4] did the revolution in the field of homomorphic computation which can perform different operations on encrypted data. Their method is called fully homomorphic encryption (FHE) which enables multiple additions and multiplications. But the problem is that with FHE, it generates large ciphertext and causes slow processing speed [5]. After these breakthroughs, Brakerski et al. proposed another somewhat homomorphic encryption (SwHE) which supports multiple additions and fewer multiplications [6]. Therefore, it reduces the ciphertext size and speeds up the computation performances. In 2011, Lauter et al. [2] showed some practical applications of SwHE in medical, financial, and advertising and pricing. Then using SwHE of [2] secure pattern matching application for analyzing personal DNA sequence was proposed by Yasuda et al. [8]. But, they did not address the pattern with a wildcard (∗) like 'AT∗G', 'AT∗', '∗AT', etc. in their research. To address this limitation, they proposed wildcards pattern matching technique using SwHE for searching real-world genome data [7]. They used packing method of [8] to match the pattern including a single wildcard which replaced a letter in the text of practical genome data. For example, for a DNA alphabet set $\Sigma = \{A, C, T, G\}$, pattern 'AT∗' matches any of the texts like 'ATC', 'ATG', 'ATA'. Here Yasuda et al. [7] addressed only a letter in the text to be replaced by a wildcard character occurred in the pattern. But several letters in the text are needed to be replaced by a wildcard character appeared in the pattern that we call repetitive-wildcards pattern matching. Here, we address this repetitive-wildcards pattern matching in encrypted domain. Therefore, searching pattern like 'AT∗CG∗AAG∗TT∗AGG' securely in the text of cloud database is our concern of research where '∗' replaces one or several letters in the text. In reality, we have been motivated by the DNA search method used in mtDB (see http://www.mtdb.igp.uu.se/ for the on-line version of DNA searching) where wildcard '∗' has been represented by a gap. In this research, we address only one wildcards symbol '∗'. If we want to support other symbols, it will increase time complexity of the method.

1.1 Recent Secure Pattern Matching Techniques

Pattern matching computation can be secured in two ways namely application specific protocol and generalized protocol. We emphasized on application specific protocol. In 2008, Jha et al. implemented Yao's protocol to secure genomic computation [9]. Here they showed a modified protocol of Yao after dividing problem instance into smaller sub-circuits and sharing the result of evaluating each sub-circuit between the participants. In 2010, Blanton et al. showed secure pattern matching technique using finite automata for DNA searching [10]. In the same year, Katz et al. described a new keyword search protocol for private DNA pattern matching by modifying Yao's garbled circuit approach [11]. For the above cases, they did not work any patterns which contain a wildcard character (*) that needed to be matched with actual text. So far we have observed that secure pattern matching computation (SPMC) with single-character wildcard was first addressed by Baron et al. in 2012 [12]. They proposed a new protocol for more expressive search queries including single-character wildcard and substring pattern matching of arbitrary alphabets. Thereafter, Defrawy et al. did a comparative study among some secure pattern-matching (SPM) protocols and measured their performances for a wildcard pattern matching [15]. But none of the methods discussed so far address on repetitive-wildcards occurred in the patterns. To address this pattern matching, Hazay et al. first proposed a few protocols for important variations of the SPM problem that were significantly more efficient than their previous protocols [16]. But these protocols are not suitable for cloud computing because they did not show any implementation procedure in the cloud. To address this problem a new method is urgently necessary.

1.2 Our Contribution

In our research, we are emphasizing on SPMC in the cloud using symmetric somewhat homomorphic encryption scheme of Yasuda et al. [7]. Moreover, wildcards pattern matching has a great impact on searching real-world genome [7]. But a few schemes discussed above used a wildcard character in a pattern which will replace several letters in the text to search genome data. Here users may also want to use repetitive-wildcards in the pattern to search their genome data. In this regard, we should have a method which will be helpful for SPMC with this type of wildcards appearance. Furthermore, we want to use patterns as 'AC*CTA*T' which can match any sequences like 'AACGGCTATTACAACTGGT'. If we use method of [7] then we require here nine homomorphic multiplications but we need a method for doing this using a few homomorphic multiplications. For this novel aim, we propose a protocol and a new packing method which enable us to carry out privacy-preserving wildcards pattern matching using symmetric somewhat homomorphic encryption scheme. Our packing method is a modified version of Yasuda et al. [14] to prevent the overflow occurred in their computation when data size exceeds their limits.

1.3 Outline

Our paper is organized in the following way. Section 2 describes secure pattern matching in the cloud along with protocol and some typical applications. Moreover, a homomorphic encryption scheme for our pattern matching protocol with its security and correctness is described in Sect. 3. In addition, our proposed packing method is discussed in Sect. 4. Our pattern matching computation is discussed in Sect. 5. We also narrate the performance of our protocol both theoretically and practically in Sect. 6. Finally, we conclude our paper in Sect. 7.

2   Secure Pattern Matching in Cloud

Among the early research works in secure pattern matching, most of them are neither suitable for repetitive-wildcards pattern matching nor applicable to cloud computing. Some researchers [7,8,14] presented their contributions that could be applied to cloud. But they did not deal with the pattern containing this type of wildcards. So our protocol for SPM using symmetric SwHE and its application are discussed in the following sub-sections.

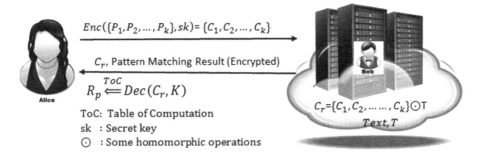

Fig. 1. Symmetric SwHE protocol for repetitive-wildcards pattern matching.

2.1   Our Protocol Using Symmetric SwHE

To describe this protocol, we consider a scenario for secure pattern matching between Alice and Bob. For example - Bob has stored plaintext $T = (a_0, \ldots, a_{l-1})$ of length l in his secure server which has a huge computation capability. Furthermore, Alice has a pattern $P = (b_{1,0}b_{1,1}\cdots b_{1,p_1-1} * b_{2,0}b_{2,1}\cdots b_{2,p_2-1} * \cdots * b_{k,0}b_{k,1}\cdots b_{k,p_k-1})$ with some wildcards which can be found in the plaintext T. Here the Alice divides the pattern into sub-patterns as $\{P_1, P_2, \ldots, P_k\}$ excluding the wildcards characters where length vector of sub-patterns as $(p_1, p_2, \ldots, p_k)$ with $p_k \leq l$. But Alice does not want to reveal his pattern to Bob. On the contrary, Bob cannot reveal his information outside his server. So homomorphic encryption property [1] can handle this situation. Fully homomorphic encryption can do any operations which have large time complexity. Somewhat homomorphic encryption [7] is helpful in our case. In addition, Bob can do the pattern matching computation by measuring the square Euclidean distance between the sub-text of T and each sub-pattern of P. For $0 \leq d \leq (ly - p_y)$ and $1 \leq y \leq k$, the square Euclidean distance E_{dis} between the sub-text T^d and each sub-pattern P_y is computed by the following equation.

$$E_{dis} = \sum_{h=0}^{p_y-1} (a_{d+h} - b_{y,h})^2 \tag{1}$$

In addition, as shown in Fig. 1, our protocol can be narrated concisely by the following points.

1. Alice has a pattern P with multiple wildcards. She breaks down the pattern P into sub-patterns $\{P_1, P_2, \ldots, P_k\}$ excluding wildcard characters and encrypts them with the homomorphic key generated by herself.
2. Then, she sends the encrypted pattern to Bob for performing a secure search.
3. Bob performs the required pattern matching computation between text T and sub-patterns $\{C_1, C_2, \ldots, C_k\}$ by Eq. (1) and returns the result containing encrypted locations to Alice.
4. Alice uses her keys to decrypt the result and uses our 'table of computation' for considering wildcards to get her desired result.

Remark 1. Here our protocol is secure under the assumption that Bob is semi-honest (also known as honest-but-curious), i.e., he always follows the protocols but tries to learn information from the protocol.

2.2 Typical Applications

SPMC has a wide area in terms of application scenarios. Moreover, the size of data is increasing very rapidly. Secure computation needs where security is the main phenomena to compute like patient's electronic health records, human genome database, digital forensics, bioinformatics, network intrusion detection, etc. Healthcare centers may upload their patient's data to a cloud server. Thus, the patient may allow the doctors to check medical reports or DNA records stored in the database. SPM is being used widely nowadays due to publicly availability of Genbank database [17] which contains an annotated collection of DNA sequences. The Genbank is actually part of the international nucleotide sequence database collaboration which includes the DNA data bank of Japan (DDBJ), the European molecular biology laboratory (EMBL), and Genbank at the national center for biotechnology information (NCBI). SPM also be used in forensics application to search a particular digital content from a large set of digital contents to protect the copyright. We hope that our packing method and protocol will be helpful for many pattern matching applications in the cloud computing platform.

Used Notations. The symbol $\mathbb{Z}$ denotes the ring of integers. For a prime number p, the ring of integers is denoted by $\mathbb{Z}_p$. For a vector $A = (a_0, a_1, \ldots, a_{n-1})$, the maximum norm is $\|a\|_\infty = \max |a_i|$. Let $\langle T, P \rangle$ denote the inner product between two vectors T and P. The ciphertexts ct_{add} and ct_{mul} denote homomorphic addition and multiplication of text m' and encrypted text $ct = Enc(m, sk)$ respectively. Also b_{y,i_y} denotes i_y-th character of y-th sub-pattern. The distribution $D_{\mathbb{Z}^n}$ indicates the n-dimensional discrete Gaussian distribution.

3   Security Using Homomorphic Encryption

In this section, we review the symmetric SwHE scheme of [7] and its correctness. In 2011, Brakerski and Vaikunthanathan [6] proposed the correctness of this scheme.

3.1   Symmetric SwHE Scheme

Yasuda et al. [7] showed a symmetric SwHE based on the public key SwHE scheme of [2]. For this scheme, we need to consider some parameters as follows:

- q: modulus q is an odd prime such that $q \equiv 1(\bmod\ 2n)$ which defines the ring $R_q = R/qR = \mathbb{Z}_q[x]/f(x)$ for a ciphertext space.
- $f(x)$: a cyclotomic polynomial where $f(x) = x^n + 1$.
- n: an integer which represents the lattice dimension for the ring $R_q = \mathbb{Z}_q[x]/f(x)$. It also represents the degree of polynomials which is a power of 2 such as 1024 or 2048.
- σ: a parameter which defines a discrete Gaussian error distribution $\chi = D_{\mathbb{Z}^n,\sigma}$ with the standard deviation $\sigma = 4 \sim 8$ practically.
- t: a prime $t < q$ which defines the message space of the scheme as $R_t = \mathbb{Z}_t[x]/f(x)$, the ring of integer polynomials modulo $f(x)$ and t.

Now we can discuss the key generation, encryption, homomorphism, and decryption property of this scheme as follows:

Key generation. Generate a ring element $R \ni s \leftarrow \chi$ for our secret key $sk = s$;

Encryption. For a given plaintext $m \in R_t$, encryption algorithm first samples $a \leftarrow R_q$ and $e \leftarrow \chi$ then encryption can be defined by a ciphertext pair $(c_0, c_1) = ct$ as follows:

$$Enc(m, sk) = (c_0, c_1) = (as + te + m, -a)$$

Homomorphic Operations.· Generally, homomorphic operations like addition ($\boxplus$) and multiplication ($\boxtimes$) are between two ciphertexts. But in our case, one is plaintext m' and another is ciphertext $ct = Enc(m, sk)$. So the homomorphic operation between our ciphertext $ct = (c_0, c_1)$ and plaintext m' can be defined as

$$\begin{cases} ct_{add} = ct \boxplus m' = (c_0 \boxplus m', c_1) \\ ct_{mul} = ct \boxtimes m' = (c_0 \boxtimes m', c_1 \boxtimes m') \end{cases} \quad (2)$$

where the plaintext m' is considered an element in R_q for the above computation. We can also define the subtraction as similar to addition as $ct \boxplus (-m)' = (c_0 \boxplus (-m)', c_1)$.

Decryption. For a ciphertext $ct \in (R_q)^2$ and $t \in R_t$ with the secret key $sk = s$, a general decryption can be defined as

$$Dec(ct, sk) = [\tilde{m}]_q \bmod t \text{ where } \tilde{m} = c_0 + c_1 s.$$

In the same way, homomorphic decryption can be defined by the following ways:

$$\begin{cases} Dec(ct_{add}, sk) = [\tilde{m}_{add}]_q \bmod t \\ Dec(ct_{mul}, sk) = [\tilde{m}_{mul}]_q \bmod t \end{cases}$$

where $\tilde{m}_{add} = c_0 + m' + c_1 s$ and $\tilde{m}_{mul} = c_0 m' + c_1 m' s$.

3.2 Security of This Scheme

We can show the security of this scheme by polynomial ring learning with errors (ring-LWE) assumption as done by Lauter et al. [2]. Let the ring $R_q = \mathbb{Z}_q / f(x)$ where $f(x) = (x^n + 1)$ is the cyclotomic polynomial over degree n. Let $s \leftarrow R_q$ be a uniformly random ring element. The assumption is given by any polynomial number of samples of the form

$$(a_i, b_i = a_i \cdot s + e_i) \in (R_q)^2$$

where a_i is uniformly random in R_q and e_i is drawn from the error distribution χ. Here the b_i's are computationally indistinguishable from uniform in R_q. Therefore, it is hard to distinguish (a_i, b_i) from a uniformly random pair (a_i, b_i). Moreover, Lyubashevsky et al. [18] showed that ring-LWE assumption is reducible to the worst-case hardness of problems on ideal lattices that is assumed to be secure against the quantum computer.

Remark 2. Recently, Castryck et al. [25] showed provably weak instances of ring-LWE. But these kinds of weak instances do not affect our scheme.

3.3 Correctness of this Scheme

The correctness of this scheme depends on how the decryption can recover the original result from the ciphertext after some homomorphic operations. We can write the decryption process as

$$\begin{cases} Dec(ct_{add}, sk) = Dec((ct \boxplus m'), sk) = m + m' \\ Dec(ct_{mul}, sk) = Dec((ct \boxtimes m'), sk) = m \cdot m' \end{cases} \tag{3}$$

Actually, the above process is already described in Sect. 1.1 of [6]. Here, ciphertext ct comes from $m \in R_q$ after encryption and another plaintext $m' \in R_q$. The encryption scheme in Sect. 3.1 is the presentation of SwHE and its holds if the following lemma holds as shown in [7].

Lemma 1 (Condition for successful decryption). *For a ciphertext ct, the decryption $Dec(ct, sk)$ recovers the correct result if $\langle ct, s \rangle \in R_q$ does not wrap-around mod q, namely, if the condition $\|\langle ct, s \rangle\|_\infty < \frac{q}{2}$ is satisfied, where let $\|a\|_\infty = \max |a_i|$ for an element $a = \sum_{i=0}^{n-1} a_i x^i \in R_q$. Specifically, for a fresh ciphertext ct, the ∞-norm $\|\langle ct, s \rangle\|_\infty$ is given by $\|m + te\|_\infty$. Moreover, for a homomorphically operated ciphertext, the ∞-norm can be computed by Eq. (2).*

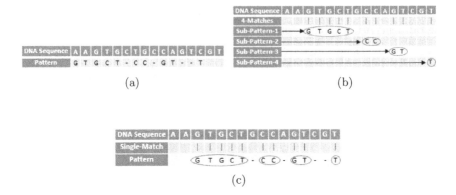

Fig. 2. (a) Our Problem domain; (b) Pattern matching for a non-binary vector of text and pattern using our sub-pattern matching concept; (c) Our pattern matching technique.

4   Packing Method for Secure Pattern Matching

Here, we skip the reviewing of some early packing methods of [2, 13] due to page limitation. However, Yasuda et al. [7] implemented the packing method of [13] for privacy preserving wildcards pattern matching using symmetric SwHE. Here, they also require three homomorphic multiplications for some pattern like 'AT*' to match some DNA sequences 'ATA', 'ATT', 'ATG', and 'ATC' over the DNA alphabet. In their research, they used a wildcard character in the pattern to replace a single letter in the text. But we like to consider the DNA sequence and pattern as shown in Fig. 2(a). Here there exist some gaps in the pattern which can be represented by a wildcard character. If we split the pattern into sub-patterns, then we get 4 different sub-patterns here. For matching these sub-patterns with the given DNA sequence, we require 4-queries i.e. 12-multiplications for the method of [7] as shown in Fig. 2(b). But if we want to do it in a few multiplications using one query as shown in Fig. 2(c), we need a different packing method than [13].

Let T be a text vector and P be a pattern vector which can be expressed as $T = (a_0, a_1, a_2, \ldots, a_{(l-1)}) \in \mathbb{Z}^l$ and $P = (b_{1,0} b_{1,1} \cdots b_{1,p_1-1} * b_{2,0} b_{2,1} \cdots b_{2,p_2-1} * \cdots * b_{k,0} b_{k,1} \cdots b_{k,p_k-1}) \in \mathbb{Z}^{|P|}$ respectively. Here the length of T is l where $l \leq n$. Moreover, pattern P can be divided into k sub-patterns as $\bar{P} = \{P_1, P_2, \ldots, P_k\}$ omitting the wildcards where the length of sub-patterns can be represented as $\{p_1, p_2, \ldots, p_k\}$. We know that pattern matching is usually done by measuring the distance between the text and pattern of the same length. That's why we need to measure the distances of every sub-pattern from every substring of text with the same length. Here we can find the distances between text and each sub-pattern by placing those distances as a coefficient of different degrees of x of an n degree polynomial. Therefore, if we use the packing method of [13] which packs all the sub-patterns as one pattern, *pattern matching result of most sub-patterns will be wrap-around the coefficient with some degrees of x.* Then it is difficult to extract each sub-pattern matching result from the resultant polynomial. As a result, it is necessary to get each sub-pattern matching result as a coefficient of different degrees of x. Now we need to pack the pattern $\bar{P}$ in a different way than packing of [13]. *To overcome the above problem that is, to avoid this wrap-around of coefficient for any degrees of x, we take the highest degrees of x as ly for the first element $b_{y,0}$ in P_y and decrease those degrees for other elements $b_{y,i}$ in that P_y with $1 \leq i \leq p_y$ and $1 \leq y \leq k$.* Therefore, using packing method of [2] and modifying packing method of [14], our packing method can be represented by the following two polynomials in the ring $R = \mathbb{Z}[x]/(x^n + 1)$ where $n \geq (k+1)l$.

1. $Poly_1(T) = \sum_{j=0}^{l-1} a_j x^j$
2. $Poly_2(\bar{P}) = \sum_{y=1}^{k} \sum_{i_y=0}^{p_y-1} b_{y,i_y} x^{ly-i_y}$

Here, multiplication of the above two polynomials helps to obtain the result of each sub-pattern P_y matching with actual text T. Therefore, degree($Poly_2(\bar{P})$) starts with ly for each sub-pattern so that one sub-pattern matching result does not wrap-around another sub-pattern matching result as a coefficient of resultant polynomial with $1 \leq y \leq k$.

Inner product property. As discussed in Sect. 3.2 of [13], the inner product of two vectors helps to compute Hamming distance and Euclidean distance. So the polynomial multiplications of text T and pattern $\bar{P}$ can be represented as

$$Poly_1(T) \times Poly_2(\bar{P}) = \left(\sum_{j=0}^{l-1} a_j x^j \right) \times \left(\sum_{y=1}^{k} \sum_{i_y=0}^{p_y-1} b_{y,i_y} x^{ly-i_y} \right)$$

$$= \sum_{y=1}^{k} \sum_{j=0}^{l-1} \sum_{i_y=0}^{p_y-1} a_j b_{y,i_y} x^{j+ly-i_y}$$

$$= \sum_{y=1}^{k} \sum_{h=0}^{ly-p_y} \sum_{i_y=0}^{p_y-1} a_{h+i_y} b_{y,i_y} x^{ly+h} + \text{terms of higher degree} + \text{terms of lower degree}$$

$$= \sum_{y=1}^{k} \sum_{d=0}^{l-p_y} \langle T^d, \bar{P}^y \rangle x^{ly+d} + \text{terms of higher degree} + \text{terms of lower degree} \qquad (4)$$

Here, T^d is the dth sub-vector $(a_d, a_{d+1}, a_{d+2}, \ldots, a_{d+p_y-1})$ of length p_y and $\bar{P}^y$ is y^{th} sub-pattern vector $(b_{y,0}, b_{y,1}, \ldots, b_{y,p_y-1})$ with $0 \leq d \leq (ly - p_y)$ and $1 \leq y \leq k$. The above result shows that one polynomial multiplication includes the simultaneous inner product of $\langle T^d, \bar{P}^y \rangle$. Furthermore, terms of higher degree mean $deg(x) > (2ly - p_y)$ and terms of lower degrees mean $deg(x) < ly$. As discussed in our protocol in Sect. 2.1, Alice has encrypted pattern ct_2 of $\bar{P}$ and Bob has the text T in the plaintext space R_t. So we can define $ct_2(\bar{P})$ for some plaintext $Poly_2(\bar{P}) \in R$ as

$$ct_2(\bar{P}) = Enc(Poly_2(\bar{P}), sk) \in (R_q)^2 \qquad (5)$$

Proposition 1. *Let $T = (a_0, a_1, a_2, \ldots, a_{l-1}) \in \mathbb{Z}^l$ be a vector of text and $P = (b_{1,0}b_{1,1} \cdots b_{1,p_1-1} * b_{2,0}b_{2,1} \cdots b_{2,p_2-1} * \cdots * b_{k,0}b_{k,1} \cdots b_{k,p_k-1}) \in \mathbb{Z}^{|P|}$ be a pattern vector where $|T| = l$. Moreover, k sub-patterns are found from the pattern, $\bar{P} = \{P_1, P_2, \ldots, P_k\}$ omitting the wildcards where the length of sub-patterns can be represented as $\{p_1, p_2, \ldots, p_k\}$ with $p_k \leq l \leq n$. If ciphertext of $\bar{P}$ can be represented by $ct_2(\bar{P})$ by Eq. (5) then under the condition of Lemma 1, decryption of homomorphic multiplication $Poly_1(T) \boxtimes ct_2(\bar{P}) \in (R_q)^2$ will produce a polynomial of R_t with x^{ly+d} including coefficient $\langle T^d, \bar{P}^y \rangle = \sum_{h=0}^{p_y-1} a_{d+h} b_{y,h} \mod t$ for $1 \leq y \leq k$, $0 \leq i_y \leq p_y$ and $0 \leq d \leq l - p_y$. Alternatively, we can say that homomorphic multiplication of $Poly_1(T)$ and $ct_2(\bar{P})$ simultaneously computes multiple inner products for $1 \leq y \leq k$ and $0 \leq h \leq (ly - p_y)$.*

5 Pattern Matching Computation

In this section, we describe Euclidean distance calculation using our packing method for pattern matching problem as shown in Eq. (1). Here we show how Bob does the homomorphic operations between his plaintext and encrypted pattern. Here we also try to show that how Euclidean distance computation can be useful in computing Hamming distance. Secure Euclidean distance has many applications like fingerprint authentication [19]. Similarly, secure Hamming distance has many applications like analysis of personal DNA sequence [8]. In this respect, let $T = (a_0, a_1, a_2, \ldots, a_{l-1}) \in \mathbb{Z}^l$ be a vector of text where $|T| = l$ and $P = (b_{1,0}b_{1,1} \cdots b_{1,p_1-1} * b_{2,0}b_{2,1} \cdots b_{2,p_2-1} * \cdots * b_{k,0}b_{k,p_k-1}) \in \mathbb{Z}^{|P|}$ be a pattern vector. Here we get sub-pattern excluding wildcards as $\bar{P} = (P_1, P_2, \ldots, P_k)$ where length vector of sub-patterns as $(p_1, p_2, \ldots, p_k)$ with $p_k \leq l \leq n$. So the squared Euclidean distance E_{dis} between T^d and P^y is given by

$$\sum_{h=0}^{p_y-1} (a_{d+h} - b_{y,h})^2 = \sum_{h=0}^{p_y-1} (a_{d+h}^2 - 2 \cdot a_{d+h} \cdot b_{y,h} + b_{y,h}^2)^2 \tag{6}$$

for each $0 \leq d \leq (ly - p_y)$ and $1 \leq y \leq k$. Here, pattern $\bar{P}_y$ occurs in the dth position of the text T if $E_{dis} = 0$. So through this equation, we can use it to carry out exact pattern matching. Moreover, if the binary vector is used then Eq. (6) also gives the Hamming distance. On the other hand, if T and P are non-binary vectors over alphabets like $\Sigma = \{A, C, T, G\}$ then we convert it unary encoded vectors $t_i p_j \in \{0, 1\}^{|\Sigma|}$ as in [7]. If d_H means Hamming distance between T^d and $\bar{P}^y$ then computation (6) gives E_{dis} that is equal to twice of Hamming distance i.e. $2d_H \langle T^d, \bar{P}^y \rangle$.

Theorem 1. *Under the condition Lemma 1, the linear combination of homomorphic operations*

$$Poly_1(T^2) \boxtimes ct_2(v_{|\bar{P}|}) \boxplus Poly_1(v_l) \boxtimes ct_2(\bar{P}^2) \boxplus (-2Poly_1(T) \boxtimes ct_2(\bar{P})) \tag{7}$$

simultaneously computes multiple values of Eq. (6) *for* $0 \leq d \leq (ly - p_y)$ *and* $1 \leq y \leq k$ *on encrypted data where* $v_{|\bar{P}|}$ *denotes an unit vector* $(1, 1, \ldots, 1)$ *of length* $|\bar{P}|$ *and* v_l *denotes another unit vector* $(1, 1, \ldots, 1)$ *of length* l. *Concretely, the homomorphic operation* (7) *gives a polynomial of* R_t *with the* x^{ly+d}-*th coefficient equals to the value of Eq.* (6) *for each* $0 \leq d \leq (ly - p_y)$ *and* $1 \leq y \leq k$ *on encrypted data.*

Proof. The property (4) shows that each x^{ly+d}-th coefficient $Poly_1(T^2) * Poly_2(v_{|\bar{P}|})$ is equal to the sum

$$(a_d^2, a_{d+1}^2, \ldots, a_{d+p_y-1}^2) \cdot (1, 1, \ldots, 1)^T = \sum_{h=0}^{p_y-1} a_{d+h}^2 \text{ for } 0 \leq d \leq (l - p_y) \text{ and}$$
$$1 \leq y \leq k$$

where A^T denotes the transpose of a vector A. Moreover, according to proposition 1, we can say that the homomorphic multiplication of $Poly_1(v_l) \boxtimes ct_2(\bar{P}^2)$ and $(-2Poly_1(T)) \boxtimes ct_2(\bar{P})$ computes two polynomials on encrypted data with the x^{ly+d}-th coefficient which are equals to $\sum_{h=0}^{p_y-1} b_{y,h}^2$ and $-2\sum_{h=0}^{p_y-1} a_{d+h} \cdot b_{y,h}$ respectively for each $0 \leq d \leq (l - p_y)$ and $1 \leq y \leq k$. Finally, we can also say by the correctness (3), it proofs that homomorphic operation in Eq. (7) produces a polynomial of R_t with x^{ly+d}-th coefficient which equals to Eq. (6) for each $0 \leq d \leq (l - p_y)$ and $1 \leq y \leq k$ on encrypted data.

Text = AAGTGCTGCCAGTCGT, Pattern = GTGCT*CC*GT*T
X = Sub-Pattern Matches Index

Index	0	1	2	3	4	5	6	7	8	9	10	11	12	13	14	15
Text	A	A	G	T	G	C	T	G	C	C	A	G	T	C	G	T
Pattern			G	T	G	C	T	-	C	C	-	G	T	-	-	T

Index	0	1	2	3	4	5	6	7	8	9	10	11	12	13	14	15
Subpattern-1		x														
Subpattern-2								x								
Subpattern-3											x					
Subpattern-4			x		x								x			x

Fig. 3. Table of Computation for finding pattern matching results.

Now we give an example to show how the computation of pattern matching is done on text using our table of computation (*ToC*) shown in Fig. 3. Let, Bob has the plaintext T = AAGTGCTGCCAGTCGT where $|T|$ = 16 and Alice has the pattern P = GTGCT*CC*GT*T with $0 \leq d \leq (16 - p_y)$ and $1 \leq y \leq 4$. Here, sub-patterns are P_1 = GTGCT, P_2 = CC, P_3 = GT, and P_4 = T. So the length vector (p_1, p_2, p_3, p_4) of sub-patterns is $(5, 2, 2, 1)$. Then Alice encrypts all sub-patterns using her key in a single polynomial by $Poly_2$ and sends it to Bob for pattern matching computation. Bob does the pattern matching according to Eqs. (6) and (7) and returns coefficients of x^{ly+d} to Alice in encrypted form. Alice then decrypts the coefficients and determine the indices where each sub-pattern matches the actual text or not using her *ToC* as shown in Fig. 3. Here, sub-patterns P_1, P_2, and P_3 match in the indices 2, 8, and 11 respectively. But sub-pattern P_4 matches in four places. Here, Alice considers only that index which is greater than the sum of the last index of sub-pattern-3 and its length ($>11+2$). So the index is 15. Finally, she computes gaps between sub-patterns and matches number of wildcards between sub-patterns. In this way, Alice finds her desired result using our protocol. Moreover, our algorithm does not match a pattern like CC*GT*GTGCT*T with given plaintext T though every sub-pattern exists in the plaintext. This mismatch happens because all sub-patterns do not occur sequentially in this case. Therefore, we can say that our algorithm accepts only sub-strings with the same order as in the main string. Furthermore, our algorithm determines only the single occurrence of the pattern P in the text T to reduce the complexity of computation.

Remark 3. Here our protocol does secure pattern matching between plaintext T of Bob and encrypted pattern $\bar{P}$ of Alice. Here Alice learns some extra information for pattern matching than she requires that also happened in the Yasuda et al. [7]. The goal of our protocol is to perform pattern matching by securing the pattern of Alice from Bob that is already preserved. Alice is securing her text using symmetric SwHE scheme in the semi-honest model. In addition, we say that our protocol acts as a building block of privacy-preserving repetitive wildcards pattern matching.

Table 1. Performance comparison for pattern matching computation with repetitive-wildcards

Parameters	Yasuda et al. method [7]	Our method
Time complexity	$\mathcal{O}(\sigma l - \delta)$	$\mathcal{O}(k(l+1) - \delta)$
Communication complexity	$\mathcal{O}(k\alpha)$	$\mathcal{O}(\alpha)$
No. of homomorphic multiplication	k	1
Text replacing behavior by a wildcard	One letter	Many letters

δ = total length of sub-patterns.
k = number of sub-patterns in the query.
α = communication cost for each query between Alice and Bob.

6   Performance Analysis

Here we evaluate our pattern matching result for both theoretically and practically in the following subsections.

6.1   Theoretical Evaluation

Usually, the performance of a computational research can be measured by complexity analysis. In this research, we address time and communication complexity analysis. Here, we also consider a performance parameter 'no. of homomorphic multiplication' due to cryptographic perspective and 'text replacing behavior by a wildcard'. Let us consider the same text T and pattern $\bar{P}$ with k sub-patterns. Now let α be the communication cost for each query between Alice and Bob. So we compare our privacy-preserving pattern matching method with that of [7] as shown in Table 1. At this point, we observe that the time complexities of the both methods are nearly same. But we have been able to reduce the communication complexity of [7] by a factor of k. Next, our method is able to handle k sub-patterns in three multiplications instead of $3k$ multiplications if we follow the method of [7]. Therefore, simplification of multiplication is done here. Moreover, in Yasuda et al. [7] method, a wildcard in the pattern replaces one letter in the text whereas in our method the same replaces many letters in the text. For designing a large pattern matching system, our pattern matching system is better than early research.

Table 2. Experimental comparison for pattern matching computation with repetitive-wildcards

n	q	k	Total time in milliseconds		δ	$\lg(t_{Adv})$
			Yasuda et al. [7]	Our method		
8192	49-bit	3	1359	437	1.00099	1150
		4	1766	438		
		5	2234	442		
16384	51-bit	3	2641	875	1.00052	2290
		4	3547	875		
		5	4437	875		
32768	53-bit	3	5375	1766	1.00027	4530
		4	7125	1786		
		5	8953	1796		
65536	55-bit	3	10750	3563	1.00014	8810
		4	14453	3564		
		5	18000	3609		
131072	57-bit	3	22500	7453	1.000073	17032
		4	30469	7453		
		5	38156	7484		

6.2 Experimental Settings and Results

We encoded the DNA alphabet set $\Sigma = \{$A, C, T, G$\}$ as $\Sigma = \{1, 2, 3, 4\}$ for simplifying our pattern matching computation. In addition, to experiment our secure protocol in Sect. 2.1, we implemented both our and Yasuda et al. [7] methods in C programming language using Pari C library (version 2.7.5) [24] and ran on a computer with Intel Core i7-4790 CPU with 3.60 GHz and 8 GB RAM. We compiled our C code using gcc 5.4.0 in Linux environment. Here, we have chosen the values of our required parameters (n, q, t, σ, k) carefully to comply with our method. We fixed the value of some parameters as $\sigma = 8, t = 2^8 n$, and vary other three parameters (n, q, k) for our experimental evaluation. We also considered the lattice dimension (n) ranging from 8192 to 131072. According to the work of [7], the value of q must be greater than $2^{11}nt\sigma = 2^{11} \cdot 2^{13} \cdot 2^{21} \cdot 2^3 = 2^{48}$ for the cipher-text space R_q. Therefore, we chose the value of modulus odd prime $q = 49 \sim 57$ bits. To serve our purpose of repetitive-wildcards pattern matching, we took three types of patterns with $k = 3 \sim 5$ where k is the number of sub-patterns existing in the pattern. We limit the value of k to $(3, 4, 5)$ to keep the lattice dimension n as low as possible for reducing the time complexity of the compu-tation. In addition, we considered mtDB as our text database of the length of 1000 and sub-patterns of length $9 \sim 15$. In these settings, we implemented both our and Yasuda et al. [7] methods for privacy-preserving repetitive wildcards pattern matching and compare their performances as shown in Table 2. Here we computed the total time for both of the methods in milliseconds (ms) required by the protocols including key generation, encryption, query, pattern matching, and decryption. From the first row of our experimental results in Table 2, we get total time taken by [7] method is 1359 ms whereas our method takes only 437 ms to match 3 sub-patterns with our text. So our system is $1359/437 \approx 3$ times faster than [7] for matching 3 sub-patterns with the text. Here same scenario preserved for the experimental results of other rows in Table 2. Therefore, our system is about k times faster than that of Yasuda et al. [7] for every parameter settings as shown in Table 2. Here, our coding is not fully optimized and the system has a low configuration as compared current high performance machine. Consequently, optimized code running on a highly configured machine can sup-port more text size and produce better results. As discussed in Sect. 4.1 of [8], we need to achieve more than 80-bit security $(\lg(t_{Adv}))$ for protecting our scheme from some distinguishing attacks. Here, we achieve the security level ranging from 1150-bit to 17032-bit for our different parameter settings and root Hermite factor $\delta < 1.0050$ as shown in Table 2. Therefore, our settings are able to pro-vide security from some distinguishing attacks. Here we also measured the time taken by key generation, encryption, pattern matching, and decryption for every parameter setting of our method. Here, the total time required for the highest settings as shown in the last row of Table 2 is 7484 ms where the time taken by key generation, encryption, pattern matching, and decryption are 47 ms, 891 ms, 6297 ms, and 249 ms respectively. Therefore, we can say that timings of key generation, encryption, and decryption at the client are low as compared to pattern matching time of our method.

Remark 4. Here we skip all the timings of key generation, encryption, pattern matching, and decryption for all parameters settings due to page limitation.

7   Conclusions

Throughout this article, we tried to show privacy-preserving repetitive-wildcards pattern matching using somewhat homomorphic encryption in the semi-honest model. For this reason, we propose a protocol and modified packing method to serve this purpose. We showed some real life applications. Here we applied our packing method in pattern matching for non-binary vectors. It is also applicable to a binary vector with multiple queries. In this article, we have discussed our method for normal text and encrypted multiple patterns. This method is also applicable when both the text and pattern are in encrypted form. Through this method, we have been able to provide a more succinct description for wildcards pattern matching computation than [7]. Furthermore, our packing method is not only applicable to SPM but also applicable to other secure computation fields. In addition, through our experimental results, we believe that our method will inspire future researchers to do large polynomial computations in a few multiplications wherever applicable.

Acknowledgment. This research is supported by KAKENHI Grant Numbers JP26540002, JP-24106008, and JP16H0175. The authors would like to thank Masaya Yasuda for his helpful comments which improve the presentation.

References

1. Rivest, R.L., Adleman, L., Dertouzos, M.L.: On data banks and privacy homomorphism. In: Foundations of Secure Computation, pp. 169–177. Academia Press (1978)
2. Lauter, K., Naehrig, M., Vaikuntanathan, V.: Can homomorphic encryption be practical? In: ACM Workshop on Cloud Computing Security Workshop, CCSW 2011, pp. 113–124, ACM, New York (2011)
3. Boneh, D., Goh, E.-J., Nissim, K.: Evaluating 2-DNF formulas on ciphertexts. In: Kilian, J. (ed.) TCC 2005. LNCS, vol. 3378, pp. 325–341. Springer, Heidelberg (2005). doi:10.1007/978-3-540-30576-7_18
4. Gentry, C.: Fully homomorphic encryption using ideal lattices. In: Symposium on Theory of Computing - STOC 2009, pp. 169–178. ACM, New York (2009)
5. Hu, Y.: Improving the efficiency of homomorphic encryption schemes. PhD diss., Worcester Polytechnic Institute, Massachusetts (2013)
6. Brakerski, Z., Vaikuntanathan, V.: Fully homomorphic encryption from Ring-LWE and security for key dependent messages. In: Rogaway, P. (ed.) CRYPTO 2011. LNCS, vol. 6841, pp. 505–524. Springer, Heidelberg (2011). doi:10.1007/978-3-642-22792-9_29
7. Yasuda, M., Shimoyama, T., Kogure, J., Yokoyama, K., Koshiba, T.: Privacy-preserving wildcards pattern matching using symmetric somewhat homomorphic encryption. In: Susilo, W., Mu, Y. (eds.) ACISP 2014. LNCS, vol. 8544, pp. 338–353. Springer, Heidelberg (2014). doi:10.1007/978-3-319-08344-5_22
8. Yasuda, M., Shimoyama, T., Kogure, J., Yokoyama, K., Koshiba, T.: Secure pattern matching using somewhat homomorphic encryption. In: ACM Workshop on Cloud Computing Security Workshop, CCSW 2013, pp. 65–76. ACM, New York (2013)
9. Jha, S., Kruger, L., Shmatikov, V.: Towards practical privacy for genomic computation. In: IEEE Symposium on Security and Privacy, 2008, pp. 216–230. IEEE (2008)
10. Blanton, M., Aliasgari, M.: Secure outsourcing of DNA searching via finite automata. In: Foresti, S., Jajodia, S. (eds.) DBSec 2010. LNCS, vol. 6166, pp. 49–64. Springer, Heidelberg (2010). doi:10.1007/978-3-642-13739-6_4
11. Katz, J., Malka, L.: Secure text processing with applications to private DNA matching. In: Proceedings of the 17th ACM Conference on Computer and Communications Security, pp. 485–492. ACM, New York (2010)

12. Baron, J., Defrawy, K., Minkovich, K., Ostrovsky, R., Tressler, E.: 5PM: secure pattern matching. In: Visconti, I., Prisco, R. (eds.) SCN 2012. LNCS, vol. 7485, pp. 222–240. Springer, Heidelberg (2012). doi:10.1007/978-3-642-32928-9_13

13. Yasuda, M., Shimoyama, T., Kogure, J., Yokoyama, K., Koshiba, T.: Practical packing method in somewhat homomorphic encryption. In: Garcia-Alfaro, J., Lioudakis, G., Cuppens-Boulahia, N., Foley, S., Fitzgerald, W.M. (eds.) DPM/SETOP -2013. LNCS, vol. 8247, pp. 34–50. Springer, Heidelberg (2014). doi:10.1007/978-3-642-54568-9_3

14. Yasuda, M., Shimoyama, T., Kogure, J., Yokoyama, K., Koshiba, Takeshi: Secure statistical analysis using RLWE-based homomorphic encryption. In: Foo, E., Stebila, D. (eds.) ACISP 2015. LNCS, vol. 9144, pp. 471–487. Springer, Heidelberg (2015). doi:10.1007/978-3-319-19962-7_27

15. Defrawy, E.K., Faber, S.: Blindfolded data search via secure pattern matching. Computer 46(12), 68–75 (2013). IEEE

16. Hazay, C., Toft, T.: Computationally secure pattern matching in the presence of malicious adversaries. J. Cryptology 27(2), 358–395 (2014). Springer, Heidelberg

17. GenBank Home on National Center for Biotechnology Information. http://www.ncbi.nlm.nih.gov/genbank/

18. Lyubashevsky, V., Peikert, C., Regev, O.: On ideal lattices and learning with errors over rings. In: Gilbert, H. (ed.) EUROCRYPT 2010. LNCS, vol. 6110, pp. 1–23. Springer, Heidelberg (2010). doi:10.1007/978-3-642-13190-5_1

19. Clancy, T.C., Kiyavash, N., Lin, D.J.: Secure smartcard based fingerprint authentication. In: Proceedings of the 2003 ACM SIGMM Workshop on Biometrics Methods and Applications, pp. 45–52. ACM, New York (2003)

20. Goldwasser, S., Micali, S.: Probabilistic encryption & how to play mental poker keeping secret all partial information. In: Proceedings of the Fourteenth Annual ACM Symposium on Theory of Computing, pp. 365–377. ACM, New York (1982)

21. ElGamal, T.: A public key cryptosystem and a signature scheme based on discrete logarithms. In: Blakley, G.R., Chaum, D. (eds.) CRYPTO 1984. LNCS, vol. 196, pp. 10–18. Springer, Heidelberg (1985). doi:10.1007/3-540-39568-7_2

22. Cohen, J.D., Fischer, M.J.: A robust and verifiable cryptographically secure election scheme. In: 26th Annual Symposium on Foundations of Computer Science, 1985, pp. 372–382. IEEE (1985)

23. Paillier, P.: Public-key cryptosystems based on composite degree residuosity classes. In: Stern, J. (ed.) EUROCRYPT 1999. LNCS, vol. 1592, pp. 223–238. Springer, Heidelberg (1999). doi:10.1007/3-540-48910-X_16

24. The PARI~Group, PARI/GP version 2.7.5, Bordeaux (2014). http://pari.math.u-bordeaux.fr/

25. Castryck, W., Iliashenko, I., Vercauteren, F.: Provably weak instances of Ring-LWE revisited. In: Fischlin, M., Coron, J.-S. (eds.) EUROCRYPT 2016. LNCS, vol. 9665, pp. 147–167. Springer, Heidelberg (2016). doi:10.1007/978-3-662-49890-3_6

Privacy-Aware Data Sharing in a Tree-Based Categorical Clustering Algorithm

Mina Sheikhalishahi[1,2(✉)], Mohamed Mejri[1],
Nadia Tawbi[1], and Fabio Martinelli[2]

[1] Department of Computer Science, Université Laval, Québec City, Canada
{mohamed.mejri,nadia.tawbi}@ift.ulaval.ca
[2] Istituto di Informatica e Telematica, Consiglio Nazionale delle ricerche, Pisa, Italy
{mina.sheikhalishahi,fabio.martinelli}@iit.cnr.it

Abstract. Despite being one of the most common approaches in unsupervised data analysis, a very small literature exists in applying formal methods to address data mining problems. This paper applies an abstract representation of a hierarchical categorical clustering algorithm (CCTree) to solve the problem of privacy-aware data clustering in distributed agents. The proposed methodology is based on rewriting systems, and automatically generates a global structure of the clusters. We prove that the proposed approach improves the time complexity. Moreover a metric is provided to measure the privacy gain after revealing the CCTree result. Furthermore, we discuss under what condition the CCTree clustering in distributed framework produces the comparable result to the centralized one.

Keywords: Distributed clustering · Algebra · Rewriting · Formal methods · Privacy

1 Introduction

Clustering is a very well-known tool in unsupervised data analysis, which has been the focus of significant research in different domains, spanning from information retrieval, text mining, scientific data exploration, to medical diagnosis [1]. Clustering refers to the process of partitioning a set of data points into groups, such that the elements in the same group are more similar to each other rather than to the ones in other groups. Despite its benefit in a wide range of applications, very few works exist to express and solve the problems of clustering algorithms in terms of formal methods [13].

In the present work, we apply the abstract representation of a categorical clustering algorithm, named CCTree [12], to formalize the process of distributed

This research has been partially supported by the EU Funded Projects H2020 C3IISP, GA #700294, H2020 NeCS, GA #675320, EIT Digital MCloudDaaS and partially by the Natural Sciences and Engineering Research Council of Canada (NSERC).

© Springer International Publishing AG 2017
F. Cuppens et al. (Eds.): FPS 2016, LNCS 10128, pp. 161–178, 2017.
DOI: 10.1007/978-3-319-51966-1_11

clustering. Distributed clustering is mainly applied when the data are originally collected at different sites [6]. Generally, for global benefit, the distributed agents are interested in obtaining a global structure of clusters on the whole data, whilst for privacy issues they are unwilling to share their own datasets, except when a desired level of privacy is guaranteed [2]. For example, the Center for Disease Control (master agent) is interested to use the result of clustering on patients' records in different hospitals (agents) to identify the trends and patterns of diseases. The result on whole dataset brings the benefit for all agents to find the better treatment. However, for privacy concerns, the hospitals are unwilling to disclose the patients' records, unless that a privacy level is satisfied [9].

In this study, we address the problem of privacy-aware distributed CCTree clustering. To this end, first each agent clusters her own dataset with the use of CCTree algorithm [12]. Then, each agent sends the abstract structure of the clusters to a master agent (honest but curious). The abstract schema of clusters is published if it preserves the required privacy of data holder. The master agent aggregates the result of clusters to get a global structure of CCTree such that each agent is able to homogenize her own clusters based on the global structure. The whole process performed by the master agent is formalized with the use of a *rewriting system*. Rewriting system as a well established mathematical structure automatically creates a new desired final result applying the correctly specified rules [3].

The contributions of the present work can be summarized as follows:

- Two rewriting systems are provided in order to automatically verify the compliance of an element of our algebraic structure to a CCTree structure, and moreover to get automatically a global CCTree structure from the abstract schema of CCTrees collected from distributed agents.
- We prove that the proposed rewriting systems terminate and produce the unique result. Furthermore, we state that under which condition the result of our distributed CCTree clustering is comparable with the centralized one.
- A metric is provided for a data holder to measure the privacy gain after revealing the structure of CCTree on her data in order to decide weather to participate in data sharing or not.

The paper is organized as follows. In Sect. 2, the required background knowledge for the proposed methodology is provided. In Sect. 3, we apply the abstract CCTree representation to formalize CCTree distributed clustering in terms of rewriting systems. In Sect. 4, we present a review of the literature. We conclude and point to the future directions of the research in Sect. 5.

2   Background

In present section, we give some required background information.

2.1   CCTree Construction

CCTree [12] is constructed iteratively through a decision tree-like structure, where the leaves of the tree are the desired clusters. The root of the CCTree contains all the elements to be clustered. Each element is described through a set of *categorical* attributes. Being categorical, each attribute may assume a finite set of discrete values, constituting its domain. At each step, a new level of the tree is generated by splitting the nodes of the previous levels, when they are not homogeneous enough. *Shannon Entropy* is used both to define a homogeneity measure called *node purity*, and to select the attribute used to split a node. In particular non-leaf nodes are divided trough the attribute yielding the maximum value for Shannon entropy. The separation is represented through a branch for each possible outcome of the specific attribute. Each branch or edge extracted from the parent node is labeled with the selected feature which directs data to the child node. A node is considered as a leaf if it respects one of the stop conditions criteria, i.e. (1) the number of elements is fewer than a threshold "μ", or (2) the node purity is better than "ε". Figure 1 depicts a simple CCTree.

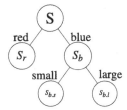

Fig. 1. A small CCTree

2.2   Rewriting Systems

A *rewriting rule* is an ordered pair, written as $x \rightarrow y$ of terms x and y. Similar to equations, rules are applied to replace instances of x by corresponding instances of y. Unlike equations, rules are not applied to replace instances of the right-hand side y [3]. A *term* over signature $\mathcal{G}$, constants $\mathcal{K}$, and variables $\mathcal{X}$ is either a variable $x \in \mathcal{X}$, a constant $k \in \mathcal{K}$, or an expression of the form $g(t_1, t_2, \ldots, t_n)$, where $g \in \mathcal{G}$ is a function symbol of n arguments, and t_i are terms [3]. A *derivation* for a rule "$\rightarrow$" is a sequence of the form "$t_0 \rightarrow t_1 \rightarrow \ldots$". An element t is *reducible* (with respect to $\rightarrow$), if there is an element u such that "$t \rightarrow u$"; otherwise it is considered as *irreducible*. A *rewrite system* R is a set of rewrite rules, $t \rightarrow u$, where t and u are term. The term u is "$\rightarrow$ *normal*" form of t, if "$t \rightarrow^* u$" and u is irreducible via $\rightarrow$, where "$\rightarrow^*$" means that continuously the transition is applied. A relation $\rightarrow$ is *terminating*, if there is no infinite derivations "$t_0 \rightarrow t_1 \rightarrow \ldots$" which means that it does not reach to a normal term. A relation $\rightarrow$ is *confluent*, if there is an element v such that "$s \rightarrow^* v$" and "$t \rightarrow^* v$" whenever "$u \rightarrow^* s$" and "$u \rightarrow^* t$" for some elements s, t and u. A relation $\rightarrow$ is *convergent*, if it is terminating and confluent. Convergent rewriting system are interesting, because all derivations lead to a unique normal form [3]. A *conditional rule* is an equational implication in which the term in the conclusion is oriented. We use the form "$x_1 = u_1 \wedge \ldots \wedge x_n = u_n \mid x \rightarrow y$" to show that under the conditions "$x_1 = u_1 \wedge \ldots \wedge x_n = u_n$" we have "$x \rightarrow y$".

2.3   Feature-Cluster Algebra

In this section, we present *feature-cluster algebra* proposed in [13] which abstracts CCTree representation in terms of a *term*. We proved in [13] that under the condition of having an order among the set of features, the proposed term *fully abstracts* CCTree structure. Full abstraction guarantees that a CCTree structure and its counterpart CCTree term can be applied one instead of the other. In what follows, we briefly present the notations of CCTree abstraction [13] which will be exploited in present study.

(I) Semiring of features: Assume that a *set of disjoint attributes*, denoted as $\mathcal{A}$, is given, where the *carrier set* of each attribute $A_i \in \mathcal{A}$ is denoted by $\mathcal{V}_{A_i}$. We call the *union* of the attributes, denoted as $\mathbb{V} = \bigcup_{A_i \in \mathcal{A}} \mathcal{V}_{A_i}$, the set of *values* or *features*. For example, the set of attributes could be $\mathcal{A} = \{color, size\}$, where $\mathcal{V}_{color} = \{red, blue\}$, and $\mathcal{V}_{size} = \{small, large\}$. Consequently, the set of features equals to $\mathbb{V} = \{red, blue, small, large\}$. Let $\mathbb{F} = \mathcal{P}(\mathcal{P}(\mathbb{V}))$ be the power set of the power set of $\mathbb{V}$. We denote $1 = \{\emptyset\} \in \mathbb{F}$ and $0 = \emptyset \in \mathbb{F}$, and the operations "$+$" and "$\cdot$" on $\mathbb{F}$ are respectively defined as "$F_i + F_j = F_i \cup F_j$" and "$F_i \cdot F_j = \{X_s \cup Y_t : X_s \in F_i, Y_t \in F_j\}$" for $F_i, F_j \in \mathbb{F}$ [13]. Hence, F belongs to $\mathbb{F}$, if it respects one of the following syntax forms: $F := 0 \mid \{\{f\}\} \mid F \cdot F \mid F + F \mid 1$, where $f \in \mathbb{V}$. Then, the quintuple $(\mathbb{F}, +, \cdot, 0, 1)$ constitutes a commutative semiring.

(II) Semiring of elements: Let us consider that the set of the attributes $\mathcal{A} = \{A_1, A_2, \ldots, A_k\}$ is given. We say s belongs to *the set of elements* $\mathbb{S}$, if $s \in \mathcal{V}_{A_1} \times \mathcal{V}_{A_2} \times \ldots \times \mathcal{V}_{A_k} \times \mathbb{N}$, where $\mathbb{N}$ is the set of *natural* numbers. Hence, $s \in \mathbb{S}$ can be written as $s = (x_1, x_2, \cdots, x_k, n)$, where $x_i \in \mathcal{V}_{A_i}$ for $1 \leq i \leq k$, and $n \in \mathbb{N}$ represents the *ID* of an element. For the sake of simplicity, we may use the alternative representation $x_i \in A_i$ instead of $x_i \in \mathcal{V}_{A_i}$. In our problem, $\mathbb{S}$ is the set of all elements that one desires to cluster. As the result of having different sets of elements to be clustered in distributed clustering, we define a semiring of the power set of all elements as follows. Two operations "$+$" and "$\cdot$" are defined on the elements of $\mathcal{P}(\mathbb{S})$ (the power set of $\mathbb{S}$) as "$S_i + S_j = S_i \cup S_j$" and "$S_i \cdot S_j = S_i \cap S_j$", respectively, for $S_i, S_j \in \mathcal{P}(\mathbb{S})$. Formally, we say S belongs to the *set of elements* $S \in \mathcal{P}(\mathbb{S})$, if it respects one of the syntax forms:

$S := \emptyset \,|\, S' \,|\, S + S \,|\, S \cdot S \,|\, \mathbb{S}$, where $S' \subseteq \mathbb{S}$. Then, the quintuple $(S, +, \cdot, \emptyset, \mathbb{S})$ is a commutative semiring [13].

Definition 1 (Feature-Cluster (Family) Term). *The set of* feature-cluster family terms *on* $\mathbb{V}$ *and* $\mathbb{S}$, *denoted as* $\mathbb{FC}_{\mathbb{V},\mathbb{S}}$ *(or simply* $\mathbb{FC}$ *if it is clear from the context), is the smallest set containing elements satisfying the following conditions:*

$$
\begin{array}{llll}
if & S \subseteq \mathbb{S} & then & S \in \mathbb{FC} \\
if & F \in \mathbb{F}_1, S \subseteq \mathbb{S} & then & F \diamond S \in \mathbb{FC} \\
if & \tau_1 \in \mathbb{FC}, \tau_2 \in \mathbb{FC} & then & \tau_1 + \tau_2 \in \mathbb{FC}
\end{array}
$$

In this case, we call S *and* $F \diamond S$ *a* feature-cluster term *and the addition of one or more feature-cluster terms is called* feature-cluster family term. *We may simply use* $\mathbb{FC}$-term *to refer to a feature-cluster family term. We define the* block *function, which receives an* $\mathbb{FC}$-term *and returns the set of its blocks as the following:*

$block : \mathbb{FC} \to \mathcal{P}(\mathbb{FC})$
$block(S) = \{S\}$, $block(F \diamond S) = \{F \diamond S\}$, $block(\tau_1 + \tau_2) = block(\tau_1) \cup block(\tau_2)$

In the case that no feature specifies S *directly, it is called an* atomic *term. The set of all atomic terms is denoted as* $\mathcal{A}$.

Definition 2 (CCTree Term). *A term resulting from a CCTree structure, or equivalently transformable to a CCTree structure, is called a* CCTree term.

Example 1. The CCTree term resulted from Fig. 1 is written as follows:

$$\tau = red \diamond S + blue \cdot small \diamond S + blue \cdot large \diamond S$$

where the symbol "$\cdot$" is used to separate the features specifying a cluster, the symbol "$+$" is applied to separate different clusters from each other, and "$\diamond$" is exploited to represent that a cluster is resulted from which main dataset. The latter property is desirable in the process of distributed clustering, where data are clustered in different agents.

Definition 3 (Term). *We call* τ *a* term, *if it has one of the following forms:* $\tau := S \,|\, F \diamond S \,|\, \tau + \tau \,|\, \tau \cdot \tau$, *where* $S := \emptyset \,|\, S' \,|\, S + S \,|\, S \cdot S \,|\, \mathbb{S}$ *and* $F := 0 \,|\, \{\{f\}\} \,|\, F + F \,|\, F \cdot F \,|\, 1$. *The set of terms on* $\mathbb{S}$ *and* $\mathbb{F}$ *is denoted as* $\mathbb{C}_{\mathbb{S},\mathbb{F}}$, *or abbreviated as* $\mathbb{C}$.

Definition 4 (Feature-Cluster Algebra). *The quintuple* $(\mathbb{C}, "+", "\cdot", 0 \diamond \emptyset, 1 \diamond \mathbb{S})$ *is an idempotent commutative semiring which is called a* feature-cluster algebra.

Definition 5 (Order Rewriting Rule). *Let an ordered set of features* $(\mathbb{V}, <)$ *be given. An* $\mathbb{FC}$-term *is called an* ordered $\mathbb{FC}$-term *on* $(\mathbb{V}, <)$, *if it is the normal form of the following rewriting rule:*

$$f_1 \cdot f_2 \diamond S \rightarrow_o f_2 \cdot f_1 \diamond S \qquad if \qquad f_1 < f_2 \quad \forall\, f_1, f_2 \in \mathbb{V}$$

Moreover, we define a rewriting rule which orders the features of an $\mathbb{FC}$*-term based on an attribute* $A \in \mathcal{A}$ *as* $f_2 \cdot f_1 \diamond S \xrightarrow{A}_o f_1 \cdot f_2 \diamond S$ *for* $f_1 \in A$*. We represent the normal form of a term* τ *applying above rewriting rule, based on attribute* A*, as* $\tau \Downarrow_A$*.*

To avoid the confusion of different representations of an $\mathbb{FC}$-term, in what follows we present the definitions of *factorized* and *non factorized* terms. In the provided examples, attributes $Color = \{r(ed), b(lue)\}$, $Size = \{s(mall), l(arge)\}$, and $Shape = \{c(ircle), t(riangle)\}$ are used to describe the terms.

Definition 6 (Factorized Term). *We define the* factorization *rewriting rule through an attribute* $A \in \mathcal{A}$*, denoted as* $\xrightarrow{A}$*, from an* $\mathbb{FC}$*-term to its factorized form as the following:*

$$f \cdot \tau_1 + f \cdot \tau_2 \xrightarrow{A} f \cdot (\tau_1 + \tau_2) \qquad for \qquad f \in A$$

we denote the normal form of applying the factorization rewriting rule on term τ *applying factorized rewriting rule, through attribute* A *as* $\tau \downarrow_A$*, and the set of factorized forms of* $\mathbb{FC}$ *is denoted by* $\mathbb{FC} \downarrow$*. A term after factorization is called a* factorized term*.*

Definition 7 (Non Factorized Term). *We define the* defactorized *rewriting rule on an* $\mathbb{FC}$*-term as "*$f \cdot (\tau_1 + \tau_2) \rightarrow_d f \cdot \tau_1 + f \cdot \tau_2$*". A normal term resulted from defactorized rewriting rule is called a* non factorized term*. A non factorized form of the term* τ *is denoted as* $\tau \uparrow$*. The set of non factorized forms of the terms of* $\mathbb{FC}$ *are denoted by* $\mathbb{FC} \uparrow$*.*

Example 2. For factorization we have: $(r \cdot s \diamond S + r \cdot c \diamond S + b \cdot s \diamond S) \downarrow_{color} = r \cdot (s \diamond S + c \diamond S) + b \cdot s \diamond S$, and for defactorization we obtain: $r \cdot (s \diamond S + c \diamond S) + b \cdot s \diamond S \rightarrow_d r \cdot s \diamond S + r \cdot c \diamond S + b \cdot s \diamond S$.

In the following, we present a set of relations on feature-cluster algebra, introduced in [13], which are applicable in our methodology for distributed clustering.

Definition 8 (Attribute Division). *Attribute division* $(\mathcal{D}_\mathcal{A})$ *is a function from* $\mathcal{A} \times \mathbb{FC}$ *to* {True, False}*, which gets an attribute and a non factorized* $\mathbb{FC}$*-term as input; it returns* True *or* False *as follows:*

$$\mathcal{D}_\mathcal{A}(A, S) = \text{False}$$
$$\mathcal{D}_\mathcal{A}(A, f \diamond S) = \text{True} \qquad if \quad f \in A$$
$$\mathcal{D}_\mathcal{A}(A, f \diamond S) = \text{False} \qquad if \quad f \notin A$$
$$\mathcal{D}_\mathcal{A}(A, f \cdot F \diamond S) = \mathcal{D}_\mathcal{A}(A, f \diamond S) \vee \mathcal{D}_\mathcal{A}(A, F \diamond S)$$
$$\mathcal{D}_\mathcal{A}(A, \tau_1 + \tau_2) = \mathcal{D}_\mathcal{A}(A, \tau_1) \wedge \mathcal{D}_\mathcal{A}(A, \tau_2)$$

The concept of attribute division is used to order the attributes presented in a term.

Definition 9 (Initial). *We define the* initial *(δ) function from $\mathcal{P}(\mathbb{FC} \uparrow)$ to $\mathcal{P}(\mathbb{F})$, which gets a set of ordered non factorized terms on $(\mathbb{V}, <)$ and returns a set of the first features of each term as follows:*

$$\delta(\emptyset) = \{0\}, \ \delta(\{S\}) = \{1\}, \ \delta(\{f \cdot F \diamond S\}) = \{f\}, \ \delta(\{\tau_1 + \tau_2\}) = \delta(\{\tau_1\}) \cup \delta(\{\tau_2\})$$

In the case that the input set contains just one term, we remove the brackets, i.e. $\delta(\{\tau\}) = \delta(\tau)$ when $|\{\tau\}| = 1$. Moreover, when the output set also contains just one element, for the sake of simplicity we remove the brackets, i.e. $\delta(X) = \{f\} = f$ for $X \in \mathcal{P}(\mathbb{FC} \uparrow)$. The initial function will be used in the process of evaluating that if a term represents a CCTree term, considering that in a CCTree the sibling features (first features in an ordered term) belong to the same attribute.

Definition 10 (Derivative). *We define the* derivative*, denoted by ∂, as a function which gets an ordered non factorized $\mathbb{FC}$-term on $(\mathbb{V}, <)$, i.e. $\partial : \mathbb{FC} \uparrow \mapsto \mathcal{P}(\mathbb{FC})$; it returns the term (set of terms) by cutting off the first features as follows:*

$$\partial(S) = \emptyset, \ \partial(f \diamond S) = \{S\}, \ \partial(f \cdot F \diamond S) = \{F \diamond S\}, \ \partial(\tau_1 + \tau_2) = \partial(\tau_1) \cup \partial(\tau_2)$$

The derivative function is defied to be used in the process of evaluating if a term represents CCTree term. More precisely, if the first level features in an ordered term (siblings in tree) belong to the same attributes, with derivative function we remove first features to evaluate if the sub-terms (sub-trees) also represent CCTree term.

Note that the functions initial *(δ) and* derivative *(∂) are overloaded to the input, depending on the input that if it is a tree or a term.*

Definition 11 (Order of Attributes). *We say attribute B is smaller or equal to attribute A on the non factorized term $\tau \in \mathbb{FC} \uparrow$, denoted as $B \preceq_\tau A$, if the number of blocks of τ that B divides, is less than (equal to) the number of blocks that A divides. Formally, $B \preceq_\tau A$ implies that:*

$$|\{\underset{i}{\tau} \in block(\tau) \mid \mathcal{D}_\mathcal{A}(B, \underset{i}{\tau}) = True\}| \leq |\{\underset{i}{\tau} \in block(\tau) \mid \mathcal{D}_\mathcal{A}(A, \underset{i}{\tau}) = True\}|$$

Given a set of attributes $\mathcal{A}$ and a term τ, the set $(\mathcal{A}, \preceq_\tau)$ is a lattice. We denote the upper bound of this set as $\sqcap_{\mathcal{A},\tau}$. This means that we have $\forall A \in \mathcal{A} \Rightarrow A \preceq_\tau \sqcap_{\mathcal{A},\tau}$.

Example 3. In the following we show how the order of attributes of a term is identified. Suppose the term $\tau = r \cdot s \diamond S + r \cdot c \diamond S + b \cdot s \diamond S$ is given. We have: $block(\tau) = \{r \cdot s \diamond S, r \cdot c \diamond S, b \cdot s \diamond S\}$. Consequently, we obtain:

$$|\{\tau_i \in block(\tau)|\mathcal{D}_\mathcal{A}(shape, \tau_i) = True\}| = 1$$
$$\leq |\{\tau_i \in block(\tau)|\mathcal{D}_\mathcal{A}(size, \tau_i) = True\}| = 2$$
$$\leq |\{\tau_i \in block(\tau)| \mathcal{D}_\mathcal{A}(color, \tau_i) = True\}| = 3$$

which means that we have "*shape* $\preceq_\tau$ *size* $\preceq_\tau$ *color*". Namely, the attribute "*color*" is the one which appears in all the blocks of term τ. We notify that in CCTree the first attribute from the root is the one which appears in all the blocks of the equivalent CCTree term. For example, in the CCTree term of Example 1, the attribute color exists in all blocks.

Features Ordering. Recalling that not having the predefined order among features creates a problem in full abstraction of terms [13]. To this end, here we propose a way to order the set of features which is appropriate to our problem. Given an $\mathbb{FC}$-term τ, we find the order of attributes according to Definition 11, whilst if for two arbitrary attributes A and A', we have $A = A'$, without loss of generality, we choose a strict order among them, say $A \prec A'$. Then in each attribute we arbitrarily (and fix) order the features.

Definition 12 (Ordered Unification). *Ordered unification ($\mathcal{F}$) is a partial function from $\mathcal{P}(\mathcal{A}) \times \mathbb{FC} \uparrow$ to $\mathbb{FC} \downarrow$, which gets a set of attributes and a non factorized term; it returns the normal form of rewriting rule $\xrightarrow{A}_o$ (Definition 5), iteratively, based on the order of attributes on received term as follows:*

$$\mathcal{F}(\emptyset, \tau \uparrow) = \tau, \quad \mathcal{F}(\{A\}, \tau \uparrow) = \tau \Downarrow_A, \quad \mathcal{F}(\mathcal{A}, \tau) = \mathcal{F}(\sqcap_{\mathcal{A}, \tau}, \mathcal{F}(\mathcal{A} - \{\sqcap_{\mathcal{A}, \tau}\}, \tau \uparrow))$$

The normal form of ordered unification is called a unified term. *By $\mathcal{F}^*(\tau)$ we mean that $\mathcal{F}$ is performed iteratively on the set of ordered attributes on τ to get the unified term.*

Ordered unification function *by automatically ordering the features of a term, as explained before, directs the shape of a term to be easily verified if it is a CCTree term.*

Example 4. To find the unified form of $\tau_1 = r \cdot s \diamond S + r \cdot c \diamond S + b \cdot s \diamond S$, we have:

$$\mathcal{F}^*(\tau_1) = \mathcal{F}(\{shape, color, size\}, \tau_1 \uparrow) = \mathcal{F}(color, \mathcal{F}(size, \mathcal{F}(shape, \tau_1)))$$
$$= r \cdot s \diamond S + r \cdot c \diamond + b \cdot s \diamond S$$

Definition 13 (Well-formed Term). Well formed function, *denoted as W, is a binary function from $\mathbb{FC} \uparrow$ to $\{$True, False$\}$, which gets a unified non factorized $\mathbb{FC}$-term $\tau \uparrow$; it returns True if $\delta(\tau \uparrow)$ is equal to one of the attributes belonging to $\mathcal{A}$; it returns False otherwise. Formally:*

$$W(\tau \uparrow) = \begin{cases} \text{True } if & \exists \ A_i \in \mathcal{A} \quad s.t. \quad \delta(\tau \uparrow) = A_i \\ \text{False} & otherwise \end{cases}$$

A unified term τ is called a well formed term, *if $W(\tau) = True$.*

An atomic term is considered as a *well formed term*. Basically, well-form function verifies if in a unified non factorized term the first level features belong to the same attribute or not, as expected for CCTree structure.

Theorem 1. *A unified term represents a CCTree term, or it is transformable to a CCTree structure, if and only if, (1) it can be written in the form $\mathcal{F}^*(\tau) = \sum_i f_i \cdot \tau_i$, such that (1) "$W(\mathcal{F}^*(\tau)) = True$", i.e. the unified form of the received term is a well formed term; and (2) the unified form of each τ_i is a well formed term as well ($W(\tau_i) = True$) and (3) each τ_i respects above requirements [13].*

3   Distributed Private CCTree Clustering

Data clustering has become increasingly exploited in a wide range of applications, spanning from molecular biology to marketing [1]. In many areas, the data are collected in different sites, for instance different hospitals. Due to the privacy issues, each data holder may prevent to publish her own dataset, unless some privacy level is guaranteed [9]. To this end, each agent computes the amount of privacy leakage when the clustering algorithm result is published comparing to the publishing of the original dataset. If this difference is higher than her desired threshold, then she will share her CCTree; Otherwise she refuses to participate in collaborative CCTree construction.

Afterwards, the result of each CCTree in each participated agent is transformed to its equivalent CCTree term. The resulted CCTree terms are reported to the master agent (honest but curious) for composition. The CCTree terms are composed automatically based on our proposed composition rewriting rules (Table 2), which creates a final CCTree term that all terms can be homogenized to it. Therefore, the composition result is reported to each agent to homogenize CCTree terms, and consequently the structure of all CCTrees. Figure 2 depicts a high level representation of such an architecture.

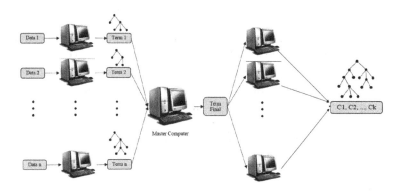

Fig. 2. Distributed clustering workflow.

In what follows, we first prove that if all agents fix the stop condition (the minimum number of elements in leaves) of CCTree equal to μ, then publishing the result as a CCTree term satisfies k-anonymous dataset (k is dependent to μ) [4]. Then, we propose *CCTree rewriting system* which automatically verifies the compliance of a term to a CCTree structure. Afterward, we come up with the *composition rewriting system*, which is exploited to find a global CCTree term from the addition of several CCTree terms (received from distributed agents). At the end of the section, we prove that the proposed methodology results in (1) a unique CCTree term from the addition of several CCTree terms, (2) the process of finding the global CCTree terminates, (3) the time complexity improves in distributed system, comparing to centralized one, and finally (4) under some condition the CCTree, resulted from the distributed architecture, is comparable to the centralized schema.

3.1 Privacy-Aware Data Sharing

In [5], a statistical framework is proposed to measure the amount of privacy which is violated through publishing the result of a classifier. We extend the same notations for publishing the result of our clustering algorithm. This privacy violation is formally measured as what follows. Given a distribution (P, U, S), where P is public data that everyone including the adversary can access, S refers to sensitive data we are trying to protect, and U is data not known by the adversary. The resulted structure of CCTree say $\mathcal{C}$, i.e. CCTree term, is available to adversary which can be used to predict U given P. Assume that t samples $\{(p_1, s_1), \ldots, (p_t, s_t)\}$ are already available to adversary. The goal is to test whether revealing the resulted $\mathcal{C}$ increases the ability of adversary to predict S values for unseen samples. It is expected that $\mathcal{C}$ would not be much more accurate than random guess, and the adversary is not able to improve her own estimation about S applying $\mathcal{C}$. Formally, this concept is measured through Bayes error, and means that for all classifiers using P the Bayes error should bed the same as the Bayes error of all classifiers using $(P, \mathcal{C}(P))$. Formally, given $\mathcal{C}$ and t samples from P and S, if $\rho(t) = \rho\{t; P, S\}$ and $\rho(t; \mathcal{C}) = \rho\{t; P, \mathcal{C}(P), S\}$ be the Bayes errors for classifiers using P only and using $P, \mathcal{C}(P)$ respectively, and considering $\bar{\rho} = \lim_{t \to \infty}$, and $\bar{\rho}(\mathcal{C}) = \lim_{t \to \infty} \rho(t; \mathcal{C})$, we have the upcoming definition from [5].

For $0 \le p \le 1$, the result of CCTree $\mathcal{C}$ is (t, p) privacy violating if $\rho(t; \mathcal{C}) \le \rho(t) - p$, and the clustering $\mathcal{C}$ is (∞, p)- privacy violating if $\bar{\rho}(\mathcal{C}) \le \bar{\rho} - \rho$.

Under this definition, if an agent finds that distributing her CCTree violates her privacy requirement, she can refuse to participate in sharing the resulting CCTree on her dataset.

3.2 CCTree Rewriting System

In order to be able to define some rules on a term to verify if it satisfies CCTree structure, it is required to define the concept of *Component* of a term. Roughly speaking, a component of a CCTree term refers to sub-tree in CCTree structure. Hence, when we want to check the compliance of a term to a CCTree structure, we need to verify it iteratively through sub-terms, as the iterative structure of CCTree.

Definition 14 (Component). *Given two ordered non factorized $\mathbb{FC}$-terms τ_1 and τ_2 on $(\mathbb{V}, <)$, we define the* component *relation, denoted by $\sim$, as the first level comparison of the terms as $\tau_1 \sim \tau_2 \Leftrightarrow \delta(\tau_1) = \delta(\tau_2)$.*

Let the ordered term $\tau \in \mathbb{FC} \uparrow$ on $(\mathbb{V}, <)$ be given. The equivalence class of $\tau' \in block(\tau)$ is called a component *of τ, and it is formally defined as:*

$$[\overset{\prime}{\tau}]_{\tau} = \{\tau_i \in block(\tau) \mid \overset{\prime}{\tau} \sim \tau_i\}$$

The set of all components of the term τ through the equivalence relation $\sim$, is denoted by "$block(\tau)/\sim$" or simply "$\tau/\sim$", i.e. we have: $\tau/\sim = \{[\tau_i]_{\tau} \mid \tau_i \in block(\tau)\}$.
We order the components of term τ according to the order of features in $\mathbb{V}$ as following:

$$[\overset{\prime}{\tau}]_{\tau} < [\overset{\prime\prime}{\tau}]_{\tau} \quad \Leftrightarrow \quad (\ \forall f' \in \delta([\overset{\prime}{\tau}]) \, , \, \forall f'' \in \delta([\overset{\prime\prime}{\tau}]) \Rightarrow f' < f'')$$

since the features are ordered strictly, the components are also ordered strictly.

Example 5. Consider the ordered form of the term τ_1 in Example 4, i.e. $\tau_1 = r \cdot s \diamond S + r \cdot c \diamond S + b \cdot s \diamond S$. The components of $\tau_1 \uparrow$ are $\{r \cdot s \diamond S, r \cdot c \diamond S\}$ (all blocks begin with r) and $\{b \cdot s \diamond S\}$ (all blocks begin with b). Moreover if in the first feature ordering we have $r > b$, then $\{r \cdot s \diamond S, r \cdot c \diamond S\} > \{b \cdot s \diamond S\}$.

To verify automatically if a term is a CCTree term, a set of conditional rewriting rules are provided in Table 1. The term $\emptyset$ in this table, refers to a *null* term. In this regard, the CCTree rewriting system is applied on a received term; the term is a CCTree term if the only irreducible term is $\emptyset$. In this rewriting system, $[[f(\tau)]]$ means that the semantics of $f(\tau)$ is replaced, whilst the result is considered as one unique term. Furthermore, $\tau_1 : \tau_2$ contains two terms τ_1 and τ_2, whilst each one is considered as a new term. Moreover, $[\tau]_i$ refers to the i'th component of "$\tau/\sim$" [13].

Table 1. CCTree rewriting system

(1) $(\tau \in \mathcal{A}) \mid \tau \to \emptyset$
(2) $(\tau \neq \mathcal{F}^*(\tau)) \mid \tau \to [[\mathcal{F}^*(\tau)]]$
(3) $(\tau = \mathcal{F}^*(\tau)) \wedge (W(\tau)) \wedge (\tau \notin \mathcal{A}) \mid \tau \to [[\Sigma_{\tau_k \in [\tau]_1} \partial(\tau_k)]] \ : \ \dots \ : \ [[\Sigma_{\tau_k \in [\tau]_{|\tau/\sim|}} \partial(\tau_k)]]$

The first rule of Table 1 specifies that if a term is an atomic term, it is directed to $\emptyset$. The second rule expresses that if a term is not in unified form, it is required to be transformed to its unified representation. The third rule specifies that if a non atomic unified term is well formed, it is divided to the derivative of its components. The last rule is used to verify whether the CCTree conditions satisfy for the following components or not, resulting from the iterative structure of CCTree. These rules are following the structure of Theorem 1 in identifying if a term is in compliance with a CCTree structure.

Example 6. Suppose that the term $\tau_1 = a_1 \diamond S + b_1 \diamond S$, with the set of attributes $A = \{a_1, a_2\}, B = \{b_1, b_2\}$, are given. We apply the CCTree rewriting rules to automatically verify if τ_1 is a CCTree term. The term τ_1 is not atomic. Moreover, we have $\tau_1 = \mathcal{F}^*(\tau_1)$ and "$W(\tau_1) = False$" since the first features of the components of τ_1 are not equal. There is no CCTree rewriting rule which can be applied, whilst this term is not $\emptyset$. This means that the received term τ_1 is not a CCTree term.

As another instance, we show that the term $\tau_2 = a_1 \diamond S + a_2 \diamond S$ with the set of attributes $A = \{a_1, a_2\}, B = \{b_1, b_2\}$, is a CCTree term.

$$(\tau_2 = \mathcal{F}^*(\tau_2)) \wedge (W(\tau_2)) \mid a_1 \diamond S + a_2 \diamond S \xrightarrow{(3)} S : S \xrightarrow{(1)} \emptyset : \emptyset$$

The condition of this conditional rewriting rule verifies that if the term is in unified form, and if in unified form all first features belong to the same attribute or not. If so, then the terms is broken to its components, to verify the same condition for following sub-terms. Since by removing the first features, atomic terms (terms without feature specifying them) are ontained each one is directed to a *null* term. There is no irreducible term except $\emptyset$, hence, τ_2 is a CCTree term.

3.3   Composition Rewriting System

To address the composition process, a set of *composition rewriting rules* (Table 2) are proposed to obtain automatically a CCTree term when a term is not a CCTree term. The *split* relation (4'th rule of Table 2) is added to the rules of Table 1 to get CCTree term from non CCTree term.

Definition 15 (Split). *Suppose that a unified term $\tau \in \mathbb{FC} \uparrow$ on $(\mathbb{V}, <)$ and the set of attributes $\mathcal{A}$, is given. Considering $\sqcap_{\mathcal{A}, \tau}$ as the upper bound attribute of τ, we define the* split *relation as what follows:*

$$split(\tau) = \begin{cases} \tau & if \quad W(\tau) = True \\ \sum_{\tau_i \in block(\tau)} \zeta(\tau_i) & if \quad W(\tau) = False \end{cases}$$

where:

$$\zeta(\tau) = \begin{cases} \tau_i & if \quad \mathcal{D}_{\mathcal{A}}(A, \tau_i) = True \\ (\sum_{a_i \in \sqcap_{\mathcal{A}, \tau}} a_i) \cdot \tau_i & if \quad \mathcal{D}_{\mathcal{A}}(A, \tau_i) = False \end{cases}$$

This means that all the blocks of τ which do not contain any feature of $\sqcap_{\mathcal{A}, \tau}$ are multiplied to the addition of the features of $\sqcap_{\mathcal{A}, \tau}$. In the following example we show how split relation is applied.

Example 7. Suppose that the term $\tau_2 = r \cdot s \diamond S + c \diamond S + b \diamond S$ is given. We have $W(r \cdot s \diamond S + r \cdot c \diamond S + b \diamond S) = False$, hence, τ_2 is not a well formed term. Considering that $\sqcap_{\mathcal{A}, \tau_2} = color$, and $\mathcal{D}_{\mathcal{A}}(colro, r \cdot s \diamond S) = True$, $\mathcal{D}_{\mathcal{A}}(colro, r \cdot c \diamond S) = True$, $\mathcal{D}_{\mathcal{A}}(colro, b \diamond S) = False$, we have: $split(r \cdot s \diamond S + c \diamond S + b \diamond S) = r \cdot s \diamond S + (r + b) \cdot c \diamond S + b \diamond S = r \cdot s \diamond S + r \cdot c \diamond S + b \cdot c \diamond S + b \diamond S$.

Actually, when a term is not a CCTree term, it is possible to infer it from its unified form when the first features of its components do not belong to the same attribute. Therefore, the split rule is proposed to generate a well formed term from a non CCTree term. In what follows, we add the split rule to the previous rewriting system, which is used when a term is not a CCTree term to obtain a CCTree term.

The composition rewriting rules to get a CCTree term from a non CCTree term is presented in Table 2. In the proposed rewriting system, $[[f(\tau)]]$ means that the semantic of $f(\tau)$ is replaced, whilst the result is considered as one unique term, not several terms. Furthermore, $\tau_1 : \tau_2$ contains two terms τ_1 and τ_2, whilst each one is considered as a new term; and $[\tau]_i$ refers to the i'th component of $\tau/\sim$. Comparing to Table 1, just the *split rule* is added. This rule guarantees that if a term is not a CCTree term, how by splitting the term based on the upper bound attribute we may get a CCTree term.

Table 2. Composition Rewriting System

(1) $(\tau \in \mathcal{A}) \mid \tau \to \emptyset$
(2) $(\tau \neq \mathcal{F}^*(\tau)) \mid \tau \to [[\mathcal{F}^*(\tau)]]$
(3) $(\tau = \mathcal{F}^*(\tau)) \wedge (W(\tau)) \wedge (\tau \notin \mathcal{A}) \mid \tau \to [[\Sigma_{\tau_k \in [\tau]_1} \partial(\tau_k)]] : \ldots : [[\Sigma_{\tau_k \in [\tau]_{|\tau/\sim|}} \partial(\tau_k)]]$
(4) $(\tau = \mathcal{F}^*(\tau)) \wedge (\sim W(\tau)) \mid \tau \to [[split(\tau)]]$

To this end, first of all, the set of attributes $\mathcal{A}$ describing the received term τ is provided. Note that in categorical clustering algorithm, the set of attributes are known beforehand. The set of attributes and non CCTree term are given to the composition rewriting system. When the conditions of the rule $(\tau = \mathcal{F}^*(\tau)) \wedge (W(\tau)) \mid \tau \to [[\Sigma_{\tau_k \in [\tau]_1} \partial(\tau_k)]] : \ldots : [[\Sigma_{\tau_k \in [\tau]_{|\tau/\sim|}} \partial(\tau_k)]]$ respects for a term τ, we save τ. Then all $[[\Sigma_{\tau_k \in [\tau]_i}]]$ of τ are replaced by their own successive terms respecting this rule. This process is repeated iteratively till reaching to atomic terms in all derivations. The result of this term is the desired CCTree term.

Example 8. Suppose that the addition of two CCTree terms is given as $\tau = a_1 \diamond S + a_2 \diamond S + b_1 \diamond S' + b_2 \diamond S'$, with the set of attributes $A = \{a_1, a_2\}, B = \{b_1, b_2\}$. It is easy to verify that τ is not a CCTree term from the rules of Table 1. We are interested to find a CCTree term from the received non CCTree term τ, with the use of composition rewriting system. To this end we have:

(i) $(\tau = \mathcal{F}^*(\tau)) \wedge (\sim W(\tau)) \mid \tau \xrightarrow{(4)} [[split(\tau)]]$

(ii) $[[split(\tau)]] = \tau' = a_1 \diamond S + a_2 \diamond S + (a_1 + a_2) \cdot b_1 \diamond S' + (a_1 + a_2) \cdot b_2 \diamond S'$

(iii) $(\tau' \neq \mathcal{F}^*(\tau')) \mid \tau' \xrightarrow{(2)} [[\mathcal{F}^*(\tau')]] = (a_1 \cdot (S + b_1 \diamond S') + a_2 \cdot (S + b_1 \diamond S')) = \tau''$

(iv) $(\tau'' = \mathcal{F}^*(\tau'')) \wedge (W(\tau'')) \mid \tau'' \xrightarrow{*(3)*} S + b_1 \diamond S'(I) : S + b_1 \diamond S'(II)$

(I) $S + b_1 \diamond S' \xrightarrow{(4)} (b_1 + b_2) \cdot S + b_1 \diamond S' \xrightarrow{(2)} b_1 \cdot (S + S') + b_2 \diamond S$
$\xrightarrow{*(3)*} S + S' : S \xrightarrow{(1)} \emptyset : \emptyset$

(II) $S + b_1 \diamond S' \xrightarrow{(4)} (b_1 + b_2) \cdot S + b_1 \diamond S' \xrightarrow{(2)} b_1 \cdot (S + S') + b_2 \cdot S$
$\xrightarrow{*(3)*} S + S' : S \xrightarrow{(1)} \emptyset : \emptyset$

To find the resulted CCTree term, we consider the terms respecting the rule (3), shown with $*(3)*$. Hence, we have them as: $(*) a_1 \cdot (S + b_1 \diamond S') + a_2 \cdot (S + b_1 \diamond S')$, $(**) b_1 \cdot (S + S') + b_2 \diamond S$, $(* * *) b_1 \cdot (S + S') + b_2 \cdot S$.

Then, since $(**)$ results from this term $S + b_1 \diamond S'$ inside $(*)$, and $(* * *)$ from term $S + b_1 \diamond S'$ inside $(*)$, we replace them to their previous form:

$$a_1 \cdot (b_1 \cdot (S + S') + b_2 \diamond S) + a_2 \cdot (b_1 \cdot (S + S') + b_2 \cdot S)$$

Since there is no more term respecting rule (3), the above term is the desired CCTree term. It can automatically be verified that the resulted term is a CCTree term (Table 1).

After that the final CCTree term, resulting from the composition of two (or more) CCTree terms, is returned to the distributed devices, the CCTree term of each agent has to be extended to the final CCTree term. The extension of each CCTree term to a final CCTree term will homogenize the structure of all CCTrees. To this end, it is enough to add a CCTree term with the final CCTree term. Then, all *split* rules applied on CCTree term in the process of its composition with final CCTree term, shows the required split in the associated CCTree structure, following the procedure of transforming a term to tree provided in [13].

3.4   Confluent Rewriting Systems

In this section, we first present what the termination and confluence of a rewriting system mean. Furthermore, through several theorems, we prove our proposed rewriting systems are terminating and confluent. Termination and confluence are the interesting properties of a rewriting system, which guarantee that firstly, applying the rewriting rules of the proposed system, there is no infinite loop of rules, and furthermore, we always get a unique result.

Termination and Confluence of a Rewriting System. A rewriting system is terminating, if there is no infinite derivation "$t_1 \rightarrow t_2 \rightarrow t_3 \rightarrow \ldots$" in R. This implies that every derivation eventually ends to a normal form [3]. Lankford theorem claims that a rewriting system R is terminating, if for some *reduction ordering* "$>$", we have "$x > y$" for all rules "$x \rightarrow y \in R$". An order is a reduction ordering, if it is *monotonic* and *fully invariant* [3]. A relation is monotonic if it preserves the order through adding or reduction a term in both sides, and it is fully invariant, if it preserves the order when a term is substituted in both sides of the relation [3]. An element t in the rewriting system R is locally confluent if for all $x, y \in R$ such that "$t \rightarrow x$" and "$t \rightarrow y$", there exists $u \in R$ such that "$x \rightarrow^* u$" and "$y \rightarrow^* u$". If every $t \in R$ is locally confluent, then $\rightarrow$ is called locally confluent. Newman's lemma expresses that a terminating rewriting system is confluent if and only if it is locally confluent [3].

Theorem 2. *The CCTree rewriting system is terminating.*

Proof. To prove this theorem we first define a *reduction order* on the rules of CCTree rewriting system. To this end, we define the *size* function which gets an

$\mathbb{FC}$-term and returns the number of features appeared in the term as follows: $size : \mathbb{FC} \rightarrow \mathbb{N}$, such that $size(S) = 1$, $size(f \diamond S) = 1$, $size(F \cdot \tau) = |F| + size(\tau)$, $size(\tau_1 + \tau_2) = size(\tau_1) + size(\tau_2)$ and we consider $size(\emptyset) = 0$, and $size(\tau_1 : \tau_2) = size(\tau_1) + size(\tau_2)$.

We say $\mathbb{FC}$-term τ_1 is smaller than $\mathbb{FC}$-term τ_2, denoted by $\tau_1 \leq \tau_2$, if the number of features in τ_1 is less than the number of features in τ_2, or equally $size(\tau_1) \leq size(\tau_2)$. This partial ordering is well-founded, since there is no infinite descending chain (number of features are limited). It is monotonic, because the property of number of features in two terms is preserved when a term is added or reduced in both sides. Furthermore, the substitution in left and right sides, preserves the order of number of features, i.e. it is fully invariant. Therefore, the proposed ordering is a reduction ordering.

Considering that $\emptyset$ is a null term containing no feature, in the first rule we have *atomic term* $> \emptyset$. In the second one, the conditional rule is just applied when the term is not equal to its unified form; whilst the ordered unification function, if applied, does not change the number of features, i.e. $\tau \geq \mathcal{F}^*(\tau)$ for $\tau \neq \mathcal{F}^*(\tau)$, since $size(\tau) = size(\mathcal{F}^*(\tau))$. Worth noticing that this rule is a one step rule, such that when the term is unified, the other rules are exploited. In the third rule, the first features of all components of the left term are removed, i.e. the size (number of features) of the left-hand term is greater than the size (number of features) in the right-hand one. Hence, the proposed reduction ordering $\leq$ on CCTree rewriting system, so the system is terminating. □

Theorem 3. *The CCTree rewriting system is confluent.*

Proof. In CCTree rewriting system, all rules are conditional and there is no term for which two (or more) conditions are satisfied at the same time. This means that the possibility of having $\tau \rightarrow \tau_1$ and $\tau \rightarrow \tau_2$ where $\tau_1 \neq \tau_2$, does not happen. Hence, the rewriting system is locally confluent. According to Newman's lemma, the CCTree rewriting system being terminating (Theorem 2) and locally confluent, it is confluent. □

Theorem 4. *The composition rewriting system is confluent.*

Proof. The only rule added to composition rewriting system comparing to CCTree rewriting system, is the rule *split*. We show that *split* rule is not contradicting the termination and confluence of rewriting system. First of all, the *split* rule is one step rule, i.e. the result of *split* rule, after one step application, is considered as the premise of other rules (which decreases the term). On the other hand, on each term, the *split* rule is applied at most equal to the number of attributes (finite). Hence, since the *split* by itself is one step rule, and for each term it is called finite times, the composition rewriting system is terminating.

On the other hand, there is no term respecting at the same time two (or more) conditions of composition rewriting system, i.e. there is no term τ for which $\tau \rightarrow \tau_1$ and $\tau \rightarrow \tau_2$, where $\tau_1 \neq \tau_2$. This means that composition rewriting system is locally confluent. Therefore, the composition rewriting system is terminating and locally confluent, and hence, from Newman's lemma, it is confluent. □

3.5 Complexity and Result Comparison Between Centralized and Distributed CCTree Clustering

In what follows, we discuss on time complexity improvement for CCTree clustering in distributed devices, compared to centralized one. Furthermore, we state under what condition the CCTree resulted from distributed schema equals to centralized one.

Theorem 5. *Let us consider N to be the total number of elements desired to be clustered, k be the number of attributes, v_{max} be the maximum number of values in an attribute, and K be the maximum number of non leaf nodes. The time complexity of constructing CCTrees in n distributed devices equals to $\frac{1}{n} \cdot O(K \times (N \times m + N \times v_{max}))$.*

Proof. In [11], the time complexity of constructing a CCTree has been calculated. Recalling again, consider N as the number of elements in whole dataset, N_i be the number of elements in node i, m be the total number of features, v_l the number of features of attribute A_l, k the number of attributes, and $v_{max} = max\{v_l\}$. For constructing a CCTree, if $K = m + 1$ be the maximum number of non leaf nodes, which arise in a complete tree, then the maximum time required for constructing a CCTree with N elements equals to $O(K \times (N \times m + N \times v_{max}))$. Now if we equally divide the dataset containing N points to n devices, it takes $O(K \times ((N/n) \times m + (N/n) \times v_{max})) = \frac{1}{n} \cdot O(K \times (N \times m + N \times v_{max}))$ to create n CCTrees, i.e. the whole required time will be divided to the number of devices. The other part of algebraic calculations requires constant time.   □

Definition 16 (Kullback-Leibler Divergence). *Let P and Q be two probability distributions on $A_1 \times A_2 \times \ldots \times A_k$, where $A_i \in \mathcal{A}$, $\forall \leq i \leq k$ (the set of attributes in CCTree clustering). Then, Kullback-Leibler divergence [7] from Q to P, denoted by $D_{KL}(P||Q)$, is a measure gained comparing the probability distribution Q with the probability distribution P, as follows:*

$$D_{KL}(P||Q) = \sum\nolimits_{X_i \in A_1 \times A_2 \times \ldots \times A_k} p(X_i) \log \frac{p(X_i)}{q(X_i)}$$

whilst whenever $\log \frac{p(X_i)}{q(X_i)} \to \infty$, then we set $\log \frac{p(X_i)}{q(X_i)}$ to 1.

From the above definition, if for two datasets D_1 and D_2 with the probability distributions P_1 and P_2, respectively, we have the result of $D_{KL}(P_1||P_2)$ is close to zero, then it means that they have almost the same data distribution. Consequently, they will produce *similar* CCTrees.

Theorem 6. *Let D_1 and D_2 be two datasets with the probability distributions P_1 and P_2 (as Definition 16), respectively. If $D_{KL}(P_1||P_2) = 0$, then $CCTree(D_1) = CCTree(D_2)$.*

Proof. The proof is resulted from the fact that the structure of CCTree is dependent to the attribute selected for dividing the data in each node. If the distribution of elements in two dataset are almost equal, it means that the same attribute in both causes the highest Shannon entropy, and hence, the one selected for data division through branches labeled the features of selected attribute.   □

Theorem 6 states that if for two datasets the probability distributions are equal, it results in having equal CCTree structure for both agents. In other words, when *Kullback-Leibler divergence* of two probability distribution tends to zero, the result of our distributed framework produces the more similar result to the centralized system. Extending the result to more than two datasets, it can be expressed as follows. Let N datasets $D_1, D_2, \ldots, D_n$ with the probability distributions $P_1, P_2, \ldots, P_n$, respectively, be given. If $D_{KL}(P_i \| P_j) = 0$ for all $1 \le i, j \le n$, then the CCTree resulted from our distributed framework equals to CCTree of centralized system. The more the probability distribution is divergent (higher Kullback-Leibler divergence result), the more it is possible that the final CCTree in distributed framework be different from the centralized one. In future work, we plan to verify this topic in more detail through real use case experiments.

4   Related Work

The problem of knowledge extraction among multiple parties involved in a data mining task has been presented in [14]. The studied methodology aims at performing data mining without data disclosure between the parties. This methodology relies on homomorphic encryption and digital envelope techniques. These techniques suffer from the drawback of being applicable to only a small set of data analysis functions. Also they impose a considerable overhead. In [8], the basic paradigms and the notions of secure multiparty computation and its relation to privacy preserving data mining has been surveyed. Still it only works on data mining algorithms that apply the proposed computations. Clifton et al. [2] propose a toolkit for different applications required in privacy preserving distributed data mining. Data transformation methods have been proposed in [10] for privacy preserving clustering. In [9], a general framework is proposed to formalize the architecture of privacy preserving data mining in collaborative system. However, to the best of our knowledge, the present study is amongst the very first efforts in applying algebraic structure for addressing data mining issues.

5   Conclusion

In the present work, an abstract representation of a categorical clustering algorithm, named CCTree, is used to address the problem of privacy-aware distributed clustering. Generally for global benefit, the distributed agents are interested to share their information to get the global structure of their own data. However, for privacy concerns, the agents in distributed system are unwilling to disclose their datasets. To address the aforementioned challenges in distributed CCTree clustering, we proposed a rewriting system which automatically returns a CCTree term, in a way that all CCTrees in distributed agents can be homogenized. The termination and confluence of the proposed rewriting system have been proven, which guarantees first of all we have no infinite loop in applying the proposed rewriting systems, and moreover, the resulted final term is unique.

In future directions, we plan to apply the proposed methodology in realistic case studies to evaluate its efficiency in distributed clustering. Moreover, we plan to generalize the proposed approach for a wide range of distributed categorical clustering where the features play an important role in identifying the clusters, thence, applicable in abstraction.

References

1. Berkhin, P.: A survey of clustering data mining techniques. In: Kogan, J., Nicholas, C., Teboulle, M. (eds.) Grouping Multidimensional Data, pp. 25–71. Springer, Heidelberg (2006)
2. Clifton, C., Kantarcioglu, M., Vaidya, J., Lin, X., Zhu, M.Y.: Tools for privacy preserving distributed data mining. SIGKDD Explor. Newsl. **4**(2), 28–34 (2002)
3. Dershowitz, N., Jouannaud, J.: Rewrite systems. In: van Leeuwen, J. (ed.) Handbook of Theoretical Computer Science, vol. b, pp. 243–320. MIT Press, Cambridge (1990)
4. Fung, B.C.M., Wang, K., Chen, R., Yu, P.S.: Privacy-preserving data publishing: a survey of recent developments. ACM Comput. Surv. **42**(4), 14:1–14:53 (2010)
5. Kantarcioğlu, M., Jin, J., Clifton, C.: When do data mining results violate privacy? In: Proceedings of the Tenth ACM SIGKDD International Conference on Knowledge Discovery and Data Mining, KDD 2004, pp. 599–604. ACM, New York (2004)
6. Kriegel, H.P., Kroger, P., Pryakhin, A., Schubert, M.: Effective and efficient distributed model-based clustering. In: Fifth IEEE International Conference on Data Mining (2005)
7. Kullback, S., Leibler, R.A.: On information and sufficiency. Ann. Math. Statist. **22**, 79–86 (1951)
8. Lindell, Y., Pinkas, B.: Secure multiparty computation for privacy-preserving data mining (2008)
9. Martinelli, F., Saracino, A., Sheikhalishahi, M.: Modeling privacy aware information sharing systems: a formal and general approach. In: 15th IEEE International Conference on Trust, Security and Privacy in Computing and Communications (2016)
10. Oliveira, S.R.M., Zaïane, O.R.: Achieving privacy preservation when sharing data for clustering. In: Jonker, W., Petković, M. (eds.) SDM 2004. LNCS, vol. 3178, pp. 67–82. Springer, Heidelberg (2004). doi:10.1007/978-3-540-30073-1_6
11. Sheikhalishahi, M., Mejri, M., Tawbi, N.: Clustering spam emails into campaigns. In: Library, S.D. (ed.) 1st Conference on Information Systems Security and Privacy (2015)
12. Sheikhalishahi, M., Saracino, A., Mejri, M., Tawbi, N., Martinelli, F.: Fast and effective clustering of spam emails based on structural similarity. In: Garcia-Alfaro, J., Kranakis, E., Bonfante, G. (eds.) FPS 2015. LNCS, vol. 9482, pp. 195–211. Springer, Heidelberg (2016). doi:10.1007/978-3-319-30303-1_12
13. Sheikhalishahi, M., Mejri, M., Tawbi, N.: On the abstraction of a categorical clustering algorithm. In: Perner, P. (ed.) MLDM 2016. LNCS (LNAI), pp. 659–675. Springer, Heidelberg (2016). doi:10.1007/978-3-319-41920-6_51
14. Zhan, Z.J.: Privacy-preserving collaborative data mining. Doctoral Dissertation (2006)

Three Views of Log Trace Triaging

Raphaël Khoury[✉], Sébastien Gaboury, and Sylvain Hallé

Laboratoire d'informatique formelle, Département d'informatique et de
mathématique, Université du Québec à Chicoutimi, Saguenay, Canada
{raphael.khoury,s1gabour}@uqac.ca, shalle@acm.org

Abstract. This paper extends previous work on execution trace triaging. We examine the problem of trace triaging along three of the four views used in the study of temporal properties, namely the automata-theoretic view, the temporal logic view and the set-theoretic view. For each case, we propose several partitions of universe of possible traces into equivalence classes, which follow naturally from the chosen view and form the basis for trace triaging.

1 Introduction

The problem of log trace triaging consists of partitioning a set of traces into meaningful equivalence classes, with respect to the evaluation of a sequential property over these traces. Stated more formally, triaging can be seen as a generalization of trace verification, replacing its two-valued (pass/fail) result with membership in one of potentially many equivalence classes—thus providing a more detailed feedback about the status of compliance or violation of the trace. As a simple example, consider the property "eventually, either a or b will hold", and the two traces cca and ccb. Checking the property in the classical way would return the same verdict ("true") for both; however, one could imagine multiple ways of creating a finer classification: separating traces that fulfill the property because a holds from those where b holds, or according to the length of their longest non-compliant prefix, and so on.

So far, log trace triaging has been the subject of scarce literature; as we shall see, the closest line of works concentrates on bug classification. However most techniques either require human intervention, lack a formal definition, or perform a form of partitioning that does not satisfy the definition of an equivalence class. There is therefore a need for an automated and formally-grounded partitioning methodology. In previous work, we introduced the basic concepts of such a trace classification, as approached from the angle of Linear Temporal Logic [27]. In particular, we introduced the concept of *trace hologram*, a tree structure resulting from the evaluation of an LTL formula on a specific trace. When interpreted as equivalence classes, manipulations on these holograms cluster event traces into various natural categories, many of which correspond to intuitive ways of grouping them.

© Springer International Publishing AG 2017
F. Cuppens et al. (Eds.): FPS 2016, LNCS 10128, pp. 179–195, 2017.
DOI: 10.1007/978-3-319-51966-1_12

However, temporal logic is but one of four equivalent *views* in which formal properties about traces can be stated and verified. These views, as defined in a paper by Chang et al., also include automata, language theory and topology [10]. Therefore, in this paper, we build on previous work by approaching the problem of trace triaging also from the automata-theoretic and language-theoretic viewpoints. We shall show that the concepts introduced earlier, namely of creating equivalence classes based on some criterion computed from the evaluation of a temporal formula, have equivalents in finite-state automata and language theory. We will describe multiple ways of classifying traces with respect to a property; in some cases, we also demonstrate that some of these classifications subsume others.

Such a partitioning of event traces into equivalence classes can have several applications in the understanding, debugging and maintenance of complex software systems. For example, in test case generation, it may be desirable to select from the possibly infinite set of possible program behaviors, a finite subset of test cases that covers every possible type of behavior of interest. One possible way of doing so could be by picking one trace in each equivalence class defined by some triaging rule. When debugging, one can use triaging to narrow down the analysis on a subset of recorded traces for which the execution has violated a property in a particular manner. Triaging can also help system administrators minimize the overhead of record-keeping, since for many applications, records of a single trace in each equivalence class can be sufficient, if we can determine that the set of classes ranges over every possible behavior of interest. Finally, equivalence classes also provide an easy way to perform trace reduction (also called trace abstraction): abstracting a trace simply amounts to replacing it with the shortest trace that belongs to the same equivalence class. For all these reasons, the study of property-based partitioning of event traces introduced in this paper shall prove to be a stepping stone towards the achievement of these goals.

In this paper, we present a theoretical framework that guides the triaging of traces into meaningful subclasses, and permits new classifications schemes to be defined, and compared with existing ones. We show how the problem of trace triaging can be examined from each of three different views of temporal specifications defined in the literature, namely temporal logic, automata and language theoretic, and that each view gives rises to different classifications. Indeed, a classification that can be easily stated and performed when operating in a given view can be difficult of impossible to express under a different view.

The remaining of this paper proceeds as follows: Sect. 2 introduces preliminary notions related to traces and formalism. In Sect. 3, we review our previous work on trace triaging, which approached the problem from the perspective pf temporal logic view. Sections 4 and 5 propose triaging based on two additional views, namely automata theoretic and language theoretic. Section 6 surveys related works. Concluding remarks are given in Sect. 7.

2   Preliminaries

Let Σ be a finite or countably infinite set of events, each of which is assumed to be a set of name-value pairs. An execution trace is a finite sequence of events, and captures the behaviour of a system at runtime. We let σ, τ range over sequences. Let Π be a set of attribute names, and V be a set of values; event i in a trace σ is a partial function $\sigma_i : \Pi \rightarrow V$ that assigns a value to attributes. Σ^* denotes the set of all traces and $acts(\sigma)$ is the set of events occurring in trace σ. We write σ_* for the ultimate event of sequence σ. The concatenation of sequences σ and σ' is given as $\sigma; \sigma'$.

2.1   Log Trace Triaging and Temporal Specifications

Trace triaging is the problem of sorting traces into meaningful categories. In other words, it is the task of devising a triaging function $\kappa : \Sigma^* \rightarrow C$, with $C \subseteq \mathbb{P}(\Sigma^*)$, the selector, that maps each trace to a class $c \in C$. For a given triaging function κ we write $[\![c]\!]_\kappa$ for the set of traces $S \subseteq \Sigma^*$ such that $\sigma \in S \Leftrightarrow \kappa(\sigma) = c$. The subscript κ is omitted when clear from context.

Let $p \in \Pi$ be some attribute, $\sigma, \sigma' \in \Sigma^*$ two traces that are identical, except that at their i-th event, $\sigma_i(p) \neq \sigma'_i(p)$; where $a(p)$ indicates the valuation of attribute p in event a. These two traces are said to be (p, i)-different. A formula φ is said to be p-invariant if, for any pair of (p, i)-different traces σ, σ', $\sigma \models \varphi \Leftrightarrow \sigma' \models \varphi$.

This concept is best illustrated through an example. Let $\varphi \equiv \mathbf{G}\,(\mathrm{p} = 0)$, and the following two traces composed of a single event: $\sigma = \{(\mathrm{p}, 0), (\mathrm{q}, 0)\}$, $\sigma' = \{(\mathrm{p}, 0)\}$. One can see that σ and σ' are $(\mathrm{q}, 0)$-different, since $\sigma(\mathrm{q}) = \{0\}$ and $\sigma'(\mathrm{q}) = \emptyset$. Intuitively, it is clear that the truth value of φ is the same for any two (q, i)-different traces, and hence that φ is q-invariant.

Let φ be a specification of property of interest in the context in which the traces are generated and triaged. Any useful selector κ should respect the two following properties (from [27]).

Definition 1 (Coherence). *A selector κ is called* coherent *if and only if:*

$$\forall c \in C : \forall \sigma, \sigma' \in [\![c]\!]_\kappa : \sigma \models \varphi = \sigma' \models \varphi.$$

Informally, this first property states that a category cannot contain both compliant and non-compliant traces. The second property states that two traces that are not meaningfully different with respect to the property of interest should be placed in the same category:

Definition 2 (Consistency). *A selector κ is called* consistent *if and only if: for each $p \in \Pi$, if φ is p-invariant and σ, σ' are two (p, i)-different traces, then $\kappa(\sigma) = \kappa(\sigma')$.*

We say that a triaging function is *reasonable* when it is both coherent and consistent. If we let $\kappa : \Sigma^* \rightarrow C$ and $\kappa' : \Sigma^* \rightarrow C'$ be two selectors, we say that κ is finer than κ' (written $\kappa \preceq \kappa'$) if $\forall \sigma \in \Sigma^* : \kappa(\sigma) \subseteq \kappa(\sigma')$.

2.2   The Four Views of Temporal Specifications

According to Chang et al. [10], a given property φ can be visualized along any one of four distinct views: temporal logic, automata, language theory and topology. In this paper, we approach the problem of trace triaging from the first three of these four views. We argue that since each view gives rise to a different property representation and a different verification mechanism, each view should also give rise to a different trace triaging paradigm. This intuition is illustrated in Fig. 1.

Varvaressos et al. [27] introduced trace holograms, as a mechanisms to generate and represent triaging functions. An hologram is an abstraction of the tree generated when verifying the satisfaction of an LTL formula on a trace. Several triaging schemes occur naturally when specific information (e.g. nodes or node labels) is deleted from the tree. Two distinct traces can thus be considered equivalent and classified into the same category. In an analogous manner, if the desired property is stated as an automaton, the verification process generates a path over the states of the automaton, which can also be abstracted to produce a trace categorization. A similar reasoning can be applied to the language theoretic representation of properties.

The ability to examine the same property along multiple alternative view has several advantages, as a given property may be more concise, or more readily understandable or checkable, given the chosen representation. Alternative representations also give rise to alternative verification algorithms, and thus to different tools. Likewise, one of the main advantages of a multi-paradigm view of trace triaging, is that a given partitioning of Σ^* might be stated in a natural and intuitive manner in a given view of temporal properties, but the same classification would be difficult to achieve if a different view of temporal properties were used.

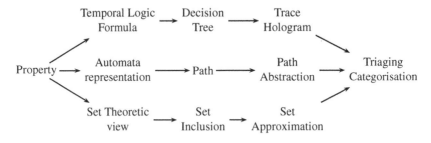

Fig. 1. The alternative views of log trace triaging

3   Temporal Logic View

In previous work [27], it was shown how the use of a formal specification of a system's expected behaviour, expressed as formulæ of Linear Temporal Logic (LTL), can be used as the basis for a classification of execution traces. By repeatedly applying the recursive rules defining the semantics of LTL operators, the evaluation of a LTL formula φ on a trace σ induces a tree. Figure 2 shows such a tree for the formula $\mathbf{G}\,(a \to \mathbf{X}\,b)$, evaluated on the trace cab; the top-level operator of that formula, $\mathbf{G}$, corresponds to the top-level node of the tree. According to the semantics of LTL, $\mathbf{G}\,\varphi$ is true if and only if φ is true for every suffix of the current trace. The tree hence spawns three child nodes, corresponding to the evaluation of $a \to \mathbf{X}\,b$ for traces cab, ab and b, respectively. Taking the first such child node, the top-level operator now becomes $\to$; this operator evaluates to $\top$ when, on the current trace, either a evaluates to $\bot$ or $\mathbf{X}\,b$ evaluates to $\top$. This, in turn, spawns to child nodes corresponding to each condition, and so on. Provided that n-ary operators are evaluated in a fixed order, this structure is uniquely defined for a given formula and a given trace.

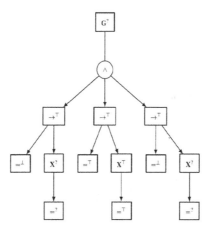

Fig. 2. Evaluating an LTL formula on a trace induces a tree.

As a first classification, we take κ to be the function that associates each trace to its hologram. We have demonstrated in earlier work that such a classification is reasonable [27]. However, different traces are likely to have different holograms. We introduce a number of systematic rules by which pieces of an hologram can be taken off. Applying these rules has for effect that traces with originally different holograms may now belong to the same category, thereby merging trace categories.

3.1   Fail-Fast Deletion

The first deletion pattern is the fail-fast deletion. It consists of deleting all children of a temporal operator node that no longer have an influence on its truth value. Figure 3 shows the procedure for the $\mathbf{G}$ operator; φ is an arbitrary subformula, and the symbols $\star_i$ represent its truth value for each event, with the additional condition that $\star_i \neq \bot$ for $1 \leq i < n$. The box φ_n hence represents the first child node that evaluates to $\bot$. One can see in Fig. 3b that all subtrees

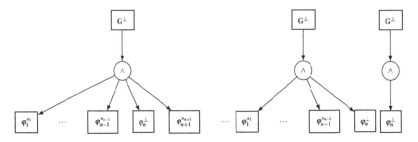

Fig. 3. Two deletion patterns for the **G** operator. (a) Original hologram (b) After fail-fast deletion (c) After polarity deletion

following φ_n are deleted. Intuitively, this represents the fact that, once the n-th event has φ evaluate to $\bot$, then $\mathbf{G}\,\varphi$ itself evaluates to $\bot$, no matter how φ evaluates on the subsequent events.

Consider for example the formula $\mathbf{G}\,(a \rightarrow \mathbf{X}\,b)$, and the two traces $caaa$ and $caac$. Originally, these two traces have different holograms; however, the application of fail-fast deletion on both holograms results in the same output, and the two traces become members of the same category. This corresponds to the intuitive notion that one does not care what follows in a trace once a violation has occurred. Note however that the trace $cacc$ is still considered distinct, since the reason for the failure is different (a "c", rather than an "a", occurred instead of the expected "b"). A dual rule for the **F** operator can also be devised, by swapping the roles of $\top$ and $\bot$.

3.2   Polarity Deletion

Fail-fast deletion applies only to temporal operators. As an extension of that rule, one may only keep nodes that are sufficient to decide on the value of an expression. For example, if the expression $\varphi \wedge \psi$ evaluates to $\bot$ because φ evaluates to $\bot$, then it is not necessary to conserve ψ, since its truth value has no effect on the result (and dually for the $\vee$ operator). Similarly, if the formula $\mathbf{G}\,\varphi$ evaluates to $\bot$ because the n-th event of a trace $\bar{\sigma}$ does not satisfy φ, it is not necessary to conserve nodes describing how φ evaluates to $\top$ on the $n-1$ previous events: the knowledge that $\sigma^n \not\models \varphi$ is sufficient to decide on the value of $\mathbf{G}\,\varphi$. More generally, it is not necessary to keep nodes of a hologram whose *polarity* (i.e. their truth value) does not contribute to the final result of the global formula. Figure 3c shows the result of polarity deletion on the hologram of Fig. 3a. Again, a dual reasoning can be made for the **F** temporal operator.

When applied to temporal operators, this deletion rule expresses the fact that two traces where the same violating sequence of events occurs are considered the same, even if this sequence is preceded by a varying number of events irrelevant to the violation. For example, using polarity deletion, the traces $bcabbbd$ and $cabbd$ get similar holograms for the formula $\mathbf{G}\,(a \rightarrow \mathbf{X}\,(b\,\mathbf{U}\,c))$. The problem with both traces is that, after the occurrence of an "a", the sequence of "b" is broken off by a "d" instead of the expected "c". The position of the "a", and the actual number of "b" seen before the offending "d" are both abstracted away.

3.3   Truncation

A simple deletion rule consists of trimming from the hologram all nodes beyond a certain depth n. An extreme case is $n = 1$, which deletes all but the root of the hologram. In such a situation, κ classifies traces only according to the global truth value of the specification. For other values of n, truncation is such that one does not distinguish traces up to a certain level of abstraction. For example, truncating the holograms for $\mathbf{G}\,((a \rightarrow \mathbf{X}\,b) \wedge (\mathbf{F}\,b \wedge \mathbf{F}\,c))$ at a depth of $n = 2$ indicates that one is interested in knowing which of the two eventualities caused the failure, but not the actual contents of the event that caused it.

4   Automata Theoretic View

We shall now adopt a different point of view, and consider properties on traces expressed as finite automata. A finite deterministic automaton $\mathscr{A}$ over the alphabet Σ is a tuple $\langle Q, q_0, \delta, S \rangle$ where Q is a finite set of states, $q_0 \in Q$ is the initial state, $\delta : Q \times \Sigma \rightarrow Q$ is a transition function and $S \subseteq Q$ is a set of accepting states.

For any automaton there exists a minimal unique (up to isomorphism) canonical automaton. In what follows, we only consider canonical automata. A path π is a sequence of states$\langle q_1, q_2, q_3, ..., q_n \rangle$, such that such that there exists a finite sequence of symbols $a_1, a_2, a_3, ..., a_n$ called the label of π such that $\delta(q_i, a_i) = q_{i+1}$ for all $i \leq n$. In fact, a path is a sequence of states consisting of a possible run of the automaton, and the label of this path is the input sequence that generates this run. A run is initial if it begins on the start initial state q_0. A run is accepting if it ends on an accepting state $s \in S$.

A sequence σ satisfies the property φ if the associated run on the property automaton is initial and accepting.

The properties of coherence and consistency stated above can be stated quite straightforwardly in a automata theoretic formalism. A selector κ is coherent iff it does not include both accepting and non-accepting paths. A selector κ is consistent if it does not distinguish between two traces that exhibit the same path over the property automaton. The converse does not hold, as two sequences can meaningfully differ, and yet exhibit the same path over the canonical automaton of a property. This means that it may not be possible to state the finest classification when examining a property in the automata-theoretic view. Instead, the finest classification expressible in automata view is one that places in the same category every sequence that exhibits the same path over the property automaton.

Proposition 1. *Let* $\kappa : \Sigma^* \rightarrow C$ *and let* φ *be a property. If selector* κ *is consistent then* $\forall \sigma, \sigma' \in \Sigma^* : \pi(\sigma) = \pi(\sigma') \Rightarrow \kappa(\sigma) = \kappa(\sigma')$.

Proposition 2. *Let* $\kappa : \Sigma^* \to C$ *and let* φ *be a property. Selector* κ *is coherent iff* $\forall \sigma, \sigma' \in \Sigma^* : \pi(\sigma)$ *is an accepting run* $\Leftrightarrow \pi(\sigma')$ *is an accepting run* $\Rightarrow \kappa(\sigma) = \kappa(\sigma')$.

The automata-theoretic view presents two interesting advantages that distinguishes it from the other representations of properties. First, it is easy to generate a "typical", or generic trace in each category C by computing the shortest run over the property automata that visits the states needed for the trace to be included in C. Secondly, for a given program, it is possible to count how many different executions of length less than n are present in each category, by adapting the algorithm proposed by Bang et al. [4]. These functionalities have multiple applications, notably for estimating the coverage of an explicit-state model checking algorithm. This counting measurement can also be used as a complexity metric, providing an alternative to cyclomatic complexity.

In the following, We propose three path-based triaging schemes that are potentially useful for log trace triaging. All are abstractions of the notion of paths, thus analogous to trace holograms.

4.1 Shallow History Based Triaging

The shallow history (i.e. the same unordered set of visited states) was first introduced by Fong [13], who showed that it is a sufficiently fine approximation to serve in the enforcement of most real-life access-control policies, and other safety properties. This notion can be used for triaging, with two sequences being considered equal iff they share the same shallow history. Formally, $\kappa_{sh} : \Sigma* \to \mathscr{P}(\Sigma) : \forall \sigma, \sigma' \in \Sigma^* : \kappa_{sh}(\sigma) = \kappa_{sh}(\sigma') \Leftrightarrow acts(\sigma) = acts(\sigma')$.

For example, the Chinese Wall Policy [7] is used to avoid conflicts of interests arising from the unrestricted flow of information. In this model, a user which accesses a data object o is forbidden to simultaneously accessing certain other data objects that are identified as being in conflict with o. A violation of the policy occurs if the user accesses conflicting data objects. Since the application of the property is not sensitive to the order or number of occurrences of each data access, it makes senses to classify log traces according to their shallow history. Other access control policies [13] behave similarly.

When abstracted to its shallow history, a trace of data access events will retain only a list of the objects accessed by each user, regardless of the number of times each object has been accessed. Since this information is sufficient to detect a violation of the security policy or to generate a useful counterexample, it is not necessary to distinguish between multiple traces that vary only with respect to other, extraneous, information.

Theorem 1. *Let property* φ *be a safety property or a guarantee property.* κ_{sh} *is a reasonable selector.*

Proof. An automata representing a safety property possesses a single distinguished end state s, with no outgoing transitions [3]. Every invalid sequence passes through this state. Since every trace σ for which $s \notin \kappa_{sh}(\sigma)$ is valid, and every trace for which $s \in \kappa_{sh}(\sigma)$ is invalid, this classification is coherent. Conversely, an automata representing a guarantee property has a single valid accepting state s with no outgoing transitions, and only those sequence that exhibits s are valid. That κ_{sh} is consistent follows immediately from Definition 1.

For non-safety and non-guarantee properties, the κ_{sh} is not necessarily reasonable.

4.2 Duplicate Deletion

The second automata-based trace classification scheme is based upon the deletion of some visited states from the path. This classification scheme is useful if we are interested in examining which behaviors are present or absent in the trace, but not in how many times each present behavior occurs. Two traces abstract into the same class iff they share the same ordered list of visited states. For example, sequences $a; a; a; b; b; c$ and $a; b; b; b; c$ and $a; b; c$ are in the same category, but $c; b; a$ is not. We consider an erasing function $\delta : \Sigma^* \to \Sigma^*$ defined as follows:

$$\delta(\sigma; a) = \begin{cases} \sigma; a, & \text{if } \nexists i \in \mathbb{N} : \sigma_i = a; \\ \sigma, & \text{otherwise.} \end{cases}$$

The selector is defined with respect to this function as $\kappa_{dd} : \Sigma^* \to \mathscr{P}(\Sigma)$: $\forall \sigma, \sigma' \in \Sigma^* : \kappa_{dd}(\sigma) = \kappa_{dd}(\sigma') \Leftrightarrow \delta(\sigma) = \delta(\sigma')$.

The ordered list of states captures meaningful information about a program's behavior in many cases, as it gives a concise summery of the different behaviors present in the trace. For example, system call trace can contain several repetitions of the same system calls, representing copying a file to memory or sending data through a network. While the actual system call numbers carry meaningful information (i.e. identifies the higher-level behavior present in the trace), the number of occurrences of each system call is not particularly relevant, and may vary between runs of the same program.

As was the case with the shallow history based classification, duplicate deletion is only reasonable for safety and guarantee properties. For liveness properties, a sequence path may alternate between two states, and the entire execution will be considered valid or invalid depending on the final state present in the path — an information that is not recorded by the duplicate deletion abstraction.

Theorem 2. *Let property φ be a safety property or a guarantee property. κ_{dd} is a reasonable classification.*

Proof. Proceeds identically as that of Theorem 1.

Theorem 3. *κ_{dd} is a finer selector than κ_{dd}.*

Proof. Follows immediately from the fact that κ_{dd} distinguishes between path that visit the same states with a different ordering, while κ_{sh} does not.

4.3   Stuttering Insensitivity

As a final automata-based classification, we consider stuttering insensitivity [14]. Stuttering is the repetition of more than one consecutive occurrence of the same token in a sequence. This notion has multiple applications, notably optimizations in model-checking [17]. Stuttering Insensitivity differs from Duplicate Deletion in that the former preserves multiple occurrences of same token in a path, as long as they are not consecutive, while the latter erases all but one occurrence of each trace-event. When using Stuttering Insensitivity as a classifier, $a; a; a; b; b; a;$ and $a; a; b; a; a$ are in the same category but $a; a; a; b; b$ is not. In this paper, we consider stuttering in the path over the automaton validating the property (stuttering in the predicates of the automata's input sequences themselves would not be a reasonable selector in the sense of Definitions 1 and 2, except in the particular case of stuttering-insensitive languages). As was the case with duplicate deletion, stuttering insensitivity is defined with respect to an erasing function $\gamma : \Sigma^* \to \Sigma^*$:

$$\gamma(\sigma; a) = \begin{cases} \sigma, & \text{if } \sigma_* = a; \\ \sigma; a, & \text{otherwise.} \end{cases}$$

The selector is defined as $\kappa_{si} : \Sigma^* \to \mathscr{P}(\Sigma) : \forall \sigma, \sigma' \in \Sigma^* : \kappa_{dd}(\sigma) = \kappa_{dd}(\sigma') \Leftrightarrow \gamma(\sigma) = \gamma(\sigma')$.

Theorem 4. *Let property φ be a safety or a guarantee property. κ_{dd} is a reasonable classification.*

Proof. Proceeds identically as that of Theorem 1.

We can now show that κ_{si} is a finer selector than κ_{dd} and κ_{sh}.

Theorem 5. $\kappa_{si} \preceq \kappa_{dd} \preceq \kappa_{sh}$.

Proof. That follows immediately from the fact that κ_{dd} distinguishes between paths that visits the same states multiples times in a non-stuttering manner, while κ_{dd} does not.

5   Language Theoretic View

The third and final view of properties which we will consider is the language theoretic-view. Language theory is a convenient representation in which properties are directly represented as sets of sequences. This allows theorems and proofs to be formulated with ease. First off, the desirable properties of consistency and coherence can be formalized in a Language Theoretic manner using the notion of *residual language*. The residual language of a sequence σ, with respect to a property φ is the set of sequences τ such that $\sigma; \tau \in \varphi$. Formally $res(\sigma_\varphi) \equiv \{\tau | \sigma; \tau \in \varphi\}$. Let φ be a property, and let $\sigma\sigma' \in \Sigma^*$ be two sequences that are identical except for the value of their ultimate event, which differ in a single path value q. φ is q-invariant iff $res(\sigma_\varphi) = res(\sigma'_\varphi)$.

Proposition 3 (Consistency). *Let $\kappa : \Sigma^* \to C$ and let φ be a property. κ is consistent iff $\forall p \in \Pi : \forall \sigma \Sigma^* : \sigma, \sigma'$ are identical except that at their ith event: $\sigma_i; (p) = \sigma_i; (p) : res(\sigma_\varphi) = res(\sigma'_\varphi) \Rightarrow \kappa(\sigma; a) \wedge \kappa(\sigma; a').$*

Proposition 4 (Coherence). *Let $\kappa : \Sigma^* \to C$ and let φ be a property. If selector κ is consistent then $\forall \sigma \in \Sigma^* : \kappa(\sigma) \subseteq \varphi \vee \kappa(\sigma) \cap \varphi = \emptyset.$*

5.1   Edit Distance Based Classification

The trace correction distance [28] is the minimal number of insertions, deletions and substitutions needed to transform a given sequence σ into a new sequence σ' such that $\sigma' \models \varphi$. It is a generalization of the Levenshtein distance. Observe that for sequences that already satisfy the property, the correction distance is 0.

The correction distance is useful because it gives users an intuitive measure of how invalid a sequence is, allowing to distinguish gradations between violations of the property. In the context of security policy enforcement [20], it provides an approximation of the amount of modifications needed to recover from a violation. Trace correction can also be used for triaging, with two sequences being considered equal iff they share the same edit distance to a valid sequence. Let $correct : \Sigma^* \to \mathbb{N}$ be a function that calculates the minimal edit distance from any sequence in Σ^* to a sequence in the property of interest, using the algorithm presented in [28]. Selector κ_{ed} is formally defined as:

$$\kappa_{ed} : \Sigma * \to \mathscr{P}(\Sigma) : \forall \sigma, \sigma' \in \Sigma^* : \kappa_{ed}(\sigma) = \kappa_{ed}(\sigma') \Leftrightarrow correct(\sigma) = correct(\sigma')$$

Theorem 6. *κ_{ed} is a reasonable classification.*

Proof. That κ_{ed} is coherent holds trivially from the fact that every sequence σ such that $\sigma \models \varphi$ has correction 0, and no invalid sequence does. Let σ, σ' be two φ-invariant sequences and let n be the correction distance for σ. Since σ and σ' are φ-invariant, they differ with respect to only one path event e. Since φ is invariant with respect to e, the correction of the distance necessarily implies either modifying this event for both traces, or for neither. Since the two traces do not differ with respect to any other event, their respective edit distance are the same.

5.2   Classifications Based on Subwords

As a final classification strategy, we consider two schemes based upon the presence or absence of subwords of a given length k. The subwords (or factors) of length k of a sequence σ are the sequences of length k that occur inside a word. For example the sequence $a; b; a; b; a; b; a$ contains the factors of length 2 $a; b$ and $b; a$ and the factors of length 3 $a; b; a$ and $b; a; b$. Subwords are frequently used as an abstraction for the behavior of complex systems.

Let $sub_k(\sigma)$ be the set of subwords of length k present in a sequence σ. We define κ_{s_k} as follows:

$$sub_k(\sigma) : \Sigma * \to \mathscr{P}(\Sigma) : \forall \sigma, \sigma' \in \Sigma^* : \kappa_{s_k}(\sigma) = \kappa_{s_k}(\sigma') \Leftrightarrow sub_k(\sigma) = sub_k(\sigma')$$

Theorem 7. $\forall j, k \in \mathbb{N} : j < k \Rightarrow \kappa_{s_k}$ *is a finer classifier than* κ_{s_j}.

While subword are frequently used in trace analysis, they are only a coherent classification in the case of *locally testable properties* [6]. Membership of a word in a locally testable languages are defined by a set of factors of bounded length k of that word, irrespective of the order of occurrences or their frequency. As shown in [26] these include a number of security-relevant properties. The classification is not generally consistent, unless care is taken to merge classes that differ only with respect to the presence of two p-different subwords for a p-invariant property.

Theorem 8. *Let property* φ *be a locally testable property.* κ_{s_k} *is a coherent classification.*

Proof. That κ_{s_k} is coherent follows immediately from the definition of locally testable properties, which can be defined by the inclusion or exclusion of finite length subwords.

5.3   Residual Language

We can use the residual language of a sequence as the basis for classification, with the intuition that two sequence are equivalent iff the same set of continuations will lead to a valid sequence:

$$\kappa_{res} : \Sigma * \to \mathscr{P}(\Sigma) : \forall \sigma, \sigma' \in \Sigma^* : \kappa_{res}(\sigma) = \kappa_{res}(\sigma') \Leftrightarrow res(\sigma) = res(\sigma')$$

The residual language is a useful notion, notably with respect to runtime enforcement [25]. Observe that the set of possible residual languages correspond to the states of a deterministic finite automata that accept the words of the language accepted by this automata, with each state defining a different residual.

Theorem 9. κ_{res} *is a reasonable classification.*

Proof. The classifier κ_{res} is coherent, each possible residual corresponds to a state of the DFA that accepts φ, and any state is either accepting or not accepting. Likewise, the classifier κ_{res} is consistent, since any p-different sequence σ, σ' exhibit the same path over the DFA that accepts a p-invariant property, and thus exhibit the same residual language.

We can now show that κ_{res} is a coarser classification than κ_{dd} and κ_{si}.

Theorem 10. $\kappa_{si} \preceq \kappa_{dd} \preceq \kappa_{res}$

Proof. Follows immediately from the fact that the residual language of a sequence σ is uniquely defined by the final state of the path of σ over the DFA that accepts sequences in the property of interest. Let $[\![c]\!]$ be an equivalence class of sequences, classified using κ_{res}. For every sequence σ in $[\![c]\!]$, the path $\pi(\sigma)$ in the DFA of the corresponding property end in the same state d. It is easy to see that any two traces that share the same classification according to κ_{dd}, will also have the same final state. Conversely, two sequence may exhibit the same final state, but differ in other parts of the sequence and thus be classified differently according to κ_{dd}. The selector κ_{dd} is thus finer than κ_{res}.

Interestingly, the comparison between κ_{res} and the automata-based classifications is the only case in which we were able to compare selectors that originate with different views of the target property. In other cases we were only able to show that a selector was finer than another selector of the same type. This motivates the use of multiple representations of the property of interest. Likewise, we also showed how certain views were more adequate to classify certain types of properties, such as safety and guarantee properties for the automata-based view, or locally testable languages for κ_s.

6   Related Work

6.1   Logic-Based Approaches

From a logical point of view, the notion of hologram bears resemblance to the concept of Henkin witness [16], of which it can be seen as a generalization. Parallels can also be drawn with multi-valued logics, such as LTL_3 [19] and RV-LTL [5], which provide truth values in addition to the classical $\top$ and $\bot$. For example, in the case of LTL_3, a trace σ evaluates to $\top$ with respect to a property φ if all extensions σ' are such that $\sigma; \sigma' \models \varphi$ (and dually for $\bot$). A trace is associated with a third truth value, ?, when there exist extensions σ' and σ'' such that $\sigma; \sigma' \models \varphi$ and $\sigma; \sigma'' \not\models \varphi$.

These truth values can be seen as one possible partition of the set of traces with respect to a property. The present paper generalizes this idea, and introduced many more ways of creating equivalence classes with respect to a property, which are not related to the concept of possible extensions.

6.2   Bug Classification

A second line of work relates to the classification of software bugs. The most common way of categorizing bugs is based on their assessed severity [8]. This approach makes sense from a business standpoint, since it allows project managers to easily prioritize the resolution of bugs. However, severity is generally distributed across a handful of qualitative levels, such as "catastrophic", "essential" and "cosmetic". Some approaches rather suggest to classify bugs by ease of reproduction [15] and by type (e.g. system bugs, code bugs, etc.) [30]. Other categorizations reported include HP's three-dimensional scheme (origin, type, mode) and IBM's Orthogonal Defect Classification's six-dimensional scheme (type, source, impact, trigger, phase found and severity) [29]. The IEEE also defines a standard for the classification of software anomalies using 18 attributes [1]. All these categories, however, require human intervention (apart from basic fields such as date), and are based on a qualitative evaluation of the reported bugs.

Other approaches attempt to classify bugs through automated means. Most of these works use clustering techniques borrowed from data mining, mostly based on textual data [2,31], which can be mined either to directly separate bugs from non-bugs [22], or to generate labels (categories) from the most frequent terms [23].

Closer to the goals introduced earlier are approaches applying data mining to execution traces for classification [21]. A number of patterns (i.e. orderings of atomic events) are first defined based on the problem domain, and the most frequent patterns occurring in a set of traces are used as the basis of a feature vector that is then fed to a clustering algorithm. However, contrarily to the approach we will present, this technique requires a set of traces to perform computation; the category to which a trace belongs is not intrinsic, and rather depends on the set of other traces on which the algorithm was applied. Moreover, since this approach, as with all data mining techniques, is based on statistical computations, the clusterings obtained do not necessarily correspond to intuitive ways of grouping traces.

6.3   Trace Abstraction

Our proposed approach also relates to *trace abstraction*, which is widely used in program maintenance and other tasks that require a solid comprehension of complex programs. Cornelissen et al. survey four of these techniques [12]. The first is subsequence summarization, [18], which assigns consecutive events that have equal or increasing nesting levels (in terms of method calls) to the same group; when a level decrease is encountered and the difference exceeds a certain threshold, called the gap size, a new group is initiated. The second, stack depth limitation [11,24], removes events from a trace that exceed some maximum level of nesting in method calls. Language-based filtering removes events based on their characteristics: for example, getters and setters, or private method calls, are taken out from the trace. Finally, sampling techniques simply keep every n-th event of a trace [9].

The main difference between these methods and the one we propose is that in our case, the classification has solid theoretical foundation, and more importantly are based on some property of the trace. This allows us to reason about the equivalence classes; moreover, the property is preserved despite the abstraction process. In contrast, Cornelissen's survey rather compares these techniques with respect to informal criteria, such as the proportion of a trace that is taken off, or the processing time required to compute each filter.

7   Conclusion

In this paper, we have shown how techniques borrowed from runtime verification can be adapted to the classification of event traces. First, we introduced the concept of a partition of the set of event traces, and in particular the case of *coherent* and *consistent* classification functions. For an arbitrary trace property φ, we then presented different classification functions based on φ, depending on whether it is expressed as a temporal logic formula, a finite-state automaton, or a first-order expression over languages.

The approach itself lends itself to a number of extensions and refinements. At the moment, all violations of a specification are considered equally. From a bug triaging perspective, it would be interesting to assign a weight to various parts of a specification; hence a violation of $\varphi \wedge \psi$ when φ is false could be given more weight than when ψ is false. Similarly, the number of times a property is violated could be integrated in the computation: a trace failing $\mathbf{G}\,\varphi$ ten times in a row could be given a higher value than a trace where φ is false only once. Similarly for a finite-state machine, a numerical score could be assigned to each non-accepting state, so that violating the property bears a different cost depending on the final state that is reached. In turn, these numerical values could be used to infer the equivalent of a severity metric, providing a systematic and automated alternative to the qualitative and manual assessment currently in use.

The set of all possible combinations of deletion rules forms a lattice over the inclusion relation $\sqsubseteq$ on categories. This is one of the first conditions for one to be able to apply basic data mining on $\varSigma^*$, where $\sqsubseteq$ can act as a generality relation. It would be possible, for example, to search for the tightest set of deletion rules that still puts all observed buggy traces into a single category, thereby providing a "common point" to all the bug instances found and hinting at a possible repair.

References

1. IEEE standard classification for software anomalies. Technical report 1044-2009. IEEE (2010)
2. Alenezi, M., Magel, K., Banitaan, S.: Efficient bug triaging using text mining. JSW **8**(9), 2185–2190 (2013)
3. Alpern, B., Alpera, B., Schneider, F.B.: Recognizing safety and liveness. Distrib. Comput. **2**, 117–126 (1986)
4. Bang, L., Aydin, A., Bultan, T.: Automatically computing path complexity of programs. In: Nitto, E.D., Harman, M., Heymans, P. (eds.) Proceedings of the 2015 10th Joint Meeting on Foundations of Software Engineering, ESEC/FSE 2015, Bergamo, Italy, 30 August - 4 September 2015, pp. 61–72. ACM (2015)
5. Bauer, A., Leucker, M., Schallhart, C.: Comparing LTL semantics for runtime verification. J. Log. Comput. **20**(3), 651–674 (2010). http://dx.doi.org/10.1093/logcom/exn075
6. Beauquier, D., Pin, J.: Languages and scanners. Theor. Comput. Sci. **84**(1), 3–21 (1991)
7. Brewer, D.F.C., Nash, M.J.: The Chinese wall security policy. In: S&P, pp. 206–214. IEEE Computer Society (1989)
8. Carstensen, P.H., Sørensen, C., Tuikkar, T.: Let's talk about bugs!. Scand. J. Inf. Syst. **7**(6), 33–54 (1995)
9. Chan, A., Holmes, R., Murphy, G.C., Ying, A.T.T.: Scaling an object-oriented system execution visualizer through sampling. In: 11th International Workshop on Program Comprehension (IWPC 2003), 10–11 May 2003, Portland, Oregon, USA, pp. 237–244. IEEE Computer Society (2003). http://dx.doi.org/10.1109/WPC.2003.1199207
10. Chang, E., Manna, Z., Pnueli, A.: The safety-progress classification. In: Bauer, F.L., Brauer, W., Schwichtenberg, H. (eds.) Logic and Algebra of Specification. NATO ASI Series, vol. 94, pp. 143–202. Springer, Heidelberg (1993)

194   R. Khoury et al.

11. Cornelissen, B., van Deursen, A., Moonen, L., Zaidman, A.: Visualizing testsuites to aid in software understanding. In: Krikhaar, R.L., Verhoef, C., Lucca, G.A.D. (eds.) CSMR, pp. 213–222. IEEE Computer Society (2007). http://dx.doi.org/10.1109/CSMR.2007.54
12. Cornelissen, B., Moonen, L.: On large execution traces and trace abstraction techniques. Technical report, Delft University of Technology, Software Engineering Research Group (2008)
13. Fong, P.W.L.: Access control by tracking shallow execution history. In: S&P, pp. 43–55. IEEE Computer Society (2004)
14. Groote, J.F., Vaandrager, F.: An efficient algorithm for branching bisimulation and stuttering equivalence. In: Paterson, M.S. (ed.) ICALP 1990. LNCS, vol. 443, pp. 626–638. Springer, Heidelberg (1990). doi:10.1007/BFb0032063. http://dblp.uni-trier.de/db/conf/icalp/icalp90.html#GrooteV90
15. Grottke, M., Trivedie, K.S.: A classification of software faults. In: ISSRE, pp. 4.19–4.20 (2005)
16. Henkin, L.: The completeness of the first-order functional calculus. J. Symbolic Logic $14(3)$, 159–166 (1949)
17. Holzmann, G.J., Peled, D.A.: An improvement in formal verification. In: Hogrefe, D., Leue, S. (eds.) Formal Description Techniques VII. IFIP AICT, pp. 197–211. Springer, New York (1994). doi:10.1007/978-0-387-34878-0_13
18. Kuhn, A., Greevy, O.: Exploiting the analogy between traces and signal processing. In: 22nd IEEE International Conference on Software Maintenance (ICSM 2006), 24–27 September 2006, Philadelphia, Pennsylvania, USA, pp. 320–329. IEEE Computer Society (2006). http://dx.doi.org/10.1109/ICSM.2006.29
19. Leucker, M., Schallhart, C.: A brief account of runtime verification. J. Log. Algebr. Program. $78(5)$, 293–303 (2009)
20. Ligatti, J., Bauer, L., Walker, D.: Edit automata: enforcement mechanisms for run-time security policies. Int. J. Inf. Secur. 4, 2–16 (2005)
21. Lo, D., Cheng, H., Han, J., Khoo, S.C., Sun, C.: Classification of software behaviors for failure detection: a discriminative pattern mining approach. In: KDD, pp. 557–566 (2009)
22. Moha, N., Guéhéneuc, Y.G., Leduc, P.: Automatic generation of detection algorithms for design defects. In: ASE, pp. 297–300. IEEE Computer Society (2006)
23. Nagwani, N.K., Verma, S.: CLUBAS: an algorithm and Java based tool for software bug classification using bug attributes similarities. J. Softw. Eng. Appl. $5(6)$, 436–447 (2012)
24. Rountev, A., Connell, B.H.: Object naming analysis for reverse-engineered sequence diagrams. In: Roman, G., Griswold, W.G., Nuseibeh, B. (eds.) ICSE, pp. 254–263. ACM (2005). http://doi.acm.org/10.1145/1062455.1062510
25. Sridhar, M.: Model-checking in-lined reference monitors. Ph.D. thesis, The University of Texas at Dallas, Richardson, Texas, August 2014
26. Talhi, C., Tawbi, N., Debbabi, M.: Execution monitoring enforcement under memory-limitation constraints. Inf. Comput. $206(2–4)$, 158–184 (2008)
27. Varvaressos, S., Lavoie, K., Gaboury, S., Hallé, S.: A generalized monitor verdict for log trace triaging. In: PCODA, pp. 13–18. IEEE Computer Society (2015)
28. Wagner, R.A.: Order-n correction for regular languages. Commun. ACM $17(5)$, 265–268 (1974)
29. Wagner, S.: Defect classification and defect types revisited. In: DEFECTS 2008, Proceedings of the 2008 Workshop on Defects in Large Software Systems, pp. 39–40 (2008)

30. Wiszniewski, H.K.B., Mork, H.: Classification of software defects in parallel programs. Technical report 2, Faculty of Electronics, Technical University of Gdansk, Poland (1994)

31. Xuan, J., Jiang, H., Ren, Z., Yan, J., Luo, Z.: Automatic bug triage using semi-supervised text classification. In: SEKE, pp. 209–214. Knowledge Systems Institute Graduate School (2010)

Crypto and Communication Security

A Multi-round Side Channel Attack on AES Using Belief Propagation

Hélène Le Bouder[1]([⊠]), Ronan Lashermes[1], Yanis Linge[2], Gaël Thomas[3], and Jean-Yves Zie[4]

[1] LHS-PEC TAMIS, INRIA, Campus Beaulieu, 35042 Rennes, France
`helene.le-bouder@inria.fr`
[2] STMicroelectronics, 190 Avenue Coq, 13106 Rousset, France
[3] Orange Labs, 44 Avenue de la République, 92320 Châtillon, France
[4] CEA-TECH, Centre de Microélectronique de Provence,13120 Gardanne, France

Abstract. This paper presents a new side channel attack to recover a block cipher key. No plaintext and no ciphertext are required, no templates are built. Only the leakage measurements collected in many different rounds of the algorithm are exploited. The leakage is considered as a Hamming weight with a Gaussian noise. The chosen target is the Advanced Encryption Standard (AES). Bayesian inference is used to score all guesses on several consecutive round-key bytes. From these scores a Belief Propagation algorithm is used, based on the relations of the KeyExpansion, to discriminate the unique correct guess. Theoretical results according to various noise models are obtained with simulations.

Keywords: Side channel analysis · Hamming weight · AES · Key expansion · Multi-round attack · Bayesian inference · Belief propagation

1 Introduction

Security is a key component for information technologies and communication. Even if an encryption algorithm is proved secure mathematically, cryptanalysis has another dimension: physicals attacks. These attacks rely on the interaction of the computing unit with the physical environment.

The Side Channel Analyses (SCA) are physical attacks based on observations of the circuit behavior. They exploit the fact that some physical values (timing, power consumption, electromagnetic emissions (EM)) of a device depend on intermediate values of the computation. This is the so-called leakage of information of the circuit.

The Advanced Encryption Standard (AES) has been chosen as a target because it is the most widespread block cipher. Yet, our approach would be the same for any other block cipher.

Motivations: Generally the SCA as in [1,2] links a text with a measurement. This induces that the attack is often on the first or last round. But the framework described in [3] suggests that other kinds of attack-path are possible.

© Springer International Publishing AG 2017
F. Cuppens et al. (Eds.): FPS 2016, LNCS 10128, pp. 199–213, 2017.
DOI: 10.1007/978-3-319-51966-1_13

Our first idea is to draw an attack-path linking a leakage measurement with another one. Another approach in SCA are template attacks [4,5] which compare traces from the targeted device with traces from a profiling device.

In this paper, the main motivation was to build an attack which uses only traces, no text and no template. We are in the case of an attacker who can just observe a leakage but has no access to the device's input/output.

The great majority of side-channel attacks published in the literature follows a divide and conquer strategy. In the case of AES, bytes of a round-key are attacked one at a time. So the other main motivation in our approach is to attack different round-keys of the AES and use links between them to improve the probability to find the correct guess.

Contribution: This paper presents a new side channel attack. It is a multi-round attack, where no template and no texts (neither plaintexts nor ciphertexts) are used; only leakage measurements are required. In our attack the leakage is considered as a Hamming weight with a Gaussian noise. Bayesian inference is used to obtain scores for the possible values of the different round-key bytes. Then, the main idea is to use a Belief Propagation (BP) algorithm to cross information between them, in order to have a key which respects the rules of KeyExpansion.

Organization of this paper: The paper is organized as follows. The general context is first introduced in Sect. 2. Our attack is divided in two steps. A first analysis on each round is described in Sect. 3. Then in Sect. 4, the results of the analysis of this first step are linked using the BP algorithm. Results are presented in Sect. 5. Finally the conclusion is drawn in Sect. 6.

2   Preliminaries

2.1   The Targeted Encryption Algorithm: AES

The algorithm: The Advanced Encryption Standard is a standard established by the NIST [6] for symmetric key cryptography. It is a block-cipher. The encryption first consists in mapping the plaintext T of 128 bits into a two-dimensional array of $4 \cdot 4 = 16$ bytes called the State. Rows and columns are respectively noted l and c. Then, after a preliminary xor (the bit-wise xor is noted $\oplus$) between the input and the key K_0, the AES executes 10 times a round-function that operates on the State. The operations used during these rounds are:

- **SubBytes**, composed of non-linear transformations: 16 S-boxes noted SB, working independently on individual bytes of the State.
- **ShiftRows** noted SR, a byte-shifting operation on each row of the State.
- **MixColumns** noted MC, a linear matrix multiplication on $GF(2^8)$, working on each column of the State.
- **AddRoundKey** a xor between the State and the round-key K_r, $r \in [\![0, 10]\!]$.

The derived key: K denotes the master key. The size of the master key is 128 bits. K_r is the round-key used at round r, K_r is represented by a two-dimensional array of $4 \cdot 4$ bytes, like the State. $K_r^{l,c}$ is the round-key byte at row l and column c. The round-key K_{r+1} depends on the round-key K_r with $K_0 = K$. More precisely, the round-keys are computed with a KeyExpansion function described by the system of Eq. (1), where SB is the S-Box function and Rcon is a constant matrix of size $4 \cdot 10$.

$$\begin{cases} K_{r+1}^{l,0} = K_r^{l,0} \oplus Rcon(l,r) \oplus SB\left(K_r^{l+1 \bmod 4,3}\right) \ \forall l \in [\![0,3]\!] \\ K_{r+1}^{l,c} = K_r^{l,c} \oplus K_{r+1}^{l,c-1} \hspace{3.3cm} \forall l \in [\![0,3]\!] \text{ and } c \in [\![1,3]\!] \end{cases} \quad (1)$$

2.2   Overview of Our Attack and State of the Art

In this paper, we wanted to build an attack which uses only traces, no text and no template. In our attack, all the round-keys have already been precomputed, as is the case of most software AES implementations. So using the leakage of the KeyExpansion as done by Mangard in [7] is impossible, the attacker just observe leakage from AES round functions.

Actually in the state of the art, there are two kinds of approaches in SCA.

One consists in a divide and conquer strategy to attack one part (*e.g.* byte) at a time, as in classical attacks [1,2]. An attacker gives a score (for example a probability or a correlation) to each key byte guess. The difficulty is to enumerate all possible round-key guesses in a way that minimizes the rank of the correct round-key byte. This problem is indeed the focus of many papers as [8,9].

Recently in different works as [10–14], a new method consists in directly using links between variables of an algorithm. Information of each trace feeds a BP algorithm or a SAT-solver which usually converges to the correct key. The first time that BP was used in SCA on AES, was in the attack of Veyrat-Charvillon *et al.* [14]. They use BP on the whole AES algorithm to derive a global template attack.

Grosso *et al.* [15] compared both approaches and concluded that BP is a little bit better.

The presented work was made in parallel and independently from the recent works [14,15]. The strategy was chosen to be applied to a real experimental attack. Our attack presented is divided in two parts:

1. a divide and conquer attack focuses on key bytes of different rounds (Sect. 3);
2. linking the information obtained for each byte of every round-key (Sect. 4).

So, one contribution in our attack is to merge these two approaches and take advantage of both.

2.3   Attack-Path

An attack-path is an exploitable relation between some observables (data or measurements) and the target, here the key K. Generally the attack-path in

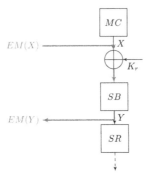

Fig. 1. Attack path

SCA as [1,2] links a text with a measurement. In our attack, we want to link two EM or power leakage measurements. Finally the attack-path is between two rounds (AddRoundKey of round r and the S-boxes of round $r+1$); it is illustrated in Fig. 1. The attacker has no text at her disposal, she then needs an important leakage as it is her only source of information. More precisely, the most leaking functions in AES are MC and SB, so the leakages used in this attack are at the output of both computations.

Hence this attack is possible on every rounds except rounds 0 and 10. Indeed there is no MC before the xor with K_0 and there is no SB after K_{10}.

In the following, $\mathcal{K}$ denotes the discrete random variable on a targeted key byte $K_r^{l,c}$, a guess is noted k and $\mathbb{K}$ is the set of guesses k, $\mathbb{K} = [\![0, 255]\!]$. The correct value is noted $\hat{k}$ (i.e. $K_r^{l,c} = \hat{k}$).

X denotes the discrete random variable on the byte at the input of AddRoundKey, an event is noted $X = x$ with $x \in [\![0, 255]\!]$. Likewise, Y denotes the discrete random variable on the byte at the output of SubBytes, an event is noted $Y = y$ with $y \in [\![0, 255]\!]$.

The mathematical model for the leakage is a Hamming weight (HW) with an additive Gaussian noise. This model is the classic model used in [1,2].

2.4 Theoretical Attack-Path

Before presenting our attack in practice, the relevance of the theoretical attack-path is proved; *i.e.* whether with only pairs (h_x, h_y) of Hamming weights (without noise) it is possible to deduce the value $\hat{k}$. This approach is similar to algebraic attacks [16–18].

The function HW is not invertible, the set $HW^{-1}(h)$, whose cardinal depends on the value of h, is the fiber of h by HW:

$$HW^{-1}(h) = \{x \text{ such that } HW(x) = h\}.$$

For the good guess value $\hat{k}$, the following equation is verified:

$$SB(\hat{k} \oplus x) = y.$$

The attacker has only pairs (h_x, h_y). For each pair only a subset of guesses k is possible. Let $\mathbb{K}_{(h_x, h_y)}$ be such a subset of guesses:

$$\mathbb{K}_{(h_x, h_y)} = \{k \text{ such that } \exists x \in HW^{-1}(h_x) \text{ and } HW\left(SB\left(k \oplus x\right)\right) = h_y\}.$$

Let $\mathbb{K}(\hat{k})$ be the intersection of the sets $\mathbb{K}_{(h_x, h_y)}$ built with all 256 possible values of x, and the unknown and correct key $\hat{k}$:

$$\mathbb{K}(\hat{k}) = \bigcap_{x=0}^{255} \mathbb{K}_{(h_x, h_y)}.$$

The correct guess $\hat{k}$ belongs to $\mathbb{K}(\hat{k})$. Thus, the first natural idea is to use a sieve to discriminate the wrong guesses.

We have studied all the cases for each key byte value $\hat{k}$. The sieve is not enough, because there exists some value $\hat{k}$ such that one wrong guess is not discriminated:

$$\mathbb{K}(\hat{k}) = \{\hat{k}, k\}.$$

However it can be observed that the sets $\mathbb{K}(\hat{k})$ are all different, as illustrated in the following example. Besides they can be computed once and for all, for every possible value of the correct key $\hat{k}$; for example:

$$\begin{aligned} \mathbb{K}(25) &= \{25, 62\} \\ \mathbb{K}(62) &= \{62\} \end{aligned} .$$

If the attacker has used all possible pairs (h_x, h_y), she has computed the set $\mathbb{K}(\hat{k})$. Since all the sets $\mathbb{K}(\hat{k})$ are different, the attacker can discriminate the correct key $\hat{k}$. The attack-path is valid.

2.5   Leakage Model

Our model for the leakage is a Hamming weight (HW) with an additive Gaussian noise. In this paper, for a given discrete random variable Z, the discrete random variable representing the Hamming weight of Z is noted H_Z, the event "the Hamming weight of Z is h_z" is denoted $H_Z = h_z$ for $h_z \in [\![0, 8]\!]$. H'_Z denotes the continuous random variable representing the "measured" Hamming weight; an event is noted $H'_Z = h'_z$, with $h'_z \in \mathbb{R}$ such as:

$$h'_z = h_z + \delta; \tag{2}$$

with δ an event of the Gaussian random variable $\mathcal{N}\left(0, \sigma_Z{}^2\right)$. For a continuous random variable H'_Z, $F_{H'_Z}$ denotes its probability density function. The probability density function associated to $\mathcal{N}\left(0, \sigma_Z{}^2\right)$ is given by:

$$\mathcal{F}_{\sigma_Z}(z) = \frac{1}{\sigma_Z \cdot \sqrt{2\pi}} \cdot \exp\left(-\frac{1}{2} \cdot \left(\frac{z}{\sigma_Z}\right)^2\right). \tag{3}$$

3   Attack on Each Round-Key Byte

In practice, the attacker does not have pairs of Hamming weights, but leakage measurements.

3.1   Points of Interest

In order to use observed Hamming weights h'_z, the time when they can be observed in the trace must be identified. The points of interest, denoted *PoI*, are a set of points which correspond to the moments of information leakage. The detection of *PoI* is a critical point when performing an SCA attack but it is not the subject of this paper. We consider that *PoI* can be found using the method of [19], without a profiling phase.

3.2   Getting Observed Hamming Weights from Physical Measures

In this paragraph, the *PoI* are known and we assume that the noise follows a normal distribution $\mathcal{N}(0, \sigma_Z{}^2)$. Physical measures are obtained, as an example, with an oscilloscope.

The goal of our attack is to succeed without using a template approach, the attacker may not have a profiling device. In this case, the attacker has to guess the standard deviation σ_Z of the noise. A guess is noted σ_G. She considers the 9 theoretical Gaussian distributions $\mathcal{N}\left(h, \sigma_G^2\right)$ centered in the different Hamming weights $h \in [\![0,8]\!]$. They are added to create a new distribution from which a new standard deviation σ_H is computed:

$$\sigma_H = std \left(\sum_{h \in [\![0,8]\!]} \binom{8}{h} \mathcal{N}\left(h, \sigma_G\right) \right).$$

She computes the mean $\overline{M}$ of the measured values $M = (m_i)_{1 \leq i \leq n}$ at a PoI. Then the observed hamming weights are computed as follow:

$$h'_i = \left(m_i - \overline{M}\right) \cdot \frac{\sigma_H}{std(M)} + 4.$$

If the attack succeeds, σ_G is a good approximation.

3.3   Bayesian Inference

In this part, the goal is to build a probability for each guess k given a set of measurements of n pairs $(H'_X, H'_Y) = (h'_x, h'_y)$ that a round-key byte $\mathcal{K}$ equals k. The main idea is to study the joint probability. This kind of approach is used in stochastic attacks [20] or in the attack of Linge *et al.* [19].

Throughout the paper, the following relations are used. A set of n pairs (h_x, h_y) is denoted $\{(h_x, h_y)\}_n$, the i-th pair is denoted $(h_x, h_y)_i$. Likewise a set of n pairs (h'_x, h'_y) is denoted $\{(h'_x, h'_y)\}_n$ and the i-th pair is denoted $(h'_x, h'_y)_i$.

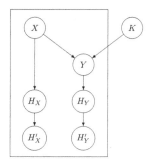

Fig. 2. Modeling the problem with a graph. An arrow means influence between two variables. The variables in the rectangle have a different value at each execution, while the value of the variables outside the rectangle is fixed throughout the attack.

The probability A_k for a guess k given the measurements (H'_X, H'_Y), (4) is defined as follow.

$$A_k = \Pr\left[\mathcal{K} = k | \{(h'_x, h'_y)\}_n\right].\tag{4}$$

The context can be represented with a belief network (as in [21]). It is a graph where the nodes are variables as illustrated in Fig. 2.

At the start of the attack all guesses are equiprobables, the prior distribution is uniform:

$$\forall k \in \mathbb{K}, \quad \Pr\left[\mathcal{K} = k\right] = \frac{1}{256}.\tag{5}$$

Probabilities $\Pr\left[(H_X, H_Y) = (h_x, h_y) | \mathcal{K} = k\right]$ can be precomputed once and for all by enumeration on the value x.

So the attacker wants to evaluate the probability of A_k, given by Eq. (4), i.e. the probability of $\mathcal{K} = k$ given a set of measurements. The Bayes theorem implies:

$$A_k = \frac{\overbrace{F_{(H'_X, H'_Y)}\left(\{(h'_x, h'_y)\}_n | \mathcal{K} = k\right) \cdot \Pr[\mathcal{K} = k]}^{A1_k}}{\underbrace{F_{(H'_X, H'_Y)}\left(\{(h'_x, h'_y)\}_n\right)}_{A0_k}}.$$

The denominator $A0_k$ can be obtained by normalization, there is no need to compute it. The pairs $(H'_X, H'_Y)_i$ are independent and identically distributed; i.e. all the pairs have the same distribution of probabilities and all the pairs are mutually independent. It means that a pair $(H'_X, H'_Y)_1$ cannot be predicted with the previous pair $(H'_X, H'_Y)_2$; thus:

$$A1_k = \prod_{i=1}^{n} \underbrace{F_{(H'_X, H'_Y)}\left((h'_x, h'_y)_i | \mathcal{K} = k\right)}_{A2_k}.$$

Now, the probability of a single pair is needed.

$$A2_k = F_{(H'_X, H'_Y)}\left((h'_x, h'_y)|\mathcal{K} = k\right).$$

The law of total probability implies that:

$$A2_k = \sum_{(h_x, h_y)} \underbrace{F_{(H'_X, H'_Y)}\left((h'_x, h'_y)|(h_x, h_y)\right)}_{A3_k} \cdot \Pr\left[(h_x, h_y)|\mathcal{K} = k\right].$$

$$A3_k = F_{(H'_X, H'_Y)}\left((h'_x, h'_y)|(h_x, h_y)\right)$$

The pair (H_X, H_Y), the variable H'_X and the variable H'_Y are independent. For a fixed h_x, H'_X and H_Y are independent, thus:

$$F_{H'_X}\left(h'_x|(h_x, h_y)\right) = F_{H'_X}\left(h'_x|H_X = h_x\right).$$

Likewise, for a fixed h_y, H'_Y and H_X are independent, thus:

$$F_{H'_Y}\left(h'_y|(h_x, h_y)\right) = F_{H'_Y}\left(h'_y|H_Y = h_y\right).$$

Thus:

$$A3_k = F_{H'_X}\left(h'_x|H_X = h_x\right) \cdot F_{H'_Y}\left(h'_y|H_Y = h_y\right).$$

But $F_{H'_X}(h'_x|H_X = h_x)$ follows the normal distribution centred in h_x, so:

$$F_{H'_X}\left(h'_x|H_X = h_x\right) = \mathcal{F}_{\sigma X}\left(h'_x - h_x\right).$$

Likewise:

$$F_{H'_Y}\left(h'_y|H_Y = h_y\right) = \mathcal{F}_{\sigma Y}\left(h'_y - h_y\right).$$

Finally, the probability A_k, that a round-key byte $\mathcal{K}$ equals k for some given measurements of (H'_X, H'_Y), is proportional to the product[1]:

$$A_k \propto \prod_{i=1}^{n} \sum_{(h_x, h_y)} \mathcal{F}_{\sigma X}\left(h'_{x,i} - h_x\right) \cdot \mathcal{F}_{\sigma Y}\left(h'_{y,i} - h_y\right) \cdot \Pr\left[(h_x, h_y)|\mathcal{K} = k\right]. \quad (6)$$

Note that, in the previous equation, the Gaussian noise hypothesis can be relaxed by replacing the Gaussian probability density functions ($\mathcal{F}_{\sigma X}$ and $\mathcal{F}_{\sigma Y}$) by whatever probability density function the attacker can come up with.

At the end of this part, the attacker has a probability for each guess k on every key byte of round 1 to 9.

---

[1] $h'_{x,i}$ is the i-th measurement h'_x.

4   Crossing Information from Round-Key Bytes with BP

4.1   Goal

The round-key bytes are linked by KeyExpansion relations (1). There are $16 \cdot 9$ round-key bytes linked together using $16 \cdot 8$ equations. It is supposed that the correct key is the one minimizing the ranks of its round-key byte values across all 9 rounds. In this part, this additional information is crossed with the estimations to improve the probabilities $\Pr[\mathcal{K} = k]$ and to have a key which respects the rules of KeyExpansion. To this end, in this part a technique known as Belief Propagation (or sum-product algorithm) [22] is used.

BP was first used by Gallager [23] for decoding low-density parity-check (LDPC) codes. It was then rediscovered by Tanner [24] and formalized by Pearl [25]. The first time that BP was used in SCA on AES, in the attack of Veyrat-Charvillon *et al.* [14], then it is studied in [15].

4.2   Factor Graph

The BP algorithm relies on a bipartite graph called a factor graph (or Tanner graph). To each node in the factor graph is associated some information.

The nodes of a factor graph are of two kinds:

- variable nodes, in our case representing round-key bytes;
- factor nodes, in our case representing equations used in the KeyExpansion.

An edge links a variable node with a factor node, when the equation represented by the factor node involves the byte represented by the variable node. A part of the factor graph associated with the KeyExpansion is illustrated in Fig. 3.

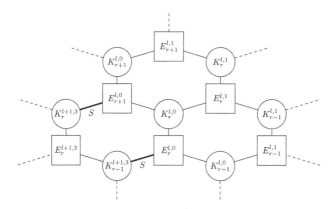

Fig. 3. Part of the factor graph associated with the AES KeyExpansion. Circles are variable nodes (round-key bytes) and squares are factor nodes (equations). Equations are labeled using the same indexes as the round-key byte they define, i.e. equation $E_r^{l,c}$ is the equation used to create $K_r^{l,c}$. The S-labeled edges remind the use of the S-box in the equation for that particular byte.

In the following, the notation $N(\cdot)$ applied to a node is used to denote the set of neighbours of that node. Thus $N(\mathcal{K})$ is the set of equations involving round-key byte $\mathcal{K}$, and $N(E)$ is the set of round-key bytes composing equation E. Finally, a factor node E "is satisfied" when the corresponding KeyExpansion equation is satisfied.

4.3 Algorithm

The BP algorithm in the general case is summed up in Algorithm 1.

Algorithm 1. Belief Propagation Algorithm.

Inputs: Experimental distributions A_k of every round-key byte $\mathcal{K}$; m the maximal number of iterations of BP.

Outputs: Final distributions B_k deduced using KeyExpansion relations.
  for all round-key byte $\mathcal{K}$ **and** value k **and** equation E **do**

$$\mu_{\mathcal{K} \to E}(k) = A_k.$$

  end for
  for $j = 1$ **to** m **do**
    for all round-key byte $\mathcal{K}$ **and** value k **and** equation E **do**

$$\mu_{E \to \mathcal{K}}(k) = \sum_{(k_1,k_2) \in \mathbb{K}^2} E(k,k_1,k_2) \cdot \mu_{\mathcal{K}_1 \to E}(k_1) \cdot \mu_{\mathcal{K}_2 \to E}(k_2)$$

      with $N(E) \setminus \{\mathcal{K}\} = \{\mathcal{K}_1, \mathcal{K}_2\}$.
    end for
    for all round-key byte $\mathcal{K}$ **and** value k **and** equation E **do**

$$\mu_{\mathcal{K} \to E}(k) \propto A_k \prod_{E_1 \in N(\mathcal{K}) \setminus \{E\}} \mu_{E_1 \to \mathcal{K}}(k).$$

    end for
  end for
  for all round-key byte $\mathcal{K}$ **and** value k **do**

$$B_k \propto A_k \prod_{E \in N(\mathcal{K})} \mu_{E \to \mathcal{K}}(k).$$

  end for

In our case, the input of BP are the probabilities A_k found in (6). For a key byte $\mathcal{K}$, BP computes B_k a better belief, from the initial value A_k. As already stated, nodes in the factor graph exchange information messages with their neighbours. More precisely, since the graph is bipartite, two types of messages are exchanged:

– variable to factor messages between a variable node (key byte) $\mathcal{K}$ and a factor node (equation) E, denoted $\mu_{\mathcal{K} \to E}(k)$;

- factor to variable messages between a factor node E and a variable node $\mathcal{K}$, denoted $\mu_{E \to \mathcal{K}}(k)$.

B_k is computed according to the input probability A_k and to the probabilities $\Pr[\mathcal{K} = k|E]$ conditional on factor node E in $N(\mathcal{K})$ to be satisfied using the following equation:

$$B_k \propto A_k \prod_{E \in N(\mathcal{K})} \Pr[\mathcal{K} = k|E]. \tag{7}$$

$N(E) \setminus \{\mathcal{K}\} = \{\mathcal{K}_1, \mathcal{K}_2\}$. Thanks to the law of total probability, $\Pr[\mathcal{K} = k|E]$ can the be obtained by summing $\Pr[\mathcal{K}_1 = k_1] \cdot \Pr[\mathcal{K}_2 = k_2]$ over all the possible values for k_1 and k_2 such that factor node E is satisfied. Thus, the following equation holds:

$$\Pr[\mathcal{K} = k|E] = \sum_{(k_1, k_2) \in \mathbb{K}^2} E(k, k_1, k_2) \cdot \Pr[\mathcal{K}_1 = k_1] \cdot \Pr[\mathcal{K}_2 = k_2]. \tag{8}$$

$\Pr[\mathcal{K}_1 = k_1]$ and $\Pr[\mathcal{K}_2 = k_2]$ are needed to compute $\Pr[\mathcal{K} = k|E]$ which depends on:

$$E \in N(\mathcal{K}) \cap N(\mathcal{K}_1) \cap N(\mathcal{K}_2).$$

Hence, using Eq. (7) directly on $\mathcal{K}_1$ and $\mathcal{K}_2$ would create a self-convincing loop for node $\mathcal{K}$. To avoid that problem, the factor corresponding to node E is removed from the product in Eq. (7) in that case:

$$\Pr[\mathcal{K}_1 = k_1] \propto A_{k_1} \prod_{E_1 \in N(\mathcal{K}_1) \setminus \{E\}} \Pr[\mathcal{K}_1 = k_1|E_1]. \tag{9}$$

However, it can be shown [22,23] that the Eqs. (7), (8) and (9) do not hold in general because they require an independence assumption on the probabilities used in the different products. In [26], authors show that in practice, the equation can be replaced by approximation, the BP gives excellent results. So, the Eqs. (7), (8), and (9) are respectively replaced by:

$$B_k \propto A_k \prod_{E \in N(\mathcal{K})} \mu_{E \to \mathcal{K}}(k) \tag{10}$$

$$\mu_{E \to \mathcal{K}}(k) = \sum_{(k_1, k_2) \in \mathbb{K}^2} E(k, k_1, k_2) \cdot \mu_{\mathcal{K}_1 \to E}(k_1) \cdot \mu_{\mathcal{K}_2 \to E}(k_2) \tag{11}$$

$$\mu_{\mathcal{K} \to E}(k) \propto A_k \prod_{E_1 \in N(\mathcal{K}) \setminus \{E\}} \mu_{E_1 \to \mathcal{K}}(k) \tag{12}$$

To complete the description of the BP algorithm, an initialization step is done before applying the above equations. The variable to factor messages $\mu_{\mathcal{K} \to E}(k)$ are initialized with the prior probabilities A_k corresponding to round-key byte $\mathcal{K}$.

In summary, after an initialization phase, BP works by alternatively applying Eqs. (11) then (12) for every edge $(\mathcal{K}, E)$ in the graph. At the end of the execution, the returned value B_k is computed using Eq. (10). The number of iterations is not precisely defined but BP converges rapidly.

At the end, the attacker deduces from the BP outputs B_k, 9 probable round-keys. The attack succeeds if one of these 9 probable round-keys is an actual round-key, i.e. it is derived from the correct master key using the KeyExpansion.

Finally it is interesting to note that using BP for enhancing the probabilities on the different round-keys would work better as the number of rounds increases. Indeed, each new round brings independent information on the key that can be crossed with all other rounds.

5   Results

5.1   Simulation Results

The simulations are done with the programming language julia (v0.4). They would correspond to an attack against a typical unprotected 8-bit software implementation of AES. Plaintexts are randomly generated. Measured Hamming weights are simulated with a noise according to $\mathcal{N}(0, \sigma^2)$ for various standard deviations σ. To facilitate the simulation the noise is supposed to be the same on X and Y: $\sigma = \sigma_X = \sigma_Y$.

We emphasize that to overcome floating point arithmetic issues, the normalization steps in both the Bayesian attack and the BP algorithm are not performed. As such, we work with scores corresponding to the logarithm of probabilities instead of probabilities directly.

Simulation to retrieve a key byte from pairs of noisy Hamming weights: First, at the level of a single byte using Bayesian inference (Sect. 3.3). For different noise standard deviation σ and different numbers of traces n, the average rank of the good key byte has been computed, for 100 simulated attacks for each possible value of the key $\hat{k}$. The results are displayed in Table 1.

Using BP on simulation results: Now, the attack on the whole master key is simulated to see the additional benefit of BP. The algorithm returns 9 round-keys. The measure used here is then the minimum of the Hamming distances

Table 1. Average rank of the good key byte $\hat{k}$ according to the noise standard deviation σ and the number of traces n, for 100 simulated attacks for each possible value of the key $\hat{k}$.

$n\backslash\sigma$	0.1	0.2	0.3	0.5	1.0	1.5	2.0	3.0
100	1.2	1.3	2.3	14	66	96	107	119
1000	1	1	1	1	7.1	35	66	97
10000	1	1	1	1	1	2.2	12	48
100000	1	1	1	1	1	1	1.1	7.3

Table 2. Hamming distance between the best key found by BP and the correct master key K according to the noise standard deviation σ and the number of traces n, estimated over 100 simulated attacks.

$n\backslash\sigma$	0.1	0.2	0.3	0.5	1.0	1.5	2.0	3.0
100	0	0	0	0	59	51	53	54
1000	0	0	0	0	0	39	46	51
10000	0	0	0	0	0	0	0	40
100000	0	0	0	0	0	0	0	0

Table 3. Success of the attack according to the noise standard deviation σ and the number of traces n, for 100 simulated attacks. ✓ indicates the attack always succeeds even if not using BP, ✓ indicates the attack succeeds only with using BP and × indicates the attack fails.

$n \backslash \sigma$	0.1	0.2	0.3	0.5	1.0	1.5	2.0	3.0
100	✓	✓	✓	✓	×	×	×	×
1000	✓	✓	✓	✓	✓	×	×	×
10000	✓	✓	✓	✓	✓	✓	✓	×
100000	✓	✓	✓	✓	✓	✓	✓	✓

between the guessed round-keys and the correct round-keys, where the minimum is taken over the nine round-keys. The results are summarized in Table 2. As it can be seen, the results are sharply separated, either the attack always succeeds or it always fails completely. Nonetheless, the number of traces required for the attack to succeed using BP is an order of magnitude below of what is required without BP. Finally the improvement of BP on the attack is illustrated in the Table 3.

Using the BP algorithm considerably improves the success rate. It makes it possible to reduce the number of traces required for the attack to succeed. For example, when σ is equal to 0.1, only 100 traces are required thanks to BP, as opposed to 1000 traces without BP.

6   Conclusion

This paper presents a new side channel attack targeting the AES key. The first motivation for this paper was to realize an attack without texts and without templates, using only leakage measurements. The leakage is considered as a Hamming weight with an additive Gaussian noise. On each round 1 to 9 of the AES, two points of leakage are required to define the attack path without any text.

First, with a Bayesian inference approach a score is assigned to each round-key byte for all rounds from 1 to 9. Then, the second step is to use the KeyExpansion rules to aggregate the knowledge on the round-key bytes to discriminate the correct key. A belief propagation is used for that purpose.

Simulation results have shown that the attack is effective, using the BP algorithm is a very good way to enhance the chances to recover the key. Even in the presence of a strong noise the attack can succeed. The BP algorithm approach can be used in combination with any other attack able to score all round-key bytes on several consecutive rounds. Additionally, it shows that increasing the number of rounds in a crypto-algorithm in order to make it resist classical cryptanalysis can weaken it with respect to our attack.

Finally, we would like to explore if masked implementations are effectively protecting against this attack.

Acknowledgment. The authors would like to thank Christophe Clavier (University of Limoges, France), Guillaume Reymond (Tiempo, France), Assia Tria (CEA-TECH, France), and Antoine Wurker (Eshard, France) for their valuable contributions to the development and understanding of the issues discussed in the paper. This work was initiated while Hélène Le Bouder was at École des Mines de Saint-Étienne. This work was partially funded by the French National Research Agency (ANR) as part of the program Digital Engineering and Security (INS-2013), under grant agreement ANR-13-INSE-0006-01 and by the French DGCIS (Direction Générale de la Compétitivité de l'Industrie et des Services) through the CALISSON 2 project.

References

1. Kocher, P., Jaffe, J., Jun, B.: Differential power analysis. In: Wiener, M. (ed.) CRYPTO 1999. LNCS, vol. 1666, pp. 388–397. Springer, Heidelberg (1999). doi:10.1007/3-540-48405-1_25
2. Brier, E., Clavier, C., Olivier, F.: Correlation power analysis with a leakage model. In: Joye, M., Quisquater, J.-J. (eds.) CHES 2004. LNCS, vol. 3156, pp. 16–29. Springer, Heidelberg (2004). doi:10.1007/978-3-540-28632-5_2
3. Le Bouder, H., Lashermes, R., Linge, Y., Robisson, B., Tria, A.: A unified formalism for physical attacks. IACR Cryptology ePrint (2014)
4. Hanley, N., Tunstall, M., Marnane, W.P.: Unknown plaintext template attacks. In: Youm, H.Y., Yung, M. (eds.) WISA 2009. LNCS, vol. 5932, pp. 148–162. Springer, Heidelberg (2009). doi:10.1007/978-3-642-10838-9_12
5. Archambeau, C., Peeters, E., Standaert, F.-X., Quisquater, J.-J.: Template attacks in principal subspaces. In: Goubin, L., Matsui, M. (eds.) CHES 2006. LNCS, vol. 4249, pp. 1–14. Springer, Heidelberg (2006). doi:10.1007/11894063_1
6. NIST: Specification for the advanced encryption standard. FIPS PUB 197 (2001)
7. Mangard, S.: A simple power-analysis (SPA) attack on implementations of the AES key expansion. In: Lee, P.J., Lim, C.H. (eds.) ICISC 2002. LNCS, vol. 2587, pp. 343–358. Springer, Heidelberg (2003). doi:10.1007/3-540-36552-4_24
8. Veyrat-Charvillon, N., Gérard, B., Renauld, M., Standaert, F.-X.: An optimal key enumeration algorithm and its application to side-channel attacks. In: Knudsen, L.R., Wu, H. (eds.) SAC 2012. LNCS, vol. 7707, pp. 390–406. Springer, Heidelberg (2013). doi:10.1007/978-3-642-35999-6_25
9. Belaïd, S., Coron, J.-S., Fouque, P.-A., Gérard, B., Kammerer, J.-G., Prouff, E.: Improved side-channel analysis of finite-field multiplication. In: Güneysu, T., Handschuh, H. (eds.) CHES 2015. LNCS, vol. 9293, pp. 395–415. Springer, Heidelberg (2015). doi:10.1007/978-3-662-48324-4_20

10. Martin, D.P., O'Connell, J.F., Oswald, E., Stam, M.: Counting keys in parallel after a side channel attack. In: Iwata, T., Cheon, J.H. (eds.) ASIACRYPT 2015. LNCS, vol. 9453, pp. 313–337. Springer, Heidelberg (2015). doi:10.1007/978-3-662-48800-3_13

11. Bogdanov, A., Kizhvatov, I., Manzoor, K., Tischhauser, E., Witteman, M.: Fast and memory-efficient key recovery in side-channel attacks. IACR Cryptology ePrint, 795 (2015)

12. Gérard, B., Standaert, F.-X.: Unified and optimized linear collision attacks and their application in a non-profiled setting. In: Prouff, E., Schaumont, P. (eds.) CHES 2012. LNCS, vol. 7428, pp. 175–192. Springer, Heidelberg (2012). doi:10.1007/978-3-642-33027-8_11

13. Ye, X., Eisenbarth, T., Martin, W.: Bounded, yet sufficient? How to determine whether limited side channel information enables key recovery. In: Joye, M., Moradi, A. (eds.) CARDIS 2014. LNCS, vol. 8968, pp. 215–232. Springer, Heidelberg (2015). doi:10.1007/978-3-319-16763-3_13

14. Veyrat-Charvillon, N., Gérard, B., Standaert, F.-X.: Soft analytical side-channel attacks. In: Sarkar, P., Iwata, T. (eds.) ASIACRYPT 2014. LNCS, vol. 8873, pp. 282–296. Springer, Heidelberg (2014). doi:10.1007/978-3-662-45611-8_15

15. Grosso, V., Standaert, F.-X.: ASCA, SASCA and DPA with enumeration: which one beats the other and when? In: Iwata, T., Cheon, J.H. (eds.) ASIACRYPT 2015. LNCS, vol. 9453, pp. 291–312. Springer, Heidelberg (2015). doi:10.1007/978-3-662-48800-3_12

16. Courtois, N.: How fast can be algebraic attacks on block ciphers? In: Symmetric Cryptography. Dagstuhl Seminar Proceedings, vol. 07021 (2007)

17. Nover, H.: Algebraic cryptanalysis of AES: an overview. University of Wisconsin, USA (2005)

18. Courtois, N.T., Bard, G.V.: Algebraic cryptanalysis of the data encryption standard. In: Galbraith, S.D. (ed.) Cryptography and Coding 2007. LNCS, vol. 4887, pp. 152–169. Springer, Heidelberg (2007). doi:10.1007/978-3-540-77272-9_10

19. Linge, Y., Dumas, C., Lambert-Lacroix, S.: Using the joint distributions of a cryptographic function in side channel analysis. In: Prouff, E. (ed.) COSADE 2014. LNCS, vol. 8622, pp. 199–213. Springer, Heidelberg (2014). doi:10.1007/978-3-319-10175-0_14

20. Schindler, W., Lemke, K., Paar, C.: A stochastic model for differential side channel cryptanalysis. In: Rao, J.R., Sunar, B. (eds.) CHES 2005. LNCS, vol. 3659, pp. 30–46. Springer, Heidelberg (2005). doi:10.1007/11545262_3

21. Barber, D.: Bayesian Reasoning and Machine Learning, 04-2011 edn. Cambridge University Press, Cambridge (2011)

22. Kschischang, F.R., Frey, B.J., Loeliger, H.-A.: Factor graphs and the sum-product algorithm. IEEE Trans. Inf. Theory $47(2)$, 498–519 (2001)

23. Gallager, R.G.: Low-density parity-check codes. IRE Trans. Inf. Theory $8(1)$, 21–28 (1962)

24. Tanner, R.M.: A recursive approach to low complexity codes. IEEE Trans. Inf. Theory $27(5)$, 533–547 (1981)

25. Pearl, J.: Reverend bayes on inference engines: a distributed hierarchical approach. In: National Conference on Artificial Intelligence, pp. 133–136. AAAI Press (1982)

26. Chung, S.-Y., David Forney Jr., G., Richardson, T.J., Urbanke, R.L.: On the design of low-density parity-check codes within 0.0045 dB of the Shannon limit. IEEE Commun. Lett. $5(2)$, 58–60 (2001)

Anonymizable Ring Signature Without Pairing

Olivier Blazy[1(✉)], Xavier Bultel[2], and Pascal Lafourcade[2]

[1] Xlim, Université de Limoges, Limoges, France
olivier.blazy@unilim.fr
[2] LIMOS, Université Clermont Auvergne, Clermont-Ferrand, France

Abstract. Ring signature is a well-known cryptographic primitive that allows any user who has a signing key to anonymously sign a message according to a group of users. Some years ago, Hoshino *et al.* propose a new kind of ring signature where anybody can transform a digital signature into an anonymous signature according to a chosen group of users; authors present a pairing-based construction that is secure under the gap Diffie-Hellman assumption in the random oracle model. However this scheme is quite inefficient for large group since the generation of the anonymous signature requires a number of pairing computations that is linear in the size of the group. In this paper, we give a more efficient anonymizable signature scheme without pairing. Our anonymization algorithm requires n exponentiations in a prime order group where n is the group size. Our proposal is secure under the discrete logarithm assumption in the random oracle model, which is a more standard assumption.

1 Introduction

Anonymizable Signature [7] is a kind of ring signature where anybody who has a signature produced by a group member can transform it into an anonymous signature within the group: someone can check that the anonymous signature has been produced by the group member signature but it is not possible to guess who is he. In practice, such a scheme allows a user to delegate to a proxy the task to anonymize a given signature. For example, during the reviews of an academic conference, each reviewer can sign his review before sending it to the program chair. Then the program chair anonymizes the given signature for the program committee and sends the review and the anonymous signature to the author of the paper. Then the author is convinced that the review comes from one of the member of the program committee but do not know who is the reviewer. The reviewer does not need to know the other members of the program committee.

Authors of [7] propose a pairing-based scheme secure under the gap Diffie-Hellman assumption in the random oracle model. In this scheme, the anonymous signature is a proof of knowledge of a valid signature within the group. However, this scheme is quite inefficient for large groups: the anonymization requires a

---

This research was conducted with the support of the "Digital Trust" Chair from the University of Auvergne Foundation.

F. Cuppens et al. (Eds.): FPS 2016, LNCS 10128, pp. 214–222, 2017.
DOI: 10.1007/978-3-319-51966-1_14

number of pairing computation which is linear on the size of the group. In this paper, we propose GAWP (for *Get Anonymizable signature Without Pairing*), an efficient pairing-free anonymous signature scheme. This scheme is based on the Schnorr signature [9] and uses the same methodology as [7]. Moreover, our scheme is provably secure under the discrete logarithm assumption in the random oracle model.

Related works: Ring signatures have been introduced by Rivest *et al.* in [8]. Such a signature scheme allows a user to sign a message anonymously within a group. Since the user only needs the public keys of all the members of the group and his secret key, this primitive does not require any group manager as in group signatures [2]. More recently, formal security definitions for ring signatures have been proposed [1]. In [7], Hoshino *et al.* define *anonymizable signatures* that extend the concept of ring signatures adding the possibility to transform any signature into an anonymous signature within a chosen group. Authors formally define the security models of this new primitive and propose a secure instantiation based on the BLS signature [3]. This scheme requires pairing and is proven secure in the random oracle model. To the best of our knowledge, it is the only one anonymizable signature scheme of the literature. Finally, *relinkable signatures* [10] are close to anonymous signatures: this primitive allows a proxy who have the *relink key* to change the group of an anonymous signature. However, a signature cannot be anonymized by anybody. Moreover, the signatures are anonymous for everybody in anonymous signature, but they are not anonymous for the proxy in relinkable signatures.

Outline: In the next section, we present the cryptographic background required for our work. In Sect. 3 gives the formal definitions of an anonymizable signature and the corresponding security models. Then we present the scheme GAWP in Sect. 4 and we analyze its security before concluding in the last section.

2 Background

In this section, we recall some definitions and cryptographic notions.

Definition 1 (Discrete Logarithm). *Let $\mathbb{G}$ be a multiplicative group of prime order p and $g \in \mathbb{G}$ be a generator. The* discrete logarithm problem *(DL) is to compute x given (g, g^x). The* discrete Logarithm hypothesis *states that there exists no polynomial time algorithm that solves DL with non-negligible advantage.*

Zero-knowledge proofs: [6] A *proof of knowledge* is a two-party protocol between two polynomial time algorithms P (the *prover*) and V (the *verifier*). It allows the prover P to convince the verifier V that he knows a solution s to the instance $\mathcal{I}$ of a problem $\mathcal{P}$. Such a protocol is said *zero-knowledge proof of knowledge* (ZKP) if it satisfies the following properties:

Completeness: If P knows s, then he is able to convince V (*i.e.*, V outputs `"accept"`).

Soundness: If P does not know s, then he is not able to convince V (*i.e.*, V outputs `"reject"`) except with negligible probability.

Zero-knowledge: V learns *nothing* about s except $\mathcal{I}$.

Honest-verifier ZKP (HZKP) is a weaker notion of ZKP which is restricted to case where the verifier is *honest*, *i.e.*, V correctly runs the protocol.

If we only have one flow from the prover to the verifier, we say that the ZKP is *non-interactive* (NIZKP). In the litterature, *sigma protocols* are ZKP with three exchanges between the prover and the verifier: a commitment, a challenge, and a response. By example, the Schnorr protocol [9] is a signma protocol that allows to prove the knowledge of the discrete logarithm of an instance $(g, k = g^x)$: the prover chooses $r \xleftarrow{\$} \mathbb{Z}_p^*$ and sends $R = g^r$. Then the verifier sends the challenge $c \xleftarrow{\$} \mathbb{Z}_p^*$ to the prover, who responds with the value $z = r + x \cdot c$. The verifier accepts the proof iff $g^z = h \cdot k^c$.

If the challenge is chosen on a large set, it is possible to transform a sigma protocol into a NIZKP using the Fiat-Shamir heuristic [5] replacing the challenge by the digest of a hash function on the commitment. It is also possible to transform such a NIZKP into a signature scheme in the random oracle model by using the message together with the commitment as input in the hash function to compute the challenge. For example, the Schnorr signature is obtained using this transformation on the Schnorr protocol: to sign a message m with the secret key $x \in \mathbb{Z}_p^*$, the signer picks r and computes $h = g^z$ and $z = r + x \cdot H(h, m)$. Using the public key $k = g^x$ and the signature (h, z), anybody can check that $g^z = h \cdot k^{H(h,m)}$ to validate the signature on m.

Finally, our scheme uses the generic transformation of ZKP designed by [4]. The authors propose a generic transformation from the ZKP of the solution to some problem instance to a ZKP of the solution to one problem instance out of n problem instances (without revealing this problem instance). This transformation holds with any sigma protocol and works as follows: consider n instances $\{I_i\}_{1 \leq i \leq n}$ and a prover who only knows the solution s_1 of the instance I_1. The prover sends n commitment h_i for $1 \leq i \leq n$ and receives an unique challenge c. For all the instances $\{I_i\}_{2 \leq i \leq n}$, the prover chooses a challenge c_i such that he is able to prove the knowledge of the solution of I_i using h_i and the challenge c_i as in the original sigma protocol (note that since he chooses the challenge by himself, he does not need to really know the corresponding secret). Finally, he computes $c_1 = c \oplus c_2 \oplus \ldots \oplus c_n$ and proves the knowledge of I_1 using h_1 and the challenge c_1 as in the original sigma protocol (note that, in this case, the prover must to know the secret s_1 to conclude the proof). Then the verifier check the proof for all pairs (h_i, c_i) and checks that $c = c_1 \oplus \ldots \oplus c_n$. The computational and space cost of the resulting ZKP is n times the cost of the primary ZKP. It is possible to use the Fiat-Shamir transformation on such a ZKP to obtain an equivalent NIZKP.

3   Security Models

We first give a formal definition of an *Anonymizable Ring Signature*.

Definition 2 (Anonymizable ring signature (ARS)). *An ARS is a tuple of algorithms (Init, Gen, Sig, Ver, Ano, AVer) such that:*

Init(1^t) : *This algorithm outputs an init value from security parameter t.*
Gen(init): *This algorithm outputs a signing key pair (ssk, svk) from init.*
Sig(ssk, m): *This algorithm outputs a signature σ on the message m using the signing key ssk.*
Ver(svk, σ, m): *This algorithm returns 1 when σ is a valid signature of m for the verification key svk. Else it returns 0.*
Ano(L, σ, m, svk): *This algorithm outputs an anonymous signature $\widehat{\sigma}$ on the message m according to the set of public key L from the signature σ and the corresponding verification key svk.*
AVer(L, $\widehat{\sigma}$, m): *This algorithm returns 1 when $\widehat{\sigma}$ is a valid signature of m for the set of verification keys L. Else it returns 0.*

In what follow, we denote by $out_{\mathcal{O}}$ the set of all the values outputted by the oracle $\mathcal{O}$ during an experiment. The first security requirement is the *unforgeability*. An ARS is unforgeable when it is not possible to forge a signature without the corresponding secret key, and to forge an anonymous signature without a signature valide for one of the group members. In this model, we give to the attacker the possibility to ask anonymous and regular signatures for chosen messages and chosen users to some signing oracle. Of course, to win the attack, the attacker must forge a signature that does not come from these oracles.

Definition 3 (EUF-CMA security). *Let P be an ARS of security parameter t and let $\mathcal{A} = (\mathcal{A}_1, \mathcal{A}_2)$ be a polynomial time adversary. We define the existential unforgeability against chosen message attack experiment for $\mathcal{A}$ as follows:*

$\mathbf{Exp}_{P,\mathcal{A}}^{\text{euf-cma}}(t, n)$:
$init \leftarrow Init(1^t)$
$\forall\ i \in \{0, \dots, n\}, (ssk_i, svk_i) \leftarrow Gen(init)$
$I \leftarrow \mathcal{A}_1^{\mathcal{GO}(\cdot), \mathcal{SO}(\cdot), \mathcal{AO}(\cdot)}(t, \{svk_i\}_{0 \le i \le n})$
$(L_*, \widehat{\sigma}, m) \leftarrow \mathcal{A}_2^{\mathcal{GO}(\cdot), \mathcal{SO}(\cdot), \mathcal{AO}(\cdot)}(t, \{svk_i\}_{0 \le i \le n}, \{ssk_i\}_{i \in I})$
$if\ ((AVer(L_*, \widehat{\sigma}, m) = 1)\ and\ (L^* \subset \{svk_i\}_{0 \le i \le n, i \notin I})$
    $and\ (\forall\ svk \in L_*, (svk, m, *) \notin out_{\mathcal{SO}})\ and\ ((L_*, m, \widehat{\sigma}) \notin out_{\mathcal{AO}}))$
then output 1 else output 0.

Where oracles are defined as follows:

$\mathcal{GO}(\cdot)$ *is a key generation oracle that increments $n \leftarrow n + 1$, generates $(ssk_n, svk_n) \leftarrow Gen(init)$ and returns it.*
$\mathcal{SO}(\cdot)$ *is a signing oracle that takes (svk_i, m) as input. It computes $\sigma \leftarrow Sig(ssk_i, m)$ and returns (svk_i, m, σ).*
$\mathcal{AO}(\cdot)$ *is an anonymization oracle that takes (svk_i, m, L) as input. It computes $\sigma \leftarrow Sig(ssk_i, m)$ and $\widehat{\sigma} \leftarrow Ano(L, \sigma, m, svk_i)$ and returns $(L, m, \widehat{\sigma})$.*

We define the advantage of the adversary $\mathcal{A}$ against the EUF-CMA experiment by $\mathsf{Adv}_{P,\mathcal{A}}^{euf\text{-}cma}(t,n) = \Pr[\mathsf{Exp}_{P,\mathcal{A}}^{euf\text{-}cma}(t,n) = 1]$. We define the advantage on EUF-CMA experiment by $\mathsf{Adv}_P^{euf\text{-}cma}(t,n) = \max_{\mathcal{A}\in\text{POLY}(t)}\{\mathsf{Adv}_{P,\mathcal{A}}^{euf\text{-}cma}(t,n)\}$. We say that a ARS scheme P is EUF-CMA secure when the advantage $\mathsf{Adv}_P^{euf\text{-}cma}(t,n)$ is negligible for any polynomially bounded n.

The second security requirement is the anonymity. Loosely speaking, an ARS is anonymous when it is not possible to guess who has produced the signature used to compute an anonymous signature. In this security model, the adversary chooses two users and a message m, and it receives an anonymous signature produced from the signatures on m computed by one of the two users included in a bigger set L. The goal is to guess who is the user chosen by the challenger. To help him, the adversary have access to some signing oracles.

Definition 4 (Anonymity). *Let P be an ARS of security parameter t and let $\mathcal{A} = (\mathcal{A}_1, \mathcal{A}_2)$ be polynomial time adversary. We define the anonymity experiment for adversary $\mathcal{A}$ against P as follows:*

$\mathsf{Exp}_{P,\mathcal{A}}^{anon}(t,n)$:
$b \leftarrow \{0,1\}$
$init \leftarrow \mathsf{Init}(1^t)$
$\forall\ i \in \{0,\dots,n\}, (\mathsf{ssk}_i, \mathsf{svk}_i) \leftarrow \mathsf{Gen}(init)$
$(i_0, i_1, L, m) \leftarrow \mathcal{A}_1^{\mathcal{GO}(\cdot),\mathcal{SO}(\cdot),\mathcal{AO}(\cdot)}(t, \{(\mathsf{ssk}_i, \mathsf{svk}_i)\}_{0\leq i\leq n})$
If i_0 *OR* $i_1 \notin L$ *then Abort*
$\hat{\sigma} \leftarrow \mathsf{Ano}(L, \mathsf{Sig}(\mathsf{ssk}_{i_b}, m), m, \mathsf{svk}_{i_b})$
$b' \leftarrow \mathcal{A}_2^{\mathcal{GO}(\cdot),\mathcal{SO}(\cdot),\mathcal{AO}(\cdot)}(t, \hat{\sigma})$
output $b = b'$.

Where $\mathcal{GO}(\cdot)$, $\mathcal{SO}(\cdot)$ *and* $\mathcal{AO}(\cdot)$ *are defined as in Definition 3.*

The advantage of the adversary $\mathcal{A}$ against anonymity is $\mathsf{Adv}_{P,\mathcal{A}}^{anon}(t,n) = \left|\Pr[\mathsf{Exp}_{P,\mathcal{A}}^{anon}(t,n) = 1] - \frac{1}{2}\right|$. *We define the advantage on anonymity experiment by* $\mathsf{Adv}_P^{anon}(t,n) = \max_{\mathcal{A}\in\text{POLY}(t)}\{\mathsf{Adv}_{P,\mathcal{A}}^{anon}(t,n)\}$ *where* $\text{POLY}(t)$ *is the set of all the algorithm that are polynomial in t. We say that a ARS scheme P is anonymous when the advantage* $\mathsf{Adv}_P^{anon}(t,n)$ *is negligible for any polynomially bounded n.*

4   Constructions

In this section, we present our scheme called GAWP (for *Get ARS Without Pairing*). We use the same design methodology as in [7]: to anonymize the signature σ of a message m, a user computes a non-interactive zero knowledge proof of the knowledge of σ according to one verification key out of all the verification keys of the group. Our scheme is based on the well known Schnorr signature (see Sect. 2). Particularly, the signature and the verification algorithm are the same as in the Schnorr signature: let g be the generator of a prime order group, then the signature algorithm outputs $h = g^r$ and $z = r + \mathsf{ssk} \cdot H(h, m)$ where r is a random value, ssk the signing key and m the message. To validate a signature,

Prover P		Verifier V
z		k, h, m, H
$s \xleftarrow{\$} \mathbb{Z}_p^*$		$c \xleftarrow{\$} \mathbb{Z}_p^*$
$S = g^s$	$\xrightarrow{\quad S \quad}$	
$\alpha = s + z \cdot c$	$\xleftarrow{\quad c \quad}$	
	$\xrightarrow{\quad \alpha \quad}$	Check that:
		$g^\alpha \overset{?}{=} S \cdot (h \cdot k^{H(h,m)})^c$

Fig. 1. Protocol $\varPi_0$

a user checks that $g^z = h \cdot \mathsf{svk}^{H(h,m)}$ where svk is the public verification key such that $\mathsf{svk} = g^{\mathsf{ssk}}$. Then, our goal is to give a way to prove the knowledge of a valid Schnorr signature according to one of the verification keys of the group. Note that the first part of the signature $h = g^r$ does not leak any information about the signing key ssk. Then this value can be public in the anonymized signature. The last step is to prove the knowledge of the second part of the signature z according to h, m, H and the set of verification key L of all members of the group. More precisely, our aim is to prove the knowledge of z such that $g^z = h \cdot \mathsf{svk}^{H(h,m)}$ for one $\mathsf{svk} \in L$, h, m and H. In the following, we first give the zero-knowledge proof that allows to prove the knowledge of a Schnorr signature. Next, we give the concrete construction of GAWP, and finally, we analyze its security.

Proof of knowledge construction: Let $\mathbb{G}$ be a group of prime order p, g be a generator of $\mathbb{G}$ and n be an integer. Let k and h be two elements of $\mathbb{G}$, m be a bit-string and $H : \{0,1\}^* \to \mathbb{Z}_p^*$ be a hash function. Finally, for all $i \in \{1, \dots, n\}$, we set the instance tuple $t_i = (k_i, h, m, H)$.

In the following, we show how to build $\varPi$, a non-interactive zero knowledge proof of knowledge of $z \in \mathbb{Z}_p^*$ such that there exists an instance $(k, h, m, H) \in \{t_i\}_{1 \leq i \leq n}$ such that $z = \log_g(h \cdot k^{H(h,m)})$. We first describe in Fig. 1 the interactive case $\varPi_0$ where $n = 1$, hence there is only one instance $t = (k, h, m, H)$. It is a variant of the Schnorr protocol [9]. This proof is a sigma-protocol.

Lemma 1. *The ZKP $\varPi_0$ is complete, sound, and honest-verifier zero-knowledge.*

The proof of Lemma 1 is similar to the proof of the Schnorr protocol properties [9]. As $\varPi_0$ is honest-verifier zero knowledge and a sigma protocol, we can use the generic transformation of [4] to obtain the interactive version of our proof for any $n \geq 1$. Finally, using this transformation and the Fiat-Shamir heuristic on $\varPi_0$, we build the non-interactive proof $\varPi$ in the random oracle model.

Theorem 1. *The NIZKP $\varPi$ is complete, sound, and zero-knowledge in the random oracle model.*

Proof. It is a direct implication of [4] and Lemma 1.

Notation: We denote by $\Pi.\mathsf{Proof}(z, t, \{t_i\}_{1 \le i \le n})$ the algorithm that generates such a proof where z is the secret, $t = (k, h, m, H) \in \{t_i\}_{1 \le i \le n}$ is the instance corresponding to z such that $g^z = h \cdot k^{H(h,m)}$ and $\{t_i\}_{1 \le i \le n}$ is the set of all the instances. We denote by $\Pi.\mathsf{Verif}(\pi, \{t_i\}_{1 \le i \le n})$ the algorithm that checks the validity of the proof π according to the set of instances $\{t_i\}_{1 \le i \le n}$.

Scheme 1 (GAWP scheme). $GAWP = (\mathsf{Init}, \mathsf{Gen}, \mathsf{Sig}, \mathsf{Ver}, \mathsf{Ano}, \mathsf{AVer})$ *is an ARS such that:*

$\mathsf{Init}(1^t)$**:** *This algorithm chooses a group $\mathbb{G}$ of prime order p according to the security parameter t. It then chooses a generator g of $\mathbb{G}$ and a hash function $H : \{0, 1\}^* \to \mathbb{Z}_p^*$. It outputs $(\mathbb{G}, p, g, H)$.*

$\mathsf{Gen}(\mathsf{init})$**:** *This algorithm picks $x \xleftarrow{\$} \mathbb{Z}_p^*$, computes $\mathsf{ssk} = x$ and $\mathsf{svk} = g^x$ and returns $(\mathsf{ssk}, \mathsf{svk})$.*

$\mathsf{Sig}(\mathsf{ssk}, m)$**:** *This algorithm picks $r \xleftarrow{\$} \mathbb{Z}_p^*$, computes $h = g^r$, $M = H(h, m)$ and $z = r + \mathsf{ssk} \cdot M$ and returns $\sigma = (h, z)$.*

$\mathsf{Ver}(\mathsf{svk}, \sigma, m)$**:** *Using $\sigma = (h, z)$, if $g^z = h \cdot \mathsf{svk}^{H(h,m)}$ then this algorithm returns 1, else it returns 0.*

$\mathsf{Ano}(L, \sigma, m, \mathsf{svk})$**:** *Using $\sigma = (h, z)$, this algorithm computes a zero-knowledge proof of the knowledge of the witness z such that there exists $k \in L$ such that $g^z = h \cdot k^{H(h,m)}$ without revealing neither z nor k. More precisely, it uses the non-interactive zero-knowledge proof scheme Π to computes $\widehat{\sigma} = \Pi.\mathsf{Proof}(z, (\mathsf{svk}, h, m, H), \{(k, h, m, H)\}_{k \in L})$ and returns it.*

$\mathsf{AVer}(L, \widehat{\sigma}, m)$**:** *This algorithm computes $b = \Pi.\mathsf{Verif}(\widehat{\sigma}, \{(k, h, m, H)\}_{k \in L})$ and returns it.*

Security Analysis: We have the following theorem.

Theorem 2. *If there is no polynomial time algorithm $\mathcal{A}$ that solves the discrete logarithm problem with a non-negligible probability, then $\mathsf{Adv}_{GAWP}^{euf\text{-}cma}(t, n)$ and $\mathsf{Adv}_{GAWP}^{anon}(t, n)$ are both negligible in t for any polynomially bounded n in the random oracle model.*

We show this, through the two following lemmas

Lemma 2. *An ARS is unforgeable under the hardness of the discrete logarithm problem.*

Proof. We are going to show that is we have a polynomial adversary $\mathcal{A}$ able to forge our scheme in a polytnomial time with non negligible probability ϵ, then we can build a simulator $\mathcal{B}$ able to break the discrete logarithm problem with a similar polynomial time with probability ϵ/q where q is the number of users in the system.

Let assume $\mathcal{B}$ receives a discrete logarithm challenge $\mathsf{svk}_* \in \mathbb{G}$. We are going to build a sequence of games, allowing $\mathcal{B}$ to use adversary $\mathcal{A}$ to compute x such that $g^x = \mathsf{svk}_*$.

We first start the simulation by picking a random user and setting his public key as svk_*, all the user users have keys generated honestly (in other words the simulator $\mathcal{B}$ knows their corresponding signing keys). This means that if the adversary wants to corrupt some users, we can give him the corresponding secret keys.

When answering signing queries:

- If the signer is an honest user, $\mathcal{B}$ simply computes the signature honestly using the associated (known) secret signing keys.
- If the user, is the expected challenge user, then $\mathcal{B}$ picks a random $r \in \mathbb{Z}_p^*$, computes h^r, and simulates the Zero-Knowledge proof $\hat{\sigma}$ to say that this is indeed a valid signature for a set of users L containing the challenge user i_*. Under the Zero Knowledge property (hence the programmabilty of the ROM), this simulation is indistinguishable from a real signature.

After a polynomial number of signing queries, the adversary picks a user i_*' and returns a signature on an unsigned message/set of users. For the forgery to be valid, the signature has to be valid, the set of users should only contain uncorrupted users, and never have signed the said message.

From the adversary point of view honest signatures, and simulated ones are indistinguishable, hence with probability $1/q$ the adversary is going to pick the expected user as his challenge one.

Now using the extractability of the random oracle, $\mathcal{B}$ can recover the value ssk_* used to generate the proof (this can simply be done by rewinding the random oracle on the final proof computation). Hence after a polynomial time $\mathcal{B}$ is able to recover the discrete logarithm associated with the challenge with probability ϵ/q. $\square$

Lemma 3. *The previous scheme is anonymous in the Random Oracle Model.*

Proof. Let us assume there exists an adversary $\mathcal{A}$ against the Anonymity of our scheme, we are going to build a simulator $\mathcal{B}$ in the Random Oracle Model.

- We start from a game $\mathcal{G}_{0,0}$ where the simulator does everything honestly and picks the identity i_0. This includes generating honestly all the secret keys and signing.
- We now change the generation of the challenge signature. The user still picks a random $r \in \mathbb{Z}_p^*$ but now simulates the Zero-Knowledge proof $\hat{\sigma}$. This is done by programming the random oracle, so that the challenge value fits with the guess done in the first part of the proof. This leads to the game $\mathcal{G}_{1,0}$. Using Theorem 1, this game is indistinguishable from the previous one.
- A simulated challenge signature for the identity i_1 is exactly the same (as the simulation does not require the knowledge of the key), hence game $\mathcal{G}_{1,1}$ is identical to the previous one.
- Finally, the simulator $\mathcal{B}$ switches back to an honest signature this time made by using the secret key i_1 to generate $\hat{\sigma}$. Once again, under the random oracle model, this game is indistinguishable from the previous one. $\square$

Efficiency: In GAWP, the signature algorithm requires one exponentiation, and the anonymization algorithm requires $2 \times n$ exponentiations where n is the size of the group. In the scheme [7], the signature requires one exponentiation, but the anonymization requires $n+1$ exponentiations and $2 \times n + 1$ pairing computations. Moreover, this scheme requires $2 \times n$ pairing computations and n exponentiations in the verification algorithm of an anonymous signature when our scheme requires only $2 \times n + 1$ exponentiations. Thus GAWP is more efficient than the scheme [7] that becomes impractical when the group contains a lot of members.

5   Conclusion

In this paper, we show that pairings are not needed in anonymizable ring signature: we design a paring-free scheme that is more efficient and secure under a more standard assumption as the previous scheme in [7]. Particularly, the anonymization algorithm and the anonymous verification algorithm in [7] are very inefficient for large groups comparing to ours since it requires a number of pairing computations that is linear in the size of the group. The next step will be to design an anonymizable ring signature that can be proven secure without the random oracle heuristic.

References

1. Bender, A., Katz, J., Morselli, R.: Ring signatures: stronger definitions, and constructions without random oracles. In: Halevi, S., Rabin, T. (eds.) TCC 2006. LNCS, vol. 3876, pp. 60–79. Springer, Heidelberg (2006). doi:10.1007/11681878_4
2. Boneh, D., Boyen, X., Shacham, H.: Short group signatures. In: Franklin, M. (ed.) CRYPTO 2004. LNCS, vol. 3152, pp. 41–55. Springer, Heidelberg (2004). doi:10.1007/978-3-540-28628-8_3
3. Boneh, D., Lynn, B., Shacham, H.: Short signatures from the Weil pairing. J. Cryptology **17**(4), 297–319 (2004)
4. Cramer, R., Damgård, I., Schoenmakers, B.: Proofs of partial knowledge and simplified design of witness hiding protocols. In: Desmedt, Y.G. (ed.) CRYPTO 1994. LNCS, vol. 839, pp. 174–187. Springer, Heidelberg (1994). doi:10.1007/3-540-48658-5_19
5. Fiat, A., Shamir, A.: How to prove yourself: practical solutions to identification and signature problems. In: Odlyzko, A.M. (ed.) CRYPTO 1986. LNCS, vol. 263, pp. 186–194. Springer, Heidelberg (1987). doi:10.1007/3-540-47721-7_12
6. Goldwasser, S., Micali, S., Rackoff, C.: The knowledge complexity of interactive proof systems. SIAM J. Comput. **18**, 186–208 (1989)
7. Hoshino, F., Kobayashi, T., Suzuki, K.: Anonymizable signature and its construction from pairings. In: Joye, M., Miyaji, A., Otsuka, A. (eds.) Pairing 2010. LNCS, vol. 6487, pp. 62–77. Springer, Heidelberg (2010). doi:10.1007/978-3-642-17455-1_5
8. Rivest, R.L., Shamir, A., Tauman, Y.: How to leak a secret. In: Boyd, C. (ed.) ASIACRYPT 2001. LNCS, vol. 2248, pp. 552–565. Springer, Heidelberg (2001). doi:10.1007/3-540-45682-1_32
9. Schnorr, C.P.: Efficient identification and signatures for smart cards. In: Brassard, G. (ed.) CRYPTO 1989. LNCS, vol. 435, pp. 239–252. Springer, Heidelberg (1990). doi:10.1007/0-387-34805-0_22
10. Suzuki, K., Hoshino, F., Kobayashi, T.: Relinkable ring signature. In: Garay, J.A., Miyaji, A., Otsuka, A. (eds.) CANS 2009. LNCS, vol. 5888, pp. 518–536. Springer, Heidelberg (2009). doi:10.1007/978-3-642-10433-6_35

Security Analysis of WirelessHART Communication Scheme

Lyes Bayou[1(✉)], David Espes[2], Nora Cuppens-Boulahia[1],
and Frédéric Cuppens[1]

[1] LabSTICC, Télécom Bretagne, 2 Rue de la Châtaigneraie, Césson Sévigné, France
lyes.bayou@telecom-bretagne.eu
[2] LabSTICC, University of Western Brittany, Brest, France

Abstract. Communication security is a major concern in industrial process management. Indeed, in addition to real-time requirements, it is very important to ensure that sensing data sent by field sensors are not altered or modified during their transmission. This is more true in Wireless Sensor Networks where communication can be hijacked and false data injected. Therefore wireless communication protocols include several security mechanisms to ensure data confidentiality and integrity. In this paper, we present an attack against WirelessHART, the leading wireless communication protocol in industrial environment. We show that an insider attacker can bypass security mechanisms and inject false commands in the network. Such attacks can have harmful economical consequences or even more can threaten human lives. We propose also some solutions that can be applied for detecting and mitigating this kind of attacks.

1 Introduction

Industrial Control Systems (ICS) are computed-based systems used for monitoring and managing industrial installations and facilities. We can find such systems in airports, power plants, gas refineries, etc. The architecture of these systems relies on several sensors and actuators deployed throughout the industrial installation. Sensors are responsible for gathering different kinds of information about the industrial process such as temperature, pressure, flow, etc. These information are sent to a controller that processes them and sends back commands to actuators. As results, an actuator can for example open a valve to increase the flow of a chemical component or stop a pump when the oil tank is filled.

The security in Industrial Control Systems is a major concern. Indeed, these systems manage installations that play an important economical role. Even more, targeting these systems can lead not only to economical losses but can also threaten human lives [1].

Therefore and as these systems depend on sensing data, it is important to secure communication channels between these sensors and the main controllers. This issue is more challenging in Wireless Sensor Networks as the use of wireless communications brings its own security weaknesses.

© Springer International Publishing AG 2017
F. Cuppens et al. (Eds.): FPS 2016, LNCS 10128, pp. 223–238, 2017.
DOI: 10.1007/978-3-319-51966-1_15

Based on the analysis of the communication scheme, we present in this paper an attack against WirelessHART [2], the leading wireless communication protocol in the industrial environment. We show that although this protocol implements several mechanisms to ensure the integrity and confidentiality of exchanged data, an insider attacker can use its own credential to bypass security mechanisms and inject false commands in the network. Using this weakness, we describe three scenarios that can be used to launch an attack against a WSN. Such attacks can have harmful economical consequences or even more can threaten human lives.

Several tests were conducted on a simulated network to prove the feasibility of these attacks and to assess its potential impact on the functioning of the industrial process.

The rest of the paper is organized as follows. In Sect. 2, we give a brief description of the functioning of a WirelessHART network, its communication scheme and how data are exchanged and secured. We detail in Sect. 3, the functioning of the broadcast attack and give three different scenarios that use this attack. Section 4 presents results of the three scenarios on a simulated WSN. Some countermeasures that can be used to detect such attacks are discussed in Sect. 5. In Sect. 6, we discuss prior works on the security of WirelessHART. Finally, Sect. 7 presents the conclusion and future works.

2   Background

WirelessHART [2] is the first standardized wireless communication protocol specially developed for industrial process management. It uses a time-synchronized, self-organized and self-healing mesh architecture to provide a reliable and real-time communication. It is included in version 7 of the HART standard, released in 2007, and was approved as a IEC 62591 standard in 2010.

2.1   Topology of a WirelessHART Network

A typical WirelessHART network is composed of the following devices:

- A Gateway that connects the wireless network to the plant automation network, allowing data to flow between the two networks. It can also be used to convert data and commands from one protocol to another one;
- A Network Manager that is responsible for the overall management, scheduling, and optimization of the wireless network. It generates and maintains all of the routing information and also allocates communication resources;
- A Security Manager that is responsible for the generation, storage, and management of cryptographic keys;
- Access Points that connect the Gateway to the wireless network through a wired connection;
- Field devices deployed in the plant field and which can be sensors or actuators;
- Routers used for forwarding packets from one network device to another;
- Handheld devices that are portable equipments operated by the plant personnel used in the installation and during the maintenance of network devices.

2.2   WirelessHART Stack

The WirelessHART protocol is composed of 4 layers. It is based in its physical layer upon the IEEE 802.15.4 standard [3]. It defines its own data link layer and network layer and shares the same application layer with the wired HART protocol (in the addition of wireless commands). A brief description of each layer is given below:

- Application Layer (AL): it is a command based layer. It is used to send sensing data from field devices to the Network Manager, and to send commands from the Network Manager to the field devices. It supports both common HART commands (inherited from the wired version) and WirelessHART commands.
- Transport Layer (TL): it provides mechanisms to ensure packets fragmentation and defragmentation. It ensures data delivery without loss, duplication or misordering to its final destination. It supports acknowledged and unacknowledged transactions.
- Network Layer (NL): it ensures end-to-end integrity and confidentiality. It provides routing features. It receives packets from the DLL and checks if they have to be transmitted to the AL or have to be resent to the DLL to be forwarded to the next device.
- Data Link Layer (DLL): it is responsible of preparing packets for transmission, sending and receiving packets, managing time slots and maintaining informations about neighborhood. It provides hop-by-hop authentication.
- Physical Layer (PhL): it is based on the IEEE 802.15.4-2006 standard and operates in the 2.4 GHz. It is responsible of wireless transmission and reception.

2.3   WirlessHART Communication

The Network Manager is one of the most important devices in a WirelessHART network. It is responsible for the overall management, scheduling, and optimization of the wireless network. It generates and maintains graphs and routing information and also allocates communication resources.

Communication Type. In WirelessHART there are 05 packet types, called Data Link Protocol Unit (DLPDU), that can be exchanged between devices:

- Data DLPDU: encapsulates packets from the NL. It is used to exchange sensing data and AL commands.
- Ack DLPDU: is used by a device that receives an unicast packet, to send back to the sender device an acknowledgment of the reception of that packet.
- Keep-alive DLPDU: is used by a device that spends a defined time without sending any packets, to inform its neighbors that it is still active.
- Advertise DLPDU: is used for providing information to neighboring devices trying to join the network;

- Disconnect DLPDU: is used by a device to inform its neighboring devices that it is leaving the network.

Ack, Advertise, Keep-Alive and Disconnect DLPDUs are generated and processed in the Data Link Layer and are not propagated to the network layer or forwarded through the network. This means that these DLPDUs are only used in local communication between neighbors. The Data DLPDU is the only kind of packet that is transmitted in an end-to-end communication. During the transmission, data fields in the payload are enciphered.

Communication Scheduling. To provide reliable and collision free communication, WirelessHART uses *Time Division Multiple Access* (TDMA) and *Channel hopping* to control the access to the wireless medium. The time is divided in consecutive periods of the same duration called slots. Each communication between two devices occurs in one slot of 10 ms. Superframes are collection of slots repeated continuously with a fixed repetition rate.

Typically, two devices are assigned to one time slot (one as the sender and a second as the receiver). Only one packet is transmitted in one slot from the sender to the receiver which has to reply with an acknowledgment packet in the same slot. In the case of a broadcast message, there is one sender and multiple receivers and the message is not acknowledged.

In addition to the TDMA, WirelessHART uses channel hopping to provide frequency diversity and avoid interferences. Thus, the 2.4 GHz band is divided into 16 channels numbered from 11 to 26 which provide up to 15 communications in the same slot (Channel 26 is not used).

Communication Routing. WirelessHART implements in the Network Layer, two methods of routing packets throughout the network, i.e., graph routing and source routing.

- Graph routing: a graph is a collection of directed paths that connect network devices. It is build by the Network manager based on its knowledge of the network topology and connectivity. Every graph has a unique graph identifier that is inserted in the network packet header. Each device receiving this packet, must forward it to the next hop belonging to that graph. This routing method is used for normal communications, in both upstream (from a device to the network manager) and downstream (from the network manager to a specific device) directions.
- Source routing: it is a single directed route between a source and a destination device. The complete route is completely inserted in the network packet header by the sender device. Each intermediate device propagates the packet to the next device indicated in the source route field. This method of routing is used only for testing routes, troubleshooting network paths or for ad-hoc communications.

Communication Security. WirelessHART implements several mechanisms to ensure data confidentiality, authenticity and integrity in both hop-by-hop and end-to-end transmissions.

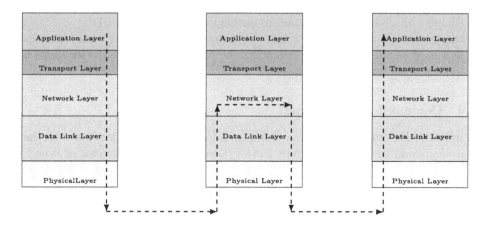

Fig. 1. WirelessHART communication scheme

Indeed, as WirelessHART builds a mesh network, sensors are located several hops from the network manager. Thus, these sensors rely on their neighbors to forward their packets from/to the network manager. Therefore, as illustrated in Fig. 1, the several forwards of packets between neighbor devices are called *the hop-by-hop transmission* and the communication between the sending sensor and the network manager is called *the end-to-end communication*.

Security at Data Link Layer: The hop-by-hop transmission security is provided by the Data Link Layer (DLL) using a cryptographic key called "Network Key" shared by all devices composing the wireless network. It defends against attackers who are outside the network and do not share its secret.

Each DLPDU is authenticated by the sending device using *the network key*. Therefore, before processing any received DLPDU, a device must check the keyed Message Integrity Code (MIC) to authenticate the identity of the sending device. We must note that the DLPDU itself is not enciphered but authenticated by a four-byte MIC generated with CCM* mode (Combined Counter with CBC-MAC) using the AES-128 block cipher.

Security at Network Layer: The end-to-end security is provided by the Network Layer (NL) using a cryptographic key called "Session Key" known only by the two communicant devices. It defends against attackers who may be on the network path between the source and the destination (Inside attacker).

The network layer also uses a keyed Message Integrity Code (MIC) for the authentication of the Network Protocol Data Unit (NPDU). Additionally, it is used to encrypt and decrypt the NPDU payload. The end-to-end security is session oriented i.e., it provides a private and secure communication channel between a pair of network devices. Each session is defined by two elements:

– the session key: it is a dedicated 128-bits cryptographic key. It is used to encipher the NPDU payload and to authenticate the whole NPDU.
– the session counter: it is a 32 bits value that defends against replay attacks and used as the nounce for generating the NPDU MIC. Each device keeps a history of received nonce counter.

2.4   Communication Scheme

WirelessHART implements unicast and broadcast communications in both the Data Link and the Network Layers. In the Data link layer, the unicast or broadcast communication is set by configuring the packet with unicast or a broadcast destination address, by using the unicast or the broadcast graph and also by using the dedicated transmission slots. Indeed, the Network Manager configures each wireless sensor to be at the beginning of each slot either a sender, a receiver or to stay idle.

As illustrated in Fig. 2, when a device receives unicast packet, it starts by authenticating it in the Data link layer (DLL) using the network key and then it is transmitted to the Network layer. There, the destination NL address is checked. If it matches the device's address, the packet is authenticated a second time using the unicast session key and its payload is deciphered and sent to the Application Layer to be executed. Otherwise, the packet is sent back to the DLL to be forwarded to the next hop device.

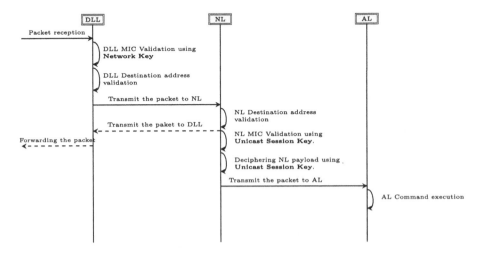

Fig. 2. Unicast packet processing sequence

In a broadcast communication, a packet sent by the Network manager is propagated to all devices in the wireless network. As illustrated in Fig. 3, each time a device receives a broadcast packet, it starts by authenticating it firstly in the Data link layer (DLL) using the network key and then in the Network layer (NL) using the broadcast session key. If the packet passes authentication validations, it will be deciphered and sent to the Application Layer (AL) to be executed. A copy of the packet is also sent back to the DLL to be forwarded to other devices.

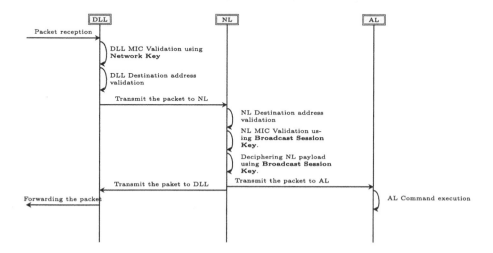

Fig. 3. Broadcast packet processing sequence

On another hand, in the Network Layer, four sessions are set up as soon as any device joins the network. They allow the transmission of sensing data from a device to the Network Manager, and the transmission of commands from the Network Manager to a field device.

1. unicast session with the NM: it is used by the network manager to manage the device.
2. broadcast session with the NM: it is used to globally manage devices. For example this can be used to roll a new network key out to all network devices. All devices in the network have the same key for this session.
3. unicast session with the Gateway: it carries normal communications (for example process data) between the gateway and the device.
4. broadcast session with the Gateway: it is used by the gateway to send the identical application data to all devices.

In addition, each device has a join session key which cannot be deleted. The Join_key is the only key that is written once connecting to the device's maintenance port. It can also be updated by the Network Manager once the device is successfully connected. All other keys are distributed by the Network Manager.

3   Communication Scheme Attack

The idea of the attack is that a malicious insider attacker uses its own credentials to bypass the authentication mechanism and injects false command into the network. These false commands will be authenticated as legitimate commands and executed by receiving devices. Depending on the nature of injected false commands, consequences on the network can be more or less harmful.

As indicated in the previous Section, end-to-end communications are secured by session keys. In unicast communications, the session key is only known by the two communicant devices while in broadcast communications, the session key is shared by all devices connected to the network.

Therefore to launch the command injection attack, the malicious insider attacker will use Broadcast Session credentials to perform this kind of attacks. Indeed, as part of the network, the malicious node is configured with *the broadcast session key* and the *session counter*.

The command injection attack can be performed in several ways such as: a Direct command injection attack, a Bounced command injection attack and an On-the-fly command injection attack.

3.1   Scenario 1: Direct Command Injection Attack

In a Direct Command Injection Attack a malicious insider node forges a fake broadcast packet and forwards it to its neighbors.

As illustrated in Fig. 4, at the moment T the malicious node *Device*5 uses its knowledge on the broadcast session credential i.e., the broadcast session key and the session counter, to forge a broadcast packet. The source address in the NL is set to the Network Manager address and the destination addresses in both network and data link layers are set to the broadcast address. The malicious insider node will send the forged packet using its own broadcast link in the same way as if it was a legitimate packet sent by the network manager. Receiving nodes, *Device*8 and *Device*9, will authenticate the packet using the broadcast session key and execute the injected false command.

Using this attack, a malicious insider node can inject any false command and send it to its neighbors using the broadcast graph.

3.2   Scenario 2: Bounced Command Injection Attack

In WirelessHART both DLL and NL destination addresses can be either unicast or broadcast addresses and all combinations are allowed. So, a packet can have unicast DLL destination address and a broadcast NL destination address.

In a Bounced Command Injection Attack a malicious insider node forges a fake broadcast packet and sends it to its parent node. As illustrated in Fig. 5, this kind of attacks is composed of the following steps:

1. At the moment T the malicious node *Device*5 uses its knowledge of the broadcast session credential i.e., the broadcast session key and the session counter,

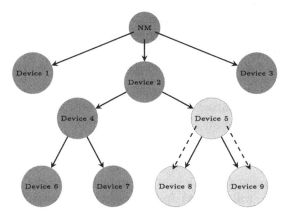

Fig. 4. Direct broadcast attack

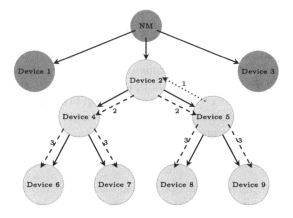

Fig. 5. Bounced broadcast attack

to forge a broadcast packet. The source address in the NL is set to the Network Manager address and the NL destination address is set to the broadcast address.

In the DLL, the source address is set to the *Device*5 address and the destination address is set to its parent's address i.e., *Device*2. The malicious insider node will send the forged packet using its own normal link between itself and the parent node.

2. The receiving node *Device*2 authenticates the packet in the DLL as a legitimate unicast packet and transmitted it to the upper layer.

   In the NL, the packet is identified as a broadcast packet sent by the Network Manager. It is authenticated and deciphered using the broadcast session key. The packet is then transmitted to the application layer to be executed.

   A copy of the packet is also transmitted to the DLL to be forwarded to *Device*2 neighbors i.e., *Device*4 and *Device*5.

3. Both *Device*4 and *Device*5 process the received packet as a legitimate broadcast packet sent by the Network manager and propagate it to their neighbors.
4. As results, the injected false command packet is received and executed by *Device*2, *Device*4, *Device*5, *Device*6, *Device*7, *Device*8 and *Device*9.

This scenario allows a malicious insider node by using its parent node as a relay to increase the impact of the attack. By this way, the injected false command is propagated to all parent node's children.

3.3 Scenario 3: On-the-fly Command Injection Attack

In an On-the-fly command injection attack, a malicious insider node that receives a broadcast packet, will forward to its neighbors a modified version of the received packet.

As illustrated in Fig. 6, this attack is performed according to the following steps:

1. The Network Manager sends a broadcast packet.
2. The broadcast packet is forwarded to devices and received by the malicious insider node *Device*5.
3. All receiving node execute the command sent by the network manager and forward it to devices in their neighborhood.
4. The malicious node *Device*5 uses its knowledge of broadcast session credential i.e., the session key and the session counter, to modify the received broadcast packet and send it to its neighbors.
5. As results, the injected false command packet is received and executed by *Device*8 and *Device*9.

As in the direct command injection attack, a malicious insider node can inject any false command and sent it to its neighbors using the broadcast graph. The difference is that an on-the-fly injection command attack is a stealth attack as the injected packet is hidden inside a legitimate communication flow.

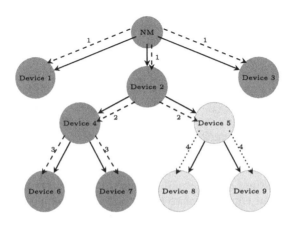

Fig. 6. On-the-fly broadcast attack

3.4   Discussion

Described scenarios showed the feasibility of the broadcast attack and that it can be performed in several ways. We must note that although we can launch the attack at any chosen time T, the malicious node must wait for an appropriate time slot to be able to send the forged packet. For example in the case of the direct command injection, the malicious node must wait for the next broadcast slot to send the false command to its neighbors. But as all devices are configured with this kind of slots, it is always possible for a malicious node to send its false command. According to the WirelessHART [2], by default each device is configured with one sending unicast slot and one sending broadcast slot each 1 min. Thus, the average waiting time T_{Avg} between the attack launching time and the false command injection time is: $T_{Avg} = T_{sending\_broadcast}/2 = 30$ s in the case of a direct attack and $T_{Avg} = T_{sending\_unicast}/2 + T_{sending\_broadcast}/2 = 60$ s for a bounced attack. The on-the-fly attack duration depends on the industrial process and broadcast commands sending frequency. In average, this frequency is around 1 h.

By comparing the 3 scenarios, we can see that the bounced command injection increases the spreading area of the attack by using the parent of the malicious node as a relay. Also, the on-the-fly command injection attack is interesting as it hides the attacks inside a legitimate flow. Nevertheless, the drawback of this attack is that the malicious node must wait to the transmission by the network manager of a broadcast packet which can take a long time to happen.

Finally, we must note that in all these scenarios, the malicious insider node has the choice between executing or not the injected false command. Indeed, depending on the attack's goal, the malicious node can launch the attack with or without executing it. For example, by not executing the false command, the malicious node can mislead administrators in their investigations to discover the origin of the network disturbances.

4   Attack Implementation

To test the broadcast attack, we use WirelessHART NetSIM [4], a simulator that we develop for assessing the security of WirelessHART SCADA-based systems.

As illustrated in Fig. 7(a), the simulated wireless network is composed of a network manager and 9 wireless sensors. Wireless sensors are configured to send periodically each 4 s simulated sensing data to the Network Manager. Figure 7(b) illustrates the routing graphs. The broadcast graph is indicated by dotted green arrows.

For testing the three scenarios, we launched the broadcast attack at $T = 800$ s and the *Device*5 is configured to be the malicious insider attacker. The injected false command is the command 961 that is used to set a new *network key*. This command has 2 parameters: *the new network key*, and T' the time when it will be changed. In all the three scenarios $T' = 920$ s.

As illustrated in Fig. 8(a) i.e., in the normal case, the size of sensing data received by the Network Manager is about 720 bytes each 4 s. We observe that

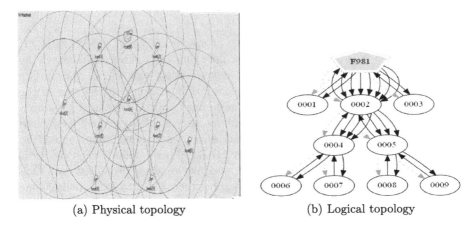

(a) Physical topology   (b) Logical topology

Fig. 7. Simulation network topology (Color figure online)

for the three scenarios of the broadcast attack, the size of received data by the Network Manager falls immediately at $T = 920$. This indicates that the Network manager stops receiving sensing data from some wireless sensors.

Indeed at $T = 920$ *infected devices* will execute the injected false command and start to use the received network key to calculate the DLL MIC. When received by a device that has not been infected by the attack, the packet do not pass the MIC validation step and is rejected. Consequently, packet sent by *infected devices* will be rejected and not received by the Network Manager.

In comparison with the normal case, in the direct command injection attack the data received by the Network Manager, illustrated in Fig. 8(b), falls from 720 bytes to 480 bytes. This represents a decrease of 33%. Indeed, 3 devices i.e., *Device*5, *Device*8 and *Device*9, are infected by this attack.

In the case of the bounced command injection attack, shown in Fig. 8(c), we record a decrease of 77% in the data received by the Network Manager. This indicates that this kind of attacks, allows a malicious node to use its parent device as a relay to propagate the attack to a great number of devices. As result, 7 devices are infected by the attack, i.e., *Device*5, *Device*2, *Device*4, *Device*6, *Device*7, *Device*8 and *Device*9.

In the on-the-fly command injection attack, we configure the Network Manager to broadcast, at $T = 800$ s to all devices, a command to change the network key at $T' = 920$ s. The malicious attacker will modify this command and send a false command to its children devices. This attack has the same impact as in the case of a direct command injection command. As a variant, we choose that the malicious node does not execute the false command, which explains the difference of the impact between the direct and on-the-fly broadcast attacks. As indicated in Fig. 8(d), the received data by the network manager decreased by 22% as only 2 devices are infected i.e., *Device*5 and *Device*6.

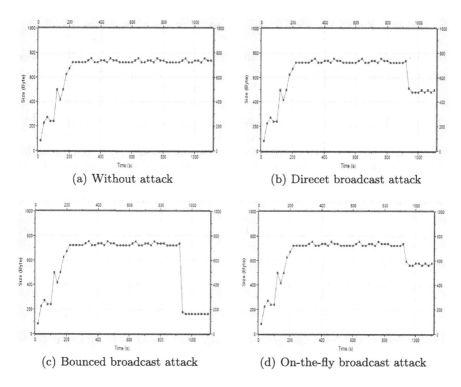

(a) Without attack   (b) Direcet broadcast attack

(c) Bounced broadcast attack   (d) On-the-fly broadcast attack

Fig. 8. Sensing data received by the network manager.

5   Countermeasures Discussion

The broadcast communication is an important feature in WirelessHART. It allows the Network Manager to configure all devices composing the wireless network by only sending a single packet. It avoids a costing time and resources process of sending a single packet to each device. But as shown in this paper, this feature creates a dangerous breach in the communication scheme security. As it is complicated to ban broadcast communications, we propose hereafter, some ideas to reduce the exposition to this vulnerability.

– Broadcast packet validation after the reception of 2 identical packets: this condition aims to stop direct and on-the-fly command injections. Indeed, as WirelessHART builds a meshed network, best practices in industrial sensor networks recommends that each node has at least 2 or 3 parents. Consequently, each sensor will receive the broadcast packet more than once. Thus, according to this rule, each node must wait till the reception of the same packet from another of its parents before it executes and forwards it. Nodes located at one hop do not have to apply this rule as they receive the broadcast packet directly from the Network Manager. This countermeasure adds a latency in the transmission of broadcast packets and can, in some cases, block their forwarding.

– DLL and NL addresses validation: in the case of the bounced command injection attack, DLL and NL headers of the injected packet indicate contradictory informations. Indeed, the source address in the DLL header indicates that the packet has been sent by a children node i.e., the malicious node, while the source address in the NL header indicates that the packet has been sent by a parent node i.e., the network manager. Therefore, implementing in the NL a security mechanisms that rejects packets indicating such contradictory informations can mitigate this kind of attacks. We must note that even if this solution do not complain with the layer separation principle, in practice WirelessHART layers already use information provided by other layers such as addresses.

– Use of an IDS for monitoring node's behavior: indeed, except rethinking deeply the communication scheme of WirelessHART, as implementing asymmetric cryptography for packet's authentication, that is a costly process, the use of an IDS will increase significantly the security of such networks. Indeed, this kind of system by monitoring exchanged packets, are able to detect the injection of a false packet or the modification of a packet during its transmission.

In conclusion, the two first countermeasures are partial solutions that do not prevent all scenarios. The second solution is the costless one as it adds a reduced overhead. The use of an IDS is the more efficient solution. Indeed, although it requires the installation of dedicated equipments for traffic monitoring, it is the only solution that detects all possible scenarios. Nevertheless, given that WSNs are distributed systems, we must pay attention to the scheme used to deploy the IDS as it directly impacts the information gathering capability.

6   Related Works

Most of dedicated studies on WirelessHART focus mainly on the evaluation of the performances of this protocol and its capabilities to operate in an industrial environment and its capacity to meet real-time requirements [5–7].

On the other hand, security analysis conducted on WirelessHART are based on the specifications of the standard without conducting any tests. Thus, in [8] Raza et al. discuss the strengths and the weaknesses of security mechanisms and analyze them against the well known threats in the wireless sensor networks. They conclude that WirelessHART is strong enough to be used in the industrial process control environment. Alcazar and Lopez identify in [9] vulnerabilities and threats in several wireless communication protocols used in industry i.e., ZigBee PRO, WirelessHART and ISA100.11.a. They analyze in detail the security features of each of these protocols. For them, WirelessHART offers strong authentication capabilities before and after deployment. However, they recommend to add a rekeying process to WirelessHART to enforce its resilience to sniffing attacks and thereby key disclosure.

But although WirelessHART implements several security mechanisms, it stays vulnerable to dangerous attacks. Thus, in a previous work, we develop WirelessHART NetSIM [4], a simulator for assessing the security of WirelessHART SCADA-based systems. It can be used to test attacks and countermeasures on WSN. It includes several scenarios for testing simple and complex kinds of attacks. Using this simulator, we give the first description of a Sybil attack specially tailored to target WirelessHART based SCADA systems [10]. We demonstrate that an insider attacker using this weakness can isolate partially or more again totally wireless sensors from the SCADA network. This attack targets the security authentication in the data link layer and is based on the knowledge of the network key by all devices composing the wireless network.

Nevertheless, this attack do not allow the injection of false commands into the network as security mechanisms in the upper layer will stop injection attacks. Therefore, the presented attack in this paper is more dangerous than the previous one, as it permits the injections of any false command by circumventing security mechanisms implemented in the Network Layer.

7   Conclusion

In this paper, we analyze the security of the communication scheme in WirelessHART, the most widely used wireless protocol in SCADA systems. We show that an insider attacker can bypass implemented security mechanisms and inject false commands into the network. These false commands will be authenticated as legitimate commands and executed by receiving devices.

The attack is based on the use of *the broadcast session* credentials that are shared by all devices composing the wireless network. We give also the description of three different scenarios that exploit this weakness. Tests conducted, using a simulator dedicated to WirelessHART security assessment, confirm the feasibility of the attack and its potentially harmful impact. In these tests we choose the network key change command as injected false command. By this way, we were able to break the reception by the network manager of sensing data from wireless sensors. Other scenarios can be developed to take advantage of this weakness. For example, the source routing method can be used to inject false commands to a greater number of sensors.

On the other hand, proposed solutions do not totally mitigate the broadcast attack. Indeed, the broadcast communication is an important feature that cannot be removed. Therefore, and except changing deeply the communication scheme implemented by WirelessHART, the use of an Intrusion Detection System (IDS) is the best operational manner to detect and mitigate this kind of attacks. Further research must be made to study the best way to apply IDS to WSN in industrial environments.

References

1. Huang, Y.L., Cárdenas, A., Amin, S., Lin, Z.S., Tsai, H.Y., Sastry, S.: Understanding the physical and economic consequences of attacks on control systems. Int. J. Crit. Infrastruct. Prot. **2**(3), 73–83 (2009)
2. HART Communication Foundation: WirelessHART. http://www.hartcomm.org
3. IEEE: IEEE 802.15.4-2006: Standard for Local and metropolitan area networks-Part 15.4: Low-Rate Wireless Personal Area Networks (LR-WPANs). http://www.ieee.org
4. Bayou, L., Espes, D., Cuppens-Boulahia, N., Cuppens, F.: WirelessHART NetSIM: a WirelessHART SCADA-based wireless sensor networks simulator. In: Bécue, A., Cuppens-Boulahia, N., Cuppens, F., Katsikas, S., Lambrinoudakis, C. (eds.) CyberICS/WOS-CPS -2015. LNCS, vol. 9588, pp. 63–78. Springer, Heidelberg (2016). doi:10.1007/978-3-319-40385-4_5
5. Han, S., Zhu, X., Mok, A.K., Chen, D., Nixon, M.: Reliable and real-time communication in industrial wireless mesh networks. In: 17th IEEE RTAS, USA, pp. 3–12. IEEE Computer Society (2011)
6. Kim, A.N., Hekland, F., Petersen, S., Doyle, P.: When HART goes wireless: understanding and implementing the WirelessHART standard. In: Proceedings of 13th IEEE International Conference on Emerging Technologies and Factory Automation, ETFA, Hamburg, Germany, pp. 899–907. IEEE (2008)
7. Song, J., Han, S., Mok, A., Chen, D., Lucas, M., Nixon, M.: WirelessHART: applying wireless technology in real-time industrial process control. In: Real-Time and Embedded Technology and Applications Symposium, RTAS 2008, pp. 377–386. IEEE, April 2008
8. Raza, S., Slabbert, A., Voigt, T., Landernäs, K.: Security considerations for the WirelessHART protocol. In: Proceedings of 12th IEEE International Conference on Emerging Technologies and Factory Automation, ETFA, Spain, pp. 1–8. IEEE (2009)
9. Alcaraz, C., Lopez, J.: A security analysis for wireless sensor mesh networks in highly critical systems. IEEE Trans. Syst. Man Cybern. Part C **40**(4), 419–428 (2010)
10. Bayou, L., Espes, D., Cuppens-Boulahia, N., Cuppens, F.: Security issue of WirelessHART based SCADA systems. In: Lambrinoudakis, C., Gabillon, A. (eds.) CRiSIS 2015. LNCS, vol. 9572, pp. 225–241. Springer, Heidelberg (2016). doi:10.1007/978-3-319-31811-0_14

Malware and Antivirus

Function Classification
for the Retro-Engineering
of Malwares

Guillaume Bonfante$^{(\boxtimes)}$ and Julien Oury Nogues

Carbone Team, Lorraine University - CNRS - LORIA, Nancy, France
guillaume.bonfante@univ-lorraine.fr

Abstract. In the past ten years, our team has developed a method called morphological analysis that deals with malware detection. Morphological analysis focuses on algorithms. Here, we want to identify programs through their functions, and more precisely with the intention of those functions. The intention is described as a vector in a high dimensional vector space in the spirit of compositional semantics. We show how to use the intention of functions for their clustering. In a last step, we describe some experiments showing the relevance of the clustering and some of some possible applications for malware identification.

1   Introduction

In this contribution, we are concerned with the retro-engineering of malware. In particular, we think to CERTs (Computer Emergency Response Team) where people must determine the content of some attacks; usually, they are asked to give answers quite quickly. Saving time is not just an option. This task is awfully complicate, and demands some high skills and high education. Indeed, the major part of questions are not computable, and thus only talented people may handle such issues. Since the number of attacks is arising [Sym16], we think there is a strong need to give some help, that is to provide automatic tools that output some insights on what's happening.

To get the outline of the behavior of a program, the import address table (IAT) provides a list of external functions that are called. Those include low level system calls. Naturally, those functions give good hints on the job of the program itself. As a justification of the fact, we recall that the (famous, if not the most) retro-engineering tool called IDA introduces this list on its front page as shown on the right. No doubt about it, we are aware that import tables may be hidden by malware or by packers, in particular in the case of code injection. But actually that enforces our argument: showing your import table is telling who you are.

F. Cuppens et al. (Eds.): FPS 2016, LNCS 10128, pp. 241–255, 2017.
DOI: 10.1007/978-3-319-51966-1_16

In this paper, we put the focus on functions and we report some experiment that we made about classification. We show in a second part how that can be related to malware classification. But before going further, let us come back to the context of this research. We have developed at the High Security Lab in Nancy a detection method called morphological analysis. Let us say few words about it. For deeper explanations, we refer the reader to [BKM09]. So, given some program—no matter if it is a malware or not—, we extract its control flow graph, either by a static analysis or a dynamic one. In the latter case, we use an instruction tracer that is made as stealthy as possible, in particular against anti-debugging techniques or anti-virtualization procedures. In the end, we transform the control flow graph to avoid basic obfuscations and we cut it into small pieces called sites. Sites are used as code signatures : they are identified up to some isomorphism. To sum up, the method focuses on *algorithms*. But algorithms may not reveal the *intention* behind them. Our slogan here is that *functions* can do it. There is nothing new at that point: functional models (recall SADT!) are central to software engineering (e.g. Ross [Ros77]).

Let us push a little bit further this idea of extracting the intention of a function. For the internal functions of a malware (and possibly for sane programs), there are no chances to extract it easily. Indeed, malware are awfully obfuscated, and thus two consequences: first, at the binary level, the code is completely blurred, typically, `call 0x12345678` is replaced by `push eax, jmp 0x12345678` where `eax` points to the current instruction. The replacement can be opposite, that is `jmp 0x12345678` can be replaced by `call 0x12345678, ...,` `pop eax` with `pop eax` pointing at position `0x12345678`. Second point, malware writers use tricks to hide functions. For instance, function call conventions are not followed: the signature `55 8B EC` corresponding to the standard sequence `push ebp, mov ebp, esp` is no longer operative. Thus, it becomes even difficult to identify correctly functions within a malware code. Finally, (and obviously, but for the sake of the argument, we *must* mention it!), the malware does not come with any documentation nor debugging hints. Thus, extracting the intention of internal functions of malware is difficult, and precisely this is the task of retro-analysts.

But, for the functions that occur within external calls, the situation is quite different. External calls refer to dynamically loaded libraries which—if correctly designed—provide well identified functionalities via functions. Moreover, libraries are—should be—well documented within their API. Furthermore, they are manually written, and for that reason, are one of the best sources of information for our purpose.

The goal of this paper is to show that one can extract meaningful informations from documentation in a retro-engineering perspective. We used MICROSOFT's API documents as a source. We used it because it is correctly[1] formatted and uniform, but the method may be used for other vendors. We also used it since many malware are written for WINDOWS and thus refer to MICROSOFT's system library such as `kernel32.dll` or `msvcr100.dll`.

---

[1] but not fully!

There is one objection we want to address. One may argue that external function calls are usually heavily hidden by malware obfuscations, thus it would be difficult to identify those functions via (for instance) import address tables. Second point, malware authors include statically some functions within the malware code so that they are not imported. This contribution is not about function identification. For that, we have shown that morphological analysis is able to do it, even in a hostile code. For instance, we established the correspondence between functions of two famous malware REGIN and QWERTY in [BMS15]. We recall that REGIN has been considered as one of the most sophisticated malware, see the nice report by Kaczmarek [Kac15]. In conclusion, we think that the problem is solved by combining morphological analysis and function analysis.

Our contribution has three facets. First, we associate to each function its *intention*. To do that, we use the idea of Vector Space Semantics (VSS) coming from Natural Language Processing. Each function will be associated to some vector representing its semantics. We built an IDA-plugin that shows this mapping. Second, we propose some *clustering* algorithms. Indeed, depending on the depth of the analysis, the retro-analyst may not need[2] to distinguish functions such as `calloc` or `malloc`, both dealing with memory allocation. Thus the idea of clusters. We propose different versions of clustering procedures and we compare them. In the perspective of VSS, clusters correspond actually to the concepts that generalize the ones of their underlying inhabitants. Third, we show how to relate the function clustering to a *malware detection* procedure. The idea that two programs are close when they use same function is quite common, especially for the ANDROID OS (e.g. [PZ13]). We show that clusters are even better. Doing so, we justify the relevance of clusters, and we show them in action.

But, before we enter into technical details, we would like to make a reference to the paper by Teh and Stewart in [TS12] who mention that there are good malware detectors based on multi-layer perceptron whose inputs are features extracted from executable file. However, these tools work too much as black boxes and they do not bring human readable evidences. They conclude that these tools are not that good for retro-analysis. What we do is precisely to establish a human readable correspondence between programs and functionalities.

In Sect. 2, we present how we built an initial database. It contains informations coming from MICROSOFT's documentation. On these, we had to run some specific tools that extract the "meaning" of the function, that is a weighted vector of words. These are based on Natural Language Processing libraries. In Sect. 3, we present our clustering algorithm with three variations on function distances. We compare the three classification procedures with standard classification measures and we discuss pro and cons of each measure. In Sect. 4, we relate the clustering to some external evaluation. We use MICROSOFT's classification and some customized tests.

At the time of the conference, we will publish all python scripts that we used all along, and our rough databases are available on https://github.com/JulienOuryNogues/DataBase-Function-Microsoft/.

---

[2] or must not.

2   The Semantics of Functions

We describe the procedure that maps functions within libraries to their intention. This is done in three steps: first, we associate libraries to functions, then, we associate functions to documentation and finally, we extract the intention of the function, that is, its semantics.

2.1   Extracting Function Names from Libraries

As stated in the introduction, we worked with DLL coming from microsoft libraries. Those are the most used, and certainly the most interesting since they are directly used for communications with the Operating System.

Our database is built from the 2481 DLL which are coming with the installation disc of our Windows distribution (Vista 64bits). A rapid comparison with other WINDOWS distribution shows that results/conclusions should not be very different. For each DLL, using the python library PEFILE, we get a table partly shown in Fig. 1:

Ordinal	RVA	Name
1	0x0001E688h	DllCanUnloadNow
2	0x0001E7B8h	DllGetClassObject
3	0x0001E67Eh	DllInstall
4	0x0001E642h	DllMain
5	0x0004C9A9h	DllRegisterServer
6	0x0004C9A9h	DllUnregisterServer

Fig. 1. The first 6 functions within accessibilitycpl.dll

This table contains the list of functions exported by the DLL. Each function is given by its Ordinal Number, its Relative Virtual Address and its name as should be referred by calling executables. Actually, according to MICROSOFT's policy, names are optional, only Ordinals are mandatory. We keep only those lines with a Name. Second, some Names follow a mangling format corresponding to Visual C/C++. Typically, we read :

`??0IndexOutOfRangeException@UnBCL@@QEAA@PEAVString@1@PEAVException@1@@Z`

In which case, our heuristics is to take the first alphanumeric string occuring within the sentence (with a PYTHON filter of the shape `r'\d*(\w*)'`). In the end, we got 50306 distinct names out of the DLLs (34964 directly, 15342 via 'demangling').

2.2   Extracting Function Documentation

The documentation of functions has been extracted from MICROSOFT website. We used two different ways to do it. First, we took the root of the WINDOWS

API INDEX documentation that is stored at https://msdn.microsoft.com/fr-fr/ library/windows/desktop/ff818516(v=vs.85).aspx. We visited the site from this rooting node, and we filtered pages corresponding to function documentation. Doing so, we got a source page for 6155 functions.

Compared to the 50306 functions mentioned above, that is clearly not enough. To complete it, we did some requests of the shape https://social.msdn.microsoft. com/search/en-US/windows?query= on MICROSOFT search tool. On the 44151 remaining functions, we performed the requests. Sometimes, we got more than one answer, typically for functions with close names (`printf` vs `wprintf`), in which case, we took them all! In the end, we got 24149 inputs on the total. We denote by $\mathcal{F}$ the set of functions with documentation.

Now, let us come to the typical content of a page that is presented in Fig. 2.

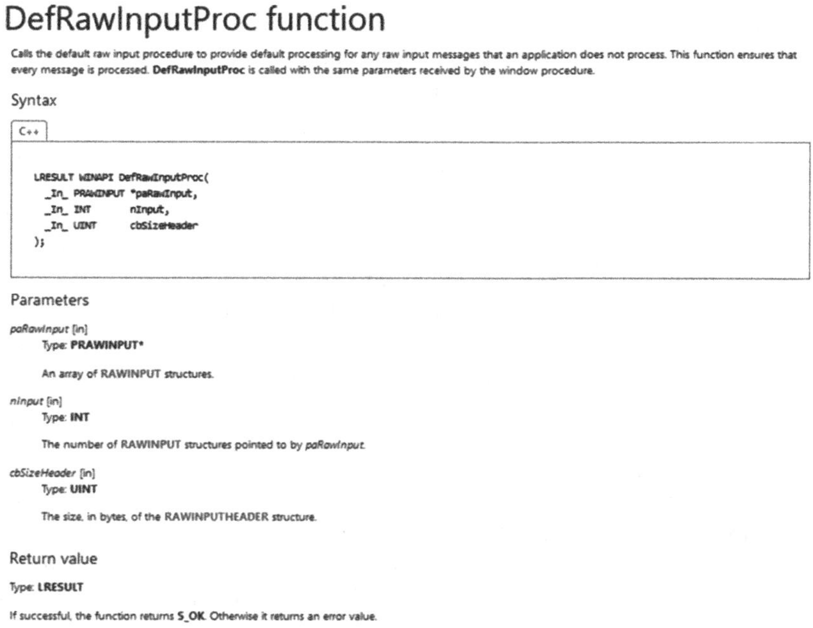

DefRawInputProc function

Calls the default raw input procedure to provide default processing for any raw input messages that an application does not process. This function ensures that every message is processed. **DefRawInputProc** is called with the same parameters received by the window procedure.

Syntax

C++

```
LRESULT WINAPI DefRawInputProc(
  _In_ PRAWINPUT *paRawInput,
  _In_ INT       nInput,
  _In_ UINT      cbSizeHeader
);
```

Parameters

paRawInput [in]
    Type: **PRAWINPUT***

    An array of RAWINPUT structures.

nInput [in]
    Type: **INT**

    The number of RAWINPUT structures pointed to by *paRawInput*.

cbSizeHeader [in]
    Type: **UINT**

    The size, in bytes, of the RAWINPUTHEADER structure.

Return value

Type: **LRESULT**

If successful, the function returns S_OK. Otherwise it returns an error value.

Fig. 2. DefRawInputProc's description

Thus, we get for each function,

- its name,
- its short description,
- its profile
- typed arguments and their description
- return value and its type.

The WINDOWS API tree describes 211 "categories/key words" among which 155 correspond to functions (versus structures). We appended within our database this category for those functions that could be properly situated within the tree.

We crossed these informations with those extracted from the PEFILE as seen in previous section, and, all in all, we have a table whose entries contain: a name, a relative virtual address, a DLL name, a WINDOWS distribution name, a short description, a profile, arguments and return value description and a WINDOWS category. The database is accessible for research purposes on our website https:// github.com/JulienOuryNogues/DataBase-Function-Microsoft.

2.3   Data Preparation, Some Natural Language Tools

Once we have a complete database, we want to perform some function classification. Indeed, for instance, the reverse-engineer may work at some abstract level for which there are no good reasons to discriminate wprintf from printf, both dealing with printing. The clustering is supposed to cope that intuition.

Function descriptions are written in English/American English, and thus in a natural language. Our classification purpose algorithm relies on what is called vector space models of meaning [Sch98] (or more abstractly distributional semantics) that has shown to be very powerful those last years by Copestake and Herbelot [CH16] or by Abramsky and Sadrzadeh [AS14]. The rise of distributional semantics is due to the fact that the method requires large amount of textual data for its learning process, and these amounts are now available. The key idea behind the model can be summed up as follows: two words are close if they occur in same contexts. Dogs and cats eat, are stroked and sleep. In some way, the concept of a pet arises from this proximity. In that paradigm, the meaning of a word (and contexts, and clusters) is represented by a vector in a high dimensional vector space whose basis is built on words themselves.

The main problem with the approach is that some words blurs the co-occurence relation that is underlying. Typically, stop words which play a grammatical role without bringing some particular concepts: "with", "to", "the", and so on. We have a first stage that removes them. To do that we use the NLTK python library (Natural Language Tool Kit [Bir15]). In a first step, we apply a part-of-speech tagger that associate to each word its category (e.g. noun, verb, adjective, determinant, etc.). Then, we keep only verbs, nouns and adjective.

For instance, printf's description is that it *submits a custom shader message to the information queue.* Applying the Part-Of-Speech Tagging, we get:

```
[('submits','NNS'), ('a','DT'), ('custom','NN'), ('shader','NN'),
('message','NN'), ('to','TO'), ('the','DT'), ('information','NN'),
('queue','NN'), ('.','.')]
```

And then,

```
[('submit','NNS'), ('custom','NN'), ('shader','NN'),
('message','NN'), ('information','NN'), ('queue','NN')]
```

Second step of our process deals with lemmatization. It is well known that some words have many inflectional forms: verbs (am, are, is, be) and nouns (singular or plural). For our purpose, there is no reasons to distinguish "submits" from "submit". Lemmatization aims to associate to each word in a sentence its *lemma*, that is the "core" word. The task is not that easy and we used the tool provided by NLTK. Applying lemmatization on our example, we get for the verb "submits": (`'submits'`,`'NNS'`,`'submit'`).

In a third step, we remove some specific words that are so common that they bring more noise to the discrimination procedure than they bring informations. The complete list is [`"none"`, `"be"`, `"specify"`, `"function"`, `"DLL"`].

We end the process by forgetting all decorations. The resulting vector on our current example is:

```
{'submits':1, 'custom':1, 'shader':1, 'message':1, 'information':1,
'queue':1}
```

The database is available on the website https://github.com/JulienOuryNogues/DataBase-Function-Microsoft.

3 Function Classification

In this section, we present some clustering methods for functions. The rough idea is to avoid dubious distinctions, between several forms of **printf** for instance. In MICROSOFT documentation, there is already a clustering of functions. Actually, functions are gathered within a tree structure that can be used for our purpose. However, it is not sufficient, for at least two reasons. First, only a third of functions occur within the tree (around 6100 over 20000). And second, MICROSOFT's classification is not used by other libraries. We prefer to have a direct method.

Generally speaking, we apply a standard classification algorithm, the k-mean to function descriptions. The main point is then to define a proper distance between functions. We propose three definitions and we compare them.

Given a word w and a function $\mathbf{f} \in \mathcal{F}$, we denote by $n(w, \mathbf{f})$ the number of occurrences of w within the (formatted as above) description of the function $\mathbf{f}$. Each function $\mathbf{f}$ is transformed into a vector $\mathbf{v_f}$ as follows:

$$\mathbf{v_f} = \sum_{w \in \mathcal{W}} n(w, \mathbf{f}) \overrightarrow{w}$$

where $\mathcal{W}$ denotes the set of english words and the family $(\overrightarrow{w})_{w \in \mathcal{W}}$ defines the (orthogonal) basis of our vector space.

Definition 1 (μ-measure). *Given two functions $\mathbf{f}$ and $\mathbf{g}$, we define $\mu(\mathbf{f}, \mathbf{g}) = \dfrac{|\mathbf{v_f} - \mathbf{v_g}|}{|\mathbf{v_f}| + |\mathbf{v_g}|}$ where $|\mathbf{v}|$ denotes the euclidian norm of the vector $\mathbf{v}$.*

The second measure we use is known as Levensthein distance. Given two words u, v on some alphabet Σ, the Levensthein measure is the number of characters that must be removed or added to the first word to reach the second one. It is denoted by $\delta(u, v)$ in the sequel. For some function $\mathbf{f}$, Name$_{\mathbf{f}}$ denotes its name (as to be opposed to its description).

Definition 2 (δ-measure). *Given two functions* $\mathbf{f}$ *and* $\mathbf{g}$, *we define* $\delta(\mathbf{f}, \mathbf{g}) = \delta(\mathrm{Name}_{\mathbf{f}}, \mathrm{Name}_{\mathbf{g}})$.

There is a slight abuse in notation, δ being used twice, but the context should be clear.

Finally, we introduce a variant of the μ-measure that is obtained by weighting words according to their relative frequency. This is known as TF-IDF (Term Frequency-Inverse Document Frequency). The intention of this measure is to decrease the weight of words that occur in a majority of documents. In the present case, each function description is considered to be a document and thus, $idf(w) = \log\left(\dfrac{|\mathcal{F}|}{|\{\mathbf{f} \in \mathcal{F} \mid n(w, \mathbf{f}) \neq 0\}|}\right)$.

The weight of a word $w \in \mathcal{W}$ in a function $\mathbf{f} \in \mathcal{F}$ is then defined as $\omega(w, \mathbf{f}) = n(w, \mathbf{f}) \times idf(w)$. From that, we define the vector $\mathbf{v'}_{\mathbf{f}} = \sum_{w \in \mathcal{W}} \omega(w, \mathbf{f})\overrightarrow{w}$. And, correspondingly, we propose:

Definition 3 (μ'-measure). *Given two functions* $\mathbf{f}$ *and* $\mathbf{g}$, *we define* $\mu'(\mathbf{f}, \mathbf{g}) = \dfrac{|\mathbf{v'}_{\mathbf{f}} - \mathbf{v'}_{\mathbf{g}}|}{|\mathbf{v'}_{\mathbf{f}}| + |\mathbf{v'}_{\mathbf{g}}|}$.

3.1 Clustering

In this section, we compare the influence of the three different measures on function clustering. We denote by d any measure among $\{\mu, \delta, \mu'\}$. We write $d(\mathbf{f}, S) = \min\{d(\mathbf{f}, \mathbf{g}) \mid \mathbf{g} \in S\}$ given $\mathbf{f} \in \mathcal{F}$ and $S \subseteq \mathcal{F}$.

We use the standard k-mean algorithm. Nevertheless, we want to make three observations. So, the algorithm is as follow:

```
def cluster(F, k): #F is the set of functions, k is the parameter
  P = choose(F, k) # P chooses a list of k initial sets
  end = False
  while(not end): # (loop 1)
    nP = [set() for i in range(k)] # nP is the next P, k empty sets
    for f in F: # (loop 2)
      nP.add(argmin ([ d(f, P[i]) for i in range(k)]))
    end = nP == P
    P = nP
```

First, we begin with a choice of the first k representative based on a density argument. This choice is important since it will modify the number of times we perform loop 1. More technically, we compute $\overline{d}(\mathbf{f}) = \dfrac{1}{|\mathcal{F}|}\sum_{\mathbf{g} \in \mathcal{F}} d(\mathbf{f}, \mathbf{g})$ for each function $\mathbf{f}$, we order that list in decreasing order. Then, we choose the (an approximation of the) largest value m such that we can find k representative $\mathcal{F}_k = \{\mathbf{f}_1, \ldots, \mathbf{f}_k\}$ such that $d(\mathbf{f}, \mathcal{F}_k) \leq m$ for any function $\mathbf{f}$ and for all $1 \leq i \leq k$, $\overline{d}(\mathbf{f}_i) = \max\{\overline{d}(\mathbf{f}) \mid d(\mathbf{f}, \mathbf{f}_i) \leq m\}$.

In the algorithm, we have to compute the distance $d(\mathbf{f}, P[i])$ from a function $\mathbf{f}$ to some cluster P, that is $\overline{d}(\mathbf{f}) = \dfrac{\sum_{\mathbf{g} \in P} d(\mathbf{f}, \mathbf{g})}{|P|}$. For μ and μ', we compute first the mean vector $\mathbf{v}_P = \sum_{\mathbf{f} \in P} \mathbf{v}_{\mathbf{f}}/|P|$ so that loop (2) costs $k \times n$ with $n = |\mathcal{F}|$. For Levenshtein measure, there is no mean words, so that you have to compute each sum separately. The cost is then (of the order) n^2.

3.2 Levenshtein Versus Vectors

With a first observation and k set to 1600 (to be compared to the 150's of window), we observe a similarity between Levenshtein's clustering and μ-clustering. In Fig. 3, we present a cluster obtained by μ-measure. Each line gives a function name followed by its corresponding vector. One observes that their names are close, it corresponds to a Levenshtein cluster!

```
waveOutMessage ,{'waveoutmessage': 1,'driver': 1,'send': 1,'device': 1,'output': 1,'message': ,'waveform-audio': 1}
waveOutGetPitch ,{'retrieve': 1,'current': 1,'setting': 1,'waveoutgetpitch': 1,'pitch': 1,'device': 1,'output': 1,'waveform-audio': 1}
waveOutSetPlaybackRate,{'set': 1,'device': 1,'rate': 1,'playback': 1,'waveoutsetplaybackrate': 1,'output': 1,'waveform-audio': 1}
waveOutRestart ,{'resume': 1,'paused': 1,'device': 1,'playback': 1,'waveoutrestart': 1, 'output': 1,'waveform-audio': 1}
waveOutPrepareHeader ,{'prepare': 1,'waveoutprepareheader': 1,'playback': 1,'waveform-audio': 1,'data': 1,'block': 1}
waveOutClose ,{'give': 1,'waveoutclose': 1,'output': 1,'device': 1,'close': 1,'waveform-audio': 1}
waveOutSetPitch ,{'set': 1,'device': 1,'pitch': 1,'waveoutsetpitch': 1,'output': 1,'waveform-audio': 1}
waveOutOpen ,{'waveoutopen': 1,'give': 1,'playback': 1,'device': 1,'output': 1,'waveform-audio': 1,'open': 1}
waveOutWrite ,{'give': 1,'send': 1,'waveoutwrite': 1,'device': 1,'output': 1,'waveform-audio': 1,'data': 1,'block': 1}
waveOutGetVolume ,{'volume': 1,'retrieve': 1,'level': 1,'current': 1,'device': 1,'output': 1,'waveform-audio': 1}
waveOutSetVolume ,{'waveoutsetvolume': 1,'set': 1,'level': 1,'volume': 1,'device': 1,'output': 1,'waveform-audio': 1}
waveOutGetPosition ,{'retrieve': 1,'give': 1,'current': 1,'playback': 1,'output': 1,'device': 1,'position': 1,'waveform-audio': 1}
```

Fig. 3. One of the categories, $k = 1600$

3.3 Experimental Protocol

Let us validate this observation. We use three similarity indices. They show different aspects of the similarities, see [Qué12] for an in depth discussion. We suppose we are given two partitions (not necessarily with same value k), $(P_i)_{i=1..n}$ and $(Q_j)_{j=1..m}$ of the set $\mathcal{F}$ of size N. Set $n_{i,j} = |P_i \cap Q_j|$, $n_{i,.} = |P_i|$ and $n_{.,j} = |Q_j|$, then, we define:
$a = \sum_{i,j} \binom{n_{i,j}}{2}$, $b = \sum_i \binom{n_{i,.}}{2} - \sum_{i,j} \binom{n_{i,j}}{2}$, $c = \sum_j \binom{n_{.,j}}{2} - \sum_{i,j} \binom{n_{i,j}}{2}$ and $d = \binom{N}{2} + \sum_{i,j} \binom{n_{i,j}}{2} - \sum_j \binom{n_{.,j}}{2} - \sum_i \binom{n_{i,.}}{2}$.

The three similarity measures we use are Rand index: $R = \dfrac{a+d}{a+b+c+d}$, Jaccard's index, $J = \dfrac{a}{a+b+c}$ and Dice's index $D = \dfrac{2a}{2a+b+c}$. Rand's index evaluates in which way two partitions agree for pairwise elements (whether they are similar or not), Jaccard's evaluates only similarities and Dice's strengthen similarities. These are the symmetric forms. If the partition $(P_i)_{i=1..n}$ is finer than $(Q_j)_{j=1..m}$, that is if $n < m$, one uses the non symmetric versions: $\tilde{R} = \dfrac{a+d+c}{a+b+c+d}$, $\tilde{J} = \dfrac{a+c}{a+b+c}$ and $\tilde{D} = \dfrac{2a+c}{2a+b+c}$ which avoids the fact that a partition in Q_i that would be perfectly split within $(P_j)_j$, that is $Q_i = \cup_{\ell=i_1,...,i_k} P_\ell$, is wrongly evaluated.

4 External Validation

Up to now, we worked without any references to other forms of evaluation. We do it in three different ways. The first objective is to evaluate the relevance of the clustering process as defined above. The second reason is that we want to justify the value of the parameter k.

4.1   Windows Categorization

WINDOWS provides its own categories. We want to compare these with our own tool. We sum up our results on the following plot:

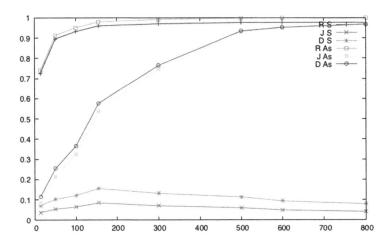

Fig. 4. Window vs μ

There are several observation that we want to make. First, Dice and Jaccard indices are closed. Thus, there are are no distance distortion (Fig. 4).

The figure shows that the clustering reaches a maximum for the symmetric Jaccard distance when the two partitions have same parameter k and the value is not very high—close to 10%–, but significant (compared to some random clusters). Differences between WINDOW'S classification and our is due to the fact that some functions use specific vocabulary. For instance, `GetProcAddress` and `LoadLibrary` which are within the category "DLL" have no common words in their vectors:

`GetProcAddress, {'library': 1, 'address': 1, 'retrieve': 1, 'dynamic-link': 1, 'specified': 1, 'variable': 1, 'dll': 1, 'export': 1}`
`LoadLibrary, {'cause': 1, 'specified': 2, 'call': 1, 'address': 1, 'load': 2, 'space': 1, 'module': 3, 'process': 1, 'other': 1}`

Third, observe that we get a good refinement of WINDOW's classification. We reach a value of 96.6% for $k = 800$ for the asymmetric Jaccard distance. Finally, on our motivating example, we get the cluster (for k = 1600): `fwprintf_s`, `wprintf_s`, `wscanf_s`, `sscanf_s`, `fscanf_s`, `fwscanf_s`, `swscanf_s`, `scanf_s`, `fprintf_s`, `printf_s`, `fread_s`, `scanf`, `wscanf`, `wprintf`, `printf`.

4.2   Do Similar Programs Share Similar Functions?

We built a database from 25 programs "grouped" in 5 categories. The first four are video players, browsers, archivers and text editors, the last one is made of MICROSOFT OFFICE's main applications. For each category, we chose the most common softwares.

Given a function clustering, $\mathcal{F} = \cup_{i=1}^{k} \mathcal{F}_i$, we define the homomorphism $\phi : \mathbb{R}^{\mathcal{F}} \to \mathbb{R}^k$ by $\phi(\mathbf{f}) = e_j$ where $\{e_1, \ldots, e_k\}$ is an orthogonal basis[3] of $\mathbb{R}^k$ and j is the (unique) index

---

[3] Being unique up to isomorphism, the definition does not depend on this choice.

such that $\mathbf{f} \in \mathcal{F}_j$. From the homomorphism, one defines the cluster distance between two vectors $\mathbf{v}$ and $\mathbf{v}'$ in $\mathbb{R}^{\mathcal{F}}$ to be $\Delta(\mathbf{v}, \mathbf{v}') = |\phi(\mathbf{v}) - \phi(\mathbf{v}')|$. In other words, applied to functions, this is the euclidian distance up to the clustering. Notice that given the definition of the homomorphism, given two functions $\mathbf{f}$ and $\mathbf{g}$, we have the inequality: $\Delta(\mathbf{v_f}, \mathbf{v_g}) \leq |\mathbf{v_f} - \mathbf{v_g}|$. With clusters, the world is smaller–in terms of dimensions– and more dense–functions being close.

From that definition, one can measure the distance between two programs:

Definition 4. *Given two programs* $\mathbf{p_1}$ *and* $\mathbf{p_2}$ *importing respectively functions* $\mathbf{f_1}, \ldots, \mathbf{f_k}$ *and* $\mathbf{g_1}, \ldots, \mathbf{g_m}$, *we define* $\mathbf{v_{p_1}} = \mathbf{v_{f_1}} + \cdots + \mathbf{v_{f_k}}$ *and* $\mathbf{v_{p_2}} = \mathbf{v_{g_1}} + \cdots + \mathbf{v_{g_m}}$. *Then, the cluster distance between programs is* $\Delta(\mathbf{p_1}, \mathbf{p_2}) = \Delta(\mathbf{v_{p_1}}, \mathbf{v_{p_2}})$. *And the normalized distance is* $\tilde{\Delta}(\mathbf{p_1}, \mathbf{p_2}) = \dfrac{\Delta(\mathbf{p_1}, \mathbf{p_2})}{\Delta(\mathbf{v_{p_1}}, \mathbf{0}) + \Delta(\mathbf{v_{p_2}}, \mathbf{0})}$ *where* $\mathbf{0}$ *is the null vector within* $\mathbb{R}^k$.

nom	IZArc2Go	WinRAR	peazip	WINZIP32	7zFM	notepad++	notepad	gvim	EditPad	PSPad	iexplore	firefox	chrome	opera	Safari	QuickTim	iTunes	vlc	realplay	wmplayer	mspaint	WINWO	POWERP	EXCE	wordpad
IZArc2Go	0.0	0.16	0.13	0.18	0.27	0.18	0.35	0.21	0.08	0.07	0.64	0.74	0.39	0.38	0.75	0.73	0.58	0.62	0.45	0.61	0.26	0.74	0.79	0.27	0.25
WinRAR	0.16	0.0	0.18	0.22	0.24	0.15	0.31	0.17	0.19	0.19	0.58	0.7	0.38	0.36	0.71	0.7	0.49	0.6	0.41	0.58	0.25	0.69	0.74	0.27	0.25
peazip	0.13	0.18	0.0	0.23	0.29	0.19	0.41	0.23	0.14	0.13	0.65	0.71	0.42	0.38	0.73	0.75	0.59	0.65	0.47	0.62	0.27	0.73	0.78	0.33	0.27
WINZIP32	0.18	0.22	0.23	0.0	0.38	0.26	0.42	0.23	0.17	0.18	0.66	0.76	0.38	0.38	0.78	0.77	0.62	0.67	0.49	0.66	0.3	0.78	0.82	0.24	0.29
7zFM	0.27	0.24	0.29	0.38	0.0	0.29	0.32	0.32	0.3	0.29	0.45	0.6	0.45	0.4	0.65	0.62	0.52	0.47	0.41	0.52	0.33	0.61	0.66	0.37	0.31
notepad++	0.18	0.15	0.19	0.26	0.29	0.0	0.28	0.2	0.21	0.18	0.6	0.72	0.38	0.37	0.71	0.71	0.48	0.6	0.44	0.57	0.32	0.72	0.78	0.29	0.3
notepad	0.35	0.31	0.41	0.42	0.32	0.28	0.0	0.3	0.39	0.37	0.44	0.63	0.48	0.51	0.61	0.6	0.47	0.45	0.41	0.54	0.32	0.55	0.6	0.38	0.31
gvim	0.21	0.17	0.23	0.23	0.32	0.2	0.3	0.0	0.24	0.22	0.59	0.7	0.35	0.36	0.69	0.68	0.5	0.6	0.42	0.55	0.3	0.71	0.76	0.32	0.3
EditPadLite7	0.08	0.19	0.14	0.17	0.3	0.21	0.39	0.24	0.0	0.08	0.66	0.74	0.39	0.39	0.75	0.74	0.61	0.64	0.46	0.64	0.27	0.75	0.8	0.23	0.25
PSPad	0.07	0.19	0.13	0.18	0.29	0.18	0.37	0.22	0.08	0.0	0.65	0.74	0.39	0.37	0.76	0.73	0.6	0.62	0.45	0.62	0.25	0.74	0.79	0.25	0.25
iexplore	0.64	0.58	0.65	0.66	0.45	0.6	0.44	0.59	0.66	0.65	0.0	0.31	0.54	0.56	0.53	0.41	0.43	0.3	0.41	0.4	0.48	0.36	0.42	0.59	0.48
firefox	0.74	0.7	0.71	0.76	0.6	0.72	0.63	0.7	0.73	0.74	0.38	0.0	0.61	0.6	0.26	0.27	0.51	0.34	0.46	0.64	0.64	0.31	0.37	0.7	0.62
chrome	0.39	0.38	0.42	0.38	0.45	0.38	0.48	0.35	0.4	0.39	0.54	0.61	0.0	0.2	0.65	0.42	0.54	0.36	0.55	0.48	0.67	0.73	0.42	0.45	
opera	0.38	0.36	0.38	0.38	0.4	0.37	0.51	0.36	0.39	0.37	0.56	0.6	0.2	0.0	0.65	0.64	0.39	0.57	0.35	0.51	0.47	0.67	0.73	0.46	0.45
Safari	0.75	0.71	0.73	0.78	0.65	0.71	0.61	0.69	0.75	0.76	0.53	0.26	0.65	0.65	0.0	0.22	0.47	0.42	0.5	0.63	0.7	0.3	0.29	0.75	0.65
QuickTimePlayer	0.73	0.7	0.75	0.77	0.62	0.71	0.6	0.68	0.74	0.73	0.41	0.27	0.65	0.64	0.22	0.0	0.45	0.42	0.47	0.5	0.66	0.21	0.34	0.73	0.64
iTunes	0.58	0.49	0.59	0.62	0.52	0.48	0.47	0.5	0.61	0.6	0.43	0.51	0.42	0.39	0.47	0.45	0.0	0.42	0.47	0.5	0.58	0.43	0.52	0.64	0.54
vlc	0.62	0.6	0.65	0.67	0.47	0.6	0.45	0.6	0.64	0.62	0.3	0.34	0.54	0.57	0.42	0.42	0.42	0.0	0.35	0.52	0.53	0.41	0.44	0.61	0.51
realplay	0.45	0.41	0.47	0.49	0.41	0.44	0.41	0.42	0.46	0.45	0.41	0.46	0.36	0.35	0.5	0.47	0.35	0.35	0.0	0.5	0.46	0.54	0.59	0.45	0.4
wmplayer	0.61	0.58	0.62	0.66	0.52	0.57	0.54	0.55	0.64	0.62	0.4	0.64	0.55	0.51	0.63	0.55	0.5	0.52	0.5	0.0	0.6	0.61	0.67	0.66	0.56
mspaint	0.26	0.25	0.27	0.3	0.33	0.32	0.32	0.3	0.27	0.25	0.48	0.64	0.48	0.47	0.7	0.66	0.58	0.53	0.46	0.6	0.0	0.84	0.89	0.27	0.12
WINWORD	0.74	0.69	0.73	0.78	0.61	0.72	0.55	0.71	0.75	0.74	0.36	0.31	0.67	0.67	0.3	0.21	0.43	0.41	0.54	0.61	0.84	0.0	0.1	0.72	0.63
POWERPNT	0.79	0.74	0.78	0.82	0.66	0.78	0.6	0.76	0.8	0.79	0.42	0.37	0.73	0.73	0.29	0.34	0.52	0.44	0.59	0.67	0.89	0.1	0.0	0.78	0.68
EXCEL	0.27	0.27	0.33	0.24	0.37	0.29	0.38	0.32	0.23	0.25	0.59	0.7	0.42	0.46	0.75	0.73	0.64	0.61	0.45	0.66	0.27	0.72	0.78	0.0	0.27
wordpad	0.25	0.25	0.27	0.29	0.31	0.3	0.31	0.3	0.25	0.25	0.48	0.62	0.45	0.45	0.65	0.64	0.54	0.51	0.4	0.56	0.12	0.63	0.68	0.27	0.0

Fig. 5. Program distance. Clustering with $k = 400$

In the table above, we computed the normalized distance between the applications of our database. Two observations. First, if one takes the closest programs (outside itself!), the result is not surprising: firefox is close to safari, gvim to notepad and safari to quicktime. These relationships differ, either applications have same purpose, or they share development.

In a second step, we use the correlation matrix above to perform some clustering for the distances in Fig. 5. For that sake, we used the k-mean algorithm with $k = 6$, that is 5 categories plus one for trash. We get the following result:

Cluster 1	Cluster 2	Cluster 3	Cluster 4	Cluster 5	Cluster 6
izarc2go	winrar	chrome	firefox	iexplore	notepad
peazip	winzip32	opera	safari	winword	mspaint
notepad++	7zFM	iTunes	quicktime	powerpnt	wordpad
gvim	editpad7	realplay	vlc		
pspad	excel	wmplayer			

The table shows that proximity is explained either by close functionalities, or by a close (past or current) development process. However, we can conclude that a such

a classification remains quite imprecise. For retro-engineering, this is not really prob-
lematic since the analyst would cope errors, but we could not use it for detection for
which false positive ratio must be low.

Finally, to show the role of function clustering, we worked directly with the direct
distance between programs $\Delta'(\mathtt{p_1},\mathtt{p_2}) = |\mathbf{v}_{\mathtt{p_1}} - \mathbf{v}_{\mathtt{p_2}}|$. The program clustering is not as
good as above.

Indeed, if we do not modify the convergence parameter (which corresponds to
some cluster distance), the algorithm converges to only one category. So, we have to
put a looser parameter (from 0.45 to 0.6) to get again some "reasonable" clusters. We
get the following table. One observes a big category still emerges. It is actually the
trash category (those who can't be compared to any others). Note also that the other
categories are not as relevant as above.

Cluster 1	Cluster 2	Cluster 3	Cluster 4	Cluster 5	Cluster 6
winrar	izarc2go	firefox	quicktime	mspaint	iexplore
winzip32	peazip	safari	vlc	wordpad	wmplayer
7zFM	gvim	realplay			winword
notepad++	editpad7				powerpnt
notepad	pspad				
chrome	excel				
opera					
iTunes					

4.3   Packer Identification

One may refine the preceding experiment as follows. The distance we define on programs does not take into account the order in which functions are used, or if they are
used once or several times. The run distance defined below takes this into consideration. Characterizing programs using function sequence as signatures is known in the
literature as behavioral detection (see for instance [JDF08]). Usually, results are not
very good due to the high ambiguity (with respect to function sequence) of program
behaviors (e.g. [BGM10]). But, what we do here is much more modest. We just want
to identify some very particular behaviors, those coming from a small set of packers.

Given a program $\mathtt{p}$ calling some functions $\mathtt{f}_1, \ldots, \mathtt{f}_k$, let us run $\mathtt{p}$ on some inputs,
one gets a sequence $w \in \{\mathtt{f}_1, \ldots, \mathtt{f}_k\}^*$ of the functions called along the computation.
We define $\mathcal{R}$ to be the set of all inputs, and for $r \in \mathcal{R}$, we define $w_{\mathtt{p},r}$ to be the sequence
of the called functions of the program $\mathtt{p}$ on inputs r. For the sake of the argument, we
will restrict runs to be finite, so are $w_{\mathtt{p},r}$ for all $r \in \mathcal{R}$.

Let us suppose given a clustering $\mathcal{F} = \cup_{i=1}^k \mathcal{F}_i$. for all $f \in \mathcal{F}, \gamma(\mathtt{f})$ denotes its cluster,
that is a number within $\{1, \ldots, k\}$. The definition extends to sequences: $\gamma(\mathtt{f}_1, \ldots, \mathtt{f}_m) =
\gamma(\mathtt{f}_1) \cdots \gamma(\mathtt{f}_m) \in \{1, \ldots, k\}^m$.

Definition 5. *Given two programs* $\mathtt{p}_1$ *and* $\mathtt{p}_2$*, we define their run distance to be*
$\overline{\delta}(\mathtt{p}_1, \mathtt{p}_2) = E(r \mapsto \delta(\gamma(w_{\mathtt{p}_1,r}), \gamma(w_{\mathtt{p}_2,r})))$*, that is the expectation of the distances of*
the runs, the words in $\{1, \ldots, k\}^*$ *being compared with respect to Levenshtein distance.*

There are infinitely many runs, so that it is hard to get the distance between two programs, actually undecidable. However, for packer identification, one may observe that packers are almost insensitive to inputs outside some self-protection mechanisms. This is for instance what is done by Calvet in [Cal10]. Thus, we will approximate run distance by the distance on one run (Fig. 6).

	calc.exe	freecell.exe	mystic-calc.exe	mystic-freecell.exe	telock98-calc.exe	telock98-freecell.exe	telock982-calc.exe
calc.exe	0.00	0.46	0.98	0.35	0.98	0.98	0.12
freecell.exe	0.46	0.00	0.97	0.2	0.97	0.95	0.45
mystic-calc.exe	0.98	0.97	0.00	0.98	0.43	0.53	0.98
mystic-freecell.exe	0.35	0.2	0.98	0.00	0.98	0.96	0.34
telock98-calc.exe	0.98	0.97	0.43	0.98	0.00	0.33	0.98
telock98-freecell.exe	0.98	0.95	0.53	0.96	0.33	0.00	0.97
telock982-calc.exe	0.12	0.45	0.98	0.34	0.98	0.97	0.00

Fig. 6. Program distance

If one uses the rough run distance, one gets a correlation matrix that reveal the similarity between the original code and its packed form. Thus, to identify packers, one use the C-prefix run distance for some $C \in \mathbb{N}$, that is $\overline{\delta}_p(\mathbf{p}_1, \mathbf{p}_2) = \min_{i > C}(E(r \mapsto \delta(\gamma(w_{\mathbf{p}_1,r})[0..i], \gamma(w_{\mathbf{p}_2,r})[0..i])))$. We take $C = 10$. The result is:

nom	calc.exe	freecell.exe	mystic-calc.exe	mystic-freecell.exe	telock98-calc.exe	telock98-freecell.exe	telock982-calc.exe
calc.exe	0.00	0.05	0.36	0.43	0.22	0.25	0.22
freecell.exe	0.05	0.00	0.39	0.36	0.22	0.25	0.22
mystic-calc.exe	0.36	0.39	0.00	0.02	0.5	0.42	0.5
mystic-freecell.exe	0.43	0.36	0.02	0.00	0.5	0.42	0.5
telock98-calc.exe	0.22	0.22	0.5	0.5	0.00	0.07	0.04
telock98-freecell.exe	0.25	0.25	0.42	0.42	0.07	0.00	0.07
telock982-calc.exe	0.22	0.22	0.5	0.5	0.04	0.07	0.00

Fig. 7. Program distance

Then, packers are correctly identified. Notice that for `telock`, we used different options (**98** or **982**) and for the rough distance, the distance were high. Not anymore with the prefix distance (Fig. 7).

4.4   Combining Morphological Analysis and Function Clustering

Let us come back to our broad objective. In our research group, we are developing morphological analysis (MA) that is used for malware identification. We recall that MA belongs to the branch of detecting method based on abstract control flow graph identification, see [BMM06] for an other example. In other words, it puts into light underlying algorithms, not functions. So, our question was the following: is there a relationship between functions and morphological analysis? Or to put it in a more precise setting: are there some specific algorithms before calling functions?

So, we came back to our application database and we applied morphological analysis. The learning process went well. To sum up, we had at least 73 specific sites (some remarkable graphs within applications). The main difference between applications is whether they are stand alone or if they are based on dynamic libraries. In the first case, we have lots of sites, in the latter one, much less.

Then, as we did above, we computed a correlation matrix that is displayed below.

	IZArc2Go	winrar	peazip	winzip32	7zfm	notepad++	notepad	gvim	editpad	pspad	iexplore	firefox	chrome	opera	Safari	quicktime	ITunes	vlc	realplay	wmplayer	mspaint	winword	powerpnt	excel	wordpad
IZArc2Go	0.00	9.89		9.57		9.04		10.96	4.48	2.45		9.94					6.74							9.86	
winrar	9.89	0.00		5.31		4.92		4.79		9.19		5.43	7.25				1.77							9.19	
peazip			0.00																						
winzip32	9.57	5.31		0.00		6.16		5.65		9.50		3.74		1.39			3.90			5.61		9.30		10.00	
7zfm					0.00																				
notepad++	9.04	4.92		6.16		0.00		2.45		9.26	3.14	3.91	5.42				5.35							9.55	
notepad							0.00																		
gvim	10.96	4.79		5.65		2.45		0.00		10.60		3.79	4.73				5.35			5.61				10.70	
editpad	4.48								0.00	6.06														7.24	
pspad	2.45	9.19		9.50		9.26		10.60	6.06	0.00			9.25				6.04							10.20	
iexplore						3.14					0.00										2.33				
firefox	9.94	5.43		3.74		3.91		3.79				0.00	3.26		2.34	2.63			3.23					9.25	
chrome		7.25				5.42		4.73		9.25		3.26	0.00	3.26			3.05				9.30			9.25	
opera				1.39									3.26	0.00			4.03								
Safari												2.34			0.00	1.89			2.34						
quicktime												2.63			1.89	0.00			2.18	2.34					
ITunes	6.74	1.77		3.90		5.35		5.35		6.04			3.05	4.03			0.00							6.04	
vlc																		0.00							
realplay												3.23			2.34	2.18			0.00						
wmplayer				5.61				5.61								2.34				0.00					
mspaint											2.33		9.30								0.00	9.30			
winword				9.30									9.30								9.30	0.00	0.97	1.05	3.28
powerpnt																						0.97	0.00	0.97	
excel	9.86	9.19		10.00		9.55		10.70	7.24	10.20			9.25				6.04					1.05	0.97	0.00	3.28
wordpad																								3.28	0.00

Some clusters occur. They are:

```
[{'winword', 'vlc', 'powerpnt', '7zFM', 'excel', 'peazip'}, {'notepad', 'wordpad'},
{'realplay', 'Safari', 'firefox', 'Quicktime'}, {'iexplore', 'mspaint'},
{'iTunes', 'chrome', 'IZArc2Go', 'pspad', 'winzip32', 'wmplayer', 'editpad',
 'gvim', 'opera', 'notepad++', 'winrar'}]
```

that brings back some of the clusters that we have seen above. For instance, we see the link between firefox, safari and quicktime. No surprises, there are differences since we are using a very different mechanism. But, a manual verification on common sites showed us that algorithmic relationships correspond to function relationship (around one third of the sites). In other words, the function analysis could be used to enrich our own methodology.

5 Conclusion

We propose a mapping from functions to their intentions via a vector of words within a natural language. It is based presently on the function documentation provided by MICROSOFT, but it could be extended to any vendors.

In a second step, we discuss the question of function clustering, the idea being to avoid dubious distinction. The clustering may be performed at different levels, depending on the expected precision.

In a third step, we relate the function clustering to other issues. We compare it with respect to MICROSOFT's own clustering. Then, we work on program identification and packer identification. In a last step we compare it to our morphological analysis.

Finally, we provide on our web-page a plugins for IDA that maps functions to their vectors, or alternatively to the url of each function. The plugins is available on our git repository.

As a perspective, we would like to explore a little bit further the natural language aspect of our approach. For instance, we did not relate words one to an other with respect to their own semantics. We think that this could strengthen the semantics of functions even more. An other idea is to look for informations in a much broader way: there are tons of tutorials, technical explanations and code samples on the web. Machine Learning techniques could be applied to these data (that could be inspired by the work of Lakhotia et al. [LL15] or Tawbi et al. [SSM+16]).

Acknowledgment. The authors would like to thank Jean-Yves Marion and Mizuhito Ogawa for early discussions and Fabrice Sabatier and Alexis Lartigue for discussions and some experiments.

References

[AS14] Abramsky, S., Sadrzadeh, M.: Semantic unification. In: Casadio, C., Coecke, B., Moortgat, M., Scott, P. (eds.) Categories and Types in Logic, Language, and Physics. LNCS, vol. 8222, pp. 1–13. Springer, Heidelberg (2014). doi:10.1007/978-3-642-54789-8_1

[BGM10] Beaucamps, P., Gnaedig, I., Marion, J.-Y.: Behavior abstraction in malware analysis. In: Barringer, H., Falcone, Y., Finkbeiner, B., Havelund, K., Lee, I., Pace, G., Roşu, G., Sokolsky, O., Tillmann, N. (eds.) RV 2010. LNCS, vol. 6418, pp. 168–182. Springer, Heidelberg (2010). doi:10.1007/978-3-642-16612-9_14

[Bir15] Bird, S.: NLTK Documentation (2015)

[BKM09] Bonfante, G., Kaczmarek, M., Marion, J.-Y.: Architecture of a morphological malware detector. J. Comput. Virol. 5(3), 263–270 (2009)

[BMM06] Bruschi, D., Martignoni, L., Monga, M.: Detecting self-mutating malware using control-flow graph matching. In: Büschkes, R., Laskov, P. (eds.) DIMVA 2006. LNCS, vol. 4064, pp. 129–143. Springer, Heidelberg (2006)

[BMS15] Bonfante, G., Marion, J.-Y., Sabatier, F.: Gorille sniffs code similarities, the case study of Qwerty versus Regin. In: Osorio, F.C. (ed.) Malware Conference, p. 8, Fajardo, Puerto Rico. IEEE, October 2015

[Cal10] Calvet, J.: Tripoux: reverse-engineering of malware packers for dummies. In: DeepSec 2010 (2010)

[CH16] Copestake, A., Herbelot, A.: Lexicalised compositionality (2016)

[JDF08] Jacob, G., Debar, H., Filiol, E.: Behavioral detection of malware: from a survey towards an established taxonomy. J. Comput. Virol. 4(3), 251–266 (2008)

[Kac15] Kaczmarek, M.: Malware instrumentation application to regin analysis. In: Freyssinet, E. (ed.) Malware Conference, p. 16, Paris, France, November 2015

[LL15] LeDoux, C., Lakhotia, A.: Malware and machine learning. In: Yager, R.R., Reformat, M.Z., Alajlan, N. (eds.) Intelligent Methods for Cyber Warfare. SCI, vol. 563, pp. 1–42. Springer, Heidelberg (2015). doi:10.1007/978-3-319-08624-8_1

[PZ13] Peiravian, N., Zhu, X.: Machine learning for android malware detection using permission and API calls. In: Proceedings of the 2013 IEEE 25th International Conference on Tools with Artificial Intelligence, ICTAI 2013, pp. 300–305, Washington, DC, USA. IEEE Computer Society (2013)

[Qué12] Quéré, R.: Some proposals for comparison of soft partitions. Ph.D. Université de La Rochelle, December 2012

[Ros77] Ross, D.T.: Structured analysis (SA): a language for communicating ideas. IEEE Trans. Softw. Eng. 3(1), 16–34 (1977)

[Sch98] Schuetze, H.: Automatic word sense discrimination. Comput. Linguist. 1(24), 97–123 (1998)

[SSM+16] Sheikhalishahi, M., Saracino, A., Mejri, M., Tawbi, N., Martinelli, F.: Fast and effective clustering of spam emails based on structural similarity. In: Garcia-Alfaro, J., Kranakis, E., Bonfante, G. (eds.) Foundations and Practice of Security. LNCS, vol. 9482, pp. 195–211. Springer, Heidelberg (2016)

[Sym16] Symantec. 2016 Internet Security Threat Report (2016)

[TS12] Teh, A., Stewart, A.: Human-readable real-time classifications of malicious executables. In: 10th Australian Information Security Management Conference (2012)

On the Feasibility of Malware Authorship Attribution

Saed Alrabaee(✉), Paria Shirani, Mourad Debbabi, and Lingyu Wang

Concordia University, Montreal, Canada
s_alraba@encs.concordia.ca

Abstract. There are many occasions in which the security community is interested to discover the authorship of malware binaries, either for digital forensics analysis of malware corpora or for thwarting live threats of malware invasion. Such a discovery of authorship might be possible due to stylistic features inherent to software codes written by human programmers. Existing studies of authorship attribution of general purpose software mainly focus on source code, which is typically based on the style of programs and environment. However, those features critically depend on the availability of the program source code, which is usually not the case when dealing with malware binaries. Such program binaries often do not retain many semantic or stylistic features due to the compilation process. Therefore, authorship attribution in the domain of malware binaries based on features and styles that will survive the compilation process is challenging. This paper provides the state of the art in this literature. Further, we analyze the features involved in those techniques. By using a case study, we identify features that can survive the compilation process. Finally, we analyze existing works on binary authorship attribution and study their applicability to real malware binaries.

1 Introduction

Authorship attribution comprises an important aspect of many forensic investigations, which is equally true in the computer world. When a malware attacks computer systems and leaves behind a malware corpus, an important question to ask is '*Who wrote this malware?*'. By narrowing down the authorship of a malware, important insights may be gained to indicate the origin of the malware, to correlate the malware to previously known threats, or to assist in developing techniques for thwarting future similar malware. Considering the fact that humans are creatures of habit and habits tend to persist, therefore, various patterns may be embedded into malware when their creators follow their habitual styles of coding.

Although significant efforts have been made to develop automated approaches for source code [18,34,41], such techniques typically rely on features that will likely be lost in the strings of bytes representing binary code after the compilation process (e.g., variable and function renaming, comments, and code organization, or the development environment, such as programming languages and

F. Cuppens et al. (Eds.): FPS 2016, LNCS 10128, pp. 256–272, 2017.
DOI: 10.1007/978-3-319-51966-1_17

text editors). Identifying the author of a malware binary might be possible but challenging. Such identification must be based on features of the malware binary that are considered to be author specific, which means those features must show only small variations in the writing of different programs by the same author and large such variations over the writing by different authors [41]. That is, authorship identification requires stylistic features that depend on authorship of the code, instead of any other properties, such as functionality. This fact implies that most existing malware analysis techniques will not be directly applicable to authorship attribution. On the other hand, several papers show that the stylistic features are abundant in binaries [13,19,38], and it may be practically feasible to identify the authorship with acceptable accuracy. Another challenge unique to malware authorship attribution is that, while software code may take many forms, including sources files, object files, binary files, and shell code, the malign nature of a malware usually dictates the focus on binary code due to the lack of source code.

In this paper, we investigate the state of the art on binary code authorship techniques and analyze them. More specifically, we first present the survey of existing techniques that are related to the analysis of authorship attribution. This paper covers related work on different representations of malware, including both source files and binaries. Second, we also look at a broader range of work on general purpose malware analysis in order to study which features are involved. Such a comprehensive study of features will allow us to consider a rich collection of features before selecting those which potentially survive the compilation process and are present in the binary code. Third, we analyze and compare binary authorship attribution systems [13,19,38]. Besides, we study their applicability to real malware binaries. Based on our analysis, we provide many important steps that should be considered by reverse engineers, security analysts, and researchers when they deal with malware authorship attribution.

2 Authorship Attribution

In this section, we review the state of the art in the broad domain of authorship attribution, including some techniques proposed for malware analysis. An important goal of this study is to collect a rich list of features that are potentially relevant to malware authorship attribution.

2.1 Source Code Authorship Attribution

Investigating source code authorship attribution techniques can help us understand the features that are likely preserved during the compilation process. Several studies have shown that certain programmers or types of programmers usually hold some features of programming. Examples are layout (spacing, indentation and boarding characters, etc.), style (variable naming, choice of statements, comments, etc.) and environment (computer platform, programming language, compiler, text editor, etc.). The authorship identification of source codes has been gaining momentum since the initial empirical work of Krsul [34]. Krsul et al. described different important applications of source code authorship techniques and found that style-related features could be extracted from malicious code as well. Burrows [16] and Frantzeskou et al. [26] use n-grams with ranking methods. Burrows and Frantzeskou have both proposed information retrieval approaches with n-grams for source code authorship attribution.

Kothari et al. [33] first collected sample source code of known authors and created profiles by using metrics extraction and filtering tools. In addition, they used style-based and character sequences metrics in classifying the particular developer. Chen et al. [22] proposed a semantic approach for identifying authorship by comparing program data flows. More specifically, they computed the program dependencies, program similarities, and query syntactic structure and data flow of the program. Burrows et al. [17] introduced an approach named Source Code Author Profile (SCAP) using byte level n-gram technique. The author claimed that the approach is language independent and n-gram profiles would represent a better way than traditional methods in order to find the unique behavioral characteristics of a specific source code author. Jang et al. [28] performed experiments to find a set of metrics that can be used to classify the source code author. They worked on extracting the programming layout, style, structure, and fuzzy logic metrics to perform the authorship analysis. Yang et al. [43] performed experiments to support the theory that a set of metrics can be utilized to classify the programmer correctly within the closed environment and for a specific set of programmers. With the help of programming metrics, they suggested developing a signature of each programmer within a closed environment. They used two statistical methods, cluster and discriminant analysis. They did not expect that metrics gathered for a programmer would remain an accurate tag for a long time. It is obvious that a one-time metrics gathering is not enough, as this should be a continuous task. The practice of authorship analysis includes metrics extraction, data analysis and classification.

A separate thread of research focuses on plagiarism detection, which is carried out by identifying the similarities between different programs. For example, there is a widely-used tool called Moss that originated from Stanford University for detecting software plagiarism [12]. More recently, Caliskan-Islam et al. [18] investigated methods to de-anonymize source code authors of C++ using coding style. They modeled source code authorship attribution as a machine learning problem using natural language processing techniques to extract the necessary features. The source code is represented as an abstract syntax tree, and the properties are driven from this tree.

2.2 Binary Code Authorship Attribution

In contrast to source code, binary code has drawn significantly less attention with respect to authorship attribution. This is mainly due to the fact that many salient features that may identify an author's style are lost during the compilation process. In [13,19,38], the authors show that certain stylistic features can indeed survive the compilation process and remain intact in binary code, which leads to the feasibility of authorship attribution for binary code. The methodology developed by Rosenblum et al. [38] is the first attempt to automatically identify authors of software binaries. The main concept employed by this method is to extract syntax-based and semantics-based features using predefined templates, such as idioms (sequences of three consecutive instructions), n-grams, and graphlets. Machine learning techniques are then applied to rank these features based on their relative correlations with authorship. A subsequent approach to automatically identify the authorship of software binaries is proposed by Alrabaee et al. [13]. The main concept employed by this method is to extract a sequence of instructions with specific semantics and to construct a graph based on register manipulation, where a machine learning algorithm is applied afterwards. A more recent approach to automatically identify the authorship of software binaries is proposed by Caliskan et al. [19]. They extract syntactical features present in source code from decompiled executable binary. Though these approaches represent a great effort on authorship attribution, it should be noted that they were not applied to real malware. Further, some limitations could be observed including weak accuracy in the case of multiple authors, being potentially thwarted by light obfuscation, and their inability to decouple features related to functionality from those which are related to authors' styles.

3   Study of Features

In this section, we present a more elaborated study of features collected during the literature review.

3.1   Features of Source Files

Program source code provides a far richer basis for writer-specific programming features. Our goal is to determine which features may survive the compilation process and be helpful for authorship identification of binary code.

Linguistic Features: Programming languages allow developers to express constructs and ideas in many ways. Differences in the way developers express their ideas can be captured in their programming styles, which in turn can be used for author identification [40]. The linguistic style is used to analyze the differences in the literary techniques of authors. Researchers have identified over 1,000 characteristics, or style markers, such as comments, to analyze literary works [20]. Moreover, it has been used to identify the author by capturing, examining, and comparing style markers [27].

Formatting: The source code formatting shows a very personal style. Formatting is also considered as a good way for programmers to make it easier when reading what was written. These factors indicate that the formatting style of code should yield writer-specific features [34]: Placement of statement delimiters, Multiple statements per line, Format of type declarations, Format of function arguments, and Length of comment lines.

Bugs and Vulnerabilities: A written program might have errors or bugs such as buffer overflow, or a pointer to an undefined memory address. These kinds of issues could be an indicator of the author.

Execution Path: The execution path may indicate the author's preference in how resolving a particular task through the selection of algorithms, as well as certain data structures, or using specific keywords such as `while` or `for`.

Abstract Syntax Tree (AST): AST is an intermediate representations produced by code parsers of compilers, and thus forms the basis for the generation of many other code representations. Such tree forms how statements and expressions are nested to produce programs. More specifically, it encompasses inner nodes representing operators (e.g., additions or assignments) and leaf nodes correspond to operands (e.g., constants or identifiers).

Control Flow Graph (CFG): It describes the order in which code statements are executed as well as conditions that need to be met for a particular path of execution to be taken. Statements and predicates are represented by nodes, which are connected by directed edges to indicate the transfer of control. For each edge, there is a label of true, false or unconditional control.

Program Dependence Graph (PDG): It is introduced by Ferrante et al. [24], which has been originally developed to perform program slicing [42]. This graph determines all statements and predicates of a program that affect the value of a variable at a specified statement.

3.2   Features of Binary Files

Compiler and System Information: A unique sequence of instructions might be an indicator of the compilers. The code may contain different system calls found only in certain operating systems. The analysis of binary code may reveal that it was written in a specific source language such as C++. This can be determined based on support routines and library calls in the binary code.

System Call: It is considered as programmatic way in which a computer program requests a service from the kernel of the operating system it is executed on, for instance, process scheduling with integral kernel services. Such system calls capture intrinsic characteristics of the malicious behavior and thus are harder to evade [21].

Errors: The binary code might have errors or bugs such as buffer overflow, or a pointer to an undefined memory address. These kinds of bugs could be an indicator of the author.

Idioms: An idiom is not really a specific feature, but rather a feature template that captures low-level details of the sequence underlying a program. Idioms are short sequences of instructions. A grammar for idiom feature follows the Backus-Naur [32] form.

Graphlet: A graphlet is an intermediary representation between the assembly instructions and the Control Flow Graph, which represents the details of a program structure [36], and is represented as a small connected non-isomorphic induced sub-graph of a large network [23]. Graphlets were first introduced by Prvzulj et al. [36] for designing two new highly sensitive measures of network locality, structural similarities: the relative graphlet frequency distance [23], and the graphlet degree distribution agreement [38].

n-grams: The n-gram feature was first used by an IBM research group [30]. An n-gram is an n-character slice of a longer string. A string is simply split into substrings of fixed length n. For example, the string 'MALWARE' can be segmented into the following 4-grams: 'MALW', 'ALWA', 'LWAR', and 'WARE'.

Opcode: An opcode is the portion of an assembly instruction that specifies the action to be performed, for instance, jmp, lea, and pop. Opcode sequences have recently been introduced as an alternative to byte n-grams [35]. Some of the opcodes (e.g. push or mov) have a high frequency of appearance within an executable file. In [39] is shown that the opcodes by themselves were capable to statistically explain the variability between malware and legitimate software.

Strings and Constants: The type of constants that used in the literature is integers, which are used in computation, as well as integers used as pointer offsets. The strings are ANSI single-byte null-terminated strings [31].

Register Flow Graph: This graph captures the flow and dependencies between the registers that annotated to cmp instruction [13]. Such graph can capture an important semantic aspects about the behavior of a program, which might indicate the author's skills or habits.

4 Implementation

This section shows the setup of our experiments and provides an overview of the collected data.

4.1 Implementation Environment

The described binary feature extractions are implemented using separate python scripts for modularity purposes, which altogether form our analytical system. A subset of the python scripts in our evaluation system is used in tandem with IDA Pro disassembler [4]. The Neo4j [10] graph database is utilized to perform complex graph operations such as k-graph (graphlet) extraction. Gephi [9] is used for all graph analysis functions (e.g., page rank) that are not provided by Neo4j. The PostgreSQL database is used to store extracted features according to its efficiency and scalability. For the sake of usability, a graphical user interface in which binaries can be uploaded and analyzed is implemented.

4.2   Dataset

The utilized dataset is composed of several files from different sources, as described below: (i) GitHub [3], where a considerable amount of real open-source projects are available; (ii) Google Code Jam [2], an international programming competition, where solutions to difficult algorithmic puzzles are available; and (iii) a set of known malware files representing a mixture of nine different families [7] provided in Microsoft Malware Classification Challenge. According to existing works, we only examine code written in C/C++. These programs are either open-source or publicly available, in which case the identities of the authors are known. Statistics about the dataset are provided in Table 1.

Table 1. Statistics about the binaries used in the evaluation

Source	# of authors	# of programs	# of functions
GitHub	50	150	40000
Google Code Jam	120	550	1065
Malware	9	36	15000
Total	179	736	46065

4.3   Dataset Compilation

To construct our experimental datasets, we compile the source code with different compilers and compilation settings to measure the effects of such variations. We use GNU Compiler Collection's gcc, Xcode, ICC, as well as Microsoft Visual Studio (VS) 2010, with different optimization levels.

4.4   Implementation Phases

The original binaries are passed to the pre-processing component, where are disassembled with IDA Pro disassembler. The second component contains two processes: (1) ASMTODB, which extracts some specific features (e.g., idioms) from the assembly files, and (2) BINTODB, which extracts the features directly from the binary files. The result of this stage is a set of features stored in the database. This phase also implements the feature ranking which is a pre-processing phase for classification.

4.5   Feature Ranking

Feature ranking is a pre-processing phase for classification. We assume that there exists a known set of program authors and a set of programs written by each of them. The task of the feature ranking algorithm is to associate the identity of the most likely author of a feature. We extract features from the program assemblies and binaries as described in the previous section in order to obtain the feature list associated with a specific author. We apply mutual information and information gain applied in Rosenblum et al. [38] and Islam et al. [19], respectively.

4.6   SQL Schema to Store All Features

Storing, ranking and processing the features in the classification phase require an appropriate SQL schema. We have chosen the PostgreSQL database system, and designed our SQL tables, the relations between them, together with the Features-to-DB APIs, so that our software modules minimize their interaction with the database.

4.7   Authorship Classification

The authorship classification technique assumes that a known set of authors with their program samples are collected. After extracting and ranking features, as described in the previous subsection, a classifier is built based on the top-ranked features, producing a decision function that can assign a label (authorship) to any given new program based on the given set of known authors. More specifically, the typical steps for authorship classification are the following:

1. Each program is first represented as an integral-valued feature vector describing those features that are present in the program.
2. Those features are ordered using the aforementioned ranking algorithm based on the mutual information between the features and the known author labels. A given number of top-ranked features are selected, and others filtered out in order to reduce both the training cost and risk of overfitting the data.
3. A cross-validation is performed on those highly-ranked features. Those features would jointly produce a good decision function for the authorship classifier.
4. The LIBLINEAR support vector machine for the actual classification is employed for the actual classification.

5   Evaluation

In this section, we present the evaluation results for the existing works on binary authorship attribution. Subsequently, we evaluate the identification and the scalability of existing works. The impact of evading techniques is then studied. Finally, binary features are applied to real malware binaries and the results are discussed.

5.1 Accuracy

The main purpose of this experiment is to demonstrate how to evaluate the accuracy of author identification in binaries.

Evaluation Settings. The evaluation of existing works is conducted using the datasets described in Sect. 4. The data is randomly split into ten sets, where one set is reserved as a testing set, and the remaining sets are used as training sets to evaluate the system. The process is then repeated 15 times (according to existing works). Furthermore, since the application domain targeted by binary authorship attribution works is much more sensitive to false positives than false negatives, we employ an F-measure as follows:

$$F_{0.5} = 1.25 \cdot \frac{P \cdot R}{0.25P + R} \tag{1}$$

Existing Works Comparison. We evaluate and compare the existing authorship attribution methods [13,18,38]. For this purpose the source code and the used database are needed. The source code of the authorship classification techniques presented by Rosenblum et al. [38] and Caliskan-Islam et al. [18] are available at [5,8], respectively; however, the datasets are not available. For the system proposed by Alrabaee et al. (OBA2) [13], we have asked the authors to provide us the source code.

Caliskan-Islam et al. present the largest scale evaluation of binary authorship attribution in related work, which contains *600* authors with *8* training programs per author. Rosenblum et al. present a large-scale evaluation of *190* authors with at least *8* training programs, while Alrabaee et al. present a small scale evaluation of 5 authors with *10* programs for each. Since the datasets used by the aforementioned techniques are not available, we compare our results with these methods using the same datasets mentioned in Table 1. The number of features used in Caliskan-Islam et al., Rosenblum et al., and Alrabaee et al. systems are *4500*, *10000*, and *6500*, respectively.

Figure 1 details the results of comparing the accuracy between existing methods. It shows the relationship between the accuracy ($F_{0.5}$) and the number of authors present in all datasets, where the accuracy decreases as the size of author population increases. The results show that Caliskan-Islam et al. approach achieves better accuracy in determining the author of binaries. Taking all three approaches into consideration, the highest accuracy of authorship attribution is close to *90%* on the Google Code Jam dataset with less than *20* authors, while the lowest accuracy is *45%* when *179* authors are involved.

As can be seen in Fig. 1, OBA2 achieves good accuracy when it deals with small scale of authors. For instance, the accuracy is approximately *84%* on GitHub dataset when the number of authors is *30*, while the accuracy drops to *58%* on the same dataset when the number of authors increases to *50*. The main reason is due to the fact that the authors of projects in Github have no restrictions when developing projects. The lower accuracy obtained by OBA2

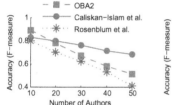 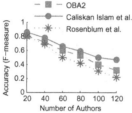 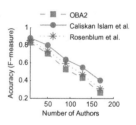

Fig. 1. Accuracy results of authorship attribution obtained by Caliskan-Islam et al. [18], Rosenblum et al. [38], and OBA2 [13], on (a) Github, (b) Google Code Jam, and (c) All datasets.

is approximately *28%* on all datasets when the number of authors is *179*. The accuracy of Rosenblum et al. approach drops rapidly to *43%*, whereas Caliskan-Islam et al. system accuracy remains greater than *60%*, if the *140* authors on all datasets are considered.

5.2 Scalability

We evaluate how well existing works scale up to *1000* authors. Since in the case of malware, an analyst may be dealing with an extremely large number of new samples on a daily basis. For this experiment, we work with *1000* users, of which are authors from the Google Code Jam. First, we extract the top-ranked features as described in Rosenblum et al. and Caliskan-Islam et al. approaches, while the features used by OBA2 are not ranked.

The results of large-scale author identification are shown in Fig. 2. As seen in Fig. 2, by increasing the number of authors, all the existing works accuracy drops significantly. For instance, Rosenblum et al. approach accuracy drops to approximately *5%* when the number of authors is greater than *600* authors. While the accuracy of OBA2 approach drops to *15%* when the number of authors reaches to *500*. However, Caliskan-Islam et al. approach accuracy drops to *20%* with an increase to over *700* authors.

Through our experiments we have observed that top-ranked features used in the Rosenblum et al. approach are mixture of compiler and user features, where leads to higher rate in false positives. OBA2 identifies author according to the way of branch handling. Therefore, when the number of authors is largely increased, distinguishing the author based on handling branches becomes limited and hard. Finally, Caliskan-Islam et al. approach relies on the features extracted from AST of compiled binary; so with the

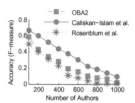

Fig. 2. Large-scale author identification results

large number of authors, these features became common and similar which make the authorship attribution harder.

5.3   Impact of Evading Techniques

In this subsection, we apply different techniques to evade the existing systems in order to study their stability. For this purpose, we randomly choose *50* authors and *8* programmes for each author. The accuracy results without applying any evading technique, and with applying evading techniques are shown in Table 2.

Refactoring Techniques. The adversary may use existing refactoring techniques to prevent authorship attribution. Hence, we use chosen dataset for the C^{++} refactoring process [1,11]. We consider the techniques of (i) Renaming a Variable (RV), (ii) Moving a Method from a superclass to its subclasses (MM), and (iii) extracting a few statements and placing them into a New Method (NM). Depth explanations of these techniques are detailed in [25]. We obtain an accuracy of *81%* in correctly classifying authors for OBA2 system, which drops to *62%* when RV is applied. The reason of this dropping in accuracy is that variable renaming affects the features used by OBA2, while OBA2 can tolerate NM, and MM. The accuracy of Caliskan-Islam et al. approach drops not greatly from *79%* to *70%*. This is due to the fact that their approach decompiles the binary into source code, and then extracts the features. Hence, the aforementioned refactoring techniques do not change much in the abstract syntax tree. However, the approach can tolerate renaming variables. Finally, Rosenblum et al. approach is the one that is mostly affected by Refactoring techniques, where the accuracy drops from *66%* to *40%*. Since their approach extracts idioms from assembly files, any of these techniques will change the idioms (sequence of assembly instructions) which cause a drop in accuracy.

The Impact of Obfuscation. We are interested in determining how existing works handle simple binary obfuscation techniques intended for evading detection, as implemented by tools such as Obfuscator-LLVM [29]. These obfuscators could apply Instruction Replacement (IR): replacing instructions by other semantically equivalent instructions, Dead Code Insertion (DCI), Register Renaming (RR), spurious control flow insertion, and can even completely Flatten Control Flow graphs (FCF). Obfuscation techniques implemented by Obfuscator-LLVM are applied to the samples prior to classifying the authors. Caliskan-Islam et al. approach is the most affected approach by FCF technique; since control flow flattening makes the decompilation process hard, which means the features cannot be extracted correctly.

Table 2. Accuracy results before and after applying refactoring techniques, obfuscation techniques, and different compilers. (AbET): Accuracy before Evading Techniques, ($\sim$): The accuracy has not affected.

System	AbET	Refactoring				Obfuscation					Compiler		
		RV	NM	MM	All	RR	IR	DCI	FCF	All	GCC	Xcode	ICC
OBA2	0.81	0.62	$\sim$	$\sim$	0.62	0.64	0.74	$\sim$	$\sim$	0.58	0.74	0.60	0.54
Caliskan-Islam	0.79	$\sim$	0.72	0.71	0.70	$\sim$	$\sim$	$\sim$	0.24	0.24	0.66	0.64	0.54
Rosenblum	0.66	0.60	0.58	0.55	0.4	0.62	$\sim$	$\sim$	0.27	0.25	0.15	0.55	0.29

The Impact of Compilers. To create experimental datasets for this purpose, we first compile the source code with GCC, VS, ICC, and Xcode compilers. Next, the effect of different compilation options, such as the source of compiler, is measured. The results show that the approach which is mostly affected by changing the compiler is Rosenblum et al.'s approach; since this approach does not distinguish between user functions or compiler functions. For instance, the accuracy observed through our experiments is 15%, when the binaries are compiled with GCC, because the GCC compiler inserts many compiler functions.

5.4   Applying Existing Works to Malware Binaries

We apply existing works to different sets of real malware: `Ramnit`, `Lollipop`, `Kelihos`, `Vundo`, `Simda`, `Tracur`, `Obfuscator.ACY`, and `Gatak`. These malware are selected due to their availability [7]. These samples contain different variants of the same malware so we assume that these variants are written by the same author or the same group of authors. Due to the lack of ground truth, we compare outputs of each approach manually to verify that they belong to same family. Details about the malware dataset are shown in Table 3. The number of compiler functions are obtained based on [37], while the fifth column shows the number of library functions acquired by F.L.I.R.T technology [4]. According to Table 3, we can observe that the percentage of compiler functions is quite high, so a pre-processing step before applying authorship attribution approaches would be demanding. For instance, the percentage of compiler functions in `Lollipop` family is *30%*. We apply existing works and cluster functions according to their features by using standard k-mean. Then we manually analysis the obtained clusters to classify them to correct/wrong clusters as shown in Table 4.

Table 3. Characteristics of malware datasets. (BF): binary functions, (CF): compiler functions, (LF): library function.

Malware	# of variants	# of BF	# of CF	# of LF
Ramnit	4	5285	1601	50
Lollipop	3	3510	1054	100
Kelihos	2	1924	847	74
Vundo	4	7923	2410	219
Simda	2	2100	689	105
Tracur	2	1657	787	100
Obfuscator.ACY	3	2762	986	310
Gatak	2	2054	860	174

Table 4. Clustering results based on the features used in existing systems. (TC): the total number of clusters, (CC): the percentage of correct clusters, (WC): the percentage of wrong clusters.

Malware	OBA2			Caliskan-Islam			Rosenblum		
	TC	CC	WC	TC	CC	WC	TC	CC	WC
Ramnit	145	60%	30%	110	47%	50%	208	18%	70%
Lollipop	90	75%	14%	185	59%	38%	220	21%	67%
Kelihos	41	88%	8%	17	90%	4%	75	34%	55%
Vundo	200	62%	14%	89	28%	68%	384	39%	48%
Simda	52	49%	50%	41	92%	5%	109	42%	51%
Tracur	44	89%	9%	53	83%	12%	124	51%	40%
Obfuscator.ACY	30	78%	21%	45	74%	24%	89	29%	70%
Gatak	29	57%	34%	51	87%	12%	79	38%	62%

6   Learnt Lessons and Concluding Remarks

Functionality or styles: During the evaluation, we have observed that the features selected by existing techniques are more closely related to the functionality of the program rather than the author's style. This argument may be supported by the evidence that a basic short program has less features than comparatively bigger, functionality-oriented programs. This shows that features are directly related to the size of the program, which usually depicts functionality but not style [13,18,38]. In order to avoid this, some existing systems could be used as preprocessing stage [14,15] applies different steps.

Feature pre-processing: We have encountered top-ranked features related to the compiler (e.g., stack frame set-up operation). It is thus necessary to filter irrelevant functions (e.g., compiler functions) in order to better identify author-related portions of code [38]. To avoid this, a filtration method based on the FLIRT technology for library identification as well as a system for compiler functions filtration such as BinComp [37] should be used. Successful distinction between the two groups of functions (library/compiler and user functions) will lead to considerable savings in time and will help shift the focus of analysis to more relevant functions.

Application type: We find that the accuracy of existing methods [13,38] depends highly on the application's domain. For example, in Fig. 1, superior accuracy is observed for the Google Code Jam dataset where the accuracy is 77% in average. This is because the approach used by Rosenblum et al. extracts SysCalls, which are more useful in the case of academia/competition code than in other cases. This can be explained by the authors' choice to systematically rely on external libraries and to implement, for instance, MFC APIs. The results also show that Alrabaee et al. rely on the application because their approach extracts the manner by which the author handles branches; for instance, the accuracy drops from *82%* to *57%* when Google Code Jam is used. After investigating the source code, we notice that the number of branches is not big, which makes the attribution even more difficult.

The source of features: Caliskan et al. [18] use a decompiler to translate the program into C-like pseudo code via Hex-Ray [6]. They pass the code to a fuzzy parser, thus abstract syntax tree is obtained, which is the source of feature extraction. In addition to Hex-Ray limitations [6], the C-like pseudo code is also different from the original code to the extent that the variables, branches, and keywords are different. For instance, we find that a function in the source code consists of the following keywords: (1-do, 1-switch, 3-case, 3-break, 2-while, 1-if) and the number of variables is 2. Once we check the same function after decompilation, we find that the function consists of the following keywords: (1-do, 1-else/if, 2-goto, 2-while, 4-if) and the number of variables is 4. This will evidently lead to misleading features.

Misleading Features: To make things worse, our re-evaluation results show that many top-ranked features are in fact completely unrelated to authors' styles. For example, many source code-level functions do not have their names identified at binary level, i.e., IDA Pro assigns a name prefixed with "sub" and postfixed with randomly generated numbers by the compiler. Experiments show that these functions with random numbers play a vital role for features to be ranked high by calculating the mutual information. This discovery shows that this technique may select many features unrelated to author styles but rather some other properties, such as compiler-generated functions.

Concluding Remarks: Binary code authorship attribution is a less explored problem compared with source code level authorship attribution due to many facts (e.g., the reverse engineering is time consuming, having limited features preserved during the compilation process). In this paper, we have first presented a literature review relevant to authorship identification of binary and source code. Subsequently, we introduce the way of extracting binary features. Then, we deeply analysis and evaluate the existing works on different scenarios such as scalability. Finally, we applied them to real set of malware binaries. It is clear that there exist many features that could potentially be useful to determine malware authorship. However, the harder part is to verify their applicability through experimental studies. We must pay special care to the following issues when we deal with binary authorship attribution:

- Dataset Size: A small amount of training set code might not be sufficient to make a good identification and a precise comparison unless very unusual indicators are present.
- Multiple Authors: The identification of authors in the case of multiple authors will be more challenging, since we have to first identify code fragments that are written by the same author.

Acknowledgments. The authors thank the anonymous reviewers for their valuable comments. Any opinions, findings, and conclusions or recommendations expressed in this material are those of the authors and do not necessarily reflect the views of the sponsoring organizations.

References

1. Refactoring tool. https://www.devexpress.com/Products/CodeRush/
2. The Google Code Jam (2008–2015). http://code.google.com/codejam/
3. GitHub-Build software better (2011). https://github.com/trending/cpp
4. IDA pro Fast Library Identification and Recognition Technology (2011). https://www.hex-rays.com/products/ida/tech/
5. The materials supplement for the paper: Who Wrote This Code? Identifying the Authors of Program Binaries (2011). http://pages.cs.wisc.edu/~nater/esorics-supp/
6. Hex-Ray decompiler (2015). https://www.hex-rays.com/products/decompiler/
7. Microsoft Malware Classification Challenge (BIG 2015) (2015). https://www.kaggle.com/c/malware-classification/data
8. Programmer De-anonymization from Binary Executables (2015). https://github.com/calaylin/bda
9. The Gephi plugin for nneo4j (2015). https://marketplace.gephi.org/plugin/neo4j-graph-database-support/
10. The Scalable Native Graph Database (2015). http://neo4j.com/
11. C++ refactoring tools for visual studio (2016). http://www.wholetomato.com/
12. Aiken, A., et al.: Moss: a system for detecting software plagiarism. University of California–Berkeley (2005). www.cs.berkeley.edu/aiken/moss.html 9
13. Alrabaee, S., Saleem, N., Preda, S., Wang, L., Debbabi, M.: Oba2: an onion approach to binary code authorship attribution. Digit. Invest. **11**, S94–S103 (2014)
14. Alrabaee, S., Shirani, P., Wang, L., Debbabi, M.: Sigma: a semantic integrated graph matching approach for identifying reused functions in binary code. Digit. Invest. **12**, S61–S71 (2015)
15. Alrabaee, S., Wang, L., Debbabi, M.: Bingold: towards robust binary analysis by extracting the semantics of binary code as semantic flow graphs (sfgs). Digit. Invest. **18**, S11–S22 (2016)
16. Burrows, S., Tahaghoghi, S.M.: Source code authorship attribution using n-grams. Citeseer (2007)
17. Burrows, S., Uitdenbogerd, A.L., Turpin, A.: Application of information retrieval techniques for source code authorship attribution. In: Zhou, X., Yokota, H., Deng, K., Liu, Q. (eds.) DASFAA 2009. LNCS, vol. 5463, pp. 699–713. Springer, Heidelberg (2009). doi:10.1007/978-3-642-00887-0_61
18. Caliskan-Islam, A., Harang, R., Liu, A., Narayanan, A., Voss, C., Yamaguchi, F., Greenstadt, R.: De-anonymizing programmers via code stylometry. In: 24th USENIX Security Symposium (USENIX Security 2015) , pp. 255–270 (2015)
19. Caliskan-Islam, A., Yamaguchi, F., Dauber, E., Harang, R., Rieck, K., Greenstadt, R., Narayanan, A.: When coding style survives compilation: de-anonymizing programmers from executable binaries. arXiv preprint arXiv:1512.08546 (2015)
20. Can, F., Patton, J.M.: Change of writing style with time. Comput. Humanit. **38**(1), 61–82 (2004)

21. Canali, D., Lanzi, A., Balzarotti, D., Kruegel, C., Christodorescu, M., Kirda, E.: A quantitative study of accuracy in system call-based malware detection. In: Proceedings of the 2012 International Symposium on Software Testing and Analysis, pp. 122–132. ACM (2012)

22. Chen, R., Hong, L., Lü, C., Deng, W.: Author identification of software source code with program dependence graphs. In: 2010 IEEE 34th Annual Computer Software and Applications Conference Workshops (COMPSACW), pp. 281–286. IEEE (2010)

23. Edwards, N., Chen, L.: An historical examination of open source releases and their vulnerabilities. In: Proceedings of the 2012 ACM Conference on Computer and Communications Security, pp. 183–194. ACM (2012)

24. Ferrante, J., Ottenstein, K.J., Warren, J.D.: The program dependence graph and its use in optimization. ACM Trans. Program. Lang. Syst. (TOPLAS) 9(3), 319–349 (1987)

25. Fowler, M.: Refactoring: Improving the Design of Existing Code. Pearson Education India, New Delhi (2009)

26. Frantzeskou, G., Stamatatos, E., Gritzalis, S., Katsikas, S.: Source code author identification based on n-gram author profiles. In: Maglogiannis, I., Karpouzis, K., Bramer, M. (eds.) AIAI 2006. IIFIP, vol. 204, pp. 508–515. Springer, Heidelberg (2006). doi:10.1007/0-387-34224-9_59

27. Holmes, D.I.: Authorship attribution. Comput. Humanit. 28(2), 87–106 (1994)

28. Jang, J., Brumley, D., Venkataraman, S.: Bitshred: feature hashing malware for scalable triage and semantic analysis. In: Proceedings of the 18th ACM Conference on Computer and Communications Security, pp. 309–320. ACM (2011)

29. Junod, P., Rinaldini, J., Wehrli, J., Michielin, J.: Obfuscator-llvm: software protection for the masses. In: Proceedings of the 1st International Workshop on Software Protection, pp. 3–9. IEEE Press (2015)

30. Kephart, J.O., et al.: A biologically inspired immune system for computers. In: Artificial Life IV: Proceedings of the Fourth International Workshop on the Synthesis and Simulation of Living Systems, pp. 130–139 (1994)

31. Khoo, W.M., Mycroft, A., Anderson, R.: Rendezvous: a search engine for binary code. In: Proceedings of the 10th Working Conference on Mining Software Repositories, pp. 329–338. IEEE Press (2013)

32. Knuth, D.E.: Backus normal form vs. backus naur form. Commun. ACM 7(12), 735–736 (1964)

33. Kothari, J., Shevertalov, M., Stehle, E., Mancoridis, S.: A probabilistic approach to source code authorship identification. In: Fourth International Conference on Information Technology, ITNG 2007, pp. 243–248. IEEE (2007)

34. Krsul, I., Spafford, E.H.: Authorship analysis: identifying the author of a program. Comput. Secur. 16(3), 233–257 (1997)

35. Kruegel, C., Kirda, E., Mutz, D., Robertson, W., Vigna, G.: Polymorphic worm detection using structural information of executables. In: Valdes, A., Zamboni, D. (eds.) RAID 2005. LNCS, vol. 3858, pp. 207–226. Springer, Heidelberg (2006). doi:10.1007/11663812_11

36. Pržulj, N., Corneil, D.G., Jurisica, I.: Modeling interactome: scale-free or geometric? Bioinformatics 20(18), 3508–3515 (2004)

37. Rahimian, A., Shirani, P., Alrbaee, S., Wang, L., Debbabi, M.: Bincomp: a stratified approach to compiler provenance attribution. Digit. Invest. 14, S146–S155 (2015)

38. Rosenblum, N., Zhu, X., Miller, B.P.: Who wrote this code? Identifying the authors of program binaries. In: Atluri, V., Diaz, C. (eds.) ESORICS 2011. LNCS, vol. 6879, pp. 172–189. Springer, Heidelberg (2011). doi:10.1007/978-3-642-23822-2_10

39. Santos, I., Penya, Y.K., Devesa, J., Bringas, P.G.: N-grams-based file signatures for malware detection. In: Proceedings of the ICEIS, vol. 2(9), pp. 317–320 (2009)
40. Shevertalov, M., Kothari, J., Stehle, E., Mancoridis, S.: On the use of discretized source code metrics for author identification. In: 2009 1st International Symposium on Search Based Software Engineering, pp. 69–78. IEEE (2009)
41. Spafford, E.H., Weeber, S.A.: Software forensics: can we track code to its authors? Comput. Secur. **12**(6), 585–595 (1993)
42. Weiser, M.: Program slicing. In: Proceedings of the 5th International Conference on Software Engineering, pp. 439–449. IEEE Press (1981)
43. Yang, K.-X., Hu, L., Zhang, N., Huo, Y.-M., Zhao, K.: Improving the defence against web server fingerprinting by eliminating compliance variation. In: 2010 Fifth International Conference on Frontier of Computer Science and Technology (FCST), pp. 227–232. IEEE (2010)

Semantically Non-preserving Transformations for Antivirus Evaluation

Erkan Ersan[1], Lior Malka[2], and Bruce M. Kapron[1(✉)]

[1] Department of Computer Science, University of Victoria, Victoria, Canada
erkanersan@gmail.com, bmkapron@uvic.ca
[2] Faculty of Graduate Studies, University of Victoria, Victoria, Canada
lior34@gmail.com

Abstract. We relax the notion of malware obfuscation to include *semantically non-preserving transformations*. Unlike traditional obfuscation techniques, these transformation may not preserve original code behaviour. Using web-based malware we focus on transformations which modify abstract syntax trees. While such transformations yield syntactically valid programs, they may yield dysfunctional samples, so that it is not clear that this is a practical approach to producing detection-evading malware. However, by implementing an automated system that efficiently filters dysfunctional samples on a virtual cloud architecture, we show that such transformations are in fact practical. Using two simple transformations, we evaluated four antivirus products and were able to create many samples that evade detection, demonstrating that semantic-preserving obfuscation is not the only effective way to mutate malware.

1 Introduction

Recent data breaches at Target, Home Depot, JPMorgan Chase, Apple iCloud, and Sony (to name a few) highlight the constant pressure that cyber-attackers put on users and corporations alike [8]. Many attacks use malware, that is software with some form of malicious functionality [4], to steal financial information, intellectual property, and private data such as usernames and passwords. An *antivirus* is a tool for malware detection. Since many organizations rely on antiviruses for protection, it is important to evaluate antivirus effectiveness.

Obfuscation is a well known technique used by malware authors to create new malware *mutations* that evade detection. Obfuscation modifies code, while retaining its behaviour [6]. For example, in the context of HTML and Javascript, *renaming* might transform the code `payload=1; print(payload)` into `x=1; print(x)`, while *partitioning* might transform the code `str =‘‘abc’’` into `str =‘‘a’’+‘‘bc’’`. See [15] for more examples.

Christodorescu and Jha [5] proposed a methodology to evaluate antivirus products against obfuscated versions of known malware. They applied this idea

Research supported by Intel as part of the Collaborative Project "Automated Antivirus Evaluation via Malware Mutations".

© Springer International Publishing AG 2017
F. Cuppens et al. (Eds.): FPS 2016, LNCS 10128, pp. 273–281, 2017.
DOI: 10.1007/978-3-319-51966-1_18

to Visual Basic malware in Microsoft Office [5]. The same methodology was used in the context of Java malware in Android applications [13,16] and Javascript malware in HTML files [15]. Industry test labs follow the same approach [3].

Our research was motivated by considering the extension of [5] to the setting of browser-delivered malware ("drive-by downloads",) using HTML- and Javascript-based malware for Internet Explorer produced by Metasploit [9]. Manual experimentation indicated that malware obfuscated using traditional techniques (along the lines of e.g. [15]) were detected, but techniques which would not obviously produce semantically equivalent code (e.g. altering HTML elements, permuting lines of JavaScript) produced malware which still delivered its payload, but was no longer detectable. This experiment, and the analysis in Sect. 5, indicates that anti-malware tools should not be designed under the assumption that all mutations must result from obfuscation. For example, [10] proposed detection of malware mutations using a method that assumes mutant malware preserves semantics, an assumption challenged by our results.

Semantically non-preserving transformations have several disadvantages compared to obfuscation. With obfuscation, millions of mutations can be generated efficiently, they are all guaranteed to work, and if one class of transformations (e.g. variable renaming) bypasses detection, then most likely other mutations in this class also bypass detection. We show that, despite their disadvantages, semantically non-preserving transformations can be efficient and practical. Our main contribution is a cloud based system that automatically and efficiently generates malware mutations. The system is generic. It will work with any antivirus, any malware, and any transformation, including obfuscation. It even supports composition of transformations. Our system also scales linearly; doubling the size of the cloud reduces the computation time by half. We evaluated four antiviruses using two simple transformations, and yet were able to create many mutations that evade detection. Our system is different from script-based approaches used in prior work due to the specific challenges of our transformations. These challenges, and our solutions are discussed in detail in Sects. 3 and 4.

Our works focuses on obfuscation of what we might call *transporter code*, that is, the HTML/Javascript code which triggers an exploit allowing the delivery of a payload written in x86 code. While obfuscation of the payload is also a well-known technique for evading detection, our abstract-syntax based approach is not directly applicable to such obfuscations.

Related work. Evaluation of antivirus effectiveness via malware mutations have been considered in [5,11,13,14,16]. A formal framework for this method has been given as well (e.g., [7]). The reason for this evaluation method is that hackers evade detection by tweaking their malware. Unlike [5,13,16], which use obfuscation, we use transformations that do not preserve the semantics of the malware. We show that our transformations yield functional and undetectable variants. Also, unlike [5,13,16], where each component is automated, but not the system as a whole, our software is fully automated and non supervised. A recent industry report that evaluated eleven antiviruses against HTML malware [3] showed that all antiviruses detected all HTML obfuscation. Our results show that evaluations which consider only transformations that preserve semantics are incomplete. In [12] a semantics-based approach to malware detection is proposed, including a definition of *non-conservative obfuscation* which is a generalization of our notion of semantically non-preserving transformation. We have not investigated the significance of our results in this broader framework.

2 Semantically Non-preserving Transformations

In formulating a notion of transformations which preserve semantics, we are faced with several choices. In the most general setting, we would need to formally model all the effects of executing a piece of code. This could involve modifications to state and side-effects involving not only memory, but also files, communication channels, etc. We will take a more practical perspective, tailored specifically to the setting of malware deployment and detection, and depends only on the ability of a piece of code to deliver a specified *payload*. See [12] for a more general approach to semantics-based notions of obfuscation.

We consider transformations $T : Code \times Aux_T \rightarrow Code$. In particular we have $T(m, r) = m'$ where m is the code to be modified and r is some auxiliary information and m' is the mutated code. The auxiliary information r depends on the transformation T. For example, in the case of variable renaming, Aux_T will consist a collection of variables and all strings to which the variables in question may be mapped. We then say that T is *semantically preserving* with respect to malware m if $T(m, r) = m'$ executes the same payload as m, for any $r \in Aux_T$. For example, obfuscation is always semantically preserving, whereas, in our above mentioned experiment, the transformation T that replaces `table` with various element names is semantically non-preserving, because there are r such that $T(m, r) = m'$ is not malware. On the other hand, if $T(m, r) = m'$ is malicious, it is not necessary that m' exploits a different vulnerability compared to m, or that m' executes other things beyond the payload of m. It only means that m' is allowed to be computationally different from m, as long as it executes the payload, and that T is allowed to output dysfunctional samples (that is, samples that do not execute the payload).

Because we admit transformations that output dysfunctional samples, we must address the issue of how generated samples may be used to test AV effectiveness. We describe our approach in Sect. 4 below, but in short we filter out dysfunctional samples by executing each sample and detecting whether it is able to deliver a payload. In practise this *post hoc* approach will produce samples that are not obtained using traditional obfuscation techniques.

3 The Generator

In this section we describe the software components that take an HTML file, possibly containing Javascript, and generate variants of this file. The variants may or may not be malware. We collectively refer to these components as the *Generator*.

As discussed previously, we focus on a simple class of transformations, namely those which apply simple modifications to the abstract syntax tree (AST) of an HTML sample document. We implemented two transformations, *permute* and *subset*, both operating only on nodes that have children. its statements as children. By *permute* we mean reordering of the children, and by *subset* we mean removing some of the children. These transformations usually do not preserve the semantics of the original HTML file.

While our goal was to apply these transformations in as general and automatic a way as possible, it is clear that blindly applying these transformations to the entire AST results in a combinatorial explosion making the approach infeasible. In particular, for an AST with n nodes, subset will generate $O(2^n)$ mutations, while permute will generate $O(n!)$. We address this issue by specializing transformations to a distinguished subset of nodes, a technique we refer to as *per-node* transformation. Currently, we have not addressed the question of general strategies for assigning transformations to nodes. For our experiments we are doing this in an *ad hoc* fashion.

4   The Infrastructure

In this section we describe the software components that take original HTML files, transform them into new HTML variants, test whether the variants are *functional* (that is, they execute the payload), and if so, whether they are detectable as malware by various antivirus products. We collectively refer to these components as the *Infrastructure*.

This Infrastructure is realized via a *producer-consumer* model wherein a *producer* inserts jobs into a queue, blocking if the queue is full, and a *consumer* removes jobs from the queue and executes them, blocking if the queue is empty. Multiple producers and consumers can run concurrently, using database tables for queues and transactions for synchronization. While the use of virtualization in testing malware detection is not new, our automated concurrent infrastructure is unique. In practice, this means that we were able to perform fully automated tests involving several antivirus products and millions of malware variants.

In more detail, generator threads produce HTML variants for the functionality workers, who test whether HTML variants execute a payload. If a variant is functional, then the functional worker produces a job for the antivirus workers, who then test whether the variant is detectable or not.

In order to maintain automation, we need a simple test to determine functionality. We chose the creation by the malware of a text file on the desktop. A possible objection to this approach is that in a real-world setting such an action would be benign in terms of impact on the target system, and that more malicious effects could be detected by other components of a detection or intrusion protection system. With respect to the first objection, we note that the degree of control required to allow the malware to perform the file creation effect would also allow it to perform more obviously malicious actions. This brings us to the second objection. Here we note that it is essential for all components of such a system to provide the highest degree of security possible. There is no guarantee that if any one component fails some other component will be able to compensate. Indeed, malware designers are able to combine evasion techniques to take advantage of weaknesses in any one detection component.

When a browser loads an HTML file, it stores it as a file in a temporary directory, and this triggers the detection mechanism of some antiviruses. However, due to the asynchronous nature of operating systems, quite often the antivirus detects the file as malware only after the browser has processed the HTML file and the malware has successfully executed. In such cases we consider the malware as being undetectable.

5   Experiments

We selected four popular antivirus products from the websites of the following companies: AVG, Kaspersky, McAfee, and Symantec. We have chosen not to disclose which product is susceptible to each method, and thus have randomly named them AV1, AV2, AV3, AV4. In all cases we downloaded the consumer grade version, and evaluated it automatically using our infrastructure.

We reviewed more than thirty Internet Explorer malware samples from Metasploit [9]. Unfortunately, not all were suitable for testing due to stability or compatibility reasons. Hence, only seven were chosen. We refer to these files, labelled $S1$ through $S7$, as the *originals*. All originals have a benign payload that creates a dummy text file on the desktop. Samples $S6$ and $S7$ did not parse with the parser of [1,2], while sample $S5$ had a payload that could not be configured. Thus, we could only experiment with the first four samples. Sample $S1$ was pure HTML, and the rest contained Javascript code. All samples were evaluated on Windows7 64-bit SP 1 and Internet Explorer 8.

Test Definitions.   We define an HTML file to be *functional* if and only if the dummy is created when the HTML file is loaded by the browser. We note that, since malware can destabilize the operating system, we have to timeout our tests, which may incorrectly label a functional variant as non functional. However, this is not a concern. The important thing is that the opposite cannot happen.

Although we use the notion of *detection*, we follow industry practise [3] and measure *prevention*. i.e., whether the payload is prevented from executing. Prevention is stronger than detection because, once malware gets control, it can do anything, including disabling the antivirus, and detection in particular.

Our antivirus evaluation consisted of two tests. In the *static* test (denoted S) we invoked the antivirus from the command line, with the HTML file as input. In the *dynamic* test (denoted D) the browser loaded the HTML file from an external HTTP server. In the static test, some antiviruses remove the file before we even have a chance to invoke the antivirus from the command line. In such a case we treat the HTML file as being detected. Conversely, in the dynamic test, if the dummy text file is created, then the payload has executed. Thus, even if the antivirus produces an alert, we consider the file as being undetected.

Analysis. The evaluation of the originals is given in Table 1. It shows four antiviruses evaluated against seven malware files, in both static and dynamic tests. We use 1 for *detected* and 0 for *undetected*. If the payload finished execution, but with high probability was later detected, then we denote it by 0*a*. Interestingly, AV3 can statically detect originals S3 through S6, and exactly those are detected in the dynamic test, but only after the payload executes. This provides a strong evidence that AV3 is signature based only, not using any runtime information. Notice that AV2 dynamically detected all malware. However, this is expected because all the samples are a few years old, on average.

Table 1. Static (S) and Dynamic (D) tests for the original samples

Sample	AV1		AV2		AV3		AV4	
	S	D	S	D	S	D	S	D
S1	0	1	1	1	0	0	0	1
S2	0	0	1	1	0	0	0	1
S3	1	1	0	1	1	0a	0	0a
S4	1	1	1	1	1	0a	0	1

We evaluated the antiviruses by submitting jobs to our system. Each job described the original, the transformation, and the antiviruses to test. These jobs, given in Table 2, show that we found thousands of new malware variants.

Table 2. Jobs showing new HTML variants generated from originals

Sample	Transformation	Generated	Functional
S1	Permute all	24	24
S1	Subset all	42	20
S2	Permute all	101674	1293
S2	Subset all	48	0
S2	Subset node 27	32768	2
S2	Subset node 20	4096	8
S3	Permute node 30	720	66
S3	Subset node 30	64	2
S3	Subset node 20	4096	8
S3	Subset node 32	524288	1
S3'	Permute node 30	108053	30
S4	Permute all	193070	7493
S4	Subset all	81494	0
S4	Subset node 10	3526	0
S4	Subset node 5	60	0

Not all jobs ran to completion, which is why some of them generated fewer variants than others under the same transformation. We suspended generator threads when we saw that others were creating functional variants. This reduced the workload on the functional workers. The transformation *Permute all* means that each node has a permute transformation, and similarly for *Subset all*. Other transformations are per node, usually assigned to Javascript nodes of the abstract syntax tree. Since they are assigned to different parts of the tree, there are no overlapping variants. The sample S3' is essentially the same as S3, but has a different AST, hence node 30 does not correspond to node 30 from S3.

Table 3. Number of Statically (S) and Dynamically (D) undetectable malware variants

Sample	Transformation	Functional	AV1		AV2		AV3		AV4	
			S	D	S	D	S	D	S	D
S1	Permute all	24	24	24	0	0	24	24	24	0
S1	Subset all	20	20	20	0	0	20	20	20	12
S2	Permute all	1293	1293	1293	1293	0	1293	1293	1293	0
S2	Subset all	0	0	0	0	0	0	0	0	0
S2	Subset node 27	2	2	2	2	0	2	2	2	0
S2	Subset node 20	8	8	8	8	0	8	8	8	0
S3	Permute node 30	66	65	65	66	0	66	66	66	0
S3	Subset node 30	2	1	1	2	0	2	2	2	0
S3	Subset node 20	8	0	0	8	0	8	8	8	0
S3	Subset node 32	1	0	0	1	0	1	1	1	0
S3'	Permute node 30	30	0	0	30	0	30	30	30	2
S4	Permute all	7493	0	0	0	0	0	5818	7493	0
S4	Subset all	0	0	0	0	0	0	0	0	0
S4	Subset node 10	0	0	0	0	0	0	0	0	0
S4	Subset node 5	0	0	0	0	0	0	0	0	0

The detection effectiveness of the antiviruses is given in Table 3. The table shows that most of the functional variants that we have created are undetectable by at least one antivirus. It proves that antiviruses cannot be evaluated based on mutations only. It also indicates that any detection mechanism that assumes that mutations must preserve the semantics of the original [10], may fail to work.

Table 3 provides the raw results, unabridged. The last three rows are all zero because these jobs did not produce functional variants, and thus have been suspended. No sample was dynamically undetectable by AV2. However, manual experiments with this antivirus showed that a *map* transformation yields statically and dynamically undetectable malware variants. The map is not an obfuscation as it replaces HTML elements with non equivalent ones. Other variants can be obtained by composing two obfuscation methods (string partitioning and BASE64 encoding). We interpret these experiments as evidence that our software is basic, and needs more transformations.

6   Conclusions

We have demonstrated that semantics-preserving obfuscation is not the only way to produce malware mutations. By relaxing the notion of obfuscation to that of semantically non-preserving transformations, we were able to obtain transformations that produce functional mutations. We developed a virtualized testing environment which allowed us, using two simple transformations, to generate thousands of samples which were undetectable by commercial AV products. Our results demonstrate the viability of obfuscation techniques that do not preserve code semantics. This does not mean that such mutations are more malicious, or should be considered as a replacement for traditional code obfuscation. Rather, they should be viewed as another threat, alone or in combination with other techniques, that anti-malware technology must be able to prevent.

References

1. jsoup: Java HTML parser. http://jsoup.org/apidocs/
2. Rhino. http://developer.mozilla.org/en-US/docs/Mozilla/Projects/Rhino
3. Abrams, R., Ghimiri, D., Smith, J.: Corporate AV/EPP comparative analysis - exploit evasion defenses. Technical report, NSS Labs (2013)
4. CERT UK. An introduction to malware (2014). www.cert.gov.uk/resources/best-practices/an-introduction-to-malware/
5. Christodorescu, M., Jha, S.: Testing malware detectors. In: Avrunin, G.S., Rothermel, G. (eds.) ISSTA 2004, ACM (2004)
6. Collberg, C., Thomborson, C., Low, D.: A taxonomy of obfuscating transformations. Technical report 148, University of Auckland, New Zealand, July 1997
7. Filiol, E., Jacob, G., Liard, M.: Evaluation methodology and theoretical model for antiviral behavioural detection strategies. J. Comput. Virol. 3(1), 23–37 (2007)
8. Granville, K.: 9 Recent Cyberattacks Against Big Business. New York Times, 5 February 2015
9. Kandias, M., Gritzalis, D.: Metasploit the penetration tester's guide. Comput. Secur. 32, 268–269 (2013)
10. Kwon, J., Lee, H.: Bingraph: discovering mutant malware using hierarchical semantic signatures. In: MALWARE 2012, pp. 104–111. IEEE Computer Society (2012)
11. Maggi, F., Valdi, A., Zanero, S.: Andrototal: a flexible, scalable toolbox and service for testing mobile malware detectors. In: Enck, W., Felt, A.P., Asokan, N. (eds.) SPSM@CCS 2013, pp. 49–54. ACM (2013)
12. Preda, M.D., Christodorescu, M., Jha, S., Debray, S.K.: A semantics-based approach to malware detection. ACM Trans. Program. Lang. Syst. 30(5), 25 (2008)
13. Rastogi, V., Chen, Y., Jiang, X.: Droidchameleon: evaluating android anti-malware against transformation attacks. In: Chen, K., Xie, Q., Qiu, W., Li, N., Tzeng, W.-G. (eds.) ASIACCS 2013, pp. 329–334. ACM (2013)
14. Rastogi, V., Chen, Y., Jiang, X.: Catch me if you can: evaluating android anti-malware against transformation attacks. IEEE Trans. Inf. Forensics Secur. 9(1), 99–108 (2014)

15. Xu, W., Zhang, F., Zhu, S.: In: MALWARE 2012, pp. 9–16. IEEE Computer Society (2012)
16. Zheng, M., Lee, P.P.C., Lui, J.C.S.: ADAM: an automatic and extensible platform to stress test android anti-virus systems. In: Flegel, U., Markatos, E., Robertson, W. (eds.) DIMVA 2012. LNCS, vol. 7591, pp. 82–101. Springer, Heidelberg (2013). doi:10.1007/978-3-642-37300-8_5

Web, Cloud, and Delegation

A Self-correcting Information Flow Control Model for the Web-Browser

Deepak Subramanian$^{(\boxtimes)}$, Guillaume Hiet, and Christophe Bidan

CentraleSupélec, Châtenay-Malabry, France
{deepak.subramanian,guillaume.hiet,christophe.bidan}@supelec.fr

Abstract. Web-browser security with emphasis on JavaScript security, is one of the important problems of the modern world. The potency of information flow control (IFC) in the context of JavaScript is quite appealing. In this paper, we adopt an earlier technique, Address Split Design (ASD), proposed by Deepak et al. [12]. We propose an alternate data-structure to the dictionaries used in ASD to keep track of secret variables. We also propose a novel approach to help track and learn from information flows. This learnt data can subsequently be used to create a more adaptive and effective IFC model. As the information about a function augments, potential leaks are also thwarted. Using such an approach, we show that more rigid security guarantees can be achieved eventually with increase in learnt data.

1 Introduction

The state of the internet has been evolving with the constant sharing of content and functionalities between websites. Many modern technologies proposed in HTML5 have served to increase capabilities of the browser while also raising new possibilities for information leakages. For example, LocalStorage provides an efficient way for persistence in the web-browser. This could cause browser-side persistent cross-site scripting if not sanitized properly. Another example is the use of WebSockets, which provides a real-time communication channel to the server. Once the channel is open, further messages in the channel do not require re-authentication or cookies since the connection is already established. There is hence a clear need to monitor the browser at a variable level as JavaScript slowly dominates the application space.

Web-browser vulnerabilities have constantly been cited among the top prevalent threats as seen clearly in lists such as the OWASP Top Ten[1]. Despite the numerous safeguards proposed over the years, including some important considerations such as the "same-origin policy" and "content security policy", these threats continue exist. Moreover it is important to have a method to provide security while preserving the user experience. It is our sincere belief that Information Flow Control (IFC) could be an effective solution to this problem. Further, the use of IFC is necessary for JavaScript since modern web-sites execute scripts

---

[1] https://www.owasp.org/index.php/Category:OWASP_Top_Ten_Project.

© Springer International Publishing AG 2017
F. Cuppens et al. (Eds.): FPS 2016, LNCS 10128, pp. 285–301, 2017.
DOI: 10.1007/978-3-319-51966-1_19

from various sources with no restrictions. The only security model available on a browser is an all-or-nothing Content-Security-Policy which can allow or deny a script based on the url. Our approach allows the page itself to function without changes while protecting secret variables from unauthorized scripts.

This paper is a logical extension an approach called Address Split Design (ASD) proposed by Deepak et al. [12]. In ASD, the authors show how the use of IFC can prevent unauthorized code from accessing sensitive information thereby preventing leakage of sensitive information. ASD maintains a dummy/public value for every secret variable and uses this public value in case of unauthorized access. In this paper, we first propose a change to how ASD maintains runtime monitoring. This proposal could reduce the number of operations that need to be performed when a secret variable is updated. We also describe a learning-based approach to information flow control on a web-browser. After the initial execution of a program using ASD, information regarding the propagation of the secret is remembered. This information is used in a self correcting mechanism for the analysis and enforcement of security on JavaScript. The bedrock of our proposed mechanism lies in correcting any possible leak through learning rather than using rigid security guarantees. Hence, in this paper, we first start with ASD as the base model and remember all the flow propagations which are used subsequently thereby accounting for all possible information flows.

The rest of the paper is organized as follows. The Sect. 2 provides a summary of the various related work. This is followed by a description of our model, address split design with dependency graphs (ASD-DG), along with relevant formalisms, in Sect. 3. The details on how reinforcement learning is applied to ASD-DG and the security guarantees that can be obtained because of learning are described in Sect. 4. There is a sum up of our approach in Sect. 5.

2   Related Work

There have been several key research since the models such as Bell and La Padula [4], and Biba [5] that have helped in shaping the field of Information Flow Control (IFC). These models established various levels of privileges and associated information to these levels. A common mechanism to achieve this is to attach security labels to information containers such as files or variables. The most simple example consists of two security labels namely, "high/sensitive" and "low/public". Information cannot flow from "High" level containers to "Low" level containers while the vice-versa is permissible. In a lattice-based design, the security lattice can contain multiple parallel or intertwined levels allowing for more complex information flow control design.

The first step in an IFC approach is to specify a policy. It consists first in defining different security labels in a lattice-based structure and then to attach these labels to the containers according to their sensitivity. Once a policy has been specified, the IFC model ensures that the execution conforms to the policy. Such an approach helps to classify information flows into legal and illegal flows. IFC models have varying mechanisms to deal with illegal information flows. These could be raising alerts, stopping execution, stopping the compilation process, modifying execution or some other customized action.

Language based IFC has been explored in great detail by label based approaches as illustrated by Sabelfeld and Myers [11]. In these approaches, the secret variables are tagged with security labels and these labels are propagated along with the information flows. In the context of IFC in JavaScript, Bielova et al. [6] provide a substantive survey with comparative studies on techniques, types of analysis (i.e. static vs. dynamic approaches) and their formal guarantees. This work has been instrumental in providing a complete picture of this research area thereby becoming a valuable stepping stone to the design of our approach.

In the field of IFC, the most important property to be satisfied by any analysis is non-interference. There are two types of non-interference based on the conditions satisfied, namely Termination-insensitive non-interference (TINI) and, Timing and Termination-sensitive non-interference (TTSNI).

TINI [1,6,7,11] is a security guarantee where, for two terminating executions of a program with the same public input, the observable public output remains unchanged regardless of the value of the secret.

TTSNI [7,10] is a security guarantee where, for two executions of a program with the same public input, the public output, the number of execution steps and time taken to generate the public output remain unchanged regardless of the value of the secret.

There are several IFC models that have been designed for the web-browser taking into account the nature of JavaScript. Relative work in this domain has been heavily biased towards dynamic approaches. This is justifiable by the highly dynamic nature of JavaScript which increases the complexity for static approaches thereby making dynamic approaches more effective.

Label-based approaches have always been in the forefront of dynamic approaches. In the context of JavaScript, Austin and Flanagan proposed the no-sensitive-upgrade [2]. Hedin and Sabelfeld [9] proposed an IFC approach for JavaScript based on a classical label-based approach previously described by Sabelfeld and Myers [11]. Hedin and Sabelfeld show the need for dynamic approaches by describing problem of the information-flow being flow sensitive in JavaScript. This increases the need to keep track of changing labels throughout the execution which becomes tedious with pure static approaches. The difference between the two approaches is that Hedin and Sabelfeld allow some upgrade instructions before the behest of the implicit information-flow. This means that, in case an implicit flow results owing to the value of a secret variable, the public output of a public value cannot be performed under any scenario in case of the no-sensitive-upgrade. However, in case of Hedin and Sabelfeld, such a public output can be allowed if and only if there was an explicit upgrade instruction before the output statement is performed.

Both these label based approaches stop further execution of a program when they encounter a possible information leak. These approaches are useful to check if a program is adherent to TINI by default without any modifications. However, they fail to continue execution of the program if there is a possibility of a leak. There exist a few dynamic preventive enforcement mechanisms in JavaScript which are able to continue execution of the program and still prevent information leakage. These mechanisms maintain more than one copy of the variable and switch contexts of the variable based on the scenario. In case there is an unauthorized public output of a secret variable, these mechanisms use a dummy/public value instead. Secure Multi-Execution (SME), faceted approach and Address Split Design (ASD) are the models known to use this approach.

The model of SME was proposed by Devriese and Piessens [7]. In SME, the information flow across labels is segregated at the process level by providing a separate process for each level of sensitivity. Let us consider a system with two levels namely a high and a low. Such a scenario would imply that there is a dedicated process for high level computations and a dedicated process for low computations. This ensures that the memory is also safely handled since the processes themselves are isolated. The low level process is the only one that can influence public output and it can only receive public input. FlowFox is a concrete implementation of SME on the Firefox web browser by De Groef et al. [8]. However, the use of SME automatically increases the time- and space-complexity for the system.

The faceted approach that has been proposed by Austin et al. [2,3] is the chief proponent of the multi-path execution approach. The authors attempt to mimic the functionality of SME with the use of a single process. It would intuitively result in a much lower time complexity. The faceted approach attains termination-insensitive non-interference since the use of a single process cannot account for timing-sensitivity. This approach works on containing multiple copies of the variables at each juncture to mimic the values of the variables in different processes in case of SME. A faceted value is represented as ¡p?$a_{private}$:a_{public}¿ where p is the principal. The principal is an access control object which determines which copy of the variable should be used. If an object c were created by using two other objects a and b, each with its own principal, there would be four possible values for this object, as shown in [FACETED APPROACH]. This growth

---

[FACETED APPROACH]

$$\text{var } a = \langle \text{p1?1} : 2 \rangle; \text{ var } b = \langle \text{p2?3} : 4 \rangle; \text{ var } c = a + b;$$
$$=> c = \langle\, \text{p1 ? } \langle\, \text{p2 ? 4 : 5} \,\rangle \, : \, \langle\, \text{p2 ? 5 : 6} \,\rangle \,\rangle;$$

---

in the number of objects is exponential. The positive effect of this phenomenon is that, only the correct copy of the object is used when it is invoked by the public output function. Just like the SME approach, the execution of multiple branches can have unintended consequences in a dynamic approach. The ZaphodFacets[2]

---

[2] https://github.com/taustin/ZaphodFacets.

is an implementation of the faceted approach as a plug-in in Firefox. It use the Narcissus JavaScript engine[3]. Cross-site scripting is handled effectively by this approach by assigning each domain into separate principal. Variables from each domain are accessed only if there is access to that principal hence significantly reducing the effects of XSS.

The ASD was proposed by Deepak et al. [12] and forms the first basis for the approach described in this paper. In this approach each secret variable is split into public and private values. ASD is similar to the faceted approach in terms of having a single process and different values for private variables. However, the key difference is that a variable can have only one private value in ASD while the faceted approach could force it to have multiple private values. Further, ASD does not execute additional branches based on the split values.

ASD seems to provide a more fine-grained IFC with function level control and its performance degradation is much more acceptable than competing approaches [12]. However, this approach does not adhere to TINI; though the secret is never given as a public output. Therefore, it suffers from lower security guarantees than SME while offering being practical. The core of this model starts with a split variable which is represented as $\lceil \text{public}^p \parallel \text{private}^s \rceil$. The split variable consists of a public value and a private value which are stored in different memory locations. The default symbol table connects the variable to its public value while the ASD mechanism overloads the symbol table at appropriate junctures to change the inferred memory location. This information is maintained in a data-structure called a dictionary that is unique to each function defined in the policy.

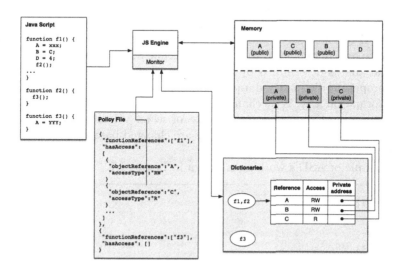

Fig. 1. Address split design [12]

---

[3] http://en.wikipedia.org/wiki/Narcissus_(JavaScript_engine).

ASD's policies allow a differentiation to read and write accesses to secret variables. These policies hence result in more fine-grained IFC which we find to be suitable as a base for our model. The working of ASD is shown in the Fig. 1. There policies and the JavaScript program are the input. The monitor which is added to the JavaScript compiler interprets these policies and creates data-structures called dictionaries. The variables which contain secret values are split to show public and private parts. The private parts of the variable are inferred from the dictionaries. These dictionaries are updated by the monitor according to information flow.

However, the tracking mechanism used in this IFC has been shown to be less efficient in write operations in comparison with read operations by the authors themselves. Further, the IFC mechanism does not consider all possible information flows and relies solely on over-approximation. We believe that with some suitable changes to this model supplemented by learning, ASD could eventually become adherent to TINI while becoming more efficient.

3   Description of Our Approach

As described in the Sect. 1, our work is an extensio of the ASD approach. Therefore, we describe the preliminaries regarding ASD in Subsect. 3.1. This is followed by the description of the dependency graph which tracks the various secrets in our approach in Subsect. 3.2. We finally discuss the evolution of the dependency graph with information flows in Subsect. 3.3.

3.1   Preliminaries on ASD

ASD is an IFC where secret variables are split to store two different values in their private and public addresses separately. The access to the secret value for a given variable is determined by the function that refers to the variable. The authors propose a dictionary data-structure to track the secret variables based on the information flow. A mechanism called the dependency tracker (DT) keeps track of the current statement and the list of secret values that are being used in the current execution. The dictionaries are changed based on the DT at every write into a variable.

An example of ASD's working is shown in Listing 1.1.

```
1 var a = 2;
2 function f1()
3 {
4   a = 3;
5   print(a);
6   var b = a;
7 };
8 f1();
```

Listing 1.1. ASD Example

Let us consider that variable a is secret and function f1 has access to a. In that case, at the beginning of the function call, $a = \lceil 2^p \parallel \text{undefined}^s \rfloor$. This notation signifies that the variable a has been split. Here, a has a public value that was initialized to 2 and a secret value that is undefined. However, when executing function f1, in line 4, the secret value is changed. This is because f1 has access to the variable a. Therefore, $a = \lceil 2^p \parallel 3^s \rfloor$.

In line 6, the variable a is read. Therefore, the dependency tracker is updated and DT = {a}. When variable b is initialized, it is split. The public value remains as undefined while the secret value is assigned as 3. Therefore, $b = \lceil \text{undefined}^p \parallel 3^s \rfloor$.

Further, any function that has access to a, is given access to b. Hence, the function f1's dictionary would be:

In the Table 1, the notation "scope(f1).b" represents the local variable of the function. Each run of the function generates a unique scope identifier which is used to identify which instance of the local variable is being used. Hence, the use of the scope identifier allows handling of local variables in all cases including recursion.

Table 1. Dictionary of function f1

Variable	Rights	Address
a	RW	@(A)
scope(f1).b	RW	@(B)

Any function that is defined in the policy is called a self-sufficient function and has its own dictionary. All other functions are called utility functions and use the dictionary of the self-sufficient function that called them. To implement the above mechanism, the symbol table is overloaded with a dictionary data-structure in ASD. There is hence a unique dictionary for every function defined in the policy.

ASD creates all dictionaries when interpreting the policies and changes every dictionary based on the monitored information flow. This creates an increased overhead when there is a large number of dictionaries. We hence propose another data-structure called the dependency graph to keep track of the information flows supplanting the existing dictionaries. We call this approach Address Split Design with dependency graphs (ASD-DG). When the dependency graph is updated, those changes will be noted by a learning mechanism. These learnt dependencies will be applied to the variables at the end of the function's || execution. In the next subsection we will discus the dependency graph and its working.

3.2   Dependency Graph

The dependency graph is a tree data-structure which contains three types of vertexes, namely, the function nodes, root nodes, and dependent nodes. The function nodes represent the various self-sufficient functions, whereas the root nodes and dependent nodes represent the various variables that contain secret values. Root nodes are created for all variables represented in the policies. Dependent nodes are created when a variable contains a secret value originating from another variable due to information flow.

In this paper, we describe the formalism along with the concepts involved in our approach. The various initial suppositions are given in [DECLARATION]. Here, the various representations used throughout the rest of the paper have been defined. We continue the representation used in ASD as part of the while language. Most rules defined in ASD hold true to ASD-DG as well. We will describe the rules that change in greater detail in parallel with the dependency graph.

The dependency graph is used to maintain data about the various variables that contain secret values due to information flow. It is a tree structure which can be defined as

$$\mathbb{DG}(V,E) \; where, \left\{ \begin{array}{c} \text{V is a set of vertexes} \\ V \ni \{\, \mathbb{DG}_f, \mathbb{DG}_{root}, \mathbb{DG}_d \,\} \\ \\ \text{E is a set of edges} \\ E \ni \{\, \mathbb{DG}_f \to \mathbb{DG}_{root}, \mathbb{DG}_{root} \to \mathbb{DG}_d \,\} \end{array} \right\}$$

[DECLARATION]

$$Let, \text{Variables } (x \in Var)$$

$$\text{Functions } (f \in F \subset Var)$$

$$\text{Statements } (S \in Stm)$$

$$\text{State } (s(f) \to \{public, secret\})$$

$$\text{Privilege } (Priv \in \{read, write, read + write\})$$

$$\text{Policy Specification } (\mathbb{P}(Var, F, Priv) \to Boolean)$$

$$\text{Dictionary } (\mathbb{D} \in Dict)$$

$$\text{Address Space[Var] } (\mathbb{A}[x] : Var \to Address)$$

$$\text{Access Control } \left(\begin{array}{l} AC_{control}(f, x) : (F, Var) \to boolean \; where, \\ \qquad\qquad control \in \{\, (r)ead, (w)rite \,\} \end{array} \right)$$

$$\text{Dependency Tracker dt} \in DT \subset Var$$

$$\text{Dependency Graph } \mathbb{DG}$$

$$\text{Dependency Graph States } \mathbb{DG}State \, \{active, inactive\}$$

$$\text{Dependency Graph Nodes } \left(\begin{array}{l} \mathbb{DG}_{node} \; where, \\ node \in \left\{ \begin{array}{l} root : \text{"Root node"}, \\ f : \text{"Function node"} \\ d : \text{"Dependent node"} \end{array} \right\} \end{array} \right)$$

$$\text{Reinforced Learning } L, \text{ collection of } \{\, (f)unction, (dt), (v)ariable \,\}$$

$$\text{Flow Type } \{FL \in (e)xplicit, (i)mplicit\}$$

The structure of the dependency graph is a simple unidirectional that can only consist of three layers. The edges are strictly only between the function nodes to root nodes or root nodes to dependent nodes. Function nodes can have any number of child root nodes. Similarly, there is no limitation on the number of child dependent nodes for root nodes. Root nodes can have two possible states, active and inactive. When interpreting the graph, the functions can access variables represented by any of the active root nodes with whom they share an edge. The state modifications occur due to information flow. Such modifications are described in greater detail along with the evolution of the graph in Subsect. 3.3. Finally, a function can access a dependent node if and only if it has access to all root nodes which are parents to that dependent node. In the formalism, the $x \rightsquigarrow f$ represents that f can access x. In the Fig. 2 f2 has access to V6. However, it cannot access V5 because f2 cannot access V1.

An example of this data structure, can be seen in the Fig. 2.

When the variables contain secret values because of information flows, they are added to the dependency graph. In our approach, we use the current DT to assign parent nodes. The DT keeps track of the current set of secret values that are influencing the information flow.

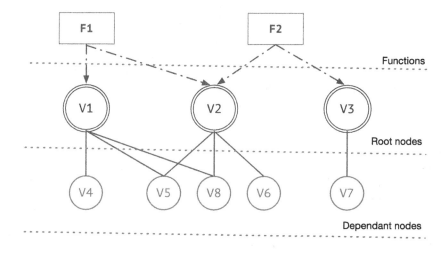

Fig. 2. Dependency graph

The rule [POLICY: FUNCTION READ ACCESS] describes the interpretation of the policy into the dependency graph. The read access constructs the link between the function nodes and the root nodes in the dependency graph. The root nodes are the initial secrets. The other secrets are added to the dependency graph because of information flows from the root nodes and hence become dependent nodes. The main purpose of the dependency graph is to overload the symbol table on a just in time basis as needed by the compiler. When a function

[POLICY: FUNCTION READ ACCESS]

$$\frac{\mathbb{P}(f, x, AC_r)}{\mathbb{DG}_f \leftarrow f; \mathbb{DG}_{root} \leftarrow x; x \rightsquigarrow f}$$

attempts to read a variable, the monitor checks the dependency graph to validate the function's permissions to perform the operation. The rules for accessing the variable are given in [RUNTIME: FUNCTION READ ACCESS]. In this equation, for a given policy, the function and variable are added to the dependency graph and then f becomes a parent of x.

3.3   Dependency Graph Evolution

In this section, we discuss the dependency graph's evolution with the various variables that are added to it over time. Variables evolve when a function performs a write operation. There have been no changes in the write operation from the original ASD in this paper. Since write permissions do not change because of information flow and are only present to protect the variable, they are maintained as a simple list. When a function writes a secret value into a public variable, this variable is split and added as a dependent node to the dependency graph. If this split variable becomes dependent on another root, it is simply moved to become a child of that root node. However, if a root node becomes dependent on another root, a dependent node pointing to that variable is created and original root node becomes inactive. An inactive root node exists only for its children. This implies that the original root variable's value has changed but there are other existing variables which contain some information about the value due to information flow.

Let us consider a statement, V2 = V4 + 4;. It can be observed in the Fig. 3 that the variable V2, which is a root variable has been changed. The figure shows that by marking the root node V2 as a grayed out node. This implies that the

[RUNTIME: FUNCTION READ ACCESS]

$$\frac{f \in \mathbb{DG}_f; x \in \mathbb{DG} \ s.t. \ x \rightsquigarrow f, \mathbb{DG}\text{State}(x) = \text{active}}{AC_r(f, x) = \text{true}; s(f) = secret}$$

$$\frac{f \in \mathbb{DG}_f; x \in \mathbb{DG} \ s.t. \ x \rightsquigarrow f, \mathbb{DG}\text{State}(x) \neq \text{active}}{AC_r(f, x) = \text{false};}$$

$$\frac{f \in \mathbb{DG}_f; x \in \mathbb{DG} , \mathbb{DG}\text{State}(x) = \text{active}, x \not\rightsquigarrow f}{AC_r(f, x) = \text{false};}$$

$$\frac{f \notin \mathbb{DG}_f;}{AC_r(f, x) = \text{false};} \qquad \frac{x \notin \mathbb{DG};}{AC_r(f, x) = \text{false};}$$

function does not have access to the variable represented by this node but it may have access to the variables represented by its children. It can also be observed that the variable V2 is now dependent on V1 and is indicated by a square in the figure.

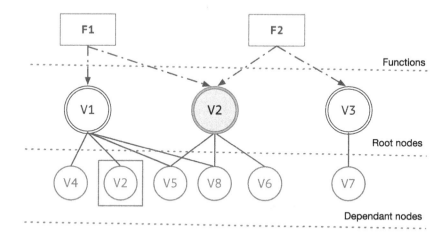

Fig. 3. Dependency graph evolution

In ASD, every dictionary containing the variable required a change when the variable was updated. However, dependency graph needs only a single operation to be performed to the same effectiveness. Every time the dependency graph changes, it is registered by the second part of model, the reinforcement learning mechanism. The use and working of the learning mechanism is described in greater detail in the following section.

4   Reinforcement Learning

The evolution of the dependency graph is continuously monitored when a function is executed and this data is used to learn about the function's characteristics. The information collected is stored as a persistent data set to be used in subsequent executions. The purpose of this learning is to understand the various paths and loops that were taken in prior executions.

The information collected contains the following: the name of the function, the dependency tracker at the time of the split, the variable being split/updated, root variable and the layout of the relevant nodes in the dependency graph. Once collected, this information is used to split/update variables at subsequent flows.

Let us consider the current state to be as shown as in the Fig. 2. We now consider functions f4, f5, and f6 as shown in the Listing 1.2.

```
1 // var V1 = secret(true/false);
2 var V10 = true;
3 var V11 = true;
4 function f4()
5 {
6   if (V1)
7     V10 = false;
8   if (V10)
9     V11 = false;
10  return V11;
11 };
12 function f5(x)
13 {
14  var y = x+1;
15  console.log(y);
16 };
17 function f6()
18 {
19  if(V10)
20  {f5(V10);}
21  else{f5(0);}
22 };
23 f4();
24 f6();
```

Listing 1.2. ASD Example

In this example, the variable V1 is a secret variable. Here we consider that the functions f4 and f6 have read access to V1. The function f5 does not have access to V1. If $V1 = \text{true}^s$, in line 7, the public variable V10 becomes a secret. In the dependency graph, its root node is V1. If $V1 = \text{false}^s$, in line 9, the public variable V11 becomes a secret with its root node being V1 due to the over-approximation of ASD.

```
1 [{function:"f4", rootVariable:"V1", split:"V10",
2                 DT:[V1], dgInfo:[{"V1", "V10"}]},
3 {function:"f4", rootVariable:"V1", split:"V11",
4                 DT:[V1], dgInfo:[{"V1", "V11"}]}]
```

Listing 1.3. ASD Example

The set of variable information shown in Listing 1.3 is the persistent data set that is maintained about the function f4 for the example in Listing 1.2. As stated above, it contains information on dependency tracker at the time of the split as well as the root node that was allocated as the parent to the variable at the end of the information flow. Each time a variable is split or its secret value is updated because of a dependency, a data set for the variable is created. This data set is added to the a persistent array of data sets if not already present. This is hence the "learnt data".

Hence, at the end of the execution of function f4, it is noted that variable V10 and V11 are dependent on the variable V1. This information is used for later executions. Now, let us consider the same function such that variable $V1 = \lceil \text{false}^p \parallel \text{false}^s \rfloor$. In this case, the line 7 is not executed. However, we know from the prior execution that V10 is dependent on V1 based on DT at the time of the split. Hence, V10 is split at the end of the execution and its private address contains the value copied from its public address, i.e. $V10 = \lceil \text{true}^p \parallel \text{true}^s \rfloor$.

Whenever, a variable is split or updated due to information flows, the changes to the dependency graph are noted into the learning mechanism. Therefore, it is represented as part of the rules [VARIABLE UPGRADE] and [VARIABLE UPDATED]. These rules stipulate the various necessary steps when a new secret value flows into a public variable and split variable respectively. In these rules, the $v.root$ represents the parent root node set the variable v and $v.root \leftsquigarrow x$ implies that the node of the variable x becomes a child node to all the root nodes of variable v. The rules show that a join operation is performed to the persistent set of learnt data along with a successful variable update or split.

[VARIABLE UPDATED]

$$\frac{f \in \mathbb{DG}_f; x \in \mathbb{DG}; x \rightarrow x'; AC_w(f,x) = \text{true}; \text{dt} = \{\}}{x^s \leftarrow A[x']; x \rightsquigarrow f; L \bowtie (f,x,\text{dt})}$$

$$\frac{f \in \mathbb{DG}_f; x \rightarrow x'; AC_w(f,x) = \text{true}; \text{dt} \neq \{\}}{x^s \leftarrow A[x']; \forall (v \in \text{dt})v.root \leftsquigarrow x; L \bowtie (f,x,\text{dt})}$$

$$\frac{f \in \mathbb{DG}_f; x \rightarrow x'; AC_w(f,x) = \text{true}; x \in \mathbb{DG}_{root}; \text{dt} \neq \{\};}{State(x) = inactive}$$

$$\frac{f \in \mathbb{DG}_f; x \rightarrow x'; AC_w(f,x) = \text{true}; \text{dt} \neq \{\}; x \in \mathbb{DG}_d}{\text{delete } x \in \mathbb{DG}_d}$$

$$\frac{f \in \mathbb{DG}_f; x \rightarrow x'; AC_w(f,x) = \text{false};}{x^p \leftarrow A[x'];} \qquad \frac{f \notin \mathbb{DG}_f;}{x^p \leftarrow A[x'];}$$

[VARIABLE UPGRADE]

$$\frac{f \in \mathbb{DG}_f; \text{dt} \neq \{\}; S(y); y \notin \mathbb{DG}}{A[y^s]; y \leftarrow \lceil A[y] \| A[y^s] \rceil; (\forall v \in \text{dt})\{v.root \leftsquigarrow y\}; L \bowtie (f,y,\text{dt});}$$

The rationale and the necessity for this split becomes evident in the execution of the function f6. The Table 2 illustrates the execution of function f6 if variable V10 was split or not. It must be noted that f6 has read access to V1 according to the policy definition.

In the Table 2 we show the execution of the function f6 after the function f4 has been executed. There are two columns where we compare ASD with ASD-DG post learning has been completed. The two cases where V1 = true^s and V1 = false^s have been considered in this example.

The first major difference is caused because of V10 being split for both values of V1 in case of ASD-DG post learning. Since the variable split is known, the DT remains the same for both cases. However, this is not the case in simple ASD. In the first case, the variable is added to the DT. The rule [SELF-SUFFICIENT

CALLED] [12] is invoked because f5 is also a self-sufficient function. Since f5 does not have access to the V11, the function call is skipped. This is in line with the dynamic policy enforcement where the secret addresses are not allowed to flow into the public addresses.

[SELF-SUFFICIENT CALLED]

$$\frac{\{\, S(f); f \in \mathbb{DG}_f; dt = \{x\}; AC_r(f,x) = \texttt{true}; \}}{s(f) = secret; dt = \{x\};}$$

$$\frac{\{\, S(f); f \in \mathbb{DG}_f; dt = \{x\}; AC_r(f,x) = \texttt{false}; FL = i\, \}}{(Skip\ S(f))}$$

$$\frac{\{\, S(f); f \in \mathbb{DG}_f; dt = \{x\}; AC_r(f,x) = \texttt{false}; FL = e\, \}}{s(f) = public; x \to A[x]; dt = \{\};} \qquad \frac{\{\, S(f); dt = \{\}; \}}{S(f);}$$

The use of the dependency graph is to compensate for the deficiencies caused by the rule [SELF-SUFFICIENT CALLED] in ASD. This rule is necessary to prevent the secret from being leaked. However, it still can cause leak on whether the variable was split. This occurs when a self-sufficient function fails to split a global variable because of that branch not being executed and this global variable being used in a subsequent self-sufficient function as a conditional in an implicit flow. In the Table 2, V10 being split affects the DT in line 1, thereby allowing/denying the execution of f5. While such a leak is only caused under specific circumstances, and the actual secret value is never leaked, it nevertheless undesirable and makes the model non-adherent to TINI. We aim to solve this issue through learning. Adding the dependency graph approach, the model gradually closes up its leaks and will eventually become adherent to TINI. Further,

Table 2. ASD-DG working

function f6()	ASD	ASD-DG post-learning
First case [V1=true[s]]		
1. {if(V10 == 1)	true, DT={V10}	true, DT={V10}
2. {f5(V10);}	~~f5(x);~~	~~f5(x);~~
3. else{f5(0);}		
4. }}		
Second case [V1=false[s]]		
1. {if(V10 == 1)	false; DT={}	false; DT={V10}
2. {f5(V10);}		
3. else{f5(0);}	DT={}; f5(0);	DT={V10};~~f5(0);~~
4. }}		

[DG LEARNING - FUNCTION ENDED]

$$\frac{exec(f) \rightarrow \texttt{completed}; L(f) \neq \varnothing}{(\forall r \in L(f))\{(\texttt{[VARIABLE UPGRADE]}/\texttt{[VARIABLE UPDATED]})(\texttt{r});\}}$$

since the dependency graph keeps track of the variables for every run, it can also observe dependencies caused by the use of `eval`, every case of a switch case and other information flows gradually over a period of time. Hence, the dependency graph and how it keeps track of various information flow is very important to the model.

The various information learnt is used by the rule [DG LEARNING - FUNCTION ENDED]. At the end of the execution of the function f, if there is any past secret information flow, additional IFC actions are performed. The learnt data contains a set of function, dependency tracker and the dependent variable. If the dependent variables have not already been split, a variable upgrade is performed based on the dependency tracker. Else, a variable update is performed.

[Proof for TINI]

Let,

$$\text{Functions} \left(f_h \bigcup f_l \equiv \overset{\forall f \in F}{\bigcup} f \right)$$

Public output functions $(f^p \in f_l)$

Secret input $x_{in.s}$

Proof:

$$(\forall f \in f_h) : \{f \leftarrow AC_r(f,x) = \textbf{true};\} \quad (\forall f \in f_l) : \{f \leftarrow AC_r(f,x) = \textbf{false};\}$$
$$(\forall f \in f_h) : \{f \leftarrow AC_w(f,x) = \textbf{true};\} \quad (\forall f \in f_l) : \{f \leftarrow AC_w(f,x) = \textbf{false};\}$$
$$\mathbb{A}[x_{in.s}] := \mathbb{A}[x_{in.s}^p] \quad \mathbb{A}[x_{in.s}] :\neq \mathbb{A}[x_{in.s}^s]$$
$$\frac{\{f(x_{in.s}) \mid f \in f_l;\}}{f \leftarrow V_{ref}(x_{in.s}); \mathbb{DG}(x) \not\leftarrow \mathbb{A}[x_{in.s}]} \quad \frac{\{f(x_{in.s}) \mid f \in f_h;\}}{f \leftarrow V_{ref}(x_{in.s}^s); \mathbb{DG}(x) \leftarrow \mathbb{A}[x_{in.s}^s]}$$
$$\frac{S_{fp} \leftarrow x_{in.s}; FL = e}{f^p \leftarrow \mathbb{A}[x_{in.s}]; S_{fp};} \quad \frac{S_{fp} \leftarrow x_{in.s}; FL = i}{(Skip\ S_{fp})}$$
$$\frac{\{f(x_{in.s}), y \not\in \mathbb{DG}, y \leftarrow x \mid f \in f_h;\}}{split(y); f \leftarrow V_{ref}(y^s); \mathbb{DG}(y) \leftarrow \mathbb{A}[y^s];}$$
$$\therefore \{S_{fp}(x_{in.s}^s) \equiv S_{fp}((x'_{in.s}^s) \mid x_{in.s} \equiv x'_{in.s}\}$$

$\textbf{However,}\ x_{in.s} \equiv x'_{in.s} \ \textbf{iff}\ \forall x \in s, \textbf{if}\ \{x \in \mathbb{DG}\} \implies \{x' \in \mathbb{DG}\}$

$\implies S_{fp}(x_{in.s}^s) \approx sS_{fp}((x'_{in.s}^s)\ \textbf{iff}\ \forall x \in s, \textbf{if}\ \{x \in \mathbb{DG}\} \implies \{x' \in \mathbb{DG}\}$

4.1 Eventual TINI

It must be noted that the premise of our model starts with not being adherent to TINI initially. This is because, ASD could leak state information of a variable at the end of the execution of a function. This leak does not mean that secret values would be printed but that it is possible to infer whether a public variable has become a dependent node or not.

The [Proof for TINI] shows that ASD-DG is only adherent to TINI if the same variables are split at the end of the execution of a given function for different values of the secret. The reinforcement learning model solves this issue by collecting information on the states of the various variables and simulating these states at the end of each function. Hence, over time, all execution paths would be covered and even dynamic flows like eval operations can be handled to a certain extent. Since the learning model would eventually ensure that the states of the variables would eventually be the same, the ASD-DG can be said to be adherent to "eventual TINI".

5 Conclusion

There is a clear and urgent need to address the various information leaks in the context of JavaScript. The dynamic nature of the language makes the standard approaches insufficient or inefficient. In this case, starting with a practical efficient approach and making it adhere to more restrictive security guarantees over time is more appropriate. We have proposed one such model and take the novel approach of using learning in the runtime environment to achieve our goals of "eventual TINI". In this process, we have also proposed a proper change to the architecture of ASD to become more efficient. Taking ASD as the base has also allowes us to account for fine-grained function level policies. We hence, propose this model as a viable IFC model for the modern web-browser. The future work of the model is to work towards a complete web-browser implementation of the proposed model.

Acknowledgments. This work has received a French government support granted to the COMIN Labs excellence laboratory and managed by the National Research Agency in the "Investing for the Future" program under reference ANR-10-LABX-07-01.

References

1. Askarov, A., Hunt, S., Sabelfeld, A., Sands, D.: Termination-Insensitive noninterference leaks more than just a bit. In: Jajodia, S., Lopez, J. (eds.) ESORICS 2008. LNCS, vol. 5283, pp. 333–348. Springer, Heidelberg (2008). doi:10.1007/978-3-540-88313-5_22
2. Austin, T.: Dynamic information flow analysis for Javascript in a web browser. Ph.D. thesis, University of California, Santa Cruz (2013)
3. Austin, T.H., Flanagan, C.: Efficient purely-dynamic information flow analysis. ACM SIGPLAN Not. **44**(8), 20 (2009)

4. Bell, D., LaPadula, L.: Secure Computer Systems: Mathematical Foundations. Technical report, DTIC.MIL (1973)
5. Biba, K.J.: Integrity Considerations for Secure Computer Systems. Technical report, The Mitre Corporation (1975)
6. Bielova, N.: Survey on JavaScript security policies and their enforcement mechanisms in a web browser. J. Logic Algebraic Program. **82**(8), 243–262 (2013)
7. Devriese, D., Piessens, F.: Noninterference through secure multi-execution. In: 2010 IEEE Symposium on Security and Privacy, pp. 109–124 (2010)
8. Groef, W.D., Devriese, D., Nikiforakis, N., Piessens, F.: FlowFox: a web browser with flexible and precise information flow control. In: Proceedings of the 2012 ACM Conference on Computer and Communications Security, pp. 748–759. ACM, Raleigh, North Carolina, USA (2012)
9. Hedin, D., Sabelfeld, A.: Information-flow security for a core of javascript. In: 2012 IEEE 25th Computer Security Foundations Symposium, pp. 3–18. IEEE, June 2012
10. Kashyap, V., Wiedermann, B., Hardekopf, B.: Timing- and termination-sensitive secure information flow: Exploring a new approach. In: 2011 IEEE Symposium on Security and Privacy, pp. 413–428. IEEE, May 2011
11. Sabelfeld, A., Myers, A.: Language-based information-flow security. IEEE J. Sel. Areas Commun. **21**(1), 5–19 (2003)
12. Subramanian, D., Hiet, G., Bidan, C.: Preventive information flow control through a mechanism of split addresses. In: 2016 ACM 9th International Conference on Security of Information and Networks. ACM, July 2016

Threat Modeling for Cloud Data Center Infrastructures

Nawaf Alhebaishi[1,2]([✉]), Lingyu Wang[1], Sushil Jajodia[3], and Anoop Singhal[4]

[1] Concordia Institute for Information Systems Engineering,
Concordia University, Montreal, Canada
{n_alheb,wang}@ciise.concordia.ca
[2] Faculty of Computing and Information Technology,
King Abdulaziz University, Jeddah, Saudi Arabia
[3] Center for Secure Information Systems, George Mason University, Fairfax, USA
jajodia@gmu.edu
[4] Computer Security Division, National Institute of Standards and Technology,
Gaithersburg, USA
anoop.singhal@nist.gov

Abstract. Cloud computing has undergone rapid expansion throughout the last decade. Many companies and organizations have made the transition from traditional data centers to the cloud due to its flexibility and lower cost. However, traditional data centers are still being relied upon by those who are less certain about the security of cloud. This problem is highlighted by the fact that there only exist limited efforts on threat modeling for cloud data centers. In this paper, we conduct comprehensive threat modeling exercises based on two representative cloud infrastructures using several popular threat modeling methods, including attack surface, attack trees, attack graphs, and security metrics based on attack trees and attack graphs, respectively. Those threat modeling efforts provide cloud providers practical lessons and means toward better evaluating, understanding, and improving their cloud infrastructures. Our results may also imbed more confidence in potential cloud tenants by providing them a clearer picture about potential threats in cloud infrastructures and corresponding solutions.

1 Introduction

Cloud computing has emerged as an attractive option for many enterprises, government agencies and organizations due to its flexibility and reduced costs. The shifting to this new paradigm is, however, still impeded by various security concerns, which are exacerbated by the lack of a clear understanding of security threats facing cloud data centers. Unlike traditional computer networks, cloud data centers usually exhibit some unique characteristics, such as the presence of significant redundancy in terms of hardware configurations, and the co-existence of both physical and virtual components. Such unique characteristics imply the need for modeling and measuring security threats specifically for cloud data centers.

© Springer International Publishing AG 2017
F. Cuppens et al. (Eds.): FPS 2016, LNCS 10128, pp. 302–319, 2017.
DOI: 10.1007/978-3-319-51966-1_20

On the other hand, modeling and measuring security threats for cloud data centers is a challenging task due to the lack of public accesses to the detailed information regarding hardware and software configurations deployed in real cloud data centers. Existing work mainly focus on high level frameworks for risk and impact assessment [19], guidelines or frameworks for cloud security metrics [2,14], and specific vulnerabilities or threats in the cloud [6,21] (a more detailed review of related work will be given in Sect. 6). However, to the best of our knowledge, there does not exist a concrete study on threat modeling and measuring for cloud data centers using realistic cloud infrastructures and well established models. Although there already exist many such threat modeling models, such as attack surface, attack tree, attack graph, and their corresponding security metrics, a systematic application of those models to concrete cloud data center infrastructures is yet to be seen.

In this paper, we present a comprehensive study on modeling and measuring threats in cloud data center infrastructures. We first provide the basis for our study as two representative cloud infrastructures, devised based on established technologies of several major players on the cloud market, e.g., Amazon, Microsoft, Google, Cisco, VMware, and OpenStack. We also provide details on the hardware and software components used in the data center to manage the cloud services. We then apply several popular threat modeling methods on such cloud infrastructures, including attack surface, attack tree, attack graph, and security metrics based on attack trees and attack graphs.

The main contribution of this paper is twofold. First, to the best of our knowledge, this is the first comprehensive study of threat modeling based on well established models and concrete cloud data center designs, which incorporate technologies used by major cloud providers on the market. Second, our study provides answers to many practical questions, such as, *How can cloud providers gather and organize knowledge concerning the security of their cloud data center and services? How can cloud providers examine the security of a cloud data center at different abstraction levels? How can cloud providers measure the security of their cloud data center before and after applying a hardening option?* Those threat modeling efforts can not only provide cloud providers practical lessons and means for understanding and improving their cloud infrastructures, but may also imbed more confidence in cloud tenants by providing them a clearer picture about potential threats in cloud infrastructures.

The remainder of this paper is organized as follows. Section 2 provides the background knowledge on threat modeling and security metrics needed later in our work. In Sect. 3, the cloud data center architecture is presented. In Sect. 4, the threat modeling is explained in details. In Sect. 5, security metrics are applied to measure the level of security. Related work are reviewed in Sect. 6, and the paper concluded in Sect. 7.

2   Background

The following briefly reviews the threat models and security metrics that are applied in this paper, including attack surface, attack tree, attack graph, attack tree-based metric (ATM), and Bayesian network (BN)-based metric.

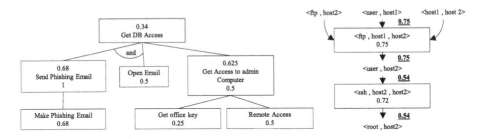

Fig. 1. Attack tree (left) and attack graph (right)

- Attack surface: Originally proposed as a metric for software security, attack surface captures software components that may lead to potential vulnerabilities. These may include entry and exit points (i.e., methods in a software program that either take user inputs or generate outputs), communication channels (e.g., TCP or UDP), and untrusted data items (e.g., configuration files or registry keys read by the software) [15]. Due to the complexity of examining source code, most existing work applies the concept in a less formal manner. For example, between an end user, the cloud provider, and cloud services, six attack surfaces can be composed [11].
- Attack tree: While attack surface focuses on what may provide attackers initial privileges or accesses to a system, attack trees demonstrate the possible attack paths which may be followed by the attacker to further infiltrate the system [20]. The left-hand side of Fig. 1 shows an attack tree example in which the attacker's goal is to get accesses to the database. In the example, there are two ways to reach the root node (the goal). First, the attacker can follow the left and middle paths at the same time (due to the *and* label), or the attacker can follow the right path for reaching the root node.
- Attack graph: As a more fine-grained model, an attack graph depicts all possible attack steps and their causal relationships [22]. In the right-hand side of Fig. 1, each triplet inside a rectangle indicates an exploit <service vulnerability, source host, destination host>, and each pair in plaintext indicates a pre- or post-condition <condition, host> of the exploits. The logic relationships between the nodes are represented based on the assumption that any exploit can be executed if and only if all of its pre-conditions are already satisfied (e.g., In Fig. 1, the first exploit requires all three pre-conditions to be satisfied), whereas any condition may be satisfied by one exploit for which the former is a post-condition.

- The above threat models are all qualitative in nature. The attack tree-based metric (ATM) quantifies the threat in an attack tree using the concept of *probability of success* [8]. The probability of each node in the attack tree is typically determined based on historical data, expert opinions, or both. In Fig. 1, a number above the label represents the overall probability of success, and a number below the label represents the probability of each node alone. The probability on the root node indicates the most risky path, which should be prioritized in security hardening. The BN-based metric [9,24] can be applied to attack graphs to calculate the probability for an average attacker to compromise a critical asset. The conditional probabilities that an exploit can be executed given its pre-conditions are all satisfied can usually be estimated based on standard vulnerability scores (e.g., the CVSS scores [16]). In Fig. 1, the probability inside a rectangle is the CVSS score divided by 10, and each underlined number represents the probability for successfully executing that exploit. In this example, the attack goal has a probability of 0.54, and if we change the *ftp* service on host2 and suppose the new probability becomes 0.4, then the new attack probability for the goal will become 0.228, indicating increased security.

3   Devising Cloud Data Center Infrastructures

In this section, we devise two cloud data center infrastructures that will be used for threat modeling in Sects. 4 and 5. To make our infrastructures more representative, we have base our infrastructures upon concepts and ideas borrowed from major players on the market, including Cisco, VMware, and OpenStack, as follows.

- Cisco presents a cloud data center design for both public and private clouds [4], which is divided into multiple layers with suggested hardware for the physical network and software used to virtualize the resources. We borrow the multi-layer concept and some hardware components, including Carrier Routing System (CRS), Nexus (7000,5000,2000), Catalyst 6500, and MDS 9000.
- VMware vSphere suggests the hardware and software components to run a private cloud data center [12]. They also tag the port numbers used to connect services together. We borrow the concepts of Authentication Server, Domain Name System (DNS), and Storage Area Network (SAN) and synthesize these to represent the main functionality of some hardware components in our cloud infrastructures.
- OpenStack is one of the most popular open source cloud operating systems [17]. We borrow following components of OpenStack: Dashboard, Nova, Neutron, Keystone, Cinder, Swift, Glance, and Ceilometer [17].

Table 1 compares the main concepts used in our infrastructures to the major cloud providers in the market, including Amazon [5], Microsoft [23], and Google [3] (some of those concepts will be discussed later in this section).

Table 1. Concepts used by major cloud providers

	AWS	Microsoft azure	Google compute
Multiple layers	×	×	×
Authentication sever	×	×	
Domain Name System	×	×	×
One service in each cluster	×	×	×
Multi-tier	×	×	×

We discuss two different infrastructures since OpenStack components can either run centrally on a single server or be distributed to multiple servers [17].

Infrastructure 1. Figure 2 illustrates our first infrastructure. The physical network provides accesses to both cloud users and cloud administrators. Cloud administrators connect to the data center through firewalls (*node* 17) and (*node* 19), an authentication server (*host* 18), and Nexus 7000 (*node* 20), which is connected to the other part of the network. For cloud users, Cisco's multi-layer concept is used [4] as follows.

- In Layer 1, a CRS (*node* 1) is used to connect the cloud to the internet, which then connects to a firewall (*node* 2, ASA 5500-X Series) while simultaneously being connected to two different types of servers (authentication servers (*host* 3) as well as DNS and Neutron Servers (*node* 4)). Those servers provide services to the cloud tenants and end users. The servers then connect to Cisco Nexus 7000 with Catalyst 6500 (*node* 5) to route the requests to destination machines.
- In Layer 2, a firewall (*node* 6, ASA 5500-X Series) connects the first layer to this layer through Nexus 5000 (*node* 7). The Nexus 5000 is used to connect rack servers through Nexus 2000, which is used to connect servers inside each rack at the computing level (*hosts* 8, 9, 10, 11, *and* 12). The Nexus 5000 (*node* 7) then connects to the next layer.
- In Layer 3, another Nexus 7000 (*node* 13) connects the previous layer to the storage. A firewall (*node* 14, ASA 5500-X Series) connects the Nexus 7000 (*node* 13) and MDS 9000 (*node* 16).

The following outlines how the cloud works. OpenStack components run on the authentication servers among which one (*host* 3) is designated for cloud tenants, and another (*host* 18) for cloud administrators. The first runs following components: Dashboard, Nova, Neutron, Keystone, Cinder, Swift, Glance, and MySql. The second runs the same components, but additionally runs Ceilometer for a billing system. The DNS server (*node* 4) runs a Neutron component that provides the address of the machine running a requested service. At the computing level (*hosts* 8, 9, 10, 11, *and* 12), all physical servers run four components: Hypervisor, Nova to host and manage VMs, Neutron agent to connect VMs to the network, and Ceilometer agent to calculate the usage. At the computing level, each physical server cluster runs the same VMs service, e.g., all *http* VMs run on the *http* server cluster, and the same occurs for application VMs, *ftp* VMs, smtp VMs, and database VMs. Finally, all physical machines and VMs run *ssh* for maintenance.

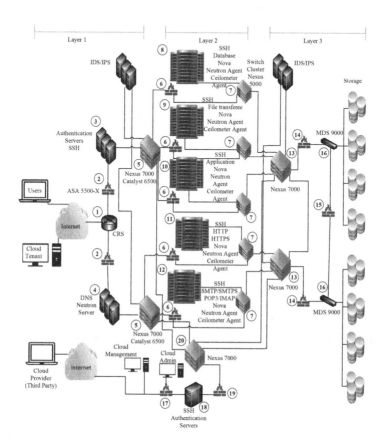

Fig. 2. Cloud data center infrastructure 1

Infrastructure 2. The second infrastructure is illustrated in Fig. 3. This infrastructure has a similar physical network as the previous, with the addition of new machines that separate OpenStack components, which are installed on the authentication servers for cloud tenants in the previous infrastructure, into many different machines. These new machines are Neutron servers (*node* 25), controller servers (*node* 36), and network nodes (*node* 34). In addition, the authentication server (*host* 23) for cloud tenants will run a Dashboard component to access and manage the VMs related to the tenant user. Moreover, Neutron server (*node* 25) serves to control the virtual network and connects to the controller node (*node* 36), which runs Nova API, Neutron API, Keystone,

Glance, Swift, Cinder, MySql, and any component needed to manage and control the cloud. The last node is a network node (*node* 34) which translate between the virtual IPs and the physical IPs to grant accesses to services running on VMs. For example, if a cloud tenant wishes to access their VMs, they will first need to connect to the Dashboard. Next, the Neutron server will send the authentication request to the keystone service on the Controller node. If the user possesses the privilege to access the VM, the controller will send a request to the network node to obtain the address for the VMs, and will then send the address to the Neutron server to connect the user to their VMs.

4   Threat Modeling

This section conducts threat modeling on the two cloud data center infrastructures that are just introduced. Since we have designed those infrastructures to be representative enough, we expect our threat models to bring useful insights to administrators of cloud infrastructures in general.

4.1   Attack Surface

In this section, we apply the attack surface concept at the resource level. Gruschka & Jensen categorize attack surfaces into those between user, service, and cloud provider [11]. The same classes are used in our discussions, with the addition of surfaces belonging to the same class. Also, we consider the service class used by Gruschka & Jensen [11] as the intermediate layer between users and the cloud provider in the sense that, if a user wishes to attack a cloud provider, he/she must pass through an attack surface consisting of services. In addition, we focus on entry and exit points [15] which indicate the means through which the attack starts and those through which data is leaked out, respectively.

In Figs. 2 and 3 it can be observed that there are three types of attack surfaces in a cloud data center. First, there are attack surfaces related to the physical network, involving hardware and software components, such as switches, routers, servers, applications, and operating systems. Second, there are virtualization-related attack surfaces, such as hypervisors and virtual switches. Last, there are cloud operating systems, such as OpenStack components (Glance, Neutron, Nova, Ceilometer, and Keystone). The first type of attack surface is similar to those in traditional networks, but components related to cloud running on top of the physical network must also be considered. On the other hand, virtualization and cloud operating systems-related attack surfaces are unique to cloud and their analysis will pose new challenges.

Attack Surface w.r.t. Users. We consider two types of users. First, the normal user using the cloud service may aim to attack either the cloud tenant who owns that service, another cloud tenant or its users using the same cloud, or the cloud provider. Second, the cloud tenant may aim to attack another cloud tenant and its users, or the cloud provider. Various surfaces can be utilized by users to attack the cloud, including the hypervisor, VMs, APIs and web services, and OpenStack components (e.g., Horizon, Keystone, Neutron, Glance, and Nova).

Example 1. A normal user wants to attack a hypervisor on the database VM server (*host* 8) to steal information about all VMs running on that machine. First, the entry point to start this attack is the database VM on the hypervisor. After he/she get initial accesses to the database VM, that VM become an exit point to attack the hypervisor. Finally, with accesses to the hypervisor, e.g., through exploiting CVE-2013-4344 [1], the attacker can get data related to all VMs run on top of this hypervisor and the hypervisor thus becomes an exit point. Next consider a cloud tenant who wants to attack another tenant hosted on the same physical machine. First, the attacker can use his/her VM as entry point to get a privilege to the hypervisor, e.g., by applying CVE-2012-3515 [1], then the attacker will use the hypervisor as an entry point to get accesses to the target VM.

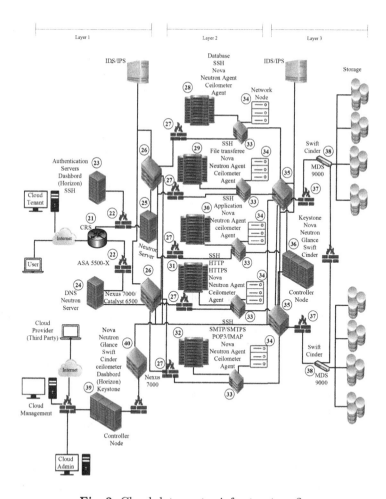

Fig. 3. Cloud data center infrastructure 2

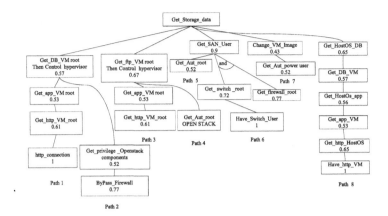

Fig. 4. Attack tree

Attack Surface w.r.t. Cloud Providers. A cloud provider here refers to an operator who has privileges to access certain components (e.g., switches, firewall, and SAN) for maintenance and management purposes. This type of attackers may use his/her accesses to resources to attack the cloud data center. All three types of attack surfaces explained before can be used by such an attacker.

Example 2. An operator who has accesses to Nexus 7000 (*node* 13) for management wants to get accesses to sensitive data related to a tenant. First, he/she can use the Nexus 7000 as an entry point to obtain a root privilege on Nexus 7000, and then use this machine as an exit point to start another attack to get data from the storage device (*node* 16).

4.2   Attack Tree

The previous section shows how attack surface may capture the initial attack attempts. To further study what may happen once an attacker gains initial privileges, we will need attack trees, which represent high level attack paths leading attackers to their goals. Figure 4 shows an attack tree for our cloud data center infrastructures. It is assumed that the root node, or goal node, is a storage device in the cloud that is susceptible to attacks by either a malicious user, a cloud tenant, or a cloud operator. Eight paths in Fig. 4 represent the possible ways to reach such a target. Each path represents a capability level of users who can follow the path; not all paths can be used by all users. For example, some paths can be followed by the cloud operator but cannot be accessed by normal users or cloud tenants. In what follows, the paths and corresponding users will be explained in further details.

– **Path 1:** This attack can be executed by a normal user to obtain data from the storage device (*node* 16). The user must first establish a connection to the *http* VM server (*host* 11) and must then acquire the root privilege on this VM.

The attacker can then connect to the application VM server (*host* 10) provided that they have obtained root privilege on that VM. After the user acquires access to the application VM, he/she may create a connection to the database VM server (*host* 8). From this point, the user can attack the database VM to obtain root privilege on that VM. Finally, the attacker can launch an attack on the hypervisor to gain access to other database VMs (*host* 8) running on the same physical machine and obtain data related to all database VMs stored on the storage device (*node* 16).

- **Path 2:** The normal user can use this path to attack the cloud storage device (*node* 38). The attacker begins the attack by surpassing the firewall (*node* 22) to obtain privilege on OpenStack (*node* 36) in order to gain a direct connection to the database VM server (*host* 28). The remainder of this attack is similar to that of path 1, and serves to gain access to the hypervisor and the storage device.

- **Path 3:** This path can be used by a cloud tenant user who has user access to the *http* VM server (*host* 11) and wishes to access *ftp* files stored on the storage device (*nose* 16). First, the cloud tenant user must obtain root privilege on the *http* VM server (*host* 11). Then, he/she will need to obtain root privilege on the application VM server (*host* 10) to start a connection to the *ftp* VM server (*host* 9). After this, the user will obtain root privilege on this VM and get the *ftp* files related to this VM. In addition, the user can attack the hypervisor to obtain the *ftp* files related to other VMs running on top of this hypervisor.

- **Path 4:** Cloud tenants who do not already possess *ftp* VM servers running on the cloud can use this path to obtain data from the storage device (*node* 16) through the *ftp* VM server (*host* 9). Cloud tenants on this path will use Open-Stack components (*host* 3) to gain privileges to access the *ftp* VM (*host* 9) belonging to another cloud tenant. In this situation, the attacker can obtain all files belonging to this VM. Furthermore, the attacker may attack the hypervisor to gain access to other *ftp* VMs running on the same physical machine.

- **Path 5:** Cloud operators with access to the admin user authentication server (*host* 18) can use this path by obtaining root access to the authentication server. They can then use this device to obtain root access on the SAN device (*node* 16) to control the data stored on the storage device.

- **Path 6:** This path can be used by a cloud operator who has access to a physical machine (e.g., a switch, firewall, or other type of machines) to attack the storage device. Suppose the attacker has user access to a switch device (*node* 13) for maintaining this device. The attacker can then obtain root access on this device as well as root access to a firewall device (*node* 14) between the switch device and the SAN (*node* 16). These two accesses may allow him/her to create a connection to the SAN device and subsequently attack the SAN in order to access the stored data.

- **Path 7:** This path may be used by a third party cloud provider who has access to the authentication server (*host* 18) of an administrator. The user must obtain root access on the authentication server and must then gain privilege on the VM image storage (*host* 18) and (*node* 16). In this case, the user may use this privilege to modify or change the VM images stored on Glance. This new image will have a backdoor that can be used by the attacker to gain access to all VMs with this image.

- **Path 8:** This path can be used by either a cloud tenant or a normal user. The goal for these attackers is to control the data belonging to other cloud tenants on the cloud. The attacker must first have access to the *http* VM sever (*host* 31) and must gain access to the Host Operating System (HOS) (*host* 31). By gaining access to the HOS, the attacker can obtain access to all VMs running on this machine. The attacker may then gain access to all application VMs (*host* 30) connected to all *http* VMs to which they have access. Subsequently, the attacker gains access to the application VMs which may run on different physical machines; the attacker may then acquire access over all HOS related to those VMs (*host* 30). The attacker can then gain root access to the database VM server (*host* 28) in order to obtain the data stored on the storage device. The attacker may also gain access to all HOS running database VMs (*host* 28).

4.3   Attack Graph

In the previous section, the attack tree shows how an attacker may follow an attack path to reach the goal. However, this is done at a higher abstraction level without details about specific vulnerabilities. We now construct attack graphs to represent specific exploits of vulnerabilities that can be use to reach the goal. Although we can apply the standard attack graph concept designed for traditional networks, special consideration must be given to the virtualization level, which is unique to cloud, and the fact that machines or VMs may have similar or identical configurations.

We construct our attack scenarios based on real vulnerabilities related to hardware and software components used in our infrastructures as listed in the National Vulnerability Database (NVD) [1]. In our attack graphs, the Common Vulnerability Scoring System (CVSS) [16] scores retrieved from the NVD are depicted inside each node after dividing it by 10 to obtain a probability value between 0 to 1, which is later used in the BN-based metric. An attack graph may be created for different types of users but we will focus on the normal user due to space limitations.

Figures 5 and 6 show two attack graphs for the data center infrastructures depicted in Figs. 2 and 3, respectively. It is assumed that the attacker has access to a cloud tenant's services. The main goal for the attacker is to steal data from the storage. The user must have access to the *http* VM as well as the application VM and database VM before reaching the goal due to the multi-tier infrastructure. The following services are assumed to be used in the data centers.

- Tectia Server version 5.2.3, for *ssh* running in all VMs.
- Apache *http* server running on *http* VM.
- Oracle version 10.1.0.2 installed on the application VM.
- Oracle version 10.2.1 on the database VM.

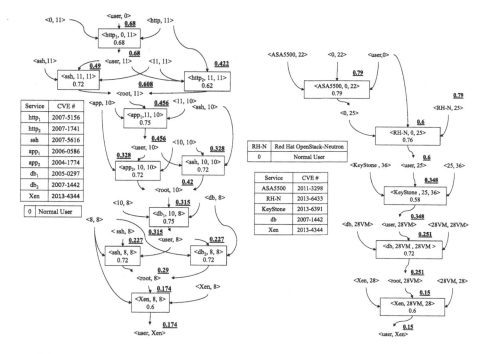

Fig. 5. Attack graph for Fig. 2   **Fig. 6.** Attack graph for Fig. 3

– Xen version 4.3.0 is running as a hypervisor to control VMs on physical machines.

Example 3. Figure 5 shows an attack graph corresponding to path 1 in the aforementioned attack tree. Between five to seven vulnerabilities are required to reach the goal. Specifically, five vulnerabilities are required if we assume the *ssh* vulnerability will be the same in the *http* server VM, application server VM, and database server VM, whereas seven vulnerabilities are required if the *ssh* vulnerability is not used to reach the goal. We divide the attack graph to four stages and in each stage the attacker will gain a different level of privileges.

– **Stage 1:** A vulnerability in the *http* server VM (*host* 11) (CVE-2007-5156) is employed by the attacker to gain user access by uploading and executing arbitrary code containing .php. in the file extension as well as unknown extensions. Then, another vulnerability on the same VM (CVE-2007-1741) is used to gain root privilege by renaming the directory or performing symlink. A *ssh* (*host* 11) vulnerability (CVE-2007-5156) can also be used to gain root privilege on the same VM.

– **Stage 2:** The attacker now can connect to the application server (*host* 10). Then, by using a vulnerability related to the application sever VM (CVE-2006-0586), the attacker is allowed to gain the user privilege by executing arbitrary sql commands through multiple parameters. To gain root privilege

on this VM, the attacker can apply this vulnerability (CVE-2004-1774) or by using an *ssh* (*host* 10) vulnerability (CVE-2007-5616), and at this point the attacker can start a connection to the database server VM.
- **Stage 3:** The attacker uses a vulnerability related to the database server (*host* 8) VM (CVE-2005-0297) to gain user access. Then, on this VM he/she can gain root access by using vulnerability (CVE-2007-1442) or an *ssh* (*host* 8) vulnerability (CVE-2007-5616).
- **Stage 4:** The attacker can then obtain data related to this database VM (*host* 8), and he/she may obtain even more data from another VM running on the same physical machine by gaining access to a hypervisor through exploiting (CVE-2013-4344).

Example 4. The attack graph in Fig. 6 is related to the infrastructure shown in Fig. 3, where OpenStack components run on more than one physical machine. The goal of this attack is to gain access to date storage in three stages. This attack graph corresponds to path 2 in the attack tree.

- **Stage 1:** A vulnerability in the firewall (*node* 22) (CVE-2011-3298) is employed by the attacker to bypass the firewall in order to connect to the Neutron server (*node* 25). The attacker can then use the Neutron vulnerability (CVE-2013-6433) to gain privileges with which he/she can use vulnerability (CVE-2013-6391) to generate EC2 token API in order to gain access to a database VM (*host* 28).
- **Stage 2:** After the attacker obtains access to the database VM (*host* 28), he/she used the database vulnerability (CVE-2007-1442) to gain root privilege on the same VM. This allows the attacker to obtain data related to this VM.
- **Stage 3:** To obtain data from another database on the same physical machine, the attacker used the vulnerability (CVE-2013-4344) to gain access to the hypervisor running on this physical machine such that he/she can access all VMs running on this machine and view the data related to these VMs.

By constructing the attack surface, attack tree, and attack graphs for the cloud data center infrastructures, we have demonstrated how each model may capture potential threats at a different abstraction layer. Nonetheless, all those models are qualitative in nature, and we will apply security metrics to measure the threats in the coming section.

5   Cloud Security Metrics Based on ATM and BN

In this section, we apply two security metrics based on the attack tree and attack graphs, respectively, to further quantify the threats modeled in the previous section.

5.1   Attack Tree Metric

In this section, an attack tree metric (ATM) will be applied based on the attack tree described in Sect. 4.2. In Fig. 7, all nodes inside the same path are considered as having AND relationships, whereas an OR relationship is assumed between different paths unless if an AND relationship is explicitly stated. Based on such assumptions, the corresponding equations are applied to calculate the probabilities. The highest probability is assigned to the root node after applying the metric. In Fig. 7, between the two probabilities in each node, the probability with (+) represents the average CVSS values and the other probability represents the metric result.

In Fig. 7, it can be observed that path 5 and 6 are the least secure paths in the attack tree. Those two paths can be followed by a cloud operator to launch an insider attack to steal data from the storage device. This metric can also be used to verify whether or not adding a new service or disabling existing services can increase security and by how much. As shown in Fig. 7, the probability to reach n_8 is 0.45; as such, if the cloud provider wishes to decide whether to increase security levels in that node, he/she can use the metric before and after applying the changes. For example, suppose the cloud provider wishes to add new rules to a firewall to prevent attacks from n_9 and n_{11} to n_8. After re-applying the ATM metric, the probability on n_8 becomes 0.348, showing increased security. Applying the ATM on other potential changes may help the cloud provider to make the right decisions in hardening the cloud.

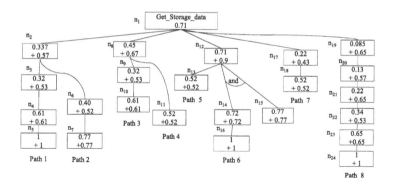

Fig. 7. Attack tree metric

5.2   Bayesian Network Metric

In this section, the BN-based security metric [9,24] will be applied to the attack graph shown in Fig. 5 to measure the threat and also the effect of certain changes made to the infrastructure. In particular, we show how the level of redundancy and diversity may affect the security of the cloud infrastructure. For redundancy, the *ssh* service running on some of the servers will be disabled to see the effect on security. As to diversity, we assume the *ssh* service may be diversified with other software, e.g., OpenSSH version 4.3, denoted as ssh_2, with a vulnerability CVE-2009-290 and a CVSS score of 6.9 [1].

Table 2 shows how security is affected by reducing redundancy and increasing diversity through disabling or diversifying some of the *ssh* instances in the infrastructure. In the left-hand side table, the first row shows that the probability for an attacker to reach the goal is 0.174 in the original configuration, and the remaining rows show the same probability after disabling one or more *ssh* instances on the three servers, e.g., the probability after disabling *ssh* on the *http* server is reduced to 0.121, which corresponds to the most secure option by disabling one *ssh* instance, and the lowest probability after disabling two and three *ssh* instances is 0.094 and 0.074, respectively.

The middle and right-hand side of Table 2 show the effect of diversifying the *ssh* instances. In the middle figure, we can observe that, after we replace the *ssh* service on *app* and *DB* servers with ssh_2, the probability for reaching the goal decreases from 0.174 to 0.171, which indicates a slight improvement in security. The next three rows of the table show that the same effect remains when one of the *ssh* instances is disabled. The last three rows show the simple fact that, when there is only one *ssh* instance left, the diversification effort has not effect.

In the right-hand side of Table 2, we change the *ssh* instance on the *http* server instead of the *app* server, as in the above case, in order to see whether different diversification options make any difference to security. We can see the probability decreases in most cases (except the fourth row), which indicates a slightly more effective option than the previous one. Overall, the best option in terms of diversification without disabling any service instance is given in the first row in the right table, with a probability 0.17, and the best option for disabling one service instance is given in the fourth row of the middle table with a probability 0.119 (disabling two instances always yields 0.094). Obviously, more options may be evaluated similarly using the BN-based metric in order to find the best option for making the cloud data center infrastructure more secure.

Table 2. The BN-based metric results for the attack graph shown in Fig. 5

$\langle user, Xen \rangle$			
http	*app*	*DB*	T
	ssh		T
T	T	T	0.174
T	F	T	0.136
T	T	F	0.136
F	T	T	0.121
T	F	F	0.106
F	F	T	0.094
F	T	F	0.094
F	F	F	0.074

$\langle user, Xen \rangle$			
http	*app*	*DB*	T
ssh_1	ssh_2	ssh_2	T
T	T	T	0.171
T	F	T	0.135
T	T	F	0.135
F	T	T	0.119
T	F	F	0.106
F	F	T	0.094
F	T	F	0.094
F	F	F	0.074

$\langle user, Xen \rangle$			
http	*app*	*DB*	T
ssh_2	ssh_1	ssh_2	T
T	T	T	0.17
T	F	T	0.133
T	T	F	0.134
F	T	T	0.12
T	F	F	0.105
F	F	T	0.094
F	T	F	0.094
F	F	F	0.074

6   Related Work

Cloud environments are usually subject to many security threats some of which exploit existing vulnerabilities related to the cloud [10]. There only exist limited efforts on threat modeling for cloud infrastructures. Ingalsbe et al. present a threat model by classifying all tenant-related components in three categories (Actor, End Points, and Infrastructure) [13] but without concrete use cases. Gruschka & Jensen identify three main entities (User, Cloud provider, and Service) and the attack surfaces between those entities [11] but again without specific details about each attack surface. We borrow this classification in devising our threat models. The original attack surface concept [15] is intended to measure the security of a software system focusing on identifying entry/exit points, communication channels, and untrusted data items from the source code. Like most existing work, our work applies those concepts but at a higher abstraction level.

Attack tree is a well known threat model which can be used for many useful analyses, such as analyzing the relative cost of attacks and the impact of one or more attack vectors [20]. Attack trees can also be used in security hardening to determine the best options to increase security within a budget [7]. Using attack trees can help to understand what kind of attackers may follow an attack tree path [18,20]. Attack graphs can be automatically generated by modeling the network and vulnerabilities, and many useful analyses may be performed using attack graphs [22]. We borrow the concepts of attack trees and attack graphs but apply them to cloud data center infrastructures that we have devised. There exist many research work on extending attack trees and attack graphs to security metrics. A probabilistic metric is applied to attack graphs to obtain an overall attack likelihood for the network [24]. Edge et al. presented protection trees [8] which are similar to attack trees but contain information on how the system can be secured, and our work borrows part of this work to apply the attack tree-based metric. A BN-based security metric applies attack graphs to measure the security level of a network [9]. The metric converts the CVSS scores of vulnerabilities into attack probabilities and then obtain the overall attack likelihood for reaching critical assets. We apply this metric to our cloud data center infrastructures in this paper. The National Institute of Standards and Technology (NIST) underline the importance of security measuring and metrics for cloud providers by providing high level definitions and requirements but no concrete methodologies [2]. Luna et al. propose a framework with basic building blocks for cloud security metrics [14]. We loosely follow the framework in this paper.

7   Conclusion

In this paper, we have conducted threat modeling and measuring for cloud data center infrastructures. First, we have shown two cloud data center infrastructures which are fictitious but represent many existing technologies adopted at real cloud data centers by major cloud providers. Three threat models were then applied to those infrastructures, namely, the attack surface, attack trees, and attack graphs, which model potential threats from different viewpoints and at different abstraction levels. We have also applied security metrics based on attack trees and attack graphs, respectively, to quantify the threats. This work will benefit cloud providers in demonstrating how threat models and metrics may assist them in evaluating and improving the security of their clouds. Future work will focus on extending the scale and scope of our existing efforts and developing automated hardening algorithms for cloud data centers to generate actionable knowledge from the threat modeling and measuring results. Another future direction is to study how cloud data center infrastructure may be best secured through simulations.

Acknowledgements. The authors thank the anonymous reviewers for their valuable comments. This work was partially supported by the National Institutes of Standard and Technology under grant number 60NANB16D287, by the National Science Foundation under grant number IIP-1266147, and by Natural Sciences and Engineering Research Council of Canada under Discovery Grant N01035.

References

1. National vulnerability database. http://www.nvd.org. Accessed 20 Feb 2015
2. National Institute of Standards and Technology: Cloud Computing Service Metrics Description (2015). http://www.nist.gov/itl/cloud/upload/RATAX-CloudServiceMetricsDescription-DRAFT-20141111.pdf. Accessed 17 June 2015
3. Adler, B.: Google Compute Engine Performance Test with RightScale and Apica (2013). http://www.rightscale.com/blog/cloud-industry-insights/google-compute-engine-performance-test-rightscale-and-apica. Accessed 26 March 2016
4. Bakshi, K.: Cisco cloud computing-data center strategy, architecture, and solutions (2009). http://www.cisco.com/web/strategy/docs/gov/CiscoCloudComputing_WP.pdf
5. Barr, J.: Building three-tier architectures with security groups (2010). https://aws.amazon.com/blogs/aws/building-three-tier-architectures-with-security-groups/. Accessed 28 March 2016
6. Dahbur, K., Mohammad, B., Tarakji, A.B.: A survey of risks, threats and vulnerabilities in cloud computing. In: Proceedings of the 2011 International Conference on Intelligent Semantic Web-Services and Applications, ISWSA 2011, New York, NY, USA, pp. 12: 1–12: 6. ACM (2011)
7. Dewri, R., Ray, I., Poolsappasit, N., Whitley, D.: Optimal security hardening on attack tree models of networks: a cost-benefit analysis. Int. J. Inf. Secur. **11**(3), 167–188 (2012)
8. Edge, K.S., Dalton, G.C., Raines, R.A., Mills, R.F.: Using attack and protection trees to analyze threats and defenses to homeland security. In: MILCOM 2006–2006 IEEE Military Communications conference, pp. 1–7, October 2006
9. Frigault, M., Wang, L.: Measuring network security using Bayesian network-based attack graphs. In: 32nd Annual IEEE International Computer Software and Applications, COMPSAC 2008, pp. 698–703, July 2008
10. Grobauer, B., Walloschek, T., Stöcker, E.: Understanding cloud computing vulnerabilities. IEEE Secur. Priv. **9**(2), 50–57 (2011)
11. Gruschka, N., Jensen, M.: Attack surfaces: a taxonomy for attacks on cloud services. In: 2010 IEEE 3rd International Conference on Cloud Computing, pp. 276–279, July 2010
12. Hany, M.: VMware VSphere in the Enterprise. http://www.hypervizor.com/diags/HyperViZor-Diags-VMW-vS4-Enterprise-v1-0.pdf. Accessed 05 Feb 2015

13. Ingalsbe, J.A., Shoemaker, D., Mead, N.R.: Threat modeling the cloud computing, mobile device toting, consumerized enterprise-an overview of considerations. In: AMCIS (2011)

14. Luna, J., Ghani, H., Germanus, D., Suri, N.: A security metrics framework for the cloud. In: 2011 Proceedings of the International Conference on Security and Cryptography (SECRYPT), pp. 245–250, July 2011

15. Manadhata, P., Wing, J.: An attack surface metric. IEEE Trans. Softw. Eng. **37**(3), 371–386 (2011)

16. Mell, P., Scarfone, K., Romanosky, S.: Common vulnerability scoring system. IEEE Secur. Priv. **4**(6), 85–89 (2006)

17. Openstack. Openstack Operations Guide. http://docs.openstack.org/openstack-ops/content/openstack-ops_preface.html. Accessed 27 Aug 2015

18. Ray, I., Poolsapassit, N.: Using attack trees to identify malicious attacks from authorized insiders. In: Vimercati, S.C., Syverson, P., Gollmann, D. (eds.) ESORICS 2005. LNCS, vol. 3679, pp. 231–246. Springer, Heidelberg (2005). doi:10.1007/11555827_14

19. Saripalli, P., Walters, B.: Quirc: a quantitative impact and risk assessment framework for cloud security. In: 2010 IEEE 3rd International Conference on Cloud Computing, pp. 280–288, July 2010

20. Schneier, B.: Attack trees. Dr. Dobb's J. **24**(12), 21–29 (1999)

21. Shaikh, F.B., Haider, S.: Security threats in cloud computing. In: 2011 International Conference for Internet Technology and Secured Transactions (ICITST), pp. 214–219, December 2011

22. Sheyner, O., Haines, J., Jha, S., Lippmann, R., Wing, J.M.: Automated generation and analysis of attack graphs. In: Proceedings of the 2002 IEEE Symposium on Security and Privacy, pp. 273–284 (2002)

23. Squillace, R.: Azure infrastructure services implementation guidelines (2015). https://azure.microsoft.com/en-us/documentation/articles/virtual-machines-linux-infrastructure-service-guidelines/. Accessed 28 March 2016

24. Wang, L., Islam, T., Long, T., Singhal, A., Jajodia, S.: An attack graph-based probabilistic security metric. In: Atluri, V. (ed.) DBSec 2008. LNCS, vol. 5094, pp. 283–296. Springer, Heidelberg (2008). doi:10.1007/978-3-540-70567-3_22

Strategies for Incorporating Delegation into Attribute-Based Access Control (ABAC)

Daniel Servos[⊠] and Sylvia L. Osborn

The University of Western Ontario, London, ON N6A 5B7, Canada
dservos5@uwo.ca, sylvia@csd.uwo.ca

Abstract. Attribute-Based Access Control (ABAC) is an emerging model of access control that has gained significant interest in both recent academic literature and industry application. However, to date there have been almost no attempts to incorporate the concept of dynamic delegation into ABAC. This work lays out a number of possible strategies for incorporating delegation into existing ABAC models and discusses the potential trade-offs associated with each strategy. Delegation strategies are categorized into families that share a number of similar properties. It is our hope that this preliminary work will aid in future ABAC based delegation research by identifying and detailing the challenges and opportunities intrinsic to each method of integrating delegation.

1 Introduction

Attribute-Based Access Control (ABAC) is a relatively new form of access control that bases access control decisions on the attributes of users, objects and the environment rather than the identity of users or the roles/clearances assigned to them. While there has been significant interest in the creation, enforcement and application of ABAC models [5,7], to date there are few works that address how delegation might be implemented or supported.

Delegation enables a user to temporarily and dynamically alter the design of an access control system after policies have been created to account for everyday changes that policies are insufficient to address. In traditional models of access control delegation is relatively straightforward. A set of permissions or a role membership is delegated directly by a delegator to a delegatee under set conditions (e.g. an expiry date). In ABAC, this is complicated by both the introduction of attributes and ABAC's identity-less nature (i.e. access decisions are made on the basis of attributes and the user's identity may be unknown). Attributes may seem like an ideal access control element to build delegation around (as is done in ABE [2,6] and Attribute Certificates [8]); however, as we will show, this naive approach comes with a number of unexpected challenges.

This paper offers a preliminarily investigation into strategies for incorporating delegation into ABAC. Potential strategies are created by evaluating the combinations of delegators, delegatable access control elements and delegatees common in most ABAC models (Sect. 2.1). The trade-offs associated with each

© Springer International Publishing AG 2017
F. Cuppens et al. (Eds.): FPS 2016, LNCS 10128, pp. 320–328, 2017.
DOI: 10.1007/978-3-319-51966-1_21

family of strategies are discussed and multiple examples are given that demonstrate how delegation might be performed (Sect. 2.2). Finally, we give conclusions and outline directions for future work (Sect. 3). It is our hope that this work will aid future research by identifying possible strategies for the creation of ABAC delegation models as well as the challenges and benefits associated with them.

2   Strategies for Incorporating Delegation in ABAC

2.1   Delegation Components

Delegation can be thought of as relating three access control components; a delegator, a delegatee and a delegatable access control element. A delegator temporarily grants a delegatee an access control element (e.g. a set of permissions or role membership) under set constraints. In RBAC delegation models, this is relatively straightforward: the delegator and delegatee are typically users and the access control element being delegated is either a set of permissions (via a temporary role)[9] or membership in an existing role [1]. ABAC, however, presents new possibilities for delegators, delegatees and delegatable elements that result in different trade-offs and limitations when combined. Each combination provides a conceivable strategy for delegation and offers particular advantages/disadvantages if used as the basis for an ABAC delegation model.

Delegatable elements are the most important characteristic of delegation as they answer *what* is being delegated, while the delegators and delegatees answer *who* and *where* (i.e. *who* is doing the delegating and *where* the elements are being delegated to). The following are the most suitable delegatable elements that we have identified in current ABAC models [5, 7, etc.]:

Attributes: Perhaps the most obvious element and one that has been explored to a limited extent (in ABE [2, 6] and Attribute Certificates [8]) are user attributes. In cases where attributes are delegatable, users are allowed to delegate their assigned attributes to a delegatee such that they are considered to be part of the delegatee's attribute set.

Permissions: Delegating permissions a delegator has obtained from a policy decision is another option. In such cases users are granted permissions as a result of their attribute set satisfying a policy and can delegate these permissions onto others while the policy remains satisfied.

Group Membership: Recent ABAC models have incorporated the concept of user groups into the core ABAC model. In HGABAC [7], groups can be directly assigned user attributes that are inherited by users through their membership. Membership in these groups provides a possible delegatable element, similar to how role membership is delegatable in some RBAC delegation models [1].

While traditional models focus on delegation between users, additional possibilities exist for ABAC. In ABAC models with group support, user groups can be delegators in the sense that attributes or other delegatable elements assigned to groups may be temporarily delegated to a delegatee. In such a case, while the

Table 1. Delegation Strategies

Strategy Name	X	DE	Y	Strategy Name	X	DE	Y
Attribute Delegation				**Permission Delegation**			
User-to-User Attribute Delegation	U	AS	U	User-to-User Permission Delegation	U	PS	U
User-to-Group Attribute Delegation	U	AS	G	User-to-Group Permission Delegation	U	PS	G
Group-to-Group Attribute Delegation	G	AS	G	' Group-to-User Permission Delegation	G	PS	U
Group-to-User Attribute Delegation	G	AS	U	Group-to-Group Permission Del	G	PS	G
User-to-Attribute Attribute Del	U	AS	A	User-to-Attribute Permission Del	U	PS	A
Group-to-Attribute Attribute Del	G	AS	A	Group-to-Attribute Permission Del	U	PS	A
User-to-Policy Attribute Delegation	U	AS	P	User-to-Policy Permission Delegation	U	PS	P
Group-to-Policy Attribute Delegation	G	AS	P	Group-to-Policy Permission Del	G	PS	P
Group Membership Delegation				**Legend**			
User-to-User Membership Delegation	U	GM	U	**U** = User	**X** = Delegator		
Group-to-User Membership Del	G	GM	U	**G** = Group	**DE** = Delegatable Element		
Group-to-Group Membership Del	G	GM	G	**P** = Policy	**Y** = Delegatee		
User-to-Group Membership Del	U	GM	G	**A** = Attribute			
User-to-Attribute Membership Del	U	GM	A	**PS** = Policy Set			
Group-to-Attribute Membership Del	G	GM	A	**AS** = Attribute Set			
User-to-Policy Membership Delegation	U	GM	P	**GM** = Group Membership			
Group-to-Policy Membership Del	G	GM	P				

group is the source of the delegatable elements, the actual instigator of the delegation would be the members of the group or another actor in the system (e.g. a group leader). Similarly, the delegatee need not be limited to a user. Delegating to a group allows a delegator to assign their delegatable elements to multiple users in one operation. This is useful in scenarios where multiple users are briefly required to take on the duties of a single delegator (e.g. an absent store manager delegating his permissions to all department managers). In cases where group membership is being delegated, it can be considered that all members in the delegatee group are also temporarily made members of the delegated group.

Delegations can also be made to a policy or attribute. When an attribute is acting as a delegatee, all users that are directly (not through delegation) assigned the same attribute also become delegatees. For example if a permission, P, is delegated to the attribute *(ROLE, {manager})* (an attribute named *ROLE* with the value "manager") all users that are assigned the attribute *ROLE* with a value of "manager" will be delegated the permission P. Using a policy as a delegatee works similarly. A delegator delegates some element to a policy they create and all users satisfying this policy are delegated the element. For example, if membership in a group, G, is delegated to the policy "*ROLE = manager AND YEARS_EMPLOYED $\geq$ 3*", users that have attributes stating that they are managers and employed for at least 3 years will be delegated membership in group G. While delegating to an attribute or policy may seem complex, it is a necessity to support delegation in a system where the identity of a user may remain unknown and access decisions are made purely on the user's attributes.

2.2   Delegation Strategies

Each delegation components described in Sect. 2.1 may be combined to create a delegation strategy. For example the combination *(Users, Permissions, Users)* represents a strategy in which users can delegate their permissions to other users, whereas *(Groups, Attributes, Policies)* would be a strategy in which groups can delegate their attributes to any user that satisfies a policy. Table 1 categorizes each strategy into families based on the element being delegated. Strategies in the same family tend to share common characteristics and challenges for systems adopting them. In this section, we discuss the advantages and limitations of each family. It is assumed that only one strategy is used at a time. While hybrid strategies are possible, and could offer advantages, they are left to future work.

Attribute Delegation. In Attribute Delegation strategies, delegatees are delegated a subset of the delegator's attributes. Delegated attributes are merged with the delegatee's directly assigned attributes (i.e. assigned through any means but delegation) and the combined attribute set is treated as the delegatee's set during policy evaluation. An example of User-to-User Attribute Delegation is shown in Fig. 1 where *direct(user)* is the user's directly assigned attributes and *effective(user)* is the user's effective attributes (i.e. the merged attribute set used for policy evaluations). In Fig. 1, Alice wants to delegate a subset of her attributes to a prospective student (Dave) so he can satisfy the policy *"role = "undergrad" AND year ≥ 2"* to view some resource. As Dave only has the value "ProspectiveStudent" for his *role* attribute and no *year* attribute, Alice must delegate both her *role* and *year* attributes for Dave to satisfy the policy. The subset Alice delegates is *{(year, {4}), (role, { "undergrad"})}* which makes Dave's effective attribute set *{(role, { "ProspectiveStudent", "undergrad")}, (year, {4})}*.

Multiple simultaneous delegations to a single user are also possible. In Fig. 1, Alice wishes to delegate to Charlie so he can satisfy the policy *"role IN { "undergrad", "grad"} AND department = "CompSci""*, and access a resource limited to CompSci students. At the same time, Bob wishes to delegate to Charlie so he can satisfy the policy *"role = "faculty" AND department = "SoftEng""* and access a resource limited to SoftEng faculty. Alice delegates *{(department, { "CompSci"})}* and Bob *{(role, { "faculty"})}*. Making Charlie's effective attributes *{(role, { "grad", "faculty"}), (department, { "SoftEng", "CompSci"})}*.

While this style of delegation is easy to implement (a subject's effective attribute set is simply used in place of their direct set), it can lead to serious problems if not carefully constrained. The first issue is the creation of conflicting policy evaluations. In Fig. 1 Alice's delegation results in Dave's effective attribute set containing two values for the *role* attribute, "ProspectiveStudent" and "undergrad". If a policy were to exist such as *"role ≠ "ProspectiveStudent""* two different results would be possible depending on the value of *role* used when evaluating the policy. A potential solution is to use a policy language that specifies clear resolutions to conflicts (e.g. prioritize attributes assigned via

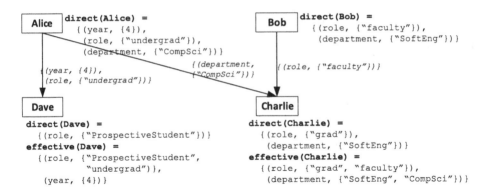

Fig. 1. Example of User-to-User Attribute Delegation. Arrows denote direction of delegation (arrow points to delegatee), boxes represent users of the system.

Fig. 2. Example of a possible attack on User-to-User Attribute Delegation.

delegation over those directly assigned or always grant access when any combination of attributes satisfies the policy). However, the issue is further complicated when multiple delegations to the same delegatee are considered simultaneously. In such cases, conflicts can arise from purely delegated attributes, making conflict handling more difficult (e.g. can not simply prioritize delegated attributes).

A second issue is the potential for users to collude to satisfy a policy that they would individually be unable to. In Fig. 2 Oscar and Mallory are trying to satisfy the policy *"year > 2 AND department = "SoftEng""*. Individually, neither can satisfy the policy as Oscar lacks a *department* attribute with a "SoftEng" value and Mallory lacks a *year* attribute with a value greater than 2. However, if Oscar delegates { *"year"*, {4}} to Mallory it creates the effective attribute set { *(year, {1, 4}), (department, { "SoftEng"})}* and Mallory can satisfy the policy if *year* is evaluated as 4. While one solution is to heavily constrain what attributes can be delegated or to use a constraint specification language [3] to enforce SoD style constraints, the simplest fix is to isolate delegated attribute sets from each other and the delegatee's directly assigned set. Thus, a user must choose what set of attributes to activate at the start of a session (similar to role activation in RBAC [4]). Isolation of attribute sets would also provide a solution to conflicting policy evaluations and aid in user comprehension. For example, Alice would know that if she delegates all of her attributes to Dave, at most Dave would have access to the same permissions as he did before in addition to the permissions Alice has access to. Users would still be able to bypass negative polices like *"year ≠ 4 AND year ≠ 1"* if not having a *year* attribute is considered to satisfy the policy by delegating a subset of their attributes that omits the *year* attribute.

A third issue resulting from merging attribute sets is losing the descriptiveness of the delegatee's attributes. In Fig. 1, after delegation, Dave's effective attribute set is no longer descriptive of Dave. Dave obtains a *year* attribute with a value of 4 while not being a student. While this makes delegation possible and allows Dave to satisfy the policy, it complicates policy creation (need to account for unexpected attribute combinations) and restricts the use of attributes to the purpose of access control (e.g. a system could not trust that an e-mail sent to an address in a user's effective attribute set was actually theirs).

The last issue is comprehension of what is being delegated and what needs to be delegated to achieve a desired result. A delegator must be familiar with the policies of the system and their own attributes. In Fig. 1, if Alice wanted to delegate a permission she was granted from satisfying the policy *"role = "undergrad" AND year ≥ 2"* she would have to understand the policy, what attribute set she has been assigned and what attribute subset to delegate. This is further complicated if delegated attribute sets are not isolated, as Alice would also have to be aware of possible conflicts and unexpected attribute combinations.

Group Membership Delegation. Group Membership Delegation requires an ABAC model which supports user groups in which members of a group inherit attributes assigned to that group. Figure 3 shows an example of how user groups work in HGABAC [7]. In this case Alice and Bob are members of the CS Faculty group and inherit the attributes *role* and *department* with values "faculty" and "CompSci" respectively. Additionally, Bob is a member of the SoftEng Undergrad group and inherits the values "undergrad" and "SoftEng" for the attributes *role* and *department*. These inherited attributes are merged with the user's directly assigned attributes to form the user's effective attribute set (similar to how attributes are merged in Attribute Delegation). In Group Membership Delegation, membership in groups are delegated as opposed to the delegator's attributes. In Fig. 3, if Alice wanted to delegate a permission she was granted from belonging to the CS Faculty group (e.g. from satisfying the policy *"role = "faculty" AND department = "CompSci""*) to Dave she would delegate her membership in the CS Faculty group such that Dave's inherited set of attributes would be *{ (role, { "undergrad", "faculty"}), (department, { "SoftEng", "CompSci"})}* leading to the effective attribute set *{ (year, {2}), (role, { "faculty", "undergrad"}), (department, { "CompSci", "SoftEng"})}* when merged with his attributes.

This method of delegation has several advantages over Attribute Delegation. User comprehension is improved as users are not required to pick individual attributes to delegate and instead only need to consider what group memberships are needed. Placing constraints on delegation becomes easier as delegators are forced to delegate whole attribute sets belonging to groups at a time (constraints can be placed on what group memberships can be delegated and by whom, rather than individual attributes). Finally, the effective attribute set of delegatees is more likely to remain descriptive of the delegatee as personal attributes (like year, age, etc.) are more likely to be directly assigned than assigned to groups.

Despite these advantages, Group Membership strategies share a number of issues in common with Attribute Delegation. Conflicting policy evaluations and user collusion is still possible, although more restrained. For collusion to be possible, groups have to be assigned the required attribute value pairs. For example, if the policy was *"role = "faculty" AND department = "SoftEng""*, Alice and Dave could still collude to satisfy the policy (by Alice delegating her membership in the CS Faculty group to Dave); however, it would not be possible for Alice and Dave to collude to satisfy the policy *"year > 1 AND department = "CompSci""* as *year* is a directly assigned attribute. Isolating attribute sets obtained through membership delegation and attribute sets obtained through normal assignment would minimize the issue and avoid unforeseen permissions being granted (e.g. if Alice delegates her membership a group to Dave, she knows that Dave would not satisfy any policy that she her self could not satisfy from her membership).

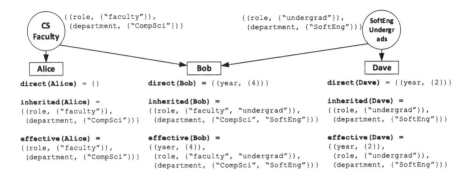

Fig. 3. Example of attribute user groups from HGABAC [7]. User groups are shown as circles and users as rectangles. Arrows denote a user being a member of a group.

Group Membership Delegation also introduces a new issue. Attributes that are directly assigned to a delegator, like the *year* attribute in Fig. 3, are undelegatable. Assuming this attribute is only directly assigned to users and never to groups, it would be impossible to delegate membership to satisfy a policy such as *"year ≥ 2"*. A system utilizing Group Membership Delegation would either have to carefully design its groups such that all desired delegation use cases can be accomplished through delegating group memberships or implement a second delegation strategy in addition to Group Membership Delegation.

Permission Delegation. Rather than delegating attributes (directly or indirectly) Permission Delegation strategies are based on delegating permissions. Delegators are able to delegate permissions they obtain by satisfying policies onto delegatees so long as the granting policy remains satisfied (e.g. if the delegator's attributes or an environmental attribute changes such that the policy granting the permission is no longer satisfied, the delegated permission is revoked). In strategies where a group is the delegator, the permissions the group can delegate is equal to the set of permissions a user would be granted if they had the same attributes as the group. For example, if the users and groups from Fig. 3 and the policy *"role = "faculty" AND department = "CompSci""* existed that granted the permission, p_1, both Alice and Bob as well as the group CS Faculty could delegate p_1. If the policy *"year $\geq$ 2 AND TIME > 9:00AM AND TIME < 5 : 00PM"* granted the permission p_2, Bob and Dave could delegate p_2 but the delegation would only be valid between 9:00AM and 5:00PM.

Permission Delegation strategies poses greater challenges in terms of implementation but resolve the issues faced by the other families. As delegated permissions are only valid while the policy granting them remains satisfied, a system would be required to either periodically check that the delegator still satisfies the policy or recheck the policy each time the delegatee uses the permission. Depending on the size of the system and the complexity of the policies, this could add significant overhead. The benefit is that no change is made to the delegatee's attribute set, limiting conflicting policy evaluations and preventing user collusion. User comprehension is also improved as users are delegated permissions directly rather than attributes that only indirectly grant permissions.

3 Conclusions and Future Work

3.1 Delegation Strategies

The ideal delegation strategy depends on the needs of the implementing system; however, a few generalizations can be made. Permission Delegation is suitable for systems requiring high user comprehension and removes the possibility of conflicting policy evaluations and user collusion. Attribute Delegation is ideal when continual policy evaluation would be difficult or low implementation complexity is desired. Group Membership Delegation provides high user comprehension with similar results to Attribute Delegation but requires group support.

Delegating to a user (X-to-User strategies) provides the closest parallel to delegation in traditional models, however, delegating to groups (X-to-Group), attributes (X-to-Attribute) or policies (X-to-Policy) can provide greater flexibility and allow for delegation to users whose identity is unknown during policy creation. X-to-Group allows for delegation to groups of users in one operation but requires group support. X-to-Policy introduces higher revocation complexity and lower user comprehension but has the greatest flexibility. X-to-Attribute provides a middle ground between the two with less flexibility than X-to-Policy but increases user comprehension while retaining the identity-less nature of ABAC.

3.2 Future Work

A number of directions are possible for future work. Using multiple strategies simultaneously could provide new possibilities for delegation. Such combinations could help overcome the limitations of individual strategies but further work is needed to evaluate any complexities or conflicts introduced. Existing policy conflict resolution techniques could help mitigate the issues faced by Attribute and Group Membership Delegation, as well as allow for hybrid strategies with minimal limitations. Additional work is required to determine if current techniques are applicable. Formalizing the strategies described in this work will allow for in-depth analysis and aid integration into existing ABAC models. Extending an existing model with each strategy would allow for a more quantitative evaluation and provide a reference model for future work. HGABAC is an ideal candidate for such extensions by virtue of its support for user groups.

References

1. Barka, E., Sandhu, R. et al.: A role-based delegation model and some extensions. In: NISSC 2000, pp. 396–404 (2000)
2. Bethencourt, J., Sahai, A., Waters, B.: Ciphertext-policy attribute-based encryption. In: SP 2007, pp. 321–334 (2007)
3. Bijon, K.Z., Krishman, R., Sandhu, R.: Constraints specification in attribute based access control. Science 2(3), 131–144 (2013)
4. Ferraiolo, D.F., Sandhu, R., Gavrila, S., Kuhn, D.R., Chandramouli, R.: Proposed NIST standard for role-based access control. Science 4(3), 224–274 (2001)
5. Jin, X., Krishnan, R., Sandhu, R.: A unified attribute-based access control model covering DAC, MAC and RBAC. In: Cuppens-Boulahia, N., Cuppens, F., Garcia-Alfaro, J. (eds.) DBSec 2012. LNCS, vol. 7371, pp. 41–55. Springer, Heidelberg (2012). doi:10.1007/978-3-642-31540-4_4
6. Servos, D., Mohammed, S., Fiaidhi, J., Kim, T.: Extensions to Ciphertext-policy attribute-based encryption to support distributed environments. Science 47(2–3), 215–226 (2013)
7. Servos, D., Osborn, S.L.: HGABAC: towards a formal model of hierarchical attribute-based access control. In: Cuppens, F., Garcia-Alfaro, J., Zincir Heywood, N., Fong, P.W.L. (eds.) FPS 2014. LNCS, vol. 8930, pp. 187–204. Springer, Heidelberg (2015). doi:10.1007/978-3-319-17040-4_12
8. Turner, S., Housley, R. et al.: An Internet Attribute Certificate Profile for Authorization. RFC 5755, January 2010
9. Wang, H., Osborn, S.L.: Static and dynamic delegation in the role graph model. Science 23(10), 1569–1582 (2011)

Physical Security

Patrolling Trees with Mobile Robots

Jurek Czyzowicz[1], Adrian Kosowski[2], Evangelos Kranakis[3(✉)],
and Najmeh Taleb[3]

[1] Dépt. d'informatique, Univ. du Québec en Outaouais, Gatineau, QC, Canada
[2] Inria - LIAFA, Paris Diderot University, Paris, France
[3] School of Computer Science, Carleton University, Ottawa, ON, Canada
`kranakis@scs.carleton.ca`

Abstract. Consider k identical robots traversing the edges of a *geometric tree*. The robots have to patrol the tree by perpetually moving along edges, but without exceeding their maximum unit speed. The robots can change direction and speed anywhere on vertices or interiors of edges. The quality of patrolling is measured by *idleness*, which is defined as the longest time period during which any point on the tree is not visited by any of the robots. Goal is to provide algorithms describing the movement of the robots along the tree so as to minimize the idleness.

Our main contribution is to show that there is an *off-line* schedule, where placing k robots at specific initial positions on a geometric tree T and making them move at unit speed, permits to achieve the optimal idle time. We extend this to a *graph tree* model (where the robots can change direction only on vertices). We also consider *on-line* schedules, working for collections of simple, identical, memoryless robots, walking with constant speed, which behave according to so-called *rotor-router* model. We conclude with a discussion of experimental work indicating that in a random setting the rotor router is efficient on tree graphs.

Keywords: Algorithms · Experiments · Idle time · Off-line · On-line · Patrolling · Robot · Rotor router · Tree

1 Introduction

Patrolling can be an important component of infrastructure security, especially when it is required to monitor physical resources enclosed within a given bounded domain from potential threats by moving perpetually along the boundary with mobile robots. The feasibility of an intrusion depends on the time during which an intruder remains undiscovered, and therefore it is important to design patrolling protocols which minimize the *idle time*, defined as the time during which boundary points are left unmonitored by a patrolling robot. For examples, discussion and a detailed survey on the use of optimization problems,

---

J. Czyzowicz and E. Kranakis—Research supported in part by NSERC Discovery grant.

F. Cuppens et al. (Eds.): FPS 2016, LNCS 10128, pp. 331–344, 2017.
DOI: 10.1007/978-3-319-51966-1_22

like patrolling, evacuation, blocking, and coverage in infrastructure security and SCADA in particular, see [23].

The present paper is concerned with patrolling geometric trees (where the robots can change direction anywhere on vertices or interiors of edges) and graph trees (where the robots can change direction only on vertices). The domain being patrolled will be a tree, i.e., connected acyclic graph, say T. Assuming that k robots are available, the main problem of interest will be to give a patrolling algorithm that optimizes the idle time on T.

1.1 Related Work

Patrolling a one-dimensional boundary with mobile robots has many applications and has been studied extensively in the robotics literature (cf. [10,16,17]) under the names of *boundary-* and *fence-patrolling*. Patrolling consists of walking perpetually around an area in order to protect or monitor it and has been defined as the act of surveillance. It is considered useful for monitoring and locating objects or humans that need to be rescued from a disaster, in ecological monitoring or detecting intrusion. Patrolling has also been used by network administrators in conjunction with mobile agents in order to detect network failures or in indexing of search engines (cf. [24]). In robotics, patrolling is often viewed as a form of terrain *coverage* and has been studied in [20,24,29].

Idle time (also called *idleness*) is the accepted measure of algorithmic efficiency of patrolling and it is related to the frequency with which the points of the environment are visited [10,16,17,24] (this last citation was also first to introduce this concept). Idleness is sometimes also viewed as average [16], worst-case [7,29], probabilistic [2] or experimentally verified [24] time elapsed since the last visit of a point [10]. In some papers the terms *blanket time* [29] or *refresh time* [27] were used instead.

A survey including diverse approaches to patrolling based on idleness criteria can be found in [28]. In [4–6] patrolling is studied as a game between patrollers and the intruder while some papers consider patrolling based on swarm or ant-based algorithms [18,25,29]. Capabilities also vary and robots may be memoryless, decentralized [25] with no explicit communication permitted either with other robots or the central station, and with local sensing [18]. In ant-like algorithms the graph nodes may be marked [29].

Theoretical approaches to patrolling in graph-based domains can be found in [10]: the two basic methods are (1) *cyclic strategies*, where a single cycle spanning the entire graph is constructed and the robots are assigned to consecutively traverse this cycle in the same direction, and (2) *partition-based strategies*, where the region is split into a number of either disjoint or overlapping portions to be patrolled by subsets of robots assigned to these regions. The environment and the time considered in the models studied are usually discrete in an underlying graph environment. When the environment is geometric, the *skeletonization* technique may be applied, with the terrain first partitioned into cells, and then graph-theoretic methods are used. Cyclic strategies usually rely either on TSP (Travelling Salesman Problem)-related solutions or spanning tree-based approaches. For example, spanning tree coverage, a technique first introduced in [19], was later extended and used in [1,16,20]. This technique is a version of the skeletonization approach where the two-dimensional grid approximating the terrain is constructed and a Hamiltonian path present in the grid is used for patrolling. In [27], polynomial-time patrolling solutions for lines and trees are proposed, where the goal is to patrol only the vertices of the graphs (note in the current paper every point of the graphs, including all the vertices and edges, is supposed to be patrolled). For the case of cyclic graphs, [27] proves the NP-hardness of the problem and a constant-factor approximation is proposed.

Patrolling with robots that do not necessarily have identical speeds has been initiated in [12]. No optimal patrolling strategy involving more than three robots has yet been proposed and the general problem is difficult and still unsolved [15,21]. Optimal patrolling involving same-speed robots in mixed domains, where regions to be traversed are fragmented by components that do not need to be monitored, is studied in [11].

Distributed control in patrolling strategies is an important alternative to the centralized. In one such approach, the authors of [13] show the convergence of the dynamical system of k robots which interact by merely bouncing against each other. Another (more popular) alternative is the rotor-router, a version of a distributed model with local control at the nodes for managing the movement of robots in a graph. The first study of rotor-routers is due to [29], which also studied multiple parallel rotor-routers experimentally and made the conjecture that a system of $k > 1$ parallel walks stabilizes with a period of length at most $2|E|$ steps ($|E|$ is the number of edges). In [9] they disprove this conjecture, showing that the period of parallel rotor-router walks can in fact, be superpolynomial in the size of graph. More interestingly, they discuss the related concept of the decomposition of the set of edges into sub-cycles, which plays an important role in understanding the periodicity of a patrolling strategy. In [14] tight bounds on the cover time (the number of steps after which each node has been visited by at least one walk, regardless of the starting locations of the walks) of k parallel rotor-router walks in a graph are provided (see also [7,29] which consider the cover time of a single walk). [22] determines the precise asymptotic value of the rotor-router cover time for all values of k for degree-restricted expanders, random graphs, and constant-dimensional tori.

Approaches emphasizing experimental results on boundary and area patrolling have been considered in [2,16,17,27]. Experimental papers related to unreliable robots performing patrolling were considered in the robotics literature [16,17,20,26].

1.2 Preliminaries and Notation

Consider a geometric graph with n vertices and m edges and k mobile robots initially placed on vertices of the graph. Let $\mathcal{A}$ be a patrolling algorithm, scheduling the movement of the robots at the same constant speed. For any algorithm $\mathcal{A}$ and any graph G let $I_{\mathcal{A}}(G, k)$ denote the idle time of the algorithm $\mathcal{A}$ for k robots on this graph; namely the supremum of "the time between successive visits of the robots at point x following algorithm $\mathcal{A}$", where the supremum is taken over all the points x of all edges of the graph G. Finally, we define

$$I(G,k) := \inf_{\mathcal{A}} I_{\mathcal{A}}(G,k), \tag{1}$$

where the infimum is over all possible patrolling algorithms $\mathcal{A}$ for G.

1.3   Outline and Results of the Paper

There is an *off-line* schedule placing the k robots at specific initial positions on a geometric tree T such that if the robots move perpetually at speed 1 it will achieve the optimal idle time $\frac{2|T|}{k}$ where $|T|$ is the sum of the length of T. Our main contribution in Sect. 2 is to show that such a schedule is an optimal one, i.e. that no other schedule can achieve a smaller idle time. We extend this to the graph tree where the patrolling robots are allowed to change direction only at vertices of the tree. In Sect. 3 we consider the *on-line* setting and construct examples of trees with port numberings on the nodes such that the resulting rotor-router has competitive ratio at least 4/3. In addition, in Sect. 3.2 we perform experimental work indicating that in a random setting the rotor-router on tree graphs is nearly optimal. To the best of our knowledge, the study considered in our paper, concerning off-line and on-line strategies for patrolling a tree has not been considered in the past. Due to space limitations all missing proofs will appear in the full paper.

2   Off-Line Algorithms

This section is concerned with the idle time for patrolling trees with a given number of robots. We distinguish patrolling on two types of domains: *geometric trees*, and *graph trees*. In the former, edge lengths are real numbers and during their traversal the robots may change direction anywhere on vertices as well as in the interior of edges. In the latter, edge lengths are positive integers and during their traversal the robots may change direction only on vertices. Note that the graph tree model will prove useful in our study of experimental results in Sect. 3.2.

2.1   Patrolling of Geometric Trees

Let $|T|$ denote the sum of lengths of the edges of T. The main theorem is the following.

Theorem 1 (Idle Time for Trees). *For any tree T and any number k of robots,*

$$I(T,k) = \frac{2|T|}{k}. \tag{2}$$

This idle time is attained when k robots traverse the tree at their maximum speed along an Eulerian cycle, while at the same time ensuring that during the traversal consecutive robots remain equidistant on this cycle.

Before proving the theorem we will prove several lemmas that will lead to the main result. As noted above, we assume throughout the discussion of the proof below that during their traversal the robots may change direction anywhere on vertices as well as in the interior of edges. Let L denote the line segment. The first lemma is well known (see [12]).

Lemma 1 (Idle Time for Lines). *For k robots on a line L, $I(L,k) = \frac{2|L|}{k}$, where $|L|$ is the length of the line L.* □

First we prove the upper bound for trees in the following lemma.

Lemma 2 (Upper Bound for Trees). *For any tree T and any number k of robots, $I(T,k) \leq \frac{2|T|}{k}$.*

Proof (Lemma 2). The upper bound $I(T,k) \leq \frac{2|T|}{k}$ is obvious since we can arrange the robots so that they traverse an Eulerian tour of the tree (staying equidistant) which has length $2|T|$. In order to make the Eulerian tour of the tree, every edge is replaced by two anti-parallel edges (of total length $2|T|$). □

To prove the lower bound, first we define the following useful concept.

Definition 1. *The cumulative idle time on a tree T is defined as $F_T(k) := kI(T,k)$, where $I(T,k)$ is the optimal idle time for k robots on the tree T.*

The main idea for the proof of the lower bound $I(T,k) \geq \frac{2|T|}{k}$ is based on proving two properties, namely:

1. Monotonicity of the *cumulative idle time* with respect to doubling the number of robots (see Inequality (3) and Lemma 3), and
2. Validity of the lower bound on caterpillar trees for k sufficiently large (see Lemma 5).

A combination of these two ideas will lead to the proof of the actual result. First we consider the monotonicity of the cumulative idle time.

Lemma 3 (Monotonicity of the Cumulative Idle Time). *For any number of robots k,*

$$F_T(2k) \leq F_T(k). \tag{3}$$

Next we define a generalization of the concept of caterpillar that will be useful for the proof.

Definition 2. *A d-caterpillar tree is a tree in which all the vertices are within distance d of a central path of the tree, where $d \geq 1$.*

Thus, the well-known concept of caterpillar is identical to 1-caterpillar. The following lemma provides a useful property that will be useful for the proof of the main theorem.

Lemma 4. *If T is a d-caterpillar with $d \geq 2$ then there is a $(d-1)$-caterpillar T' which is subtree of T and such that all the vertices of T are within distance 1 of a node of T'.*

Proof (Lemma 4). The proof is simple. The subtree T' is obtained from T by removing all its leaves. The required property for T' follows easily.   □

Lemma 5 (A Lower Bound for Caterpillar Trees). *For any caterpillar tree T, and for any real number $\epsilon > 0$ there is a sufficiently large integer k_0 such that $I(T, k) \geq \frac{2|T|}{k} - \frac{2\epsilon}{k}$, for all $k \geq k_0$.*

Now we are ready to prove the lower bound for caterpillars. We prove the following.

Lemma 6 (Idle Time for Caterpillar Trees). *For any caterpillar tree T and any number k of robots, $I(T, k) = \frac{2|T|}{k}$.*

Proof (Lemma 6). The upper bound follows from Lemma 1. We now concentrate on the lower bound. Indeed, by Lemma 5 the lower bound $I(T, k) \geq \frac{2|T|}{k} - \frac{2\epsilon}{k}$, is valid for any $k \geq k_0$, where ϵ, k_0 are selected as specified in Lemma 5. So assume that $k \leq k_0$. Choose an integer i sufficiently large such that $k \leq k_0 \leq 2^i k$. Now observe that the following inequalities are valid

$$
\begin{aligned}
I(T, k) &= \frac{F_T(k)}{k} \text{ (by definition)} \\
&\geq \frac{F_T(2^i k)}{k} \text{ (by Lemma 3)} \\
&= \frac{F_T(2^i k)}{2^i k} \cdot \frac{2^i k}{k} \\
&= I(T, 2^i k) \cdot \frac{2^i k}{k} \text{ (by definition)} \\
&\geq \left(\frac{2|T|}{2^i k} - \frac{2\epsilon}{2^i k} \right) \cdot \frac{2^i k}{k} \text{ (by Lemma 5)} \\
&= \frac{2|T|}{k} - \frac{2\epsilon}{k}.
\end{aligned}
$$

The last inequality is valid for any integer k and any real number $\epsilon > 0$. By letting $\epsilon \to 0$ the proof of the lemma is complete.   □

We are now in a position to prove the main theorem which was given at the beginning of the paper.

Proof (Theorem 1). Without loss of generality we may assume that the tree is a d-caterpillar, for some $d \geq 2$ (in fact, every tree is a d-caterpillar, for some $d \geq 2$, provided d is sufficiently large). Now the proof of Identity (2) proceeds by induction on d. Recall that Lemma 6 is precisely the base case $d = 1$. Suppose the identity in the theorem is valid for $d - 1$. By Lemma 4, the subtree T' obtained from T by removing all its leaves is a $(d-1)$-caterpillar. Clearly, Identity (2) is valid for $|T'|$, namely $I(T',k) = \frac{2|T'|}{k}$. Therefore by repeating the proof of Lemma 5 we can show that for any real number $\epsilon > 0$ there is a sufficiently large integer k_0 such that $I(T,k) \geq \frac{2|T|}{k} - \frac{2\epsilon}{k}$, for all $k \geq k_0$. In turn, using this last statement we repeat the proof of Lemma 6 to prove the desired identity. This completes the proof of Theorem 1. □

2.2 Patrolling of Graph Trees

Unlike geometric trees where a robot during patrolling may change direction at any location in the graph be that an interior point on an edge or a vertex, in graph trees a robot may change direction only on vertices of the tree. The corresponding idle time on such a graph tree T for k robots is denoted by $I'(T,k)$.

Next we provide a patrolling algorithm for the case when all the edges have integer lengths (not necessarily the same). Let $e_1, e_2, \ldots, e_{2(n-1)}$ be the sequence of edges in the order they occur in a given preorder traversal. Define a partition from a sequence of integers as follows.

1. Let $\sigma : r_0 = 0 < r_1 < \cdots < r_k = 2(n-1)$ be a sequence of integers and define sets of edges as follows: $E_i^\sigma := \{e_{r_i+1}, e_{r_i+2}, \ldots, e_{r_{i+1}}\}$, where $i + 1 < k$; (Thus, each E_i^σ is a sequence of consecutive edges in the preorder traversal;)
2. For each i, let $|E_i^\sigma| := \sum_{e \in E_i^\sigma} |e|$;
3. Define $\Delta^\sigma := \max_{i \neq j} ||E_i^\sigma| - |E_j^\sigma||$.
4. Now select a sequence $\sigma_0 : r_0 = 0 < r_1 < \cdots < r_k = 2(n-1)$ which provides the most balanced partition of the preorder traversal in the sense that it attains

$$\Delta := \min_\sigma \Delta^\sigma = \min_\sigma \max_{i \neq j} ||E_i^\sigma| - |E_j^\sigma||. \quad (4)$$

(Note that there could be more than one such sequence.) From now on when writing E_i without a superscript we will be referring to $E_i^{\sigma_0}$, where σ_0 was defined in Item 4 above.

We now define a patrolling strategy that we will analyze in detail in the sequel.

Definition 3 (Eulerian Strategy $\mathcal{ES}$). *For $i = 1, 2, \ldots, k$ the i-th robot is initially placed at the first vertex of the sequence of edges determined by the set of edges E_i. The robots move forever with speed 1.*

Theorem 2. *Consider a graph tree T with n nodes and $n-1$ edges such that all the edges have integer lengths. For any k robots:*

1. *A lower bound on any patrolling strategy is $\left\lceil \frac{2|T|}{k} \right\rceil$.*
2. *The idle time of the Eulerian patrolling strategy $\mathcal{ES}$ on the tree T satisfies $I'_{\mathcal{ES}}(T,k) \leq \left\lfloor \frac{2|T|}{k} \right\rfloor + \Delta$.*
3. *If $\Delta = 0$ then $I'_{\mathcal{ES}}(T,k) = \left\lfloor \frac{2|T|}{k} \right\rfloor$.*

When T is a line graph and $k = 2$ then the two robots can be placed to start at the endpoints of the line. Therefore in this case $\Delta = 0$ and regular patrolling provides an optimal algorithm even for arbitrary edge integer lengths. We note that in the case where all the edges have integer lengths (not necessarily the same) the robots may not be able to attain the optimal idle time $I(T, k) = \frac{2|T|}{k}$ (for geometric trees) if they all start on vertices of the tree. For example, consider three robots on a line T with three vertices and two edges one edge of length 1 and the other of length $n - 2$. For the geometric line we have that $I(T, 3) = \frac{2(n-1)}{3}$. However it is easy to see that for the line graph $I'(T, 3) = n - 2$.

3   On-Line Algorithms with Rotor-Routers

All patrolling strategies proposed in Sect. 2 are *centralized algorithms* in that the robots receive instructions from a central controller. We now describe a distributed mechanism, so-called *rotor-router*, which has been extensively studied in the literature as a *deterministic* alternative to the "random walk". Besides being distributed, the rotor-router is also an *on-line* algorithm (i.e., the environment to be patrolled is unknown), which makes it a practical tool for patrolling an unknown environment as well.

The basic idea of rotor-router is to set *locally* shared memories at the nodes of the graph. Subsequently, the robots will be updating these shared memories as they visit the vertices of the graph. For example, the rotor-router algorithm described in [29] works as follows. Let u be a vertex of the graph. Denote by $d(u)$ degree of u. Label the edges adjacent to u with numbers $1, \ldots, d(u)$ (called *ports pointers* at u). At each vertex u there is a pointer (called *exit port* at u), indicating the next (adjacent) edge to be traversed by a robot. Further, a departing robot also updates (increments) exit port.

Clearly, independently from the *initial configuration*, which is defined by initial placement of the robots, port pointers and initial exit ports at the nodes, after some transient time steps, the system reaches a *stable state*, in which the placement of the robots within the graph and the state of the exit ports repeats periodically (this is called *periodic behavior* of rotor-router). Interestingly, it has been proven (see [29]) that for a single robot such *periodicity* is only $2m$, where m is the number of edges.

3.1   Lower Bounds

For the rest of the paper we assume all edge weights are equal to 1. We know that the optimal algorithm for patrolling a graph tree of n nodes satisfies $I'(T, k) = \left\lceil \frac{2(n-1)}{k} \right\rceil$. The main problem we are interested in is whether or not the parallel rotor-routers algorithm for k robots is optimal on a tree graph with n nodes? In this subsection we prove a lower bound on the asymptotic ratio of the rotor-router on a graph tree having the form of star with three branches. The precise theorem is as follows.

Fig. 1. Proving a 4/3 lower bound for patrolling the star graph by two robots r, r'.

Theorem 3. *There is a star graph with $n+1$ vertices and edges of weight 1 and an assignment of ports pointers and exit ports such that the competitive ratio of the rotor-router algorithm for two robots is at least $\frac{4}{3}$.*

Proof. Consider the star graph depicted in Fig. 1. It has $n+1$ vertices such that one vertex is at the centre and each of its three branches has $\frac{n}{3}$ vertices. Let the three leaves of the star be named A, B, C.

The ports pointers and exit ports on the vertices of the star are initially directed as follows: (1) the ports pointers at the central node are numbers $1, 2, 3$ and oriented towards the leaves A, B, C, respectively. Further, the initial exit port at the center is 3, followed by 1 and then by 2. (2) The ports pointers and exit ports on all the vertices from the leaf A (resp. B) to the center are oriented towards the center, while the ports pointers and exit ports on all the vertices from the leaf C are oriented away from the center.

First of all observe that an optimal off-line schedule of the star graph for two robots is $\frac{2(n+1)}{2} = n+1$ as given by Theorem 1. We now propose the initialization of a rotor-router schedule and analyze its idle time.

Two robots r, r' start synchronously at the following two vertices of the graph. Robot r starts at the vertex adjacent to the leaf A while robot r' at the leaf B. The robots move at the same speed. The first robot to reach the center is r which follows port 3 towards leaf C. When robot r' reaches the center a single time unit later it will be directed towards leaf A. In the meantime robot r' will follow port 1 at the center and head towards leaf A. Observe now that when robot r' is at A robot r is a vertex away from the leaf at C. Thus the two robots are in a periodic repetition of the schedules after time exactly $\frac{2n}{3}$. It is easy to see that in the next periodic iteration of the rotor-router, robot r will head towards leaf B while robot r' towards leaf A. It follows that the idle time is exactly $\frac{4n}{3}$. This gives rise to the $\frac{4}{3}$ competitive ratio of the rotor-router and completes the proof of the theorem.   □

3.2   Experimental Results

In this section we provide experimental results based on rotor-router model. We conducted experiments to compute *idle time* for different random trees,

star graphs, variable number of robots and initial configurations. For this purpose
we have implemented the rotor-router simulator in Java. To run experiments the
simulator applied an algorithm (developed independently by David Aldous [3]
and Andrei Broder [8]) to generate *uniform random trees*. Moreover, it uses a
random number generator to generate *uniform random initial configurations*.

Random Trees. For a given tree T and a set of k robots, in addition to the
number of nodes n and robots k that affect the performance of rotor-router there
are also some *non-quantitative factors* such as: the ratio of m (number of edges)
and k, initial configuration of the system, and tree structures, that may also
affect the system's performance. To study the affect of these factors we have run
experiments for random trees on the rotor-router simulator.

In order to observe how the ratio of m and k may affect rotor-router performance we considered settings for $k = 1, \cdots, n$ robots in all experiments. Then,
we have run experiments for 100 distinctive initial configurations for each set
of $k = 1, \cdots, n$ robots on 1 random tree T (i.e., $5,000$ experiments in total)
to see how initial configurations may affect rotor-router performance. The relevant plot for these experiments is illustrated in Fig. 2. Afterwards, to study
the affect of tree structure we ran experiments for 50 different random trees,
and 100 distinctive initial configurations for each set of $k = 1, 2, \cdots, 50$ robots
on each tree (i.e., $250,000$ experiments in total). The respective plot for these
experiments is displayed in Fig. 3. In all displayed diagrams (Figs. 2 and 3), the
red, green, and blue plots represent the maximum, minimum, and average times
respectively. The black vertical lines demonstrates the %95 *confidence intervals*
for the average time.

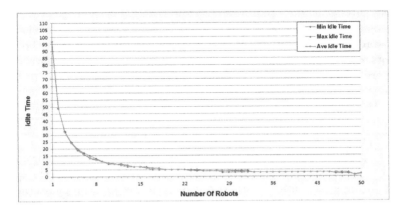

Fig. 2. Idle Time of rotor-router algorithm for 1 random tree with 50 nodes, and 100
distinctive initial configurations for each set of $k = 1, 2, \cdots, 50$ robots, drawn against
the number of participating robots in each experiment. (Color figure online)

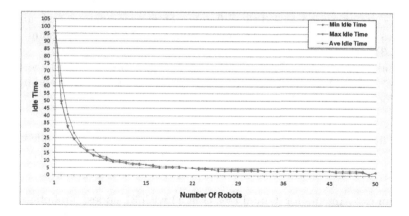

Fig. 3. Idle Time of rotor-router algorithm for 50 random trees with 50 nodes, and 100 distinctive initial configurations for each set of $k = 1, 2, \cdots, 50$ robots on each tree, drawn against the number of participating robots in each experiment. (Color figure online)

Idle Time. Idle time is the number of time steps that an edge remains unvisited by any robots. The idle time of a graph is the maximum idle time over all it's edges. To compute the idle time of tree T, we run rotor-router until the system stabilizes, when it will follow a periodic behavior afterward. Then, we run rotor-router for two more periodic cycles while keeping track of visited edges. Thereafter, we compute the idle time of each edge, and then take the maximum one as the idle time of the tree.

Figures 2 and 3 display the idle time of rotor-router algorithm for 100 distinctive initial configurations for each set of $k = 1, 2, \cdots, 50$ robots running over 1 and 50 random trees (with 50 nodes) respectively. According to these diagrams, in most cases the idle time is almost $2m/k(m = n - 1)$, which is optimal. However, there are a few cases (e.g. for $k = 2, 3$ in Fig. 3 where the points are highlighted on the plots) where the idle time is slightly more than $2m/k$ depending on the initial configuration and structure of the tree (as we also discussed for the star tree in Sect. 3.1).

According to [9], after stabilization the system is decomposed into some disjoint sub-cycles. Apparently, the robots are also divided up to some subsets traversing each sub-cycle independently, while the number of robots in each sub-cycle is proportional to the number of edges in that sub-cycle. Consequently, the idle time remains almost constant in *most cases* regardless of initial configurations and structure of the tree. In Figs. 2 and 3, locating the red (maximum), blue (minimum) and green (average) plots closely on each other confirms that idle time is independent of initial configurations and tree structure in most cases. However, apparently for some classes of trees (e.g. star graph), and number of robots (e.g. $k = 2, 3$) the initial configuration may lead the system to some sub-cycle decomposition where the number of robots and edges in each sub-cycle are not balanced up, and consequently the idle time would not be optimal. According to our results only for $k = 2, 3$ the difference between maximum and minimum idle times is noticeable, where the maximum $I(T, k)$ is $\frac{4}{3}$ of minimum $I(T, k)$ (see Fig. 3).

It is also worthy to note that although adding more robots to the system improves (reduces) the idle time, at some point where $k > m/2$ adding more robots does not change the idle time significantly.

Star Graph. In order to demonstrate the competitive ratio of the idle time we have run experiments for the star graphs named "Tripod" and "Clover" for the following settings:

1. We ran experiments for Tripod tree (Fig. 1) with 31 nodes, 2 robots, and the same initial configuration as the one in the proof of Theorem 3. We obtained the idle time of 38, which is almost $\frac{4}{3}(2m/k)$, for this setting.
2. We ran experiments for Tripod tree with 31 nodes, and 2 robots in the starting positions as in the proof of Theorem 3, but for 100 distinctive random ports pointers and exit ports. In total 100 experiments were ran and maximum, minimum and average idle times of 38, 30, and 32 were obtained respectively.
3. We ran experiments for Tripod tree with 31 nodes, $k = 2, 3, \ldots, 30$ robots, and 100 distinctive random initial configurations, i.e., $3,000$ experiments in total. We observed that the idle time was almost optimal for all cases except for $k = 2$ where the maximum, minimum and average idle time were 39, 29 and 32 respectively over 100 initial configurations.
4. First we ran experiments for Tripod tree with 106 nodes, $2 \le k \le 105$ robots, and 100 distinctive initial configurations, i.e., $10,500$ experiments. Then we replaced the tree branches of Tripod tree by random sub-trees and named the new tree "Clover". We ran experiments for Clover with 106 nodes, $k = 2, 3, \ldots, 105$ robots, and 100 distinctive initial configurations, i.e., $10,500$ experiments. Due to lack of space the results of these two types of star graphs will appear in the full paper.

In our experiments for Tripod and Clover, the maximum and minimum idle times were noticeably different for $k = 2$ as we expected. For the Tripod tree the minimum and maximum idle times are 105 (104 for Clover) and 139 (138 for crawler) receptively. This confirms the idea that for any graph similar to star graphs, which has one node in the center and three branches with length $\frac{n}{3}$ connected to it, the idle time may vary based on initial configuration. However, as our experiments shows the idle time is $\frac{4}{3}(2m/k)$ in the worse case.

4   Conclusion

Although patrolling by a team of mobile robots with the same speeds and zero visibility may look straightforward, no optimal patrolling algorithm for general graphs has been proved yet. Therefore, in order to get closer to a solution for this problem, we took one step further and studied patrolling trees by a team of k

mobile robots. We provided optimal algorithms in the off-line case and analyzed the competitive ratio of on-line patrolling algorithms for trees. In addition, we implemented a rotor-router simulator in Java and performed experiments on the competitive ratio for randomly generated trees. Some interesting open problems may be to study the off-line and on-line patrolling strategies for general graphs.

Acknowledgements. Many thanks to Leszek Gasieniec for useful conversations in the early stages of the research.

References

1. Agmon, N., Hazon, N., Kaminka, G.A.: The giving tree: constructing trees for efficient offline and online multi-robot coverage. Ann. Math. Artif. Intell. **52**(2–4), 143–168 (2008)
2. Agmon, N., Kraus, S., Kaminka, G.A.: Multi-robot perimeter patrol in adversarial settings. In: ICRA, pp. 2339–2345 (2008)
3. Aldous, D.J.: The random walk construction of uniform spanning trees and uniform labelled trees. SIAM J. Discrete Math. **3**(4), 450–465 (1990)
4. Alpern, S., Morton, A., Papadaki, K.: Optimizing randomized patrols. Operational Research Group, London School of Economics and Political Science (2009)
5. Alpern, S., Morton, A., Papadaki, K.: Patrolling games. Oper. Res. **59**(5), 1246–1257 (2011)
6. Amigoni, F., Basilico, N., Gatti, N., Saporiti, A., Troiani, S.: Moving game theoretical patrolling strategies from theory to practice: an USARSim simulation. In: ICRA, pp. 426–431 (2010)
7. Bampas, E., Gąsieniec, L., Hanusse, N., Ilcinkas, D., Klasing, R., Kosowski, A.: Euler tour lock-in problem in the rotor-router model. In: Keidar, I. (ed.) DISC 2009. LNCS, vol. 5805, pp. 423–435. Springer, Heidelberg (2009). doi:10.1007/978-3-642-04355-0_44
8. Broder, A.: Generating random spanning trees. In: 30th Annual Symposium on Foundations of Computer Science, pp. 442–447 (1989)
9. Chalopin, J., Das, S., Gawrychowski, P., Kosowski, A., Labourel, A., Uznanski, P.: Lock-in problem for parallel rotor-router walks. CoRR abs/1407.3200 (2014)
10. Chevaleyre, Y.: Theoretical analysis of the multi-agent patrolling problem. In: IAT, pp. 302–308 (2004)
11. Collins, A., Czyzowicz, J., Gasieniec, L., Kosowski, A., Kranakis, E., Krizanc, D., Martin, R., Morales Ponce, O.: Optimal patrolling of fragmented boundaries. In: Proceedings of SPAA (2013)
12. Czyzowicz, J., Gąsieniec, L., Kosowski, A., Kranakis, E.: Boundary patrolling by mobile agents with distinct maximal speeds. In: Demetrescu, C., Halldórsson, M.M. (eds.) ESA 2011. LNCS, vol. 6942, pp. 701–712. Springer, Heidelberg (2011). doi:10.1007/978-3-642-23719-5_59
13. Czyzowicz, J., Georgiou, K., Kranakis, E., MacQuarrie, F., Pajak, D.: Fence patrolling with two-speed robots. In: Proceedings of ICORES 2016, 5th International Conference on Operations Research and Enterprise Systems, Rome, Italy, 23–25 February 2016 (2016)
14. Dereniowski, D., Kosowski, A., Pajak, D., Uznanski, P.: Bounds on the cover time of parallel rotor walks. In: STACS 2014, Lyon, France, 5–8 March 2014, pp. 263–275 (2014)

15. Dumitrescu, A., Ghosh, A., Tóth, C.D.: On fence patrolling by mobile agents. Electr. J. Comb. **21**(3), P3.4 (2014)
16. Elmaliach, Y., Agmon, N., Kaminka, G.A.: Multi-robot area patrol under frequency constraints. Ann. Math. Artif. Intell. **57**(3–4), 293–320 (2009)
17. Elmaliach, Y., Shiloni, A., Kaminka, G.A.: A realistic model of frequency-based multi-robot polyline patrolling. In: AAMAS, vol. 1, pp. 63–70 (2008)
18. Elor, Y., Bruckstein, A.M.: Autonomous multi-agent cycle based patrolling. In: Dorigo, M., et al. (eds.) ANTS 2010. LNCS, vol. 6234, pp. 119–130. Springer, Heidelberg (2010). doi:10.1007/978-3-642-15461-4_11
19. Gabriely, Y., Rimon, E.: Spanning-tree based coverage of continuous areas by a mobile robot. In: ICRA, pp. 1927–1933 (2001)
20. Hazon, N., Kaminka, G.A.: On redundancy, efficiency, and robustness in coverage for multiple robots. Rob. Auton. Syst. **56**, 1102–1114 (2008)
21. Kawamura, A., Kobayashi, Y.: Fence patrolling by mobile agents with distinct speeds. In: Chao, K.-M., Hsu, T., Lee, D.-T. (eds.) ISAAC 2012. LNCS, vol. 7676, pp. 598–608. Springer, Heidelberg (2012). doi:10.1007/978-3-642-35261-4_62
22. Kosowski, A., Pająk, D.: Does adding more agents make a difference? A case study of cover time for the rotor-router. In: Esparza, J., Fraigniaud, P., Husfeldt, T., Koutsoupias, E. (eds.) ICALP 2014. LNCS, vol. 8573, pp. 544–555. Springer, Heidelberg (2014). doi:10.1007/978-3-662-43951-7_46
23. Kranakis, E., Krizanc, D.: Optimization problems in infrastructure security. In: Garcia-Alfaro, J., Kranakis, E., Bonfante, G. (eds.) FPS 2015. LNCS, vol. 9482, pp. 3–13. Springer, Heidelberg (2016). doi:10.1007/978-3-319-30303-1_1
24. Machado, A., Ramalho, G., Zucker, J.-D., Drogoul, A.: Multi-agent patrolling: an empirical analysis of alternative architectures. In: Simão Sichman, J., Bousquet, F., Davidsson, P. (eds.) MABS 2002. LNCS (LNAI), vol. 2581, pp. 155–170. Springer, Heidelberg (2003). doi:10.1007/3-540-36483-8_11
25. Marino, A., Parker, L.E., Antonelli, G., Caccavale, F.: Behavioral control for multi-robot perimeter patrol: a finite state automata approach. In: ICRA, pp. 831–836 (2009)
26. Marino, A., Parker, L.E., Antonelli, G., Caccavale, F., Chiaverini, S.: A fault-tolerant modular control approach to multi-robot perimeter patrol. In: Robotics and Biomimetics (ROBIO), pp. 735–740 (2009)
27. Pasqualetti, F., Franchi, A., Bullo, F.: On optimal cooperative patrolling. In: CDC, pp. 7153–7158 (2010)
28. Portugal, D., Rocha, R.: A survey on multi-robot patrolling algorithms. In: Camarinha-Matos, L.M. (ed.) DoCEIS 2011. IAICT, vol. 349, pp. 139–146. Springer, Heidelberg (2011). doi:10.1007/978-3-642-19170-1_15
29. Yanovski, V., Wagner, I.A., Bruckstein, A.M.: A distributed ant algorithm for efficiently patrolling a network. Algorithmica **37**(3), 165–186 (2003)

Towards Side-Channel Secure Firmware Updates
A Minimalist Anomaly Detection Approach

Oscar M. Guillen[1(✉)], Fabrizio De Santis[1], Ralf Brederlow[3], and Georg Sigl[1,2]

[1] Technische Universität München EISEC, Munich, Germany
{oscar.guillen,desantis,sigl}@tum.de
[2] Fraunhofer Institute AISEC, Munich, Germany
georg.sigl@aisec.fraunhofer.de
[3] Texas Instruments Deutschland, Freising, Germany
r-brederlow@ti.com

Abstract. Side-channel attacks represent a serious threat to the security of encrypted firmware updates: if the secret key is leaked, then the firmware is exposed and can be replaced by malicious code or be stolen. In this work, we show how simple anomaly detection measures can effectively *increase* the security of encrypted firmware updates at *minimum* cost. Our method is based on the simple observation that firmware payloads have a specific structure (machine code), which can be easily verified at runtime in order to react to side-channel attacks. This enables performing proactive measures to limit the number of measurements that can be taken when a side-channel attack is detected. We tested the viability of our approach through simulations and verified its effectiveness in practice on a TI MSP430 microcontroller using a software implementation of AES. Our approach represents a step forward towards increasing the security of firmware updates against side-channel attacks: it effectively *increases* the security of firmware updates, has only negligible overhead in terms of code size and runtime, requires no modification to the underlying cryptographic implementations, and can be used in conjunction with countermeasures such as masking and re-keying to further enhance the side-channel resistance of a device.

Keywords: Side-channel analysis · Anomaly detection · Embedded devices · Secure firmware updates · Decryption

1 Introduction

In the world of Internet-of-Things (IoT), where millions of interconnected smart devices collect and exchange potentially sensitive data, firmware update mechanisms are particularly important to prevent massive data leaks, when new firmware vulnerabilities are found or disclosed in the public community [21]. Encrypted firmware update mechanisms provide a way to fix critical vulnerabilities remotely, i.e. once embedded systems are already deployed in the field, without disclosing the firmware source code. However, while offering protection against data leaks, firmware exposure, and malicious firmware modification,

© Springer International Publishing AG 2017
F. Cuppens et al. (Eds.): FPS 2016, LNCS 10128, pp. 345–360, 2017.
DOI: 10.1007/978-3-319-51966-1_23

encrypted firmware update mechanisms may also introduce new attack vectors, such as side-channel attacks, when *unprotected* cryptographic implementations are used [5,11,20]. Although side-channel attacks have been known for more than two decades, many commercial off-the-shelf embedded devices, such as low-cost microcontrollers (MCUs), rarely include side-channel attack counter-measures, mainly due to economical reasons and performance costs [18,19]. In fact, applying side-channel countermeasures to cryptographic implementations typically translates into a significant increase in terms of code size, runtime and power consumption. These are all undesired characteristics for IoT end-node devices, such as sensors and actuators, which are typically memory constrained and battery operated devices that must be sold at low prices to meet the market requirements. Also, most wide-spread side-channel countermeasures, like mask-ing schemes, require large amount of randomness to be effective [8,10,14,26], but low-cost embedded devices are typically not equipped with true random number generators (TRNGs). Furthermore, the correct implementation of side-channel countermeasures has been proven to be complicated in many situations [2,3], and even when correctly implemented, the resistance provided by single coun-termeasures may still be futile against educated attackers [16,25]. Therefore, it is not uncommon to require the implementation of multiple countermeasures to increase the side-channel resistance of embedded devices. These and other factors have motivated researchers to continue the quest for alternative counter-measures [18].

In this work, we propose the use of anomaly detection to recognize when side-channel attacks are taking place during firmware updates in order to stop them before successful attack completion. This strategy can be combined with other side-channel countermeasures, e.g.:

- Updating the key while the firmware update is taking place in order to thwart side-channel attacks when the attacker passively collects measurements during a valid firmware update.
- Anomaly detection to recognize when side-channel attacks are taking place if the attacker actively generates the inputs to the decryption algorithm instead of using legitimate data, i.e. when not enough leakage can occur during a valid firmware update procedure due to the key being updated.
- Secure counters (e.g. similar to wrong PIN counters found in EMV cards) to prevent an attacker from interrupting the firmware update process.

In the following we will focus on the anomaly detection part, which is our new contribution. Anomaly detection is achieved by creating a model of the expected firmware characteristics (machine code) and embedding it into the device. Then, during firmware decryption, independent of the block cipher mode used, the content of the plaintext is immediately inspected after each ciphertext block is decrypted, to verify whether or not it contains valid instruction encodings and the memory addresses lie within valid ranges. If valid instruction encodings are not found or the address locations do not match the standard memory layout ranges, an alarm is raised and appropriate countermeasures can be applied, i.e. update or erase a secret-key. Under the assumption that not enough leakage can occur during a valid firmware update procedure, i.e. the key is refreshed during the update itself, the attacker will provide random inputs to the decryption algorithm instead of using legitimate data, i.e. firmware images. In this case, the resulting machine code will deviate from the expected values after a decryption and hence can be detected with high confidence using anomaly detection measures. Once an attack has been identified, a reaction may be initiated to thwart the successful completion of the attack, e.g. re-keying. Note that limiting the amount of information that can be leaked under the same key during side-channel attacks is a commonly used technique, which has been proven effective in many leakage-resilient constructions [4,17,23]. Our technique is a lightweight and practical way to effectively *enhance* the side-channel resistance of embedded systems at minimum cost. While our anomaly detection technique has the limitation that analysis must be performed after decrypting at least one ciphertext block, this provides good-enough protection against side-channel analysis in practice, as we show with experimental results in Sect. 5.

Contribution. We present a general architecture to detect and react to side-channel attacks based on anomaly detection measures. We introduce a minimal model to recognize valid firmware sequences which can be implemented in software with negligible overhead. This allows retrofitting general purpose MCUs to increase their side-channel security. Our approach is agnostic to the block-cipher used, and thus, does not require modifications to existing implementations, while also being orthogonal to available countermeasures. Furthermore, it can be applied to products already deployed in the field through a firmware update. Finally, we present implementation results, taking a Texas Instrument MSP430FR5969 MCU as target of evaluation, as well as side-channel attacks on simulated and real measurements. We show that embedding anomaly detection measures on MSP430FR5969 MCU costs only 340 bytes of code (which could be stored in ROM) and provide an effective first line of defense against side-channel attacks at almost no costs. To the best of our knowledge, this is the first work that exploits online anomaly detection measures to protect resource-constrained embedded devices against side-channel attacks, by analyzing the properties of the input data.

Organization. This work is structured as follows: Sect. 2 explains the background concepts of side-channel attacks in encrypted firmware updates. In Sect. 3, we introduce the generic architecture for our approach to anomaly detection. Section 4 discusses the implementation of this architecture on a TI MSP430 MCU. The results of side-channel analysis on the microcontroller, and their comparison with the attacks on simulated measurements, are shown in Sect. 5. Finally, we discuss possible alternatives to our approach for the future work in Sect. 6 before concluding with Sect. 7.

2   Side-Channel Analysis of Secure Firmware Updates

Before an encrypted firmware image can be written into an MCU, it must be first decrypted, e.g. using an n-bit block cipher defined by the pair $(\mathtt{Enc}, \mathtt{Dec})$:

$$\mathtt{Enc}/\mathtt{Dec} : \{0, 1\}^n \times \{0, 1\}^\kappa \to \{0, 1\}^n$$

The device receives the encrypted firmware image $\mathtt{Enc}(\mathsf{FW})$ as a sequence of ciphertexts $(c_1, c_2, \ldots, c_q) = (\mathtt{Enc}(p_1), \mathtt{Enc}(p_2), \ldots, \mathtt{Enc}(p_q))$ obtained by encrypting n-bit blocks of the firmware image using a secret key $k \xleftarrow{\$} \{0, 1\}^\kappa$. The key k is distributed out-of-band in a trusted environment to all parties. Performing decryption on the ciphertexts to retrieve the original firmware image generates side-channel leakage information. This is defined as $\mathtt{Dec}(k, c_i) \rightsquigarrow \ell_i = L(f(s, c_i))$, where L is a leakage function, f is an intermediate function of the decryption algorithm, and s is a small part of the cryptographic key, known as a sub-key. An attacker which can observe the leakage information, e.g. through the power consumption of a cryptographic device for a number of queries q, and store it as a vector $\boldsymbol{l} = (\ell_1, \ell_2, \ldots, \ell_q)$, can then perform a Differential Power Analysis (DPA) attack offline. The attack works as follows: for each input c_i, the attacker will generate all possible sub-key candidates $\{\tilde{s}_j\}$, and compute the intermediate values $f(\tilde{s}_j, c_i)$. The attacker makes use of a power consumption model M to generate hypothetical leakage values $M(f(\tilde{s}_j, c_i))$, which are later compared to the actual measurements through the use of a statistical distinguisher such as Pearson's correlation coefficient.

For anomaly detection, we define $\mathcal{P}$ as the set of all *valid* plaintexts, i.e. plaintexts which contain valid instructions and memory offsets. To conduct a successful attack, the attacker must collect enough side-channel leakage information $\boldsymbol{l}$, for a large enough q. The value q depends on the implementation of the underlying cryptographic primitive (e.g. hardware/software) and the amount of noise in the measurements. Hence, the maximum number of decryptions that an attacker could observe under the same key is determined by the size of valid firmware images and the number of different firmware updates. However, please note that q can be arbitrarily limited by refreshing the secret key during firmware updates at the cost of longer data transfers. Also note that this will also prevent the attacker from averaging the measurements to remove the noise. At this point, the attacker can only try collecting leakage information, either by generating random [15] or adaptively-chosen ciphertexts [27] $\{\tilde{c}_i\}$ to be decrypted, i.e. $\{\tilde{p}_i = \mathtt{Dec}(k, \tilde{c}_i)\}$. Hence, the resulting plaintexts $\{\tilde{p}_i\}$ will have a high probability of being invalid, that is, $\tilde{p}_i \notin \mathcal{P}$, and the attack of being detected. This scenario is particularly relevant for small, ultra-low power MCUs, which are widely seen in IoT sensor applications, where the number of updates performed is kept to a minimum in order to reduce energy consumption.

3   Architecture for Anomaly Detection

Anomaly detection is the problem of recognizing data instances that differ from an expected behavior [7]. In the context of security, anomaly detection is used

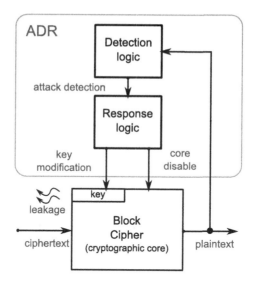

Fig. 1. Block diagram of the Anomaly Detection and Response (ADR) module and its connection to a cryptographic core.

to identify evidence of attack attempts, under the assumption that anomalies are introduced when malicious activity is taking place [9].

Figure 1 shows the proposed Anomaly Detection and Response (ADR) module and its connection to a cryptographic core. The ADR is composed of two sub-blocks: detection logic and response logic. The former is responsible for detecting if an attack is taking place, the latter is used to generate a response to the attack. Plaintext data is fed into the input of the ADR for data collection, regardless of whether decryption or encryption routines are performed by the cryptographic core. For the use-case of firmware updates, at least a block must be decrypted in order to be able to analyze the plaintext data. Within the detection logic, data characteristics from the observed plaintext will be compared against the *features* which correspond to normal behavior. An *attack-detection* signal is triggered when anomalies are found in the plaintext. The attack-detection signal is then fed into the response logic block, whose function is to react to the attack.

3.1   Detection Logic

For the scenario described in Sect. 2, an attacker will generate uniformly distributed random messages $\tilde{c}_i$, to the device. After decryption, there is a high probability that the plaintext data observed at the output $\tilde{p}_i$, will differ from the expected data. We define the alarm signal to be:

$$\text{attack-detection} = \begin{cases} 1 \ (\text{attack}), & \text{if } \tilde{p}_i \notin \mathcal{P} \\ 0 \ (\text{valid-msg}), & \text{otherwise} \end{cases} \tag{1}$$

The amount of side-channel information leaked by the device in an attack is related to the number of blocks decrypted before the attack is detected. In our approach, the plaintext is analyzed immediately after each block decryption to ensure fast detection. As soon as an anomaly is detected, an alarm signaling the attack is triggered and a response is executed to counter it.

3.2   Op-Code Analysis

We make use of a *deterministic* approach to test the features of the plaintext, i.e. the instructions encoding of a specific MCU. We associate valid instruction sequences as features that correspond to normal behavior. To test for anomalies, we examine whether the observations of the collected data are in fact valid encodings for a known Instruction Set Architecture (ISA). Assuming that the probability of appearance of any given instruction does not affect the probability of appearance of another one in the sequence, i.e. obtaining valid instructions is an independent event, the probability of generating a sequence for which all observations yield valid instructions will decrease as the sequence length increases. We define $\mathcal{V}$ as the set of all valid instructions. The probability that a sequence of instructions in a plaintext is valid may be calculated as follows:

$$\prod_{i=1}^{r} \Pr(\tilde{v}_i \in \mathcal{V}) = \left(\frac{N}{2^m} \right)^r, \tag{2}$$

where N is the number of valid plaintext encodings in the given instruction set architecture, r is the number of instructions in a plaintext sequence, and m is the bit-length of a single instruction encoding.

An alarm signaling the detection of an attack will be triggered on single occurrences (*point anomalies*), i.e. when an individual observation does not comply with the model of valid instruction encodings. Since the observations may include not only the instruction's op-codes but operands as well, inputs that do not conform to the model will be taken as anomalous only when they represent instructions, and not when they represent other type of data (thus treated as *conditional anomalies*). We will discuss the special case of long data blocks in Subsect. 4.2.

3.3   Response Measures

Once an attack is detected, a response can be applied to counter it. For this, three different measures are proposed:

(a) Modifying the key material.
(b) Delaying the next response.
(c) Disabling the cryptographic core.

For (a), we erase the key value setting it to all zeros (*i.e. zeroisation*), that is, $k = 0^\kappa$. Response (b) creates a delay in the update mechanism in order to slow down the collection of leakage information, $\{\ell_i\}$. Lastly, (c) disables the cryptographic core to prevent any further collections of leakage information $\{\ell_i\}$.

4   Implementation on a General Purpose MCU

For our experiments we chose TI's MSP430 MCU architecture. To create the function to be used for *features-recognition*, the 27 core instructions were expressed as Boolean functions. The function for an invalid instruction was determined as the complement of the concatenation of these functions. The resulting Boolean function was then reduced using Logic Friday [24], a graphical interface for the ESPRESSO logic minimizer algorithm [22]. The resulting logic function, F, is shown in Eq. 3, here b_j corresponds to the j-th bit of the instruction encoding word.

$$
\begin{aligned}
\mathrm{F} = {} & \bar{b}_{15}\bar{b}_{14}\bar{b}_{13}\bar{b}_{12} & & + \bar{b}_{15}\bar{b}_{14}\bar{b}_{13}b_{11} \\
& + \bar{b}_{15}\bar{b}_{14}\bar{b}_{13}b_{10} & & + \bar{b}_{15}\bar{b}_{14}\bar{b}_{13}b_9 b_8 b_7 \\
& + \bar{b}_{15}\bar{b}_{14}\bar{b}_{13}b_9 b_8 b_6 & & + \bar{b}_{15}\bar{b}_{14}\bar{b}_{13}b_9 b_7 b_6 \\
& + \bar{b}_{15}\bar{b}_{14}\bar{b}_{13}b_8 b_7 b_6 & & + \bar{b}_{15}\bar{b}_{14}\bar{b}_{13}b_9 b_8 b_5 \\
& + \bar{b}_{15}\bar{b}_{14}\bar{b}_{13}b_9 b_8 b_4 & & + \bar{b}_{15}\bar{b}_{14}\bar{b}_{13}b_9 b_8 b_3 \\
& + \bar{b}_{15}\bar{b}_{14}\bar{b}_{13}b_9 b_8 b_2 & & + \bar{b}_{15}\bar{b}_{14}\bar{b}_{13}b_9 b_8 b_1 \\
& + \bar{b}_{15}\bar{b}_{14}\bar{b}_{13}b_9 b_8 b_0 & &
\end{aligned}
\tag{3}
$$

Figure 2 shows the conditions to perform the checks. In order to avoid false positives (i.e. triggering an alarm when an instruction is indeed valid), operands are not analyzed. In MSP430, three types of instructions are possible: single operand arithmetic, two operand arithmetic, and conditional jumps. When an instruction is analyzed, one can determine the number of operands which follow. By skipping over the operands and analyzing the op-codes as in Eq. 1 with the Boolean function F, shown in Eq. 3, false positives are completely eliminated. The amount of false negatives that will occur before an alarm is triggered will depend on the properties of the op-code space, as given by Eq. 2.

4.1   Comparison of Instruction Set Architectures

To evaluate the choice of using the MSP430 instruction set, we compare it to the instruction set ARMv6-M (which is used in ARM Cortex-M1, M0, and M0+ cores). While the MSP430 uses only 16-bit instructions, the instruction set of

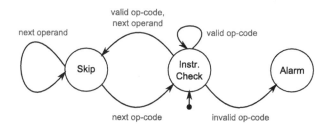

Fig. 2. State machine for the firmware code feature analyzer.

ARMv6-M uses 16-bit as well as a few 32-bit instructions. The instruction bus for both architectures is 16-bit wide, therefore, even in the case of 32-bit instructions the ARM architecture sends the instructions one 'halfword' (16-bits) at a time. Table 1 shows the percentage of valid instructions in comparison with the complete encoding space for the MSP430 and the ARMv6-M instruction sets. A column has been added to show the percentage of valid encodings if the instructions are compared making use of 16-bits for the analysis (first halfword only), or the complete 32-bits (first and second halfwords).

Figure 3 shows how the probability of randomly generating a sequence in which all instructions are valid, decreases as the number of instructions in a sequence is increased. This is based on Eq. 2 and the values from Table 1. Using both 32-bit and 16-bit instructions yields the best results for the detection of anomalies in ARM instructions. For our use-case, the 16-bit MSP430 instruction space is comparable to using both 32-bit and 16-bit instructions in the ARMv6-M instruction set, while requiring a simpler logic function for the recognition of valid instructions.

Table 1. Instruction encoding space comparison

	MSP430		ARMv6-M (1st halfword)		ARMv6-M (1st & 2nd halfwords)	
	Values	[%]	Values	[%]	Values	[%]
Encoding space	2^{16}	100	2^{16}	100	2^{32}	100
Valid encoding	57985	88.48	62894	95.97	3752681472	87.37
Invalid encoding	7551	11.52	2641	4.03	542285824	12.63

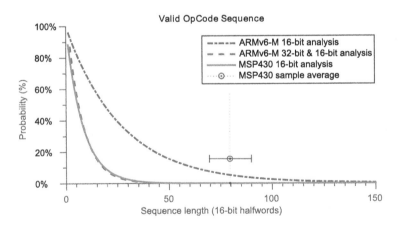

Fig. 3. Probability of generating a sequence where all values represent valid instruction encodings.

4.2   Address Analyzer for Data and Code Segments

Along with code, data-only segments may also be found inside firmware images. Typical examples of these are pre-computed tables and calibration values. The values found in data segments do not conform to the firmware properties previously described for code, therefore a supplementary analyzer is needed. Typically, MCUs make use of a unified address space for memory and peripherals. Defining segments in memory can be used to divide the code and data content. This approach prevents the occurrence of false positives caused by interpreting data as invalid instruction encodings. Figure 4 shows the state machine for the address check.

An advantage of this approach is that MCUs, such as the MSP430FR59xx family from TI, have a large address space, of which only a fraction is used. This means that, by comparing if the address obtained after decryption corresponds to a valid address space or not, the detection capabilities of the ADR can be improved. For example, Table 2 shows the memory organization of the MSP430FR5969. The address space has a range of 2^{20} addresses, which are encoded in 3 bytes, giving a total of 2^{24} possible values. This MCU has 2 kB of RAM and 63 kB of non-volatile FRAM memory. Hence, generating an address at random yields a mere $\approx 0.4\%$ probability of landing in a valid address range.

In order to avoid treating code as data and vice versa, code and data can be saved in different memory areas. To store data segments in a specific memory area, separate from the instruction encodings, minor changes need to be done to a program. Compilers, such as the ones included in newer versions of Code Composer Studio and IAR Workbench, support the *location* pragma for placing content in specific memory locations.

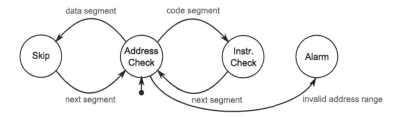

Fig. 4. State machine for the address range analysis

Table 2. Address space for the MSP430FR59x9

	Size [Bytes]	Address range [Hex]
Peripherals	4096	000000–000FFF
Bootstrap Loader (ROM)	2048	001000–0017FF
Device Descriptor Info	256	001A00–001AFF
RAM	2048	001C00–0023FF
FRAM	64512	00FF80–00FFFF

Since values inside data blocks are not analyzed, an attacker could potentially perform modifications to these values that would go undetected. To limit the chances of success of such an attack, the amount of data sent after an address should be reduced. That is, firmware images that contain large blocks of data values should be partitioned so that address checks occur often. By performing constant address checks, the probability of a modification going undetected will be reduced. To yield roughly the same probability of detection as the one that would be obtained with code checks, two address checks must be performed for every 72 half-word op-codes (i.e. 144 bytes). Therefore, 72 bytes is the maximum number of data values that should be sent between address checks, in order to maintain at least the same level of security as the one obtained with code detection.

4.3   Results

The following results were obtained for a Texas Instruments MSP430FR5969 MCU [12]. This device belongs to the new family of Ferroelectric Random Access (non-volatile) Memory (FRAM) microcontrollers from TI. For the block cipher, we make use of the unprotected AES implementation provided by Texas Instruments [13]. The code was compiled using TI's compiler v.4.4.1 under Code Composer Studio 6.1.

Table 3 shows the code foot-print of the ADR using different optimization options. The ADR function *analyzeData*, which covers the anomaly detection and response functions, has a foot-print of 340 bytes of code and 1 byte of data. In comparison, the software implementation of AES makes use of 1.88 kB of code and 267 bytes of data when compiling with whole program optimization for code size. The low code-size overhead of the ADR is accomplished by making use of Boolean functions as presented in Eq. 3.

Table 3 also shows the execution time required for the ADR to analyze a 16-bytes block of data. The time length was measured using an internal timer, TA0, set to the system clock. The timer was triggered when calling *analyzeData*

Table 3. ADR code size under different optimization parameters

Optimization level	No	Reg.	Local	Global	Interproc.	Program
	-	-O0	-O1	-O2	-O3	-O4
Size [bytes]						
.text:ADR:analyzeData	112	72	66	58	58	70
.text:ADR:analyzeOpcodeDet	352	306	272	270	270	270
.text:ADR:applyReactionMeasure	64	30	24	22	22	−
.text:ADR	528	408	362	350	350	340
Execution time [cycles/block]						
analyzeData	1614	1192	1168	1063	1064	1045

and stopped once the function returned. The number of cycles needed to step in and out of the function has been accounted for and subtracted from these numbers. The sampling size for this measurements was 10^5 ciphertexts.

5   Side-Channel Analysis

To validate the effectiveness of the ADR against side-channel attacks, we first conducted differential power analysis attacks on a simulated target and later compared them with the practical attacks on a real MCU.

5.1   Attacks on Simulated Measurements

For the simulations, a set of attacks was performed with the ADR active and another without it. The output of the S-box function in the first round of AES was selected as the target of the attack. To simulate the side-channel leakage l, we made use of the Hamming weight (HW) model. Each leakage sample ℓ_i was made Gaussian, that is, composed of a deterministic signal $HW(Sbox(s, c_i))$, and random additive noise $\eta \sim \mathcal{N}(\mu, \sigma^2)$, such that $\ell_i = HW(Sbox(s, c_i)) + \eta$. As commonly assumed in literature, we made use of additive noise following a normal distribution with zero mean and variance σ^2 [15]. Attacks were performed for 1000 tests with 5000 queries per test. For each test a randomly generated key was used. We measured the efficiency of the attack using the success rate for all 16 bytes in key k. Figure 5 shows the success rates for different noise levels, each curve shows the average of 1000 tests, each with independent keys, as well as the success rate of attacks on real measurements. Figure 5a shows a successful attack when no countermeasure is activated, while Fig. 5b shows the effect of applying key-zeroisation upon detecting the attack.

5.2   Practical Attacks on an MCU

To perform side-channel analysis, the MSP430FR5969 was configured to run at 8 MHz using the internal digitally controlled oscillator (DCO). An Agilent DSO9254A oscilloscope, configured to use a sampling rate of 200 MS/s, was then used to perform the measurements. The MSP430FR5969 was placed within an MSP-TS430RGZ48C 48-pin FRAM Target Board. To capture the power traces, a 50 Ω resistor was placed between the DVSS pin in the board and ground. A TI THS4509EVM, a 10 dB and 1900 MHz bandwidth differential amplifier module, was used to pre-amply the signal before feeding it to the oscilloscope. Figure 5 shows the success rate of a DPA attack of a software AES implementation in comparison with the simulation values. The curve depicted in Fig. 5a for the practical attack on AES is approximate to the one with a $\sigma = 22$ in our simulations model. This value shows the deviation between the simulated traces, generated with a Hamming weight model, and the actual power consumption of the target MCU.

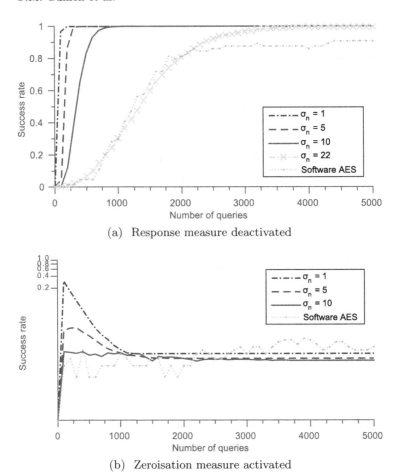

(a) Response measure deactivated

(b) Zeroisation measure activated

Fig. 5. Comparison of the success rates for DPA attacks with the proposed anomaly detection and response module activated and deactivated.

In Fig. 5b one can observe that, while for simulations some information can be leaked before the zeroisation response is applied, for the practical attack the amount of information leaked about the secret key is in fact negligible. To quantify the number of ciphertexts required to recognize an attack using deterministic firmware checks, one million tests were conducted. For each test 16-byte ciphertexts of data with uniform distribution were sent until an alarm occurred. The mean was found to be at 9.7914 ciphertexts. These results can be compared with the expectations from the ideal calculations by taking a look at the sample average in Fig. 3. When adding the address checks, the mean was found to be equal to 1.0066, which represents a challenging scenario for mounting successful side-channel attacks. Although it could be possible to collect traces from multiple devices, we believe this attack would be quite laborious and time consuming, especially if, for example, each device is programmed with an independent secret key, the anomaly detection is used in conjunction with countermeasures such as masking, or the decryption module is implemented in hardware rather than in software.

6 Discussion

We presented a minimalist, deterministic and agnostic (of the underlying cryptographic primitive) approach for performing anomaly detection to thwart side-channel attacks when the attacker actively generates the inputs to the device. Our approach is *not* intended as a drop-in replacement for other side-channel countermeasures, like masking schemes, but as a first line of defense against side-channel attacks for low-cost resource-constrained devices. Moreover, it can be combined with other software based measures, e.g. key-refreshing techniques and secure counters, to effectively enhance the resistance of firmware update mechanisms against side-channel analysis in a broader scope. The combination of the our anomaly detection approach and other measures into a complete solution is part of the future work.

Note that, even though on one hand, any upgrade to the underlying cryptographic implementation (either hardware or software) used for decrypting the firmware images would be possible without modification to the anomaly detection measure (potentially stored in ROM), on the other hand, the model underlying the anomaly detection must be adapted to each Instruction Set Architecture (ISA), i.e. if a change in the ISA is made, then the anomaly detection model must be updated accordingly. Our approach is based on a deterministic anomaly detection model, which recognizes valid instructions and memory addresses, without relying on other cryptographic primitives, i.e. hash functions or Message Authentication Codes (MACs), to detect anomalies. We believe that, in case of resource-constrained and battery operated devices, this setting represents the best compromise in terms of energy consumption, code-size and side-channel security, i.e. fastest way to recognize side-channel attacks. A first possible improvement would be to additionally apply probabilistic models in conjunction with the deterministic model, such as Hidden Markov Models (HMM), in order to verify whether a sequence of instructions within a decryption block is also legitimate. Such a probabilistic approach would probably not only require more code size and energy, but also a team of developers to run in-house verifications of the anomaly detection model, in order to ensure that encrypted software updates would pass successfully through the anomaly detection measures and not generate false positives. Yet another possible approach would be interleaving machine code and the corresponding hash values within the encrypted firmware. This approach would require considerably more energy for the transmission of the firmware (which would be at least double in length, depending on the output size of the hash function), would require the resources for the implementation of the hash function, and the corresponding energy for verifying the hash values during firmware updates. Moreover, from a side-channel security point of view, more than one input block might be needed in order to verify the hash values, depending on the input block size of the hash function, hence potentially allowing for more leakage, before the hash values can be verified and an alarm can be raised. Finally, yet another possibility would be to use authenticated encryption with associated data (AEAD) to simultaneously provide decryption with integrity verification in *one step*. At the time of writing, the Competition for Authenticated Encryption: Security, Applicability, and Robustness (CAESAR) [1] is running, with the goal of determining a portfolio of authenticated ciphers that offer advantages over AES-GCM (AES Galois Counter Mode) in terms of performance, security, and ease of correct implementations [6]. We leave the evaluation of CAESAR candidates for secure firmware updates as future work.

7 Conclusions

In this work we presented a minimalist approach to anomaly detection and reaction, as a first line of defense against side-channel attacks for encrypted firmware updates. Our solution has negligible code size and runtime overhead, can be applied to products already deployed in the field during a firmware update, and is orthogonal to existing side-channel countermeasures, such as masking schemes, which can be used in conjunction with it to increase the overall system security. Unlike many other countermeasures, the described solution is agnostic of the underlying cryptographic implementation, allowing it to be applied to any cryptographic module and does *not* require any source of randomness. In the considered application case of TI MSP430 instruction set architecture, embedding anomaly detection measures in software costs only 340 bytes, and it was proven to be practically effective against differential side-channel attacks both on simulated and real measurements, requiring *only one* decryption block on average to identify side-channel attacks.

Acknowledgments. We would like to thank the anonymous reviewers for their valuable comments and suggestions. This work was partially funded by the German Federal Ministry of Education and Research (BMBF), project SIBASE, grant number 01IS13020A.

References

1. CAESAR: Competition for authenticated encryption: security, applicability, and robustness, July 2012. http://competitions.cr.yp.to/caesar.html. This webpage is maintained by D. J. Bernstein
2. Balasch, J., Gierlichs, B., Grosso, V., Reparaz, O., Standaert, F.-X.: On the cost of lazy engineering for masked software implementations. In: Joye, M., Moradi, A. (eds.) CARDIS 2014. LNCS, vol. 8968, pp. 64–81. Springer, Heidelberg (2015). doi:10.1007/978-3-319-16763-3_5
3. Barthe, G., Belaïd, S., Dupressoir, F., Fouque, P.-A., Grégoire, B., Strub, P.-Y.: Verified proofs of higher-order masking. In: Oswald, E., Fischlin, M. (eds.) EUROCRYPT 2015. LNCS, vol. 9056, pp. 457–485. Springer, Heidelberg (2015). doi:10.1007/978-3-662-46800-5_18

4. Belaïd, S., De Santis, F., Heyszl, J., Mangard, S., Medwed, M., Schmidt, J.-M., Standaert, F.-X., Tillich, S.: Towards fresh re-keying with leakage-resilient PRFs: cipher design principles and analysis. J. Cryptographic Eng. **4**(3), 157–171 (2014)
5. Bellissimo, A., Burgess, J., Kevin, F., Secure software updates: disappointments and new challenges. In: Proceedings of the 1st USENIX Workshop on Hot Topics in Security, HOTSEC 2006, Berkeley, CA, USA, p. 7. USENIX Association (2006)
6. Bernstein, D.J.: Failures of secret-key cryptography. In: Invited Talk at FSE 2013 (20th International Workshop on Fast Software Encryption), Singapore (2013)
7. Chandola, V., Banerjee, A., Kumar, V.: Anomaly detection: a survey. ACM Comput. Surv. (CSUR) **41**(3), 15 (2009)
8. Coron, J.-S.: Resistance against differential power analysis for elliptic curve cryptosystems. In: Koç, Ç.K., Paar, C. (eds.) CHES 1999. LNCS, vol. 1717, pp. 292–302. Springer, Heidelberg (1999). doi:10.1007/3-540-48059-5_25
9. Denning, D.E.: An intrusion-detection model. IEEE Trans. Softw. Eng. **13**(2), 222–232 (1987)
10. Golić, J.D., Tymen, C.: Multiplicative masking and power analysis of AES. In: Kaliski, B.S., Koç, K., Paar, C. (eds.) CHES 2002. LNCS, vol. 2523, pp. 198–212. Springer, Heidelberg (2003). doi:10.1007/3-540-36400-5_16
11. Guillen, O.M., Brederlow, R., Ledwa, R., Sigl, G.: Risk management in embedded devices using metering applications as example. In: Proceedings of the 9th Workshop on Embedded Systems Security, WESS 2014, pp. 6:1–6:9. ACM, New York (2014)
12. Texas Instruments Inc.: SLAU367E - MSP430FR59xx Family User's Guide, August 2014
13. Texas Instruments Inc., Hall, J.H.: SLAA547A - C Implementation of Cryptographic Algorithms (Rev. A), July 2013
14. Krieg, A., Grinschgl, J., Steger, C., Weiss, R., Haid, J.: A side channel attack countermeasure using system-on-chip power profile scrambling. In: 2011 IEEE 17th International On-Line Testing Symposium (IOLTS), pp. 222–227. IEEE (2011)
15. Mangard, S., Oswald, E., Standaert, F.-X.: One for all-all for one: unifying standard differential power analysis attacks. IET Inf. Secur. **5**(2), 100–110 (2011)
16. Mangard, S., Pramstaller, N., Oswald, E.: Successfully attacking masked AES hardware implementations. In: Rao, J.R., Sunar, B. (eds.) CHES 2005. LNCS, vol. 3659, pp. 157–171. Springer, Heidelberg (2005). doi:10.1007/11545262_12
17. Medwed, M., Standaert, F.-X., Joux, A.: Towards super-exponential side-channel security with efficient leakage-resilient PRFs. In: Prouff, E., Schaumont, P. (eds.) CHES 2012. LNCS, vol. 7428, pp. 193–212. Springer, Heidelberg (2012). doi:10.1007/978-3-642-33027-8_12
18. Moradi, A., Kasper, M., Paar, C.: Black-box side-channel attacks highlight the importance of countermeasures. In: Dunkelman, O. (ed.) CT-RSA 2012. LNCS, vol. 7178, pp. 1–18. Springer, Heidelberg (2012). doi:10.1007/978-3-642-27954-6_1
19. Moradi, A., Poschmann, A.: Lightweight cryptography and DPA countermeasures: a survey. In: Sion, R., Curtmola, R., Dietrich, S., Kiayias, A., Miret, J.M., Sako, K., Sebé, F. (eds.) FC 2010. LNCS, vol. 6054, pp. 68–79. Springer, Heidelberg (2010). doi:10.1007/978-3-642-14992-4_7
20. O'Flynn, C., David Chen, Z.: Side channel power analysis of an aes-256 bootloader. In: 2015 IEEE 28th Canadian Conference on Electrical and Computer Engineering (CCECE), pp. 750–755, May 2015

21. Patton, M., Gross, E., Chinn, R., Forbis, S., Walker, L., Chen, H.: Uninvited connections: a study of vulnerable devices on the Internet of Things (IoT). In: 2014 IEEE Joint Intelligence and Security Informatics Conference (JISIC), pp. 232–235, September 2014

22. Rudell, R.L.: Multiple-valued logic minimization for pla synthesis. Technical report, DTIC Document (1986)

23. De Santis, F., Rass, S.: On efficient leakage-resilient pseudorandom functions with hard-to-invert leakages. In: Aranha, D.F., Menezes, A. (eds.) LATINCRYPT 2014. LNCS, vol. 8895, pp. 127–145. Springer, Heidelberg (2015). doi:10.1007/978-3-319-16295-9_7

24. Sontrack. Logic Friday (version 1.1.4), November 2012. http://www.sontrak.com/

25. Tillich, S., Herbst, C.: Attacking state-of-the-art software countermeasures—a case study for AES. In: Oswald, E., Rohatgi, P. (eds.) CHES 2008. LNCS, vol. 5154, pp. 228–243. Springer, Heidelberg (2008). doi:10.1007/978-3-540-85053-3_15

26. Trichina, E., De Seta, D., Germani, L.: Simplified adaptive multiplicative masking for AES. In: Kaliski, B.S., Koç, K., Paar, C. (eds.) CHES 2002. LNCS, vol. 2523, pp. 187–197. Springer, Heidelberg (2003). doi:10.1007/3-540-36400-5_15

27. Veyrat-Charvillon, N., Standaert, F.-X.: Adaptive chosen-message side-channel attacks. In: Zhou, J., Yung, M. (eds.) ACNS 2010. LNCS, vol. 6123, pp. 186–199. Springer, Heidelberg (2010). doi:10.1007/978-3-642-13708-2_12

Author Index

Printed in the United States
By Bookmasters